Slow Cooker
Winners

300 easy and satisfying recipes

Donna-Marie Pye

Robert
ROSE

Library and Archives Canada Cataloguing in Publication

Pye, Donna-Marie

    Slow cooker winners : 300 easy and satisfying recipes / Donna-Marie Pye.

Includes index.
ISBN 978-0-7788-0247-1

    1. Electric cookery, Slow. I. Title.

TX827.P9335 2010   641.5'884   C2010-903241-1

Pye, Donna-Marie

    Canada's slow cooker winners : 300 easy and satisfying recipes / Donna-Marie Pye.

Includes index.
ISBN 978-0-7788-0258-7

    1. Electric cookery, Slow. I. Title.

TX827.P9334 2010   641.5'884   C2010-903239-X

Disclaimer

The recipes in this book have been carefully tested by our kitchen and our tasters. To the best of our knowledge, they are safe and nutritious for ordinary use and users. For those people with food or other allergies, or who have special food requirements or health issues, please read the suggested contents of each recipe carefully and determine whether or not they may create a problem for you. All recipes are used at the risk of the consumer. Consumers should always consult their slow cooker manufacturer's manual for recommended procedures and cooking times.

    We cannot be responsible for any hazards, loss or damage that may occur as a result of any recipe use.

    For those with special needs, allergies, requirements or health problems, in the event of any doubt, please contact your medical adviser prior to the use of any recipe.

Design and Production: Kevin Cockburn/PageWave Graphics Inc.
Editors: Sue Sumeraj and Jennifer MacKenzie
Proofreader: Sheila Wawanash
Indexer: Gillian Watts
Photographer: Colin Erricson
Associate Photographer: Matt Johannsson
Food Styling: Kathryn Robertson
Prop Styling: Charlene Erricson

Cover image: Cinderella Stew (page 112)

We acknowledge the financial support of the Government of Canada through the Book Publishing Industry Development Program (BPIDP) for our publishing activities.

Published by Robert Rose Inc.
120 Eglinton Avenue East, Suite 800, Toronto, Ontario, Canada M4P 1E2
Tel: (416) 322-6552 Fax: (416) 322-6936
www.robertrose.ca

Printed and bound in Canada

1 2 3 4 5 6 7 8 9 CPL 18 17 16 15 14 13 12 11 10

Contents

Acknowledgments

It has been almost 10 years since I was given the opportunity to write my first book, *America's/Canada's Best Slow Cooker Recipes*. At that time, I was testing and developing recipes and delivering them to my children's preschools for input. Now I have two busy and active teenagers, who still continue to inspire me to create new and exciting meals for our slow cooker at home.

To my husband, Lawrence Greaves, for his constant support, love and encouragement throughout this project, even when I was frustrated or stressed. And for taking pots of food to his office staff, photocopying scads of recipes and evaluation forms, tasting from early morning to late at night and meeting in the hot tub for a day's wrap-up, even when we were both completely exhausted. To my daughter, Darcy, my appreciation for pitching in with meals and laundry, baking us a batch of cookies, her invaluable computer assistance — and a smile or hug, just when I needed it. And to my son, Jack, who comes home daily with a huge appetite, tells me a joke and eats whatever I put in front of him. You all add a smile to my face.

No one writes a cookbook by themselves. It is a full team effort, from concept to finished manuscript. This project would not have been possible without the help of two invaluable assistants. First, to my dear friend Leslie Huber, who spent countless hours with me, typing a manuscript, (talking), testing recipes, (talking), writing, (talking) and keeping me sane and organized when I never thought I could get things finished. It has been a journey, and I'm so glad we shared it together. To Kate Dowhan, who willingly took my retests, provided invaluable input and tested and reviewed recipes, all while raising two toddlers and experiencing a third pregnancy. It has been a pleasure working with and getting to know you.

To the countless family members, friends, co-workers at Household China & Gifts and neighbors (too many to name) who would show up at my door, slow cookers in hand, and taste whatever I would give them — no questions asked! Many thanks for offering your homes and families and your slow cookers and recipes, and for providing detailed critiques and evaluations, encouraging conversations and bottles of wine!

And to the girls who pitched in during the eleventh hour for typing assistance — Mary Taylor, Maria Burjoski, Nancy Forte, Elly Yach, Carol Parsons and my mom, Evelyn Pye — thank you, thank you, thank you!

To the entire team at Robert Rose, who have steered this book on its path, especially Bob Dees and Marian Jarkovich. It's a pleasure to work with you. You have not only made me a part of the RR family, but have also provided professional direction and expertise over the last 10 years. My appreciation to my colleagues Emily Richards and Jennifer MacKenzie for taking my phone calls and providing wonderful suggestions for the final manuscript. Your fine-tuned palates and impeccable recipe standards helped turn my recipes into a great working cookbook. To Sue Sumeraj, Jennifer MacKenzie (again) and Jo Calvert for their exceptional editing; Kevin Cockburn and the other designers at PageWave Graphics for taking manuscript typed in Times Roman, font size 12 and turning it into a cookbook for families to cherish; Kathryn Robertson, Charlene Erricson and Colin Erricson for the terrific food styling, prop styling and beautiful photographs that make the recipes come alive. It's this fine art and talent that inspires people to try the recipes that come out of my kitchen.

To the manufacturers who sent me their machines for recipe testing. Thanks to Jarden Consumer Solutions and the team at Cohn & Wolfe, who provided me with Rival Crock-Pots and didn't blink an eye when I asked for so many, in various shapes and sizes. To the staff at Cuisinart Canada for the gracious use of their slow cookers, as well as so many other supplemental materials.

To my parents, Roger and Evelyn Pye, who supported me through this past year, when it was they who needed support and strength to win their own battle. I love you both.

Finally, to the readers of *America's/Canada's Best Slow Cooker Recipes*, *Family's Best Slow Cooker Recipes* and *300 Slow Cooker Favorites*, thank you for inviting me into your kitchens and letting me cook with you for the past 10 years. I hope you will enjoy this new collection.

Cheers and happy crocking!
Donna-Marie Pye

Introduction

Kitchen appliances come and go, but the slow cooker has managed to stand the test of time. It has been almost half a century since the slow cooker arrived in stores, and it now holds a place of prominence on our counters. Most small-appliance manufacturers now include a slow cooker in their product lineup. It's a must-have for any busy, active household.

The reason for this success is that slow cookers are incredibly handy. They come in a variety of sizes, shapes and finishes, and are made to suit any type of household and kitchen decor. All cooks, from busy families to empty nesters to college students to newlyweds, can find a slow cooker to suit their needs. Not only are these appliances useful for cooking a weeknight meal, but they can help streamline preparation for a holiday gathering, when oven space is at a premium. They raise soups, stews and braises to higher levels. They can even help home cooks create delectable preserves and desserts. Who would have imagined that a pot designed to bake beans could prove to be so versatile?

My relationship with the slow cooker began more than 20 years ago, when I first used it to help put dinner on the table after a lengthy commute from my job. Once my children arrived and I began working from home, our lives reached new levels of busyness. Now, with two active, hungry teens, a full schedule of work, a husband with a demanding career and a dog that needs attention too, I still find a need for the slow cooker. It gives us a chance to sit down as a family over a home-cooked meal at least once or twice a week — something we find more difficult to do as time goes on.

Slow cookers are a breeze to use and are time-, cost- and energy-efficient. Stalwart and reliable, they require little or no tending, and very little last-minute cooking is needed. Meats and poultry braise beautifully, resulting in exceptional pot roasts, savory stews and succulent ribs, chilis and curries. Beans, peas and lentils, which are inexpensive, filling and incredibly nutritious, also benefit from long, slow cooking. Slow cookers even offer a heat-free way to cook in the summer. How many other appliances offer so many options?

In this book, you will find more than 300 recipes to explore and experiment with, featuring the best of North American regional cuisine, as well as globally inspired dishes representing cultures from around the world. I developed these recipes with convenience in mind. While most do require a few extra minutes of preparation, in some you can add all the ingredients at once. I like to use fresh ingredients, but occasionally I use a convenience-food product to make things simpler. I have incorporated many contemporary ingredients — such as balsamic vinegar, chipotle peppers, smoked paprika, roasted red peppers and edamame (soybeans) — to reflect current cooking styles and global influences.

While most of the recipes in this book serve anywhere from four to eight people, I recognized the need for recipes to suit any family and slow cooker size and have included the chapters Meals for Two and Big-Batch Dinners for a Crowd. And who doesn't deserve a break from cooking once in a while? With a bit of advance planning and the inspiring recipes in Double-Duty Dinners, you can turn tonight's dinner into tomorrow's feast, simultaneously banishing the dreaded question "Are we having that again?" The recipes in this chapter are designed to yield extras that come together quickly in a delightful second meal with minimal effort.

Slow cooking has grown up, traveled the world and come home more sophisticated, capable of a broader variety of fresh flavors, cuisines, shapes and textures. Whether you are cooking for two or serving a crowd, this book makes easy work of creating delicious, soul-satisfying meals. Happy slow cooking!

▌Slow Cooker Know-How

When cooking on Low, a slow cooker uses between 85 and 180 watts of power. The High heat setting uses almost double the power — between 160 and 370 watts.

We all have one thing in common: a busy schedule. But how do you satisfy your eclectic tastes and provide full-flavored dishes made from globally inspired recipes when you are on the go? The answer lies in one of our most trusted kitchen appliances — the slow cooker. Whether you are a family of two, three or more, a first-time cook or an experienced professional, slow cooking both saves you time and creates scrumptious, nutritious food. You can carry on with your day, working, playing or pursuing your passion, while it quietly simmers away on the counter, using its low, moist heat to coax a symphony of flavors from the food. It's like having your own private chef!

Of course, it can't do all the work — you must provide a little input. But with some preplanning and forethought, a little organization and an array of fresh ingredients, you'll have a satisfying meal waiting for you when you're ready for it. Your only job is to pour the wine and make a side dish (and sometimes even that is not necessary).

Simple by Design

Ten years ago, when I wrote my first slow cooker cookbook, I tested all the recipes in the same simple machine that was developed almost 40 years ago. Only two heat settings were available, without an automatic shutoff and with a manual Keep Warm setting. We have come a long way since then. Gone are the bland beige units with cutesy floral patterns on the sides. They have been replaced by sleek black, white and stainless-steel units designed to match our kitchen decor, all with a multitude of electronic settings.

If your slow cooker cooks at specific temperature settings, program it to cook at 200°F (100°C) for Low and 300°F (150°C) for High.

Slow cookers still operate on a high/low principle. The Low setting cooks food at around 200°F (100°C) and the High setting at about 300°F (150°C). The exact cooking temperature varies between models, so when preparing a recipe for the first time, check for doneness at the end of the minimum recommended cooking time. As you become more familiar with your model, you can adjust cooking times accordingly.

The Low setting is used for braises that require longer cooking times (8 hours or more), while the High setting is ideal for cooking and tenderizing food over a shorter time period (4 hours or less). I love the newer machines with programmable timers that allow me to preset the cooking times in half-hour increments; at the end of the set cooking time, the unit drops to a Warm heat setting that keeps the food warm without overcooking it.

Parts of a Slow Cooker

These sleek countertop appliances have some key parts, and different models offer different features. Before buying a slow cooker, you'll want to consider all of the options and decide on the model that best meets your budget and household requirements.

Casing and Insert

The appliance consists of a metal outer casing and a stoneware insert. Some stoneware is designed so that you can use it to brown meat or sauté vegetables on the stovetop before placing it in the metal casing for slow cooking. But check your manufacturer's instructions to see whether this is possible with your model. If not, it's just as easy to do your browning or sautéing in a skillet, then transfer the food to the stoneware. The recipes in this book assume the use of a skillet.

If your stoneware insert is removable, the manufacturer's directions will specify whether it is ovenproof, microwaveable and/or able to go under the broiler.

The metal casing contains thermostatically controlled heating elements, which heat up to warm the air inside the insulated metal walls, thereby cooking the meal. This low-wattage heat never makes direct contact with the stoneware, so there are no hot spots and no need for constant stirring. The slow cooker uses about the same amount of energy as a 100-watt light bulb — substantially less than a conventional oven.

Lid

All slow cookers come with a plastic or glass lid. A good lid seals in moisture and nutrients, so, while a little jiggle is acceptable, you will want to make sure the lid fits snugly. Clear lids are handy, as they allow you to see what is happening inside the slow cooker. Tempting as it might seem, it is important not to lift the lid during cooking — you can lose 20 minutes of cooking time for every lift. Look for lids that are dishwasher-safe. I have had some heat-resistant plastic ones that started out clear but with time and continued washing became opaque, making it difficult to see what was happening inside.

Glass lids get quite hot during the cooking process. When it's time to remove the lid, it's a good idea to use oven mitts or a pot holder.

Timer and Temperature Probe

Many of today's slow cookers come with a programmable timer. Some of these allow you to use preset times within the High or Low settings; others allow you to set the cooking time, then choose whether to cook on High or Low. Many machines have a Warm setting, which will kick in automatically once the preset cooking time is reached, keeping the contents warm without overcooking them. If the food is forgiving, the Warm setting can also be handy when you're taking cooked food to a potluck. Transport the food in your slow cooker and, once you reach your destination, turn on the Warm setting; the food can safely sit that way for up to 2 hours.

Some slow cookers are also equipped with a temperature probe, which works with the cooker's electronic controls to monitor the internal temperature of meat and automatically shifts to the Warm setting when the desired temperature is reached. Internal temperature is the best way to measure the doneness of some types of meats and poultry, and the probe ensures that these meats are thoroughly cooked according to specified guidelines.

> The most basic machines do not have features such as a programmable timer or a temperature probe. Before buying one, do make sure it at least has High and Low settings; otherwise, it cannot be considered a true slow cooker.

Size and Shape

Slow cookers come in an impressive range of sizes and shapes these days. Choose one that is best suited to your needs. You'd be surprised at how many households own two — one for large family meals and another for cooking side dishes, desserts and appetizers.

If you plan to make 4 to 8 servings most of the time, a 4- to 6-quart (4 to 6 L) slow cooker is the best size for you. This capacity will allow you to cook a full meal with leftovers (depending on how hungry everyone is). Most of the recipes in this book were tested in a slow cooker this size. Smaller models, in the 1½- to 3-quart (1.5 to 3 L) range, are ideal for smaller households, and for making warm dips, side dishes and appetizers for which a large pot is simply too big. If you regularly (or even occasionally) feed a crowd, or you simply like to make big batches and freeze your leftovers, you may want to invest in a 6- to 7-quart (6 to 7 L) slow cooker, which is capable of making up to 20 servings.

Slow cookers come in round, oval and rectangular models. While round slow cookers are fine for soups, stews and chilies, oval and rectangular models allow a little more flexibility when it comes to roasts and larger cuts of meat. A rectangular shape also makes more efficient use of cupboard space.

> The amount of liquid in a recipe can vary considerably, from just a few spoonfuls to enough to submerge the food completely. Ideally, the slow cooker should be no more than two-thirds full of food, with liquid at least 1 inch (2.5 cm) from the rim.

Handles, Feet and Cord Storage

Slow cookers are popular as tote-along appliances when potluck is the name of the game. Look for easy-to-grip handles that can be grasped with oven mitts on. The stoneware handles heat up when the appliance is cooking, so make sure to protect your hands accordingly.

Because slow cookers can heat up kitchen counters, many people worry about possible heat damage or even fire risk. It is always best to place your slow cooker on a solid, heat-resistant surface. However, to alleviate this problem, some manufacturers have developed slow cookers that have feet, or bases with rubberized bottoms. This feature makes using a slow cooker worry-free.

Finally, some manufacturers have developed retractable electric cords that store conveniently and efficiently inside the base of the slow cooker — a very helpful feature when storage space is at a premium.

When cleaning the slow cooker, never immerse the metal housing in water. It only needs a gentle wipe with a damp cloth to remove any dribbles or stickiness. Dry it with a clean kitchen towel so as not to damage the finish.

8 Essential Tricks of the Trade

Your slow cooker can be used to create any dish — just be adventurous! Here are my top 8 tips to help you use your appliance to its full advantage.

1. Prepare What You Can Ahead of Time

If you plan to start your slow cooker early in the day, here are a few things you can prepare the night before:

- Chop fresh vegetables, place them in airtight containers and refrigerate until the next day. Vegetables that will be used at the same time can be put into the same container to save space.
- Defrost frozen vegetables overnight in the refrigerator.
- Trim fat from meat and poultry and remove skin from poultry. Cut meat and poultry into pieces of the same size. Cubes are the best shape for even cooking, so try to get your pieces as close to cube-shaped as possible. Do *not* brown meat in advance; once it's cut to size, refrigerate it in an airtight container, keeping it separate from any other ingredients. (The exception to this rule is ground meat, which can be browned the night before; however, it still needs to be refrigerated in its own container.)

Always read the recipe all the way through first, to make sure you have the necessary ingredients and equipment, and to get a sense of the timing and what needs to happen when.

- Assemble nonperishable ingredients and cooking utensils in a convenient spot for a quick start.

Recipes in this book that lend themselves to additional advance preparation or cooking are accompanied by make-ahead instructions. Many recipes can also be completely cooked in advance and stored in the refrigerator or freezer for future use.

2. Choose Less Tender Cuts of Meat and Trim Off the Fat

The cuts of meat that benefit from slow cooking are less expensive and often from the tough shoulder area. Slow cooking breaks down the collagen in the muscles' connective tissue, leaving the meat moist and tender. Make sure to trim off all visible fat (and remove skin from poultry) before adding meat to the slow cooker. This will reduce the amount of fat you need to skim from the liquid at the end of the cooking process.

3. Cut Root Vegetables into Small Pieces

In the slow cooker, root vegetables, such as carrots, parsnips, turnips and potatoes, take longer to cook than meat pieces of the same size, so they should be thinly sliced or cut into cubes no bigger than 1 inch (2.5 cm). It's best to place them as close as possible to the bottom and sides of the stoneware, so that they benefit from proximity to the heat source.

4. Brown Meat and Sauté Vegetables First

Partial cooking or browning may add a few minutes to the preparation process, but in the end, those extra minutes will be worthwhile. Browning meat not only improves its color, but also breaks down the natural sugars, releasing their flavors. Sautéing vegetables with spices and dried herbs before slow cooking produces a richer, more intense sauce.

For browning, the first step is to cut the meat or poultry into pieces of the same size. Next, dredge it in flour, coating evenly. Add it in small batches to a small amount of oil heated over medium-high heat, either in a skillet or in your stoneware if it is designed for stovetop cooking. Stir or turn frequently to brown evenly. If you are using a skillet, transfer each batch to the slow cooker as it is browned. If you're using the stoneware, remove each batch to a plate as it is browned, then return all the meat to the stoneware after deglazing (see page 13).

Because of their hard consistency, root vegetables are well suited to the slow cooker, softening slowly and releasing their natural sugars as they simmer. Softer vegetables, such as zucchini or spinach, will turn to mush if cooked for a long time; these are best added in the last 20 minutes of cooking.

Meat should be browned in small batches, no more than a single layer over the bottom of the pan. If you overcrowd the meat, it causes too much steam, lowers the temperature and leaves meat gray instead of brown.

Sauté vegetables in a small amount of oil or butter (as called for in the recipe) heated over medium-high heat in a skillet or in stovetop-safe stoneware. For recipes that also contain browned meat, sauté the vegetables after the meat, in the same pan, either with the oil that's left or with added oil or butter. You just need to soften the vegetables — they don't need to be fully cooked or browned. If you overcook them now, they'll acquire a bland flavor during slow cooking.

After browning meat or poultry and sautéing vegetables, deglaze the pan with wine or broth to release the caramelized juices created during browning. Add a small amount of the liquid to the leftover juices and cooked-on food particles in the pan, bring it to a boil, then reduce the heat and simmer for 1 to 2 minutes while scraping up the bits stuck to the bottom of the pan. Pour this aromatic liquid over the browned meat in the slow cooker to maximize the flavor in your finished dish.

Dredging meat or poultry in flour has a two-pronged benefit. First, it adds flavor and helps the pieces brown quickly and intensely. Second, the starch in the flour acts as a thickening agent for the cooking juices once the meat is transferred to the slow cooker.

5. Don't Overdo the Liquids

Because moisture has no escape from the confines of the slow cooker, the amount of liquid in the stoneware increases as juices and steam are released from the food. Therefore, slow cooker recipes use only about half the liquid called for in conventional recipes. If you're new to slow cooking, keep in mind that the liquid may not cover the solids when you first add the ingredients to the slow cooker.

If you wind up with too much liquid when your meal is done cooking, remove the lid and increase the temperature to High if necessary, then cook, uncovered, for 30 to 45 minutes to allow some liquid to evaporate.

As a general rule, the slow cooker should be no less than half full and no more than two-thirds to three-quarters full of food once all the ingredients are added.

6. Use Whole Herbs and Spices

Whole-leaf dried herbs, such as dried thyme and oregano leaves, and whole or coarsely crushed spices release their flavor slowly throughout the long cooking process, so they are a better choice than ground herbs and spices, which tend to lose their flavor in the slow cooker. Add fresh herbs, such as basil and cilantro, during the last hour of cooking. Always taste your finished dish before serving it and adjust the salt and pepper if needed.

If you substitute fresh herbs for dried, you will need to use three times as much.

7. Resist the Temptation to Lift the Lid

Always cook with the slow cooker lid on. The lid traps heat as it rises and converts it into steam, which is what cooks the food. Removing the lid will result in major heat loss, which the slow cooker can't quickly recover. You will need to extend the cooking time by at least 20 minutes each time you lift the lid. Do so only when it is time to check for doneness, when adding ingredients or when stirring is recommended.

8. Experiment with Water Baths

Delicate dishes, such as custards, puddings and cheesecakes, are cooked to perfection in a hot-water bath, or bain-marie. In conventional cooking, this technique involves setting the filled baking dish in a larger pan filled with hot water before placing it in the oven. Heat is transferred from the hot water to the dish, cooking the contents gently and slowly, so that it doesn't curdle or form a crust. The technique works wonders in the slow cooker, too: custards, puddings and cheesecakes stay creamy and smooth, and cheesecakes do not crack. The challenge, however, is finding a dish that will fit properly in the slow cooker. Standard 4-cup (1 L) or 6-cup (1.5 L) ovenproof baking bowls work well in larger slow cookers. If you are making a cheesecake, a 7-inch (18 cm) springform pan should fit nicely.

These water baths add to the heat of your dish. So that you can safely and easily remove the dish from the slow cooker, you'll want to make foil handles to place under the dish when putting it in the stoneware. Cut a 2-foot (60 cm) piece of foil in half lengthwise. Fold each strip in half lengthwise and crisscross the strips in the bottom of the stoneware, bringing the ends up to clear the rim. Place the dish in the slow cooker and pour in enough water to come 1 inch (2.5 cm) up the sides of the dish. Cover the slow cooker with its lid, making sure the ends of the foil are tucked between the rim and the lid. Use the foil handles as lifters to remove the pan from the slow cooker.

Adapting Conventional Recipes

While this book is filled with an array of recipes to suit any palate, it's easy to alter your favorite pot roast, family stew or chili from conventional oven or stovetop directions to

If a recipe in this book instructs you to add or stir ingredients partway through, the resulting heat loss has been accounted for in the overall cooking time.

If the dish fits snugly in the slow cooker, add the water first. Since the water level will rise when you add the filled dish, test it first by pouring about 1 cup (250 mL) water into the stoneware. Add the filled pan and make sure the water rises 1 inch (2.5 cm) up the sides of the dish. If it rises any more than that, remove the pan and ladle some water out.

a slow-cooking method. You'll just need to follow a few simple guidelines:

- Select a recipe that uses a less tender cut of meat, such as beef brisket or blade roast, short ribs, stew meat, pork shoulder, or chicken or turkey drumsticks or thighs. These will become fork-tender and develop savory flavor during long cooking.

- Start by browning meats as you would for conventional recipes. Then sauté aromatic vegetables, such as onions, garlic, celery and carrots, with dried herbs and spices.

- If you have chosen a recipe with a heavy emphasis on meat, add some vegetables for a convenient way to cook a complete meal all at once. Keep in mind that root vegetables tend to cook more slowly than meat, so cut them into bite-size pieces and place them on the bottom and around the sides of the slow cooker, with the meat on top.

- Soak dried beans, peas and lentils until completely soft before adding them to the slow cooker; otherwise, the sugar and acid in other foods will prevent them from softening (see Basic Beans on page 120 for information on soaking beans).

- Reduce the amount of liquid you use by about half, as moisture is high and evaporation low in the slow cooker.

- If the recipe calls for uncooked rice, add $\frac{1}{4}$ cup (60 mL) extra liquid per $\frac{1}{4}$ cup (60 mL) rice. Long-grain parboiled (converted) white rice will yield the best results in all-day cooking.

- Add pasta and seafood in the last hour of cooking time. Pasta should be cooked to the tender but firm stage before it is added.

- Add tender vegetables, such as peas, broccoli, Brussels sprouts, cauliflower, kale and chard, in the last 15 to 60 minutes of the cooking process. Frozen vegetables, such as peas, corn and green beans, should be thawed first, then added in the last 15 to 30 minutes.

- Stir in cream, milk, sour cream and cheese just before serving. Dairy products can break down during extended cooking.

The chart on page 16 will give you an idea of how to adapt cooking times from your favorite conventional oven or stovetop recipes. These times are approximate; you are the best judge of when your food is perfectly cooked.

Organization is the key to successful slow cooking. You can prep many of your ingredients the day before and store them in airtight containers or storage bags in the refrigerator. Cover chopped potatoes with water to keep them from turning brown. Ground meat can be browned the day before, as long as it is fully cooked and refrigerated overnight. Chops, roasts, cubed meat and poultry must all be prepared just before cooking.

When adding ingredients to the slow cooker, leave at least 2 inches (5 cm) between the top of the food and the rim of the slow cooker so the food can come to a simmer.

Conventional Oven or Stovetop Time	Slow Cooker Time
15 to 30 minutes	1 1/2 hours on High
	3 hours on Low
1 hour	3 1/2 hours on High
	6 to 7 hours on Low
2 hours	4 1/2 hours on High
	9 to 10 hours on Low
3 hours	5 1/2 hours on High
	10 to 11 hours on Low

Food Safety Considerations

The U.S. Department of Agriculture assures us that, in a slow cooker that is used properly (the lid is left on and food is cooked at the appropriate heat level for the appropriate length of time), foods will reach their safe internal cooked temperature quickly enough to inhibit bacterial growth.

With that concern off the table, here are a few other kitchen safety details to consider when slow cooking:

- Always start with fresh or thawed meat and poultry. Using frozen or partially frozen meat will increase the time required for the meat's internal temperature to reach the "safe zone" in which bacteria growth is inhibited.
- In general, defrost frozen vegetables, such as peas and corn, before adding them to the slow cooker. This prevents them from slowing down the cooking process. Defrost them in the refrigerator overnight, or place them under cold running water to thaw and separate.
- Cook all ground meat and ground poultry completely before adding it to the slow cooker. (There are some exceptions, and proper cooking directions are given for these in the individual recipes.) If you are cooking ground meat the night before, chill it separately from other ingredients.
- Do not refrigerate uncooked or partially cooked meat or poultry in the slow cooker stoneware, as the insert will become very cold and will slow the cooking process. Partially cook meat or poultry only when transferring it immediately to the slow cooker. Do not refrigerate for later cooking.
- Precut meats and vegetables should be stored separately in the refrigerator. After cutting uncooked meat, never use

Once a dish is completely cooked, you can keep food warm by switching to the Low or Warm setting (many machines will automatically switch to Warm at the end of the preset cooking time). Fully cooked food is safe on these settings for up to 2 hours. Do not use the Warm setting for cooking — it is too low a temperature to cook food safely.

the same cutting board or knife for other foods without thoroughly washing these utensils with soap and hot water first.

- When cooking whole poultry or meatloaf, use a meat thermometer to accurately test doneness. Insert the thermometer into the thickest part of the thigh or loaf. The U.S. Department of Agriculture recommends cooking poultry and meatloaf to an internal temperature of 165°F (74°C); Health Canada recommends ensuring that the temperature has reached 170°F (77°C).
- Remove leftovers from the stoneware and refrigerate in small portions as quickly as possible.
- Do not reheat cooked food in the slow cooker. Frozen leftovers can be thawed in the refrigerator or microwave, then reheated in a conventional oven or microwave oven, or in a saucepan on the stove.

Know the Limitations

While I am the first to extol the virtues of slow cooking, it's important to remember that, as with any kitchen appliance, slow cookers do have some limitations. If you understand what cooks well in a slow cooker and what doesn't, you won't have any unwanted surprises.

First off, don't even entertain the idea of cooking premium, expensive cuts of meat, such as prime rib or beef filets. As mentioned earlier, slow cooking is designed to tenderize tough, inexpensive cuts of meat by breaking down collagen and fatty tissue. Cuts meant for grilling, broiling and sautéing should be left to those formats for best results.

Nor is it wise to use the slow cooker as a baking tool for items such as cookies and pies, which need dry heat. While we can achieve many wonderful desserts in the slow cooker, traditional baking methods remain the best ways to cook these items.

Although I have included many seafood recipes in this book, fish and shellfish require too short a cooking time to reap the full benefits of the slow cooker. Most of these recipes call for making a base of sauce or braised vegetables first, then adding the seafood at the end, to steam.

Finally, take care when working with dairy products and eggs, as it is easy to overcook, separate or toughen these ingredients. To avoid these problems, the recipes that contain dairy products or eggs are very specific about cooking times.

Check for doneness at the minimum time suggested, especially the first time you make a recipe.

For ease of cleanup, spray the stoneware insert with nonstick cooking spray before adding food. Do not subject the stoneware to sudden changes in temperature. Before cleaning it, let it come to room temperature, then fill it with hot, soapy water and let it soak for an hour or so. Use a nylon scrubber to remove cooked-on pieces. Most stoneware can also be cleaned in the dishwasher.

Ingredient Essentials

When I was developing and testing the recipes in this book, the basic ingredients I used were of standard size and consistency. The recipes make some assumptions about what is standard when it comes to basic ingredients; these distinctions are detailed below. For the best results, always use the recommended ingredient, exactly as called for, unless other options are indicated in a tip.

- Dried herbs are crumbled whole leaves, not ground.
- Table salt is used for cooking unless otherwise indicated. Where a recipe says "season to taste," I used kosher salt.
- All eggs used are large eggs; expect different results if you substitute medium or extra-large eggs.
- I used 2% milk and yogurt unless otherwise specified.
- When sour cream is added to the slow cooker, I used 14%. If using sour cream as a topping or adding it at the end of the cooking process, you can use a lower-fat (5%) version.
- I used salted butter.
- Fresh vegetables and fruits are medium-size unless otherwise indicated. Any inedible peels, skins, seeds and cores are removed unless otherwise indicated.
- "Onions" means regular cooking onions unless otherwise indicated.
- Canned tomatoes are diced, not whole, unless whole is specified.
- Rice is long-grain parboiled (converted), unless otherwise indicated.
- I used fresh, oven-ready lasagna noodles rather than the dried, no-boil type. For all other pasta shapes, I used dried pasta.
- Where recipes call for vegetable oil to brown meats and sauté vegetables, I used a canola/sunflower oil combination.
- When choosing poultry, look for air-chilled products, which have a firmer texture and will hold their shape better and be more tender after the long slow-cooking process.
- Avoid "seasoned" meats and poultry, which have been treated with additional water and sodium phosphate or other ingredients and tend to make slow-cooked foods watery and salty.

For baking recipes, eggs should be brought to room temperature before use; otherwise, they can be used directly from the refrigerator.

When I call for chopped or minced garlic, I used fresh garlic, not the preserved minced garlic available in stores.

When greasing stoneware, I sprayed it with nonstick cooking spray.

Breakfasts, Breads and Beverages

Pear and Honey Oatmeal

Makes 4 to 6 servings

Shake off the night's cobwebs with a bowl of this hearty oatmeal. Steel-cut oats traditionally take a much longer time to cook than quick-cooking rolled oats do. Cooking the oatmeal overnight gives you a chance to sit down to a hot breakfast in the morning, before heading out the door.

Tips

This oatmeal dish is also great served with fresh sliced bananas or apples.

For an extra-nutty flavor, try toasting the oatmeal first. Melt 2 tbsp (30 mL) butter in nonstick skillet. Add oatmeal and cook, stirring, over medium-high heat for 4 minutes or until browned and fragrant. Transfer to slow cooker stoneware and continue with cooking as directed.

- **4-quart slow cooker, stoneware greased**

2 cups	steel-cut or large-flake (old-fashioned) rolled oats	500 mL
1/4 tsp	ground cinnamon	1 mL
4 3/4 cups	water	1.175 L
1	ripe pear	1
1 tbsp	liquid honey	15 mL
	Plain yogurt (optional)	

1. In prepared slow cooker stoneware, combine oats, cinnamon, and water.

2. Cover and cook on Low for 8 hours or overnight.

3. Just before serving, dice pear. Spoon oatmeal into individual serving bowls and top with diced pear. Drizzle with honey and, if desired, serve with a dollop of yogurt.

Steel-cut (or Irish) oats are more coarsely ground and have a chewier texture than Scottish (or rolled) oats. Scottish oats are ground into a meal, making for a creamier porridge. Rolled oats (also known as large-flake or old-fashioned oats) are steamed first, then rolled, which allows them to cook a little faster. Make sure you don't use quick-cooking rolled oats in this recipe.

Cherry Vanilla Irish Oatmeal

There's no question that steel-cut oats are superior in flavor to instant oatmeal, but the extended cooking time, constant stirring and sticky pot to clean can put off even the most loyal oatmeal enthusiast. Using a slow cooker eliminates the stovetop surveillance and mess, plus the oatmeal can be kept warm for late risers.

Tips

If you find the oats a bit thick after cooking, just thin the mixture with a little extra soy milk or water.

Soy milk stands up well to slow cooking, since it has been processed in such a way that it can withstand the high temperatures. Skim and 2% milk tend to break down and curdle during long cooking.

- **4-quart slow cooker, stoneware greased**

4 cups	vanilla-flavored soy milk	1 L
4 cups	water	1 L
1¾ cups	steel-cut or large-flake (old-fashioned) rolled oats	675 mL
½ cup	dried cherries or cranberries	125 mL
⅔ cup	pure maple syrup, divided	150 mL
½ tsp	salt	2 mL
¼ tsp	ground allspice	1 mL
½ cup	fresh or frozen blueberries, thawed if frozen (optional)	125 mL
½ cup	chopped pecans (optional)	125 mL

1. In prepared slow cooker stoneware, combine soy milk, water, oats, cherries, ½ cup (125 mL) of the maple syrup, salt and allspice.

2. Cover and cook on Low for 8 hours or overnight.

3. Turn off slow cooker and stir in remaining maple syrup. Add additional water, if necessary, to achieve desired thickness. If desired, serve garnished with blueberries and pecans.

Baked Apple Breakfast Cobbler

Makes 4 to 6 servings

There's nothing like starting the day with a warm breakfast, except maybe smelling it cooking while you are still in bed. That's the beauty of this slow cooker breakfast cobbler. Prepare all of the ingredients and assemble it right after dinner. Then, before you head to bed, press the Start button. You will love the smell you wake up to!

Tips

To toast almonds, spread nuts in a single layer in a shallow baking pan or rimmed baking sheet. Bake in a 350°F (180°C) oven, stirring or shaking once or twice, for 5 to 10 minutes or until golden brown and fragrant.

You can use low-fat granola for this recipe.

- **Minimum 4-quart slow cooker, stoneware greased**

6	apples, peeled, cored and quartered	6
1 tbsp	freshly squeezed lemon juice	15 mL
2 tbsp	pure maple syrup	30 mL
1 tsp	ground cinnamon	5 mL
2 cups	prepared granola cereal	500 mL
2 tbsp	butter, melted	30 mL
1/4 cup	toasted slivered almonds	60 mL
	Vanilla-flavored yogurt	

1. Place apples in bottom of prepared slow cooker stoneware. Drizzle with lemon juice and gently toss to coat. Drizzle with maple syrup and sprinkle with cinnamon. Top with granola and drizzle with butter.

2. Cover and cook on Low for 8 hours or until apples are tender and sauce is bubbling.

3. Spoon into serving bowls and top with almonds and a dollop of yogurt.

> The best baking apples are those that maintain their shape but become nice and tender and have a sweet-tart flavor that really says "apple" when they're cooked. Some of the best varieties for this dish are Cortland, Golden Delicious, Granny Smith, Braeburn and Jonagold.

Tunisian Breakfast Couscous

Makes 4 servings

Israeli, or pearl, couscous is a staple in Middle Eastern cooking. It is a pearl-size pasta that cooks much the same as other pasta of the same size. I was curious about how it would work as a breakfast cereal, and the results are hearty and satisfying, with just a bit of texture. Slow cooking allows it to develop a nice richness. Make sure not to use the quick-cooking variety of couscous.

Tip

If you make the cereal the night before, let it cook for 6 hours on Low, then switch your slow cooker to Warm before you go to bed. That way the cereal won't overcook, and everyone can help themselves as they make their way down to the kitchen for breakfast.

• **4-quart slow cooker, stoneware greased**

1½ cups	Israeli couscous	375 mL
¼ tsp	salt	1 mL
¼ tsp	ground cinnamon or cardamom	1 mL
2 cups	water	500 mL
3 tbsp	butter	45 mL
2 tbsp	liquid honey	30 mL
1 cup	chopped apricots	250 mL
½ cup	chopped toasted almonds	125 mL
	Plain yogurt	
	Additional liquid honey (optional)	

1. In prepared slow cooker stoneware, combine couscous, salt, cinnamon, water, butter, honey, apricots and almonds.

2. Cover and cook on Low for 6 hours or overnight (see tip, at left).

3. Stir well (the cereal will be thick) and serve with yogurt. Drizzle with honey, if desired.

Fruit and Fiber Breakfast Pudding

Makes 6 servings

My husband is a fan of hot breakfast cereals. He loves to experiment with all kinds of grains and seeds, to find new ways to get more fiber. Recently, my mother introduced me to hemp nuts, which I love to sprinkle over the top for some extra crunch. Add some fresh blueberries, too, if you wish.

Tip

To grease stoneware, use a nonstick vegetable spray or use the cake pan grease available in specialty cake decorating shops or bulk food stores.

- **4-quart slow cooker, stoneware greased**

³/₄ cup	steel-cut or rolled oats	175 mL
¹/₄ cup	pot barley	60 mL
¹/₄ cup	medium-ground bulgur	60 mL
¹/₂ cup	slivered dried apricots	125 mL
¹/₂ cup	dried cranberries or raisins	125 mL
1 tbsp	flax seeds	15 mL
2 tbsp	packed brown sugar	30 mL
1 tbsp	butter	15 mL
¹/₂ tsp	salt	2 mL
¹/₂ tsp	ground cinnamon	2 mL

1. In prepared slow cooker stoneware, combine oats, barley, bulgur, apricots, cranberries, flax seeds, brown sugar, butter, salt and cinnamon.

2. Cover and cook on Low for 8 hours or overnight. Serve warm.

Bulgur is one of the oldest processed grains. It is made by soaking and cooking the whole wheat kernel, drying it and then removing part of the bran and cracking the remaining kernel into small pieces. It is great as a grain in salads and as a nutritious extender and thickener for meat dishes and soups. Bulgur will absorb twice its volume in water and can be used in place of rice in any recipe.

Savory Brunch Bread Pudding

Makes 4 to 6 servings

More commonly known as a "strata," this layered dish makes a great brunch when you have company over, because it can be assembled the night before, then cooked in the morning. When I tested this dish, it earned the comment "Absolutely delicious!" Serve it with a mixed fruit salad.

Tip

You might think that bread starts to go stale days after it is made, but the process actually begins as soon as the loaf leaves the oven and starts to cool. How quickly it goes stale depends on what ingredients went into it, how it was baked and how it is stored. For this recipe, purchase the loaf a day or two ahead. You can also use ordinary white bread; just cut each slice into quarters.

- **4- to 5-quart slow cooker, stoneware greased**

2 tbsp	butter	30 mL
8 oz	mushrooms, sliced	250 g
1	onion, minced	1
1	loaf day-old Italian bread, cut into 12 to 16 slices	1
8 oz	prosciutto, chopped	250 g
2 cups	shredded Cheddar or fontina cheese	500 mL
3	eggs	3
2½ cups	whole milk	625 mL
1 tbsp	chopped fresh parsley	15 mL

1. In a nonstick skillet, melt butter over medium-high heat. Sauté mushrooms and onions for 5 to 7 minutes or until tender and liquid has evaporated. Set aside.

2. Place half the bread slices in a single layer on the bottom of prepared slow cooker stoneware. Top with prosciutto, cheese and mushroom mixture. Place remaining bread over top.

3. In a blender or food processor, blend eggs and milk until well combined. Pour evenly over mixture in slow cooker.

4. Cover and cook on Low for 3 to 4 hours or until top is golden brown. Sprinkle with parsley before serving.

Make Ahead

This dish can be assembled up to 12 hours in advance. Prepare through step 3, cover and refrigerate overnight. The next day, let stoneware stand at room temperature for 10 minutes, then place in slow cooker and proceed with step 4.

Cluck and Murphy Breakfast Casserole

Makes 8 to 10 servings

In diner talk, "Cluck" refers to eggs and "Murphy" (a common Irish surname) to the potato's rich Irish heritage. Though filling enough as a main dish, this breakfast casserole can also be served in smaller portions, as a tasty side for pancakes or French toast. It's also great served as an easy dinner with a crisp green salad.

Tip

The stoneware inserts in most slow cookers are dishwasher-, microwave- and oven-safe, up to 400°F (200°C), depending on the manufacturer. However, unless the manufacturer indicates otherwise, most are not safe to be used on top of the stove. Check the manufacturer's instructions for further information.

- **Minimum 4-quart slow cooker, stoneware greased**

8 oz	bacon, cut into 1-inch (2.5 cm) pieces	250 g
1	onion, chopped	1
1	red bell pepper, chopped	1
8 oz	mushrooms, sliced	250 g
1 tbsp	Dijon mustard	15 mL
1/2 tsp	salt	2 mL
1/2 tsp	freshly ground black pepper	2 mL
6	eggs, lightly beaten	6
3/4 cup	sour cream	175 mL
1	package (2 lbs/1 kg) frozen hash brown potatoes, thawed	1
2 cups	shredded Cheddar cheese	500 mL
1 tbsp	chopped fresh parsley	15 mL

1. In a nonstick skillet over medium heat, cook bacon, stirring, for 7 to 8 minutes or until crisp. Reserving drippings in pan, transfer bacon to a plate lined with paper towels to drain. Once cool enough to handle, crumble bacon.

2. Discard all but 1 tbsp (15 mL) of the reserved drippings. Add onion, red pepper and mushrooms; cook over medium heat, stirring occasionally, for 5 to 6 minutes or until vegetables are tender. Stir in mustard, salt and pepper.

3. In a large bowl, whisk together eggs and sour cream. Spread half of the potatoes in prepared slow cooker stoneware. Spread onion mixture evenly over top. Sprinkle with cheese. Spread remaining potatoes over top. Pour egg mixture evenly over top and sprinkle with crumbled bacon.

4. Cover and cook on Low for 3 to 4 hours or until eggs are set and edges are brown. Do not overcook. Sprinkle with parsley and serve immediately.

Make Ahead

This casserole can be assembled up to 12 hours in advance. Prepare through step 3, cover and refrigerate overnight. The next day, let stoneware stand at room temperature for 10 minutes, then place in slow cooker and proceed with step 4.

Southwestern Holiday Hash Browns Bake

Makes 6 to 8 servings

This simple make-ahead dish is sure to please a hungry morning crowd. It has everything a good breakfast plate should have: sausage, eggs and hash browns. Serve with sliced fresh tomatoes — or with salsa for a little zing on the side.

Tip

Slices of Southwest Cornbread (page 73) make a nice accompaniment to this recipe. Cook up a pan to help feed extra-hungry visitors.

● **Minimum 4-quart slow cooker, stoneware greased**

4 cups	frozen hash brown potatoes, thawed	1 L
1 lb	smoked cured chorizo sausage, chopped	500 g
1	can (14 to 19 oz/398 to 540 mL) black beans, drained and rinsed	1
1 cup	frozen corn	250 mL
1	red bell pepper, chopped	1
1	onion, chopped	1
2 cups	shredded Monterey Jack cheese	500 mL
8	eggs	8
2 cups	whole milk	500 mL
1/2 tsp	salt	2 mL
1/4 tsp	cayenne pepper	1 mL
2 tbsp	chopped fresh cilantro	30 mL

1. In a large bowl, combine potatoes, sausage, beans, corn, red pepper and onion. Transfer to prepared slow cooker stoneware. Sprinkle with cheese.

2. In a blender, combine eggs, milk, salt and cayenne; pulse until well blended. Pour egg mixture evenly over potato mixture. Cover and let stand for 30 minutes before cooking.

3. Cover and cook on Low for 3 to 4 hours or until eggs are set and edges are browned. Do not overcook. Sprinkle with cilantro and let stand for 5 minutes before cutting.

Make Ahead

This casserole can be assembled up to 12 hours in advance. Prepare through step 2, cover and refrigerate overnight. The next day, let stoneware stand at room temperature for 10 minutes, then place in slow cooker and proceed with step 3.

Fresh cilantro, also known as coriander or Chinese parsley, has a distinctive smell and flavor that suits hearty chilis, as well as Southeast Asian and Indian dishes. To maximize its fairly short refrigerator shelf life, wash it well, spin dry and wrap in paper towels, then store in a plastic bag in the fridge. If the cilantro has roots attached, leave them on — they help keep the leaves fresh.

Slow Cooker Western Omelet

Makes 4 servings

One evening after dinner, I decided to experiment with a few extra ingredients I had in my refrigerator. With a combination of ham, eggs, cheese and a few vegetables, I set out to create a slow cooker omelet. The results were astounding. This casserole is a little firmer than a stovetop omelet, but it is still nice and tender. You can enjoy it hot or at room temperature, and it is delicious served with a tossed green salad and toast.

Tip

To grease stoneware, use a nonstick vegetable spray or use the cake pan grease available in specialty cake decorating shops or bulk food stores.

- **Minimum 4-quart slow cooker, stoneware greased**

12	eggs	12
1/4 cup	olive oil	60 mL
1 tsp	Dijon mustard	5 mL
1/3 cup	all-purpose flour	75 mL
1/2 tsp	salt	2 mL
1/4 tsp	freshly ground black pepper	1 mL
1	onion, finely chopped	1
1/2 cup	diced ham	125 mL
1/2	green bell pepper, finely chopped	1/2
1 cup	shredded Cheddar cheese	250 mL
2 tbsp	chopped fresh parsley (or 1 tbsp/15 mL dried)	30 mL

1. In a blender or food processor, combine eggs, oil and mustard; blend until mixed. Add flour, salt and pepper; pulse a few times until flour has been incorporated into egg mixture.

2. Pour egg mixture into prepared slow cooker stoneware. Sprinkle onion, ham, green pepper, cheese and parsley evenly over egg mixture.

3. Cover and cook on Low for 3 1/2 to 4 hours or until eggs are set and edges are browned. Do not overcook or eggs will toughen. Serve immediately.

Since eggs need to cook at a low temperature to remain tender, the slow cooker treats them very kindly. It's important to cook them on Low so you have more control and will get better results. If you cook them on High, it will toughen the protein and make the eggs too rubbery.

Overnight Blueberry French Toast

Makes 6 to 8 servings

This unique breakfast dish, filled with the rich flavor of heavenly blueberries, is perfect for any holiday breakfast or brunch. Turn the slow cooker on early in the morning, and by the time the rest of the house is up, you will have a fabulous dish to serve. Be sure to serve it with maple syrup and, for extra decadence, a little whipped cream.

Tip

Packages of frozen blueberries are almost a "pantry staple" in our house. We use them in just about everything. I often pick up a few bags when I see them on sale. There is no need to defrost the berries before using them in this recipe.

- **Minimum 5-quart slow cooker, stoneware greased**

1 cup	lightly packed brown sugar	250 mL
1¼ tsp	ground cinnamon	6 mL
¼ cup	butter, melted	60 mL
12	slices white, whole wheat or whole-grain bread	12
1½ cups	fresh or frozen blueberries	375 mL
5	eggs, lightly beaten	5
1½ cups	whole milk	375 mL
1 tsp	vanilla extract	5 mL
½ tsp	salt	2 mL
	Maple syrup, whipped cream and fresh blueberries (optional)	

1. In a bowl, combine brown sugar, cinnamon and butter, mixing well. Sprinkle one-third of the mixture evenly over bottom of prepared slow cooker stoneware. Cover with 6 bread slices. Sprinkle with another third of the sugar mixture and scatter berries over top. Top with remaining bread slices. Sprinkle with remaining sugar mixture.

2. In a large bowl, beat eggs, milk, vanilla and salt. Pour evenly into slow cooker. Press down lightly on bread slices. Cover and refrigerate overnight.

3. Place stoneware in slow cooker. Cover and cook on Low for 3 to 4 hours or until eggs are set and browned. Serve with maple syrup, a dollop of whipped cream and blueberries, if desired.

Slow-Cooked Baked Apple Pancake

Makes 4 servings

Everyone loves this giant family-breakfast pancake, and we also eat it as a breakfast-for-dinner meal. It is great served with tiny pork sausages and fresh maple syrup.

Tip

To prevent condensed moisture on the slow cooker lid from dripping onto the cake batter, place two clean tea towels, each folded in half (so you will have four layers), across the top of the stoneware before covering and cooking. The towels will absorb the moisture generated during cooking.

Variation

Substitute ripe pear slices for the apples and use cardamom in place of the cinnamon.

- **4- to 5-quart slow cooker**

1 tbsp	granulated sugar	15 mL
1/2 tsp	ground cinnamon	2 mL
1/4 cup	butter	60 mL
6	apples, peeled and thinly sliced	6

Pancake

2 cups	all-purpose flour	500 mL
2 tsp	baking powder	10 mL
1/4 tsp	salt	1 mL
1/4 cup	butter, softened	60 mL
2 tbsp	granulated sugar	30 mL
2	eggs, lightly beaten	2
3/4 cup	plain yogurt or sour cream	175 mL
	Maple syrup	

1. In a small bowl, combine sugar and cinnamon; set aside.

2. In a nonstick skillet, melt butter over medium-high heat. Add apples and cook, stirring often, for 5 minutes or until tender and translucent. Transfer to slow cooker stoneware and sprinkle with half the sugar mixture.

3. *Pancake:* In a bowl, combine flour, baking powder and salt. In another bowl, using an electric mixer, cream butter and sugar until light and fluffy. Beat in eggs until incorporated. Add flour mixture alternately with yogurt, making two additions of flour mixture and two of yogurt, beating well after each addition. Spread batter over apples (batter will be very thick) and sprinkle with remaining sugar mixture.

4. Place two clean towels across top of stoneware (see tip, at left). Cover with lid and cook on High for 2 1/2 to 3 hours or until a tester inserted in the center comes out clean. Serve drizzled with maple syrup.

Blueberry Banana Bread

Makes 18 slices

I have made this bread for years (but not in the slow cooker). In fact, raccoons went to town with a loaf of it on one of our camping trips when the cooler was not closed properly! I decided to adapt it to the slow cooker after reviewing other similar recipes. The results were fantastic. It is tender and moist, but a little swipe of butter on it is good, too.

Tips

Some people may wonder why you would try this in the slow cooker, rather than in the oven. Baking in the slow cooker allows you a little more freedom, time-wise, to walk away from the baking (something you wouldn't do if baking in the oven).

I like to use a silicone loaf pan in the slow cooker. If you have a round slow cooker, try using a round silicone cake pan that fits snugly inside the slow cooker casing.

Variation

This banana bread is also good made with $\frac{1}{2}$ cup (125 mL) chocolate chips or chopped walnuts instead of the blueberries.

- **Minimum 5-quart slow cooker**
- *9- by 5-inch (23 by 12.5 cm) loaf pan, greased*
- *Wire trivet to fit in slow cooker*

$1\frac{1}{2}$ cups	all purpose flour	375 mL
$1\frac{1}{2}$ tsp	baking powder	7 mL
$\frac{1}{2}$ tsp	salt	2 mL
$\frac{1}{4}$ tsp	baking soda	1 mL
$\frac{1}{3}$ cup	butter, softened	75 mL
$\frac{2}{3}$ cup	granulated sugar	150 mL
1	egg	1
3	small bananas, mashed	3
$\frac{1}{2}$ cup	fresh or frozen blueberries	125 mL
$\frac{1}{2}$ cup	chopped walnuts (optional)	125 mL

1. In a bowl, combine flour, baking powder, salt and baking soda.

2. In a large bowl, using an electric mixer, cream butter and sugar until light and fluffy. Beat in egg. Stir in banana until incorporated. Using a rubber spatula, stir in flour mixture just until moistened. Spoon mixture into prepared loaf pan, smoothing top.

3. Set pan on wire trivet in slow cooker. (Do not add water.) Cover slow cooker, but prop lid open slightly by placing a chopstick or bamboo skewer between the lid and stoneware (to allow steam to escape). Cook on High for $3\frac{1}{2}$ to 4 hours or until a tester inserted in the center of loaf comes out clean. (Do not remove the lid for the first 2 hours of cooking time.)

4. Transfer loaf pan to a wire rack. Let stand for at least 20 minutes to cool. With a knife, loosen sides of loaf. Turn out onto rack to cool completely. Slice when cool enough to handle.

Robb's Cheesy Dill Bread

Makes 16 to 18 slices

This recipe was given to me by my friend Robb Wilson. He says he never makes it the same way twice, because he throws together whatever cheese and fresh herbs he has on hand. It took some creative testing to decipher his recipe, but the end result was great.

Tip

Yeast used in baking is dehydrated and dormant. Active dry yeast needs to be dissolved in warm water to be activated. Quick-rising or instant dry yeast comes in smaller granules and can be added directly to the dry ingredients. For this recipe, use the active dry type.

• **4-quart slow cooker, stoneware greased**

2 tsp	cornmeal	10 mL
1	package ($1/4$ oz/7 g) active dry yeast	1
2 tsp	granulated sugar	10 mL
2 cups	lukewarm water, divided	500 mL
3 cups	all-purpose flour	750 mL
1 cup	whole wheat flour	250 mL
$1/2$ cup	chopped fresh dill	125 mL
$1/3$ cup	freshly grated Parmesan cheese, divided	75 mL
$1/2$ tsp	salt	2 mL
2 tbsp	vegetable oil	30 mL
1 tbsp	milk	15 mL

1. Preheat slow cooker metal casing to High (without stoneware inside). Sprinkle prepared slow cooker stoneware with cornmeal, tapping to coat evenly; line bottom of stoneware with parchment paper. Set aside.

2. Stir yeast and sugar into $1/2$ cup (125 mL) of the lukewarm water. Let stand for 10 minutes or until frothy.

3. In a large bowl, combine all-purpose flour, whole wheat flour, dill, $1/4$ cup (60 mL) of the Parmesan and salt. Make a well in the center and pour in the yeast mixture, the remaining lukewarm water and oil. Using a wooden spoon, stir until well blended.

4. Transfer dough to a well-floured work surface and knead for 8 to 10 minutes or until smooth and elastic. Add more flour, if needed, to prevent sticking.

5. Form dough into a round, place in prepared slow cooker stoneware and brush with milk. Sprinkle top with the remaining Parmesan. Let stand for 5 minutes before placing stoneware in preheated metal casing.

6. Cover and cook on High for $2^1/2$ to 3 hours or until top of loaf springs back when lightly pressed and edges are browned.

7. Turn off heat and let stand for 5 minutes. Remove stoneware, then loosen loaf by running a knife or spatula around outside edges. Invert stoneware onto cooling rack and give a sharp, quick shake to release loaf. Let cool before slicing.

Mary's Australian Ginger Beer

Makes 2 cups (500 mL) syrup, 8 servings

I developed this recipe for my mother-in-law. After her 50th-wedding-anniversary trip to Australia, she came home raving about the wonderful ginger beer she had enjoyed Down Under. It made perfect sense to brew the syrup slowly in the slow cooker to extract the ginger flavor. The syrup stores nicely in the refrigerator for up to 1 month. Cheers, Mary!

Tips

Ginger syrup will keep for up to 1 month in a sealed container in the refrigerator.

Lemon zest has an intense lemony flavor with very little bitterness (any bitterness is found in the white pith). Use a vegetable peeler to remove the zest (without the white pithy part) in long strips.

- **Minimum 4-quart slow cooker**

Ginger Syrup

1½ lbs	gingerroot, peeled and coarsely chopped or thinly sliced (2 cups/500 mL)	750 g
2 cups	granulated sugar	500 mL
4	2-inch (5 cm) long strips lemon zest	4
2 cups	water	500 mL
	Ice cubes	
1	bottle (32 oz/2 L) lemon-lime-flavored soda	1

1. *Ginger Syrup:* In slow cooker stoneware, combine ginger, sugar, lemon zest and water.

2. Cover and cook on Low for 5 to 6 hours.

3. Let syrup cool to room temperature. Strain through a fine-mesh sieve into a container with a lid. Discard solids.

4. To serve, place ice cubes in tall glasses, then add ¼ cup (60 mL) of the ginger syrup to each glass. Fill to the top with soda. Taste and add more ginger syrup, if desired. Serve immediately.

Hot Spiced Pumpkin Pie Latte

Makes 4 to 6 servings

This is my take on the expensive, high-end coffee shops' seasonal pumpkin beverage. After looking up a recipe on the web, I thought, Why not try it in the slow cooker? I prefer to use soy milk, as it stands up well in the heat of the slow cooker. This recipe easily doubles for a larger crowd.

Tips

This warm beverage holds well for several hours on Warm. If your slow cooker has a Warm mode, set it for an additional 2 hours.

To make your own pumpkin pie spice, combine 1/2 tsp (2 mL) ground cinnamon, 1/4 tsp (1 mL) ground ginger, 1/4 tsp (1 mL) ground nutmeg and a pinch of ground cloves.

Variation

Gingerbread Latte: Substitute 1/2 cup (125 mL) granulated sugar for the brown sugar. Omit the pumpkin purée. Instead of pumpkin pie spice, use 2 tsp (10 mL) ground ginger, 1 tsp (5 mL) ground cinnamon and 1/4 tsp (1 mL) each ground cloves and nutmeg. Garnish each mug with whipped cream and serve with a cinnamon stick.

- **3- to 4-quart slow cooker**

4 cups	soy milk or whole milk	1 L
1/4 cup	canned pumpkin purée	60 mL
1/4 cup	packed brown sugar	60 mL
1 tsp	pumpkin pie spice	5 mL
1	vanilla bean, split lengthwise	1
1/2 cup	brewed espresso (or 3/4 cup/ 175 mL strong brewed coffee)	125 mL
	Whipped cream	
	Grated nutmeg	

1. In slow cooker stoneware, whisk together soy milk, pumpkin purée, brown sugar and pumpkin pie spice; add vanilla bean.

2. Cover and cook on High for 2 hours or until hot. Remove vanilla bean and let it cool slightly.

3. When the vanilla bean is cool enough to handle, use the tip of a paring knife to scrape the seeds into the milk mixture; discard pods. Whisk in coffee to combine well.

4. Ladle into mugs and top with whipped cream and a sprinkling of nutmeg.

> Since you are only using a small amount of the canned pumpkin purée for this recipe, you can find lots of interesting ways to use up the leftovers. Why not bake up your favorite pumpkin loaf recipe to serve with the latte? The purée can also be used in waffle or pancake batter or soup. The possibilities are endless.

Hot Licorice Toddy

Makes 12 servings

Licorice root tea is known for its ability to relieve respiratory and stomach ailments. However, in this recipe, it's the basis for a soothing hot toddy that is the ultimate winter warmer. Because of its color, it's a fun beverage to serve at an adults-only Halloween party, but it's tasty for any cold-weather occasion.

Tip

You can find licorice spice tea in tea shops or health food stores.

- **Minimum 4-quart slow cooker**

12 cups	cold water	3 L
8	licorice spice tea bags	8
1	vanilla bean, split lengthwise	1
2	3-inch (7.5 cm) long strips lemon zest	2
1 cup	black sambuca	250 mL
1 cup	vodka	250 mL
	Black licorice twists	

1. Pour water into slow cooker stoneware. Place tea bags in water, draping the strings with the finger tabs over the rim. Add vanilla bean and lemon zest.

2. Cover and cook on Low for 8 to 10 hours or until tea is well steeped and steaming. Remove and discard tea bags and lemon zest. Remove vanilla bean and let it cool slightly.

3. When the vanilla bean is cool enough to handle, use the tip of a paring knife to scrape the seeds into the tea; discard pods. Stir in sambuca and vodka.

4. Reduce heat to Low or Warm. Mixture will stay warm for up to 3 hours.

5. Ladle into mugs and garnish with licorice twist.

> Black sambuca is made from a blend of distillates — including green anise seeds, star anise (hence the licorice flavor), elder flowers, elderberries, coriander and lemon peel — mixed with neutral alcohol from beets for a natural sweetness. It gets its rich black color from elderberry skins, and it is not as much of a "throat arsonist" as clear sambuca. Most liquor stores have a good selection of sambucas. If you can't find black sambuca, you can substitute the clear variety, but you won't get the black color.

Malted Café Mocha

Makes 6 to 8 servings

I have been drinking hot malt beverages since I was a child, and even today, when I need something to relax, I heat up some warm milk and mix in a spoonful of my favorite drink crystals. I decided to experiment with Ovaltine and coffee, which complement each other extremely well. The results were outstanding. This drink is yummy with sweet desserts, but also makes a delicious wintery hot chocolate–like treat.

Tips

For the freshest coffee, purchase whole beans and grind them yourself. You can find vanilla-flavored beans in the supermarket. Use 1 to 2 tbsp (15 to 30 mL) ground coffee per 6 oz (175 mL) water.

If you want to send your guests home early, use decaffeinated coffee — the combination of decaf and Ovaltine will have them falling asleep at the table.

It's best to let guests add their own liqueur to this drink; that way, even teens can enjoy it.

This beverage holds well for several hours on Warm. If your slow cooker has a Warm mode, set it for an additional 2 hours.

• **4- to 6-quart slow cooker**

4 cups	strong brewed vanilla-flavored coffee	1 L
2 cups	whole, evaporated or soy milk	500 mL
1 cup	malt beverage crystals, such as Ovaltine, original or chocolate-flavored	250 mL
¼ cup	granulated sugar	60 mL
	Kahlúa or Bailey's liqueur (optional)	
	Whipped cream	
	Grated chocolate	

1. In slow cooker stoneware, combine coffee and milk. Whisk in malt crystals and sugar. Cover and cook on High for 2 hours or until bubbling.

2. Whisk again before serving to ensure that malt crystals and sugar are dissolved. Ladle into mugs and add a splash of liqueur to each, if desired. Top with whipped cream and sprinkling of grated chocolate.

Appetizers, Dips and Spreads

Rosemary Roasted Pecans

Makes 2 cups (500 mL)

These elegant nuts perk up a plate of seasonal snacks. They are tasty served with Cranberry Baked Brie (page 42).

Tips

Because of their high fat content, nuts tend to go rancid quickly. They are best stored in an airtight container in a dark, cool, dry place. The freezer is ideal, and doesn't harm the nuts at all.

Along with a good bottle of red wine, these roasted nuts make a great hostess gift! Package them in an attractive tin tied with a ribbon.

- **3- to 6-quart slow cooker**
- *Baking sheet, lined with parchment paper*

1 tbsp	olive oil	15 mL
1 tsp	dried rosemary	5 mL
1/2 tsp	coarse salt	2 mL
2 cups	pecan halves	500 mL

1. In slow cooker stoneware, combine oil, rosemary and salt. Add pecans and toss to coat.

2. Cover and cook on High for 1 hour. Uncover and cook, stirring occasionally, for 1 hour or until lightly browned and fragrant.

3. Transfer pecans to prepared baking sheet and let cool. Once cool, store in an airtight container in the refrigerator for up to 6 weeks or in the freezer for up to 3 months.

Smoky Almonds

**Makes 2 cups
(500 mL)**

*On our trip to San
Francisco, my husband and
I stumbled across a farmer
selling freshly roasted
almonds with various
seasonings. He scooped
us out a pound, and we ate
them back at our hotel in
the wine bar while sipping
on glasses of red wine.
Believe me, you won't want
to stop nibbling on these.*

Tip

Light, heat and moisture
conspire to spoil nuts, so they
are best stored in airtight
plastic or glass containers in
a dark, cool, dry place. The
freezer doesn't harm them
at all.

- 1½- to 3-quart slow cooker
- *Baking sheet, lined with parchment paper*

2 tsp	olive oil	10 mL
½ tsp	smoked paprika	2 mL
½ tsp	kosher salt	2 mL
2 cups	natural almonds	500 mL

1. In slow cooker stoneware, combine oil, paprika and salt. Add almonds and toss to coat.

2. Cover and cook on High for 1 hour. Uncover and cook, stirring occasionally, for 1 hour or until nuts are browned and fragrant.

3. Transfer almonds to prepared baking sheet and let cool. Once cool, store in an airtight container in the refrigerator for up to 6 weeks or in the freezer for up to 3 months.

Spicy Maple Walnuts

**Makes 2 cups
(500 mL)**

*After they're transferred
to the baking sheet, these
nuts continue to toast a bit
from the intense heat of the
glaze, so don't overcook
them. I love the combined
flavors of the walnuts and
the maple syrup (one of
my favorite flavors of ice
cream) with the heat from
the hot pepper flakes.*

Variation

Pecan halves and almonds
also work well in this recipe,
in place of the walnuts.

- **4- to 6-quart slow cooker**
- *Baking sheet, lined with parchment paper*

¼ cup	butter, melted	60 mL
¼ cup	pure maple syrup	60 mL
2 tbsp	chopped gingerroot	30 mL
2 tsp	water	10 mL
½ tsp	ground ginger	2 mL
½ tsp	salt	2 mL
Pinch	hot pepper flakes	Pinch
2 cups	walnut halves	500 mL

1. In slow cooker stoneware, combine butter, maple syrup, gingerroot, water, ground ginger, salt and hot pepper flakes. Add walnuts and toss to coat.

2. Cover and cook on High for 1 hour. Uncover and cook, stirring occasionally, for 1 hour or until nuts are browned and fragrant.

3. Transfer walnuts to prepared baking sheet and let cool. Once cool, store in an airtight container in the refrigerator for up to 6 weeks or in the freezer for up to 3 months.

Grecian Braised Olives

**Makes about
4 cups (1 L)**

*I adore these olives. I
first tasted them at a
Mediterranean-themed
dinner party. As I was
putting the recipes together
for this book, I decided to
try making this appetizer in
the slow cooker, and was
pleasantly surprised by how
delicious the olives tasted.
It is nice to have a mixed
selection of olives, for color
and appearance, but one
variety will also work well.*

Tip

If you can't find a serrano
pepper, you can substitute
1 tsp (5 mL) hot pepper
flakes.

- **3- to 4-quart slow cooker**

2 cups	mixed olives, such as kalamata, green, niçoise	500 mL
2	cloves garlic, finely minced	2
1	small fennel bulb, thinly sliced	1
1	small navel orange, sliced into rings and quartered	1
1	red serrano chile pepper, sliced (optional)	1
2 tbsp	chopped fresh oregano or 1 tsp (5 mL) dried	30 mL
2 tbsp	olive oil	30 mL
	Freshly ground black pepper	

1. In slow cooker stoneware, combine olives, garlic, fennel, orange, chile pepper (if using), oregano and oil.

2. Cover and cook on Low for 4 to 6 hours or until warmed through. Season to taste with black pepper.

> Serrano chile peppers are green at first, then ripen to red, brown, orange or yellow. They are generally between 1 and 4 inches (2.5 and 10 cm) long and about ¹⁄₂ inch (1 cm) wide. The serrano is said to be about five times hotter than the jalapeño pepper.

Cranberry Baked Brie

Makes 4 to 6 servings

This is one of the most popular treats at any party. Whenever someone puts it out, everyone gravitates to the table and digs right in. I thought, Why not try it in the slow cooker? I used the tiny, 1-quart size slow cooker; however, if you don't have that size, wrap foil around the bottom and sides of the cheese to keep it enclosed. Otherwise, you will end up with a gooey mess.

Tips

Look for a Brie wheel that is no more than 1 inch (2.5 cm) thick. It should bulge slightly within the rind.

If you're serving a big group of people, you can use a larger Brie wheel and double the topping mixture. If the Brie does not fit snugly into the stoneware, make sure you wrap the bottom and sides of the cheese with foil.

Variation

You can substitute Camembert for the Brie (but remember that Camembert has a stronger aroma and flavor).

- **1- to 3-quart slow cooker**

1	wheel (7 oz/200 g) double-cream Brie cheese	1
$\frac{1}{2}$ cup	dried cranberries	125 mL
2 tbsp	packed brown sugar	30 mL
2 tbsp	water	30 mL
1 tsp	balsamic vinegar	5 mL
$\frac{1}{4}$ cup	chopped toasted pecans or Rosemary Roasted Pecans (page 38)	60 mL

1. Place Brie in slow cooker stoneware, if using 1-quart size. Otherwise, cut a 12-inch (30 cm) square of foil; center Brie on foil, then fold foil up around Brie, scrunching it around the sides to form a foil dish, leaving the top exposed.

2. In a bowl, combine cranberries, brown sugar, water, vinegar and pecans. Spoon on top of Brie.

3. Cover and cook on High for $1\frac{1}{2}$ hours or on Low for $2\frac{1}{2}$ to 3 hours, until center is soft and cheese starts to bulge around the edges. If you are using a mini slow cooker without a choice of heat settings, check Brie after 1 hour. Serve from slow cooker or transfer carefully to serving dish. Serve warm with crackers.

Goat Cheese Crostini with Fig Compote

Makes 2 cups (500 mL)

This compote can be used in a variety of ways, but as a topping on crostini it is a festive addition to gatherings that call for great friends, elegant bites and fabulous cocktails.

Variation

Softened cream cheese can be used in place of the goat cheese.

- 1½- to 3-quart slow cooker
- *Rimmed baking sheet*

Fig Compote

1 cup	chopped dried Mission figs	250 mL
1 cup	dry red wine	250 mL
¼ cup	packed light brown sugar	60 mL
½ tsp	dried thyme	2 mL
½ tsp	salt	2 mL

Crostini

1	baguette (8 oz/250 g), cut on the diagonal into 24 slices	1
3 tbsp	olive oil	45 mL
1	package (5 oz/142 g) goat cheese, softened	1
	Sprigs of fresh thyme (optional)	

1. *Fig Compote:* In slow cooker stoneware, combine figs, wine, brown sugar, thyme and salt, mixing well.

2. Cover and cook on High for 2¾ to 3 hours or on Low for 5½ to 6 hours, until figs are tender. Let cool to room temperature. Transfer to a jar with a lid and refrigerate for up to 1 month.

3. *Crostini:* Preheat broiler. Brush both sides of each baguette slice with oil and place on baking sheet. Broil for 1 to 2 minutes per side or until golden.

4. Spread each slice with goat cheese and top with compote. Garnish with thyme sprigs (if desired).

Goat cheese, or chèvre, is a traditional rich and creamy cheese made from fresh goat's milk. It has a light, tangy taste with a smooth finish. It slices easily, and maintains its shape when it's heated or browned in an oven or broiler.

Catalan Mushrooms

Makes 6 servings

This delicious appetizer also makes a great topping for grilled steak or homemade pizza, or can be stirred into pasta sauce.

Tips

To prepare mushrooms, wipe them with a damp paper towel. Don't rinse or soak them, or they'll absorb water and turn mushy when cooked.

Store mushrooms in a paper bag with the top loosely folded, or place them in a glass container and cover it with a tea towel or moist paper towel. Be sure to allow air circulation. Store in the refrigerator (not in the crisper) and use within a few days — or a week, if they are in an unopened package.

- **3- to 4-quart slow cooker**

1 lb	mushrooms	500 g
¼ cup	finely chopped fresh flat-leaf (Italian) parsley, divided	60 mL
2 tbsp	olive oil	30 mL
2 tbsp	finely chopped garlic	30 mL
1 tsp	coarse salt or sea salt	5 mL

1. Trim off all but ½ inch (1 cm) of the mushroom stems; cut mushrooms into quarters. In slow cooker stoneware, combine mushrooms, 1 tbsp (15 mL) of the parsley, oil, garlic and salt.

2. Cover and cook on High for 2 to 3 hours. Serve garnished with the remaining parsley.

Flat-leaf (Italian) parsley is more fragrant and less bitter than the curly variety.

Old-World Beer and Cheddar Fondue

Makes 4 to 6 servings

If fondue seems like a project, you'll be surprised how quickly it comes together in a slow cooker. My family enjoyed this one cool fall Saturday evening, as we sat around the table with some grilled shrimp, bread cubes and cauliflower and broccoli florets.

Tips

To ensure that the fondue works in the slow cooker, make sure your beer is boiling before you add the other ingredients.

In the slow cooker, an even, consistent temperature keeps the fondue warm and you don't have to worry about an open flame. It might not be as pretty as a fondue pot for serving, but you will have just as much fun.

• **4- to 6-quart slow cooker**

1 tbsp	butter	15 mL
1/2	small onion, chopped	1/2
1	clove garlic, finely chopped	1
1	bottle (12 oz/341 mL) lager-style beer (such as Heineken)	1
3 cups	shredded white Cheddar cheese	750 mL
2 cups	shredded Swiss cheese	500 mL
2 tbsp	cornstarch	30 mL
1 tsp	dry mustard	5 mL
1/2 tsp	freshly ground black pepper	2 mL
1/4 tsp	ground nutmeg	1 mL
	Bread cubes, broccoli and cauliflower florets, grilled shrimp and/or cooked chicken cubes	

1. In slow cooker stoneware, melt butter on High. Add onion and garlic; cover and cook for about 15 minutes or until tender and translucent.

2. Pour in beer. Cover and cook on High for 1 to 1½ hours or until bubbling.

3. In a bowl, combine Cheddar and Swiss cheese. Add cornstarch, mustard, pepper and nutmeg; toss to coat cheese.

4. Remove lid from slow cooker and reduce heat to Low or Warm. Sprinkle cheese mixture into stoneware, a handful at a time, stirring back and forth with a wooden spoon after each addition until all of the cheese is melted and the sauce is smooth and thick.

5. Cover and cook on Low or Warm for 20 to 30 minutes or until cornstarch has thickened the fondue.

6. Serve with bread, broccoli, cauliflower, shrimp and/or chicken for dipping.

Smoked Salmon Appetizer Cheesecake

Makes 8 to 10 servings

When we think of cheesecakes, we usually think of sweet combinations redolent with the scent of strawberries, cinnamon and chocolate. However, a savory cheesecake — delicate, creamy and delectable on the tongue — makes a wonderful appetizer for any occasion.

Tips

You will need a large round or oval slow cooker. Make sure it is big enough to hold the springform pan.

When preparing the filling, use a food processor, rather than a mixer, to incorporate the ingredients smoothly. The mixer has a tendency to add too much air, which, in turn, causes cracking on the top of the baked filling.

- **Minimum 5-quart slow cooker, stoneware lined with foil strips (see page 14)**
- *Food processor*
- *7-inch (18 cm) springform pan (or other pan that fits into slow cooker stoneware), greased*

Crust

2 tbsp	cracker crumbs (use buttery crackers, such as Ritz)	30 mL
1 tbsp	shredded Swiss cheese	15 mL
1 tsp	butter, melted	5 mL
1 tsp	finely chopped fresh dill	5 mL

Filling

1 tbsp	butter	15 mL
1/2 cup	chopped onion	125 mL
2	packages (each 8 oz/250 g) cream cheese, softened	2
2	eggs	2
1/3 cup	shredded Swiss cheese	75 mL
1/4 cup	light (5%) cream	60 mL
1/4 tsp	salt	1 mL
Pinch	freshly ground black pepper	Pinch
1	package (3 oz/85 g) smoked salmon, chopped	1
3 tbsp	finely chopped fresh dill	45 mL
	Sour cream, fresh dill sprigs and pink peppercorns	

1. *Crust:* In a bowl, combine cracker crumbs, Swiss cheese, butter and dill. Press mixture evenly over bottom of prepared springform pan. Refrigerate until ready to use.

2. *Filling:* In a skillet, melt butter over medium-high heat. Sauté onion for 3 to 4 minutes or until softened. Let cool slightly.

Tip

When using a springform
pan, you want to ensure that
the water does not seep into
the cheesecake. Wrap the
bottom of the pan with one
large, seamless piece of foil
that extends up the sides and
over the top of the pan. Cover
the top with a single piece
of foil that extends down
the sides of the pan. Secure
the foil with string or large
elastic bands.

3. In a food processor, combine onion mixture, cream cheese, eggs, Swiss cheese, cream, salt and pepper; process until smooth. Add salmon and dill; pulse until just mixed. (The salmon should still be in small chunks.) Spoon filling over prepared crust and cover tightly with foil (see tip, at left).

4. Place pan in prepared slow cooker stoneware. Pour in enough water to come 1 inch (2.5 cm) up sides of pan. (If pan fits snugly in stoneware, add water before inserting it; see page 14).

5. Cover and cook on High for 3 to 4 hours or until edges are set and center is slightly jiggly. Remove pan from slow cooker, transfer to a wire rack and let cool completely (still covered). Once cool, refrigerate for at least 2 hours or overnight.

Smoked salmon is readily available in the frozen seafood aisle of most supermarkets. To create it, fresh salmon fillets are cured in a brine solution with salt and sugar, then they are cold-smoked. The cold-smoking does not cook the fish, which is why smoked salmon has a smooth texture similar to the raw fillet.

Buffalo Chicken Bites

Makes 8 to 10 servings

The city of Buffalo, New York, made these appetizers famous. Generally, the sauce for Buffalo wings is made of vinegar, cayenne pepper and butter. To make this appetizer even easier, I have used ready-made sauce and added a little extra butter. Make sure you put out lots of toothpicks for this one!

Tip

When cooking predominantly white-meat poultry dishes in the slow cooker, be sure to avoid overcooking; otherwise, the meat will dry out and get rubbery.

- 3- to 4-quart slow cooker

1/3 cup	all-purpose flour	75 mL
2 tsp	smoked paprika	10 mL
1/4 tsp	salt	1 mL
2 lbs	boneless skinless chicken breasts (about 4), cut into bite-size pieces	1 kg
1/4 cup	Buffalo wing sauce	60 mL
2 tbsp	vegetable oil	30 mL
1 tbsp	butter, melted	15 mL
1 to 2 tbsp	hot pepper sauce	15 to 30 mL
	Blue cheese	

1. In a bowl, combine flour, paprika and salt. Add chicken and toss to coat. Shake off excess coating and transfer chicken to slow cooker stoneware. Discard excess coating mixture.

2. In a measuring cup or bowl, combine Buffalo wing sauce, oil, butter and hot pepper sauce. Pour over chicken and stir to combine.

3. Cover and cook on Low for 2 to $2\frac{1}{2}$ hours or until bubbling and chicken is no longer pink inside.

4. Transfer to a serving platter and crumble cheese over chicken. Serve with cocktail picks.

Red Thai Curry Wings

Makes 16 appetizer servings or 4 main course servings

These chicken wings, coated in a wonderfully sweet and spicy coconut-curry glaze, are especially great for cocktail parties because they're small yet filling.

Tips

Red curry paste is often available in the Asian food section of the supermarket. It is popular in Thai and Indian dishes, and adds a wonderful zing to most recipes. If you can't find it, use curry powder, instead.

Wings are much easier to eat when they are split. If wings are not split when you buy them, remove and discard the wing tips, then cut each wing at joint to make two pieces.

- **4- to 5-quart slow cooker**
- *Preheat broiler with rack positioned 6 inches (15 cm) from heat*
- *Rimmed baking sheet, lined with foil*

1	small onion, finely chopped	1
¾ cup	unsweetened coconut milk	175 mL
3 tbsp	fish sauce	45 mL
2 to 3 tbsp	Thai red curry paste	30 to 45 mL
3 lbs	split chicken wings (see tip, at left)	1.5 kg
2 tbsp	cornstarch	30 mL
2 tbsp	cold water	30 mL
¼ cup	finely chopped fresh cilantro (optional)	60 mL

1. In a large bowl, combine onion, coconut milk, fish sauce and curry paste; set aside.

2. Arrange chicken wings in a single layer on prepared baking sheet. Broil, turning once, for 15 to 20 minutes or until golden. Transfer wings to slow cooker stoneware. (Discard drippings.) Pour reserved coconut milk mixture over wings and toss gently to coat.

3. Cover and cook on Low for 3 to 4 hours or on High for 1½ to 2 hours, until wings are tender.

4. Using a slotted spoon, transfer chicken to a warmed platter; cover with foil to keep warm. Skim fat from sauce.

5. In a saucepan, combine cornstarch and water. Whisk in sauce and bring to a boil over high heat. Reduce heat and simmer, stirring, for 4 to 6 minutes or until thick and bubbling. Pour into serving bowl.

6. Garnish wings with cilantro, if using. Serve with sauce on the side.

Canned coconut milk is made from grated soaked coconut pulp — it's not the liquid found inside the coconut. It can be found in the Asian food section of the supermarket or in Asian food stores. Be sure you don't buy coconut cream, often used to make tropical drinks such as piña coladas.

Annika's Swedish Meatballs

Makes about 60 meatballs

My yoga instructor, Annika (a beautiful Swedish blonde, of course), passed along her grandmother's recipe for these light and delicate meatballs. They are one of the most popular dishes on the buffet table at any party, but they are also delicious served as a main course over wide egg noodles.

Tips

Soaking the bread in broth first adds a deliciously different texture to these meatballs. They are quite light and airy, not as heavy as meatballs made with dry bread crumbs.

Broth (or stock) is one of the most indispensable pantry staples. Commercial broth cubes and powders are loaded with salt and just don't deliver the flavor of homemade stock or prepared broth. I like to keep 32-oz (1 L) Tetra Paks on hand, especially the sodium-reduced variety.

If you can't find lingonberry sauce, you can use grape jelly, red currant jelly or cranberry sauce.

- **Minimum 4-quart slow cooker**
- *Preheat oven to 400°F (200°C)*
- *15- by 10-inch (38 by 25 cm) rimmed baking sheet, lined with foil*

Meatballs

¼ cup	beef broth	60 mL
2	slices white bread	2
1 lb	lean ground beef	500 g
1 lb	lean ground pork	500 g
1	large potato, peeled, cooked and mashed	1
½ cup	shredded white Cheddar cheese	125 mL
¼ cup	table (18%) cream	60 mL
1½ tsp	baking powder	7 mL
1	large onion, grated	1
1	egg, lightly beaten	1

Sauce

½ cup	beef broth	125 mL
½ cup	table (18%) cream	125 mL
¼ cup	lingonberry sauce	60 mL
2 tbsp	cornstarch	30 mL

1. *Meatballs:* Remove crusts from bread and place in a bowl; pour broth evenly over top and let soak until softened. Squeeze out excess broth.

2. In a large bowl, combine soaked bread, beef, pork, mashed potato, cheese, cream, baking powder, onion and egg. Mix well and shape into 1-inch (2.5 cm) balls.

3. Arrange meatballs in a single layer on prepared baking sheet. Bake in preheated oven, turning once, for 10 to 12 minutes or until no longer pink inside. Drain off any accumulated juices and transfer meatballs to slow cooker stoneware.

4. *Sauce:* In a large glass measuring cup, whisk together broth, cream, lingonberry sauce and cornstarch; pour over meatballs.

5. Cover and cook on Low for 6 to 8 hours or on High for 3 to 4 hours, until bubbling.

Tip

Resist the urge to lift the lid and taste or smell whatever is inside the slow cooker as it's cooking. Every peek will increase the cooking time by 20 minutes.

Make Ahead

These meatballs can be baked, cooled, transferred to an airtight container and refrigerated for 1 day. To freeze, place meatballs in a single layer on a rimmed baking sheet and freeze until firm. When frozen, transfer to an airtight storage container and freeze for up to 2 months. To assemble dish, place frozen meatballs in slow cooker stoneware, add sauce and cook on Low for 6 to 8 hours or on High for 3 to 4 hours, until bubbling.

Lingonberries (also known as cowberries or partridge berries) are a member of the cranberry family and are primarily used in Northern Europe to make jams and jellies. They are smaller and less tart than cultivated cranberries. Lingonberry sauce is found in gourmet food shops and in some supermarkets.

Moroccan Lamb Meatball Pouches

Makes about 30 meatballs

Tender, mild-flavored ground lamb is what makes these meatballs so unique. They are a wonderful alternative to beef meatballs, and are perfect for any party. The blend of dried fruit and exotic spices is typical of Moroccan cuisine.

Tips

Remember, when forming meatballs, handle the meat mixture lightly for a more tender texture.

If you don't want to go to the work of filling the pockets, cut larger pita pockets into wedges. Brush with olive oil and season with salt and pepper. Place them on a baking sheet and bake in a 350°F (180°C) oven for about 15 minutes or until golden and crisp. Serve alongside meatballs.

- **Minimum 4-quart slow cooker**
- *Preheat oven to 400°F (200°C)*
- *Rimmed baking sheet, lined with foil*

Meatballs

2 lbs	lean ground lamb	1 kg
2	eggs, lightly beaten	2
1 cup	fine dry bread crumbs	250 mL
1/2 cup	chopped fresh parsley	125 mL
1/4 cup	dried currants	60 mL
1 tbsp	ground cinnamon	15 mL
1 tsp	salt	5 mL
1/2 tsp	ground allspice	2 mL
1/2 tsp	ground cumin	2 mL
1/2 tsp	freshly ground black pepper	2 mL
1	jar (8 oz/250 mL) apple jelly	1
2 tbsp	unsweetened apple juice or cider	30 mL
1 tsp	hot pepper flakes	5 mL

Yogurt Mint Sauce

1 cup	plain yogurt (not low-fat)	250 mL
	Grated zest of 1 lemon	
1/4 cup	packed fresh mint leaves, minced	60 mL
2 tbsp	liquid honey	30 mL
	Salt and freshly ground black pepper	

30	mini pita pockets	30
	Chopped fresh parsley or mint	

1. *Meatballs:* In a large bowl, using a fork, combine lamb, eggs, bread crumbs, parsley, currants, cinnamon, salt, allspice, cumin and black pepper (do not overmix). Shape into 2-inch (5 cm) balls.

2. Arrange meatballs in a single layer on prepared baking sheet. Bake in preheated oven for 12 to 15 minutes or until no longer pink inside. Drain off any accumulated juices and transfer meatballs to slow cooker stoneware.

3. In a bowl, whisk together apple jelly, apple juice and hot pepper flakes; pour over meatballs.

Tip
Packed in airtight containers,
meatballs will keep for up to
4 months in the freezer.

4. Cover and cook on Low for 6 to 8 hours or on High for 3 to 4 hours, until bubbling.

5. *Sauce:* Meanwhile, in a bowl, combine yogurt, lemon zest, mint, honey, salt and pepper. Cover and refrigerate until ready to serve with meatballs.

6. *To assemble:* Cut ¼ inch (0.5 cm) off the top of each mini pita pocket and open up pocket. Place 1 meatball inside. Top with sauce and garnish with parsley.

Make Ahead

These meatballs can be baked, cooled, transferred to an airtight container and refrigerated for 1 day. To freeze, place meatballs in a single layer on a rimmed baking sheet and freeze until firm. When frozen, transfer to an airtight container and freeze for up to 2 months. To assemble dish, place frozen meatballs in slow cooker stoneware, add apple jelly mixture and cook on Low for 6 to 8 hours or on High for 3 to 4 hours, until bubbling.

Spanish Chorizo Dippers with Garlic Aïoli

Makes 8 servings

This tapas-style appetizer reminds me of my trip to Spain. Enjoy these dippers with a glass of red wine, some cured olives and good Spanish country-style bread.

Tips

Look for domestic cured chorizo sausages in Hispanic markets, gourmet food shops and some well-stocked supermarkets.

When making the garlic paste, be sure to work on a stable cutting board.

- **3- to 4-quart slow cooker**

1½ lbs	dry-cured chorizo sausage, cut into 1-inch (2.5 cm) thick slices	750 g
2	cloves garlic, minced	2
⅔ cup	dry red wine	150 mL
1 tbsp	minced fresh parsley	15 mL
	Country-style bread, sliced	

Garlic Aïoli

3	cloves garlic	3
¼ tsp	coarse salt	1 mL
½ cup	mayonnaise	125 mL
2 tbsp	olive oil	30 mL
1 tbsp	freshly squeezed lemon juice	15 mL
1 tsp	sweet paprika	5 mL
	Salt and freshly ground black pepper	

1. In slow cooker stoneware, combine sausage, garlic and red wine.

2. Cover and cook on Low, stirring once or twice, for 2 to 3 hours.

3. *Aïoli:* Meanwhile, with the flat side of a knife, mash garlic and salt until paste forms. (The coarse grains of salt help breakdown the garlic.) Transfer to a bowl and whisk in mayonnaise, oil, lemon juice and paprika. Season to taste with salt and pepper.

4. Serve the sausages with bread and aïoli.

Cheesy Mushroom Topping

Makes about 2 cups (500 mL)

This warm mushroom topping is very popular at parties. It is delicious served in toast cups (see box, at right) but also works well on crostini or crackers. Because it is saucy, try to find crackers shaped like scoops, to avoid messy drips or spills.

Tip
Use your favorite fresh mushrooms in this appetizer. Creminis or shiitakes can be used in place of button mushrooms.

- **3- to 4-quart slow cooker**

2 tbsp	butter	30 mL
1	onion, finely chopped	1
1/3 cup	all-purpose flour	75 mL
1 cup	heavy or whipping (35%) cream	250 mL
1 tsp	Dijon mustard	5 mL
1 lb	mushrooms, finely chopped	500 g
1/4 cup	freshly grated Parmesan cheese	60 mL
1	green onion, finely chopped	1
2 tbsp	finely chopped fresh parsley	30 mL
2 tsp	freshly squeezed lemon juice	10 mL
	Salt and freshly ground black pepper	

1. In a large skillet, melt butter over medium heat. Sauté onion for 3 to 4 minutes or until translucent. Stir in flour, blending well (mixture will be very thick). Gradually whisk in cream and mustard until blended and smooth. Transfer to slow cooker stoneware. Stir in mushrooms.

2. Cover and cook on Low for 3 to 4 hours or on High for 1½ to 2 hours, until bubbling.

3. Stir in cheese, green onion, parsley and lemon juice. Season to taste with salt and pepper.

To Make Toast Cups
Using a rolling pin, roll out 24 slices of fresh sandwich bread until very thin. Using a 3-inch (7.5 cm) round cookie cutter, cut a round out of each slice. Spray mini muffin tins with nonstick cooking spray. Carefully press bread rounds into tins. Bake at 375°F (190°C) for about 10 to 12 minutes or until golden brown. Remove toast cups from tins to a wire rack and let cool. Toast cups can be made several days ahead and stored in an airtight bag at room temperature.

Bloody Mary Dip

Makes 12 servings

My friend (and wonderful assistant) Leslie serves a cold appetizer similar to this one at every gathering, and it is always gone in no time. Together, we turned it into a warm dip. All your friends will be asking you for the recipe!

Tips

To avoid tears when chopping onions, put the onions in the freezer for a few minutes first.

Tomato paste is now available in tubes in many supermarkets and delis. It keeps for months in the refrigerator.

- 1- to 1½-quart slow cooker

1	stalk celery, finely chopped	1
½	onion, finely chopped	½
1½ cups	prepared tomato pasta sauce	375 mL
⅓ cup	sliced pimento-stuffed olives	75 mL
¼ cup	vodka	60 mL
2 tbsp	tomato paste	30 mL
1 tsp	celery seeds	5 mL
1 tsp	prepared horseradish	5 mL
Dash	hot pepper sauce	Dash
24	cooked peeled large shrimp (thawed if frozen)	24

1. In slow cooker stoneware, combine celery, onion, pasta sauce, olives, vodka, tomato paste, celery seeds, horseradish and hot pepper sauce.

2. Cover and cook on Low for 2 to 3 hours or until warmed through and vegetables are tender.

3. Serve with shrimp for dipping. Dip will stay warm on Low for up to 2 hours (stir occasionally).

> Prepared horseradish is a condiment made of grated horseradish root, vinegar and sometimes cream. It will keep for months in the refrigerator; when it starts to darken, it is losing flavor and should be replaced.

Cheesy White Bean and Artichoke Dip

Makes about 2 cups (500 mL)

This bean dip is an awesome alternative to high-fat chip and guacamole dips. Serve it with baked pita wedges or a plate of crudités. If you are a real garlic lover, feel free to add a few more cloves to the mix.

Tips

Use the plain canned artichoke hearts for this recipe, not the marinated ones.

To make baked pita wedges, cut pita pockets into wedges. Brush with olive oil and season with salt and pepper. Place on a baking sheet and bake in a 350°F (180°C) oven for about 15 minutes or until golden and crisp.

- 1½- to 4-quart slow cooker, stoneware greased
- *Food processor*

2 cups	cooked or canned white kidney beans (see page 120), drained and rinsed	500 mL
2 tbsp	freshly squeezed lemon juice	30 mL
1	can (14 oz/398 mL) artichoke hearts, drained and finely chopped	1
1 cup	shredded Swiss cheese or Monterey Jack cheese	250 mL
½ cup	grated Parmesan cheese	125 mL
½ cup	light sour cream	125 mL
⅓ cup	mayonnaise (regular or light)	75 mL
2	cloves garlic, minced	2
1 tsp	Worcestershire sauce	5 mL
¼ tsp	hot pepper sauce, or to taste	1 mL
¼ tsp	freshly ground black pepper	1 mL
4	slices bacon, cooked crisp and crumbled	4
2 tbsp	chopped green onions	30 mL
	Baked pita wedges (see tip, at left) or melba toast	

1. In a food processor, purée beans and lemon juice until smooth. Transfer to a medium bowl and stir in artichokes, Swiss cheese, Parmesan cheese, sour cream, mayonnaise, garlic, Worcestershire sauce, hot pepper sauce and pepper. Spoon into prepared slow cooker stoneware. Sprinkle bacon and green onions over top.

2. Cover and cook on High for 2 hours or on Low for 4 hours, until bubbling.

3. Let cool slightly before serving, as mixture will be very hot. Serve with pita wedges.

Warm Chipotle Black Bean Dip

Makes 10 to 12 servings

This is a great party dip that can be assembled up to 2 days ahead. It's perfect for serving at big football get-togethers with friends.

Tips

To ripen tomatoes, place them in a brown paper bag and store at room temperature. Never store tomatoes in the refrigerator, as it destroys their delicate flavor.

Once opened, transfer canned chipotle peppers and their sauce to a glass jar with a tight-fitting lid and store in the refrigerator for up to 10 days. For longer storage, transfer the peppers and sauce to a freezer bag and gently press out the air, then seal the bag. Manipulate the bag to separate the peppers, so it will be easy to break off a frozen section of pepper and sauce without thawing the whole package.

- **4- to 6-quart slow cooker**
- *Food processor*

1	tomato, seeded and diced	1
	Coarse salt	
2 tbsp	olive oil	30 mL
1	large onion, finely diced	1
3	cloves garlic, minced	3
1 tbsp	chili powder	15 mL
4 cups	cooked or canned black beans (see page 120), drained and rinsed, divided	1 L
1 tsp	minced chipotle peppers in adobo sauce, plus 1 tbsp (15 mL) adobo sauce	5 mL
1 tbsp	cider vinegar	15 mL
1 cup	fresh or frozen corn kernels (thawed if frozen)	250 mL
2 cups	shredded Cheddar cheese or Tex-Mex cheese blend, divided	500 mL
1/4 cup	chopped fresh cilantro	60 mL
	Freshly ground black pepper	
	Tortilla chips	

1. Place tomato in a colander set in the sink or a bowl and sprinkle with 1 tsp (5 mL) salt. Let stand until juices drain off.

2. In a large skillet, heat oil over medium-high heat. Reduce heat to medium, add onion and sauté for 4 to 6 minutes or until softened and translucent. Add garlic and chili powder; sauté for 1 minute. Add half the black beans, chipotle peppers, adobo sauce and 1/4 cup (60 mL) water; bring to a boil. Boil, stirring, for 2 to 3 minutes or until liquid is reduced by half.

3. Transfer bean mixture to a food processor, add vinegar and process until smooth. Let cool for 8 to 10 minutes or until steam subsides, then transfer to slow cooker stoneware. Stir in the remaining beans, tomato, corn, 1 cup (250 mL) of the cheese and cilantro. Season to taste with salt and black pepper.

Tip

Cooking times can vary a great deal between slow cooker manufacturers. Always let your food cook for the minimum amount of time before testing for doneness.

4. Cover and cook on Low for 3 to 4 hours or on High for 1 to 2 hours, until bubbling. Sprinkle with remaining cheese, cover and cook for 20 minutes or until cheese has melted.

Make Ahead

This dip can be assembled up to 2 days in advance. Prepare through step 3, cover and refrigerate.

When ready to cook, place stoneware in slow cooker and proceed with step 4.

A chipotle pepper is a red jalapeño chile, dried and smoked using a special process. Chipotles have a unique warm heat and smoky flavor, and are often canned in a red adobo sauce made from ground chiles, herbs and vinegar.

Roasted Garlic and Red Pepper Hummus

Makes about 3 cups (750 mL)

My friends and I love this dip so much that it comes along on our annual Winter Girls' Getaway. It is so simple to cook the chickpeas in the slow cooker, then purée the ingredients in the food processor. Just make sure the chickpeas are very tender before you process them; otherwise, your hummus won't be smooth and creamy. Serve with warm pita wedges, a plate of crudités or whole-grain crackers.

Tip

When cooking chickpeas, do not add salt to the cooking liquid. It will toughen the chickpeas and they won't absorb water properly during cooking.

- 1½- to 4-quart slow cooker
- *Preheat oven to 400°F (200°C)*
- *Food processor*

2 cups	dried chickpeas, rinsed and drained	500 mL
6 cups	boiling water	1.5 L
1	head garlic	1
	Olive oil	
½ cup	tahini (sesame seed paste)	125 mL
1	jar (12 oz/340 mL) roasted red peppers, drained (see tip, page 327)	1
⅓ cup	freshly squeezed lemon juice	75 mL
	Kosher salt	
¼ tsp	hot pepper sauce, or to taste	1 mL
	Chopped fresh parsley	

1. Place chickpeas in slow cooker stoneware and add boiling water.

2. Cover and cook on High for 3½ to 4 hours or until chickpeas are tender but still hold their shape. Drain, reserving ½ cup (125 mL) of the cooking water. Let cool to room temperature.

3. Meanwhile, peel away outer skins from garlic head, leaving skins of individual cloves intact. With a sharp knife, cut ¼ to ½ inch (0.5 to 1 cm) from the top of the head, exposing individual cloves. Place, base down, on a square of foil or in a garlic baker. Drizzle exposed cloves with oil until well coated; enclose in foil or cover with lid of baker. Bake in preheated oven for 30 to 35 minutes or until cloves feel soft when pressed. Let cool to room temperature, then remove roasted cloves with a cocktail fork or squeeze them out of their skins.

4. In a food processor, combine chickpeas, garlic, tahini, red peppers, lemon juice, salt and hot pepper sauce; purée until smooth. Hummus should be medium-thick. If it's too thick, add some of the reserved cooking water to thin.

5. Transfer hummus to a shallow bowl, drizzle with oil and garnish with parsley.

Orange Cranberry Relish

Makes about 1½ cups (375 mL)

No Thanksgiving dinner would be complete without a bowl of cranberry relish on the table. It's a holiday classic. This version is also delicious as a topping for Cranberry Baked Brie (page 42). Offer to bring the cranberry sauce, and tote along the baked Brie, too — you will be the most popular guest.

Tip
This relish is best made a day or two ahead, so the flavors can meld together and the sauce can congeal.

Variation
Cranberry Chutney: Add 1 finely chopped shallot to the slow cooker. When the cooking is finished, add ¼ cup (60 mL) chopped nuts (such as walnuts or pecans) and 1 tbsp (15 mL) sherry vinegar; let cool and refrigerate in an airtight container for up to 5 days.

- **1½- to 3-quart slow cooker**

1 cup	granulated sugar	250 mL
1 tbsp	grated orange zest	15 mL
½ cup	freshly squeezed orange juice	125 mL
1 tsp	freshly squeezed lemon juice	5 mL
1 tsp	grated gingerroot	5 mL
1	bag (12 oz/340 g) fresh or frozen cranberries (thawed if frozen)	1
½ tsp	freshly ground white pepper	2 mL

1. In slow cooker stoneware, combine sugar, orange zest, orange juice, lemon juice, ginger, cranberries and white pepper.

2. Cover and cook on Low for 3½ to 4 hours or until cranberry skins split.

3. Let cool, then transfer to an airtight container and refrigerate for up to 1 week or freeze for up to 2 months.

Rhubarb Chutney

Makes about 2 cups (500 mL)

There is no better sauce to have with pork or chicken than this overlooked springtime treat! It's spicy, fruity and delicious, and works for the classic cheese and chutney sandwich, too.

Tip

Grating gingerroot is easiest if you keep a nub of it in the freezer. (Ginger tends to get moldy and soft too quickly when it's stored in the refrigerator.) Use a Microplane-style grater for best results. Microplanes have tiny razor-like edges that make quick and easy tasks of both grating and cleaning. You will find Microplanes in good kitchenware and department stores.

- 1½- to 4-quart slow cooker
- *Two 8-ounce (250 mL) canning jars and lids (optional)*

2 tbsp	olive oil	30 mL
1	medium onion, finely chopped	1
1	6-inch (15 cm) cinnamon stick	1
4 cups	chopped rhubarb (½-inch/1 cm pieces)	1 L
½ cup	raisins	125 mL
½ cup	packed light brown sugar	125 mL
1 tbsp	minced gingerroot	15 mL
½ tsp	dry mustard	2 mL
1 tbsp	sherry vinegar	15 mL

1. In a skillet, heat oil over medium-high heat. Sauté onion for 5 to 6 minutes or until translucent. Transfer to slow cooker stoneware.

2. Add cinnamon stick, rhubarb, raisins, brown sugar, ginger and mustard, stirring to combine.

3. Cover and cook on High for 2½ to 3 hours or on Low for 5½ to 6 hours, until thickened and rhubarb has softened. Discard cinnamon stick and stir in vinegar.

4. If desired, pour into canning jars, leaving ¼ inch (0.5 cm) headspace. Seal with prepared discs and bands and process in a boiling water canner for 5 minutes (see page 65). Alternatively, let cool, transfer to an airtight container and refrigerate for up to 3 weeks.

Carolyn's Fiery Red Pepper Jelly

Makes five 8-oz (250 mL) jars

This is my favorite condiment to have in the fridge and to give as a hostess gift. I love it on a cracker with cream cheese or as a filling for tiny cheese tartlets I serve at Christmas. A friend in my book club gave me the original recipe, and I adapted it for the slow cooker. You will need to process this jelly in a boiling water bath to ensure safe storage.

Tip

When handling hot peppers, wear rubber gloves and make sure you keep your hands away from your face and eyes. Wash hands and utensils afterwards.

- **4- to 6-quart slow cooker**
- *Five 8-ounce (250 mL) canning jars and lids*

2	habanero chile peppers, seeded and finely chopped	2
1	red bell pepper, seeded and chopped	1
1 1/4 cups	apple cider vinegar	300 mL
5 cups	granulated sugar	1.25 L
1	pouch (3 oz/85 mL) liquid fruit pectin	1

1. In a food processor or blender, purée habaneros and red pepper until as smooth as possible. Add vinegar and process until even smoother. Transfer to slow cooker stoneware. Gradually stir in sugar.

2. Cover and cook on High for 2 1/2 hours, stirring twice, until bubbling around the edges. (Do not overcook, or the jelly will taste burnt.) Remove the stoneware insert. Stir in pectin until completely blended.

3. Pour into canning jars, leaving 1/4 inch (0.5 cm) headspace. Seal with prepared discs and bands and process in a boiling water canner for 5 minutes (see page 65).

Summertime Slow Cooker Strawberry Preserves

Makes about six 8-oz (250 mL) jars

Thanks to my mother, Evelyn Pye, for passing this recipe along to me. She started making these preserves a few years ago, while she wintered in Florida, where local strawberries are available in January. She wanted to capture the fresh, sweet flavor of the berries without losing any time on the golf course. Slow cooker to the rescue!

Tips

Use a potato masher to crush strawberries one layer at a time. Alternatively, you can pulse them in a food processor; just make sure you don't overprocess and turn them into a purée.

To test if preserves are set enough, place 2 or 3 small plates in the freezer. Place 1 tsp (5 mL) of hot preserves on a plate and return to freezer for 1 minute. Remove from freezer. Preserves should wrinkle slightly when edges are pushed with a finger. If not, continue cooking for 20 to 30 minutes. Repeat the test until preserves wrinkle.

These preserves are a little thinner than jam, and the texture will vary depending on the juiciness of your berries. They make a wonderful sauce served over ice cream, angel food cake or freshly baked scones or muffins.

- **3- to 6-quart slow cooker**
- *Six 8-ounce (250 mL) canning jars and lids*

8 cups	strawberries (approx.)	2 L
2 tbsp	freshly squeezed lemon juice	30 mL
2	packages (each 1.75 oz/49 or 57 g) powdered fruit pectin	2
3 cups	granulated sugar	750 mL

1. In a large bowl, using a potato masher, crush strawberries one layer at a time (or pulse in a food processor until chunky). Measure $4\frac{1}{2}$ cups (1.125 L) crushed berries. Transfer to slow cooker stoneware.

2. Add lemon juice and gently stir in pectin. Let stand for 10 minutes. Gradually stir in sugar.

3. Cover and cook on Low, stirring twice, for $2\frac{1}{2}$ hours. Increase temperature to High and cook for 2 to $2\frac{1}{2}$ hours or until preserves thicken slightly (see tip, at left). Preserves will continue to thicken as they cool.

4. Pour into canning jars, leaving $\frac{1}{4}$ inch (0.5 cm) headspace. Seal with prepared discs and bands and process in a boiling water canner for 5 minutes (see page 65).

Making Preserves and Condiments

One of the best ways to dress up any meal is to add a spoonful of a condiment on the side. Often, if I have cooked a large cut of meat or poultry and I don't have time to make gravy, I will just add a spoonful of chutney or relish to each plate. Condiments dress up even the simplest cooking, such as a fillet of fish, a steak, a chop or a grilled burger.

Most of the recipes here make only a small batch — just a jar or two — so you can refrigerate or freeze any amount you may not use right away for longer storage. However, it is best to process some preserves in a boiling water canner, to ensure safe, long-term storage by destroying normal levels of heat-resistant microorganisms. This method is best for the Summertime Slow Cooker Strawberry Preserves (page 64) and Carolyn's Fiery Red Pepper Jelly (page 63).

When you process a jar of preserves, its contents expand and gases are vented from the jar. The resulting change in the internal pressure causes the lid to be pulled down onto the jar, forming a vacuum seal. This seal prevents microorganisms and air from entering the jar and contaminating the food.

It is important to note that the cooking time before the preserves are placed in the jar is not part of the processing time. Once the preserves have cooked in the slow cooker, ladle them into clean, sterilized canning jars and seal with two-piece metal lids, then process in a boiling water canner for the time recommended in the recipe.

Once removed from the canner, jars should be stored upright and allowed to cool, undisturbed, for 24 hours. Sealed lids should have a concave appearance. In fact, you will likely hear "popping" sounds shortly after the jars have been removed from the canner, which indicate that the jars have sealed. Label and store jars in a cool, dark place and, for best results, use within 1 year.

Preserves and condiments make terrific holiday and hostess gifts, particularly when they're prettily packaged. And although the preserving recipes in this chapter are easy to make, offering them to friends is much more than a small gesture — it's a personal one, demonstrating the best sentiments, whatever the season.

Canning Preparation

Wash canning jars. Fill boiling water canner two-thirds full of water. About 30 minutes before filling jars, bring canner to a simmer over high heat. Ten minutes before filling jars, place jars, canning funnel and ladle in canner rack; return water to a simmer.

About 10 minutes before filling jars, heat a small saucepan of water until hot (180°F/82°C) but not boiling . Add lid discs, remove from heat, cover pan and let stand to soften sealing compound.

Steps to Boiling Water Canner Processing

This method is safe only for tested recipes created specifically for home canning of high-acid foods. Do not use this method for any low-acid foods or those containing animal products or oil. Consult a recently published, detailed home canning cookbook or government website for more information.

1. Ladle hot, cooked food into clean, sterilized canning jars, leaving $\frac{1}{4}$ inch (0.5 cm) headspace for jams and jellies and $\frac{1}{2}$ inch (1 cm) headspace for relish and chutneys. (Headspace is the

distance from the rim of the jar to the surface of the food or liquid inside.) Overfilling or underfilling a jar can result in seal failure.

2. Remove air bubbles by sliding a narrow spatula between the jar and the food. You can readjust the headspace, if necessary, by adding more hot food. Place a heated metal lid disc on top of each jar, wipe rims, then screw on metal bands, evenly and firmly, just until fingertip-tight.

3. Place jars on an elevated rack in a canner filled with boiling water. When all jars are in the canner or the canner is full, lower the rack into the water. Be sure the water covers the jars by at least 1 inch (2.5 cm); add boiling water, if required. Place the lid on the canner and turn heat to high.

4. When the water returns to a full rolling boil, begin counting the "heat processing" time.

5. When the time has elapsed, turn off the heat and remove the canner lid. Allow the boil to subside, then use tongs to lift jars, without tilting them, and place them upright on a towel to cool in a draft-free place. (Do not retighten screw bands.) Let jars stand, undisturbed, for 24 hours. Check that lids curve downward. Refrigerate any jars that are not sealed, and use within 3 weeks. Store sealed jars in a cool, dark place for up to 1 year.

Soups

Mexican Minestrone with Cornmeal Dumplings

Makes 6 to 8 servings

There are few things in the world I can eat twice a day for a few consecutive days, but this has proved to be one of them. Super-hearty and delicious, this soup won't disappoint you, I promise, even if you decide you don't want to eat it for six meals in a row.

Tips

Here's a foolproof way to chop an onion: Peel the onion and halve it from top to base. Place each half cut side down on a cutting board. Slice horizontally across each half. Holding the slices together, slice vertically.

Mild green chiles are found in the Mexican foods section of the supermarket. They are sold whole or chopped.

To make sure the dumplings cook through, don't lift the lid of the slow cooker until you are ready to test for doneness.

- Minimum 4-quart slow cooker

1 tbsp	vegetable oil	15 mL
1	onion, finely chopped	1
3	cloves garlic, minced	3
2	potatoes, peeled and coarsely chopped	2
1	can (19 oz/540 mL) chili-style stewed tomatoes, with juice	1
1	can (4½ oz/127 mL) chopped mild green chiles, with liquid	1
2 cups	cooked or canned black beans (see page 120), drained and rinsed	500 mL
2 cups	cooked or canned chickpeas (see page 120), drained and rinsed	500 mL
1 cup	frozen corn kernels, thawed	250 mL
1 cup	chopped green beans	250 mL
1 cup	diced carrots	250 mL
1 tbsp	chopped canned chipotle peppers in adobo sauce	15 mL
1 tsp	ground cumin	5 mL
4 cups	chicken or beef broth	1 L
	Freshly squeezed juice of 1 lime	

Dumplings

⅓ cup	all-purpose flour	75 mL
¼ cup	cornmeal	60 mL
1 tbsp	baking powder	15 mL
⅛ tsp	freshly ground black pepper	0.5 mL
1	egg	1
1 tbsp	milk	15 mL
2 tsp	vegetable oil	10 mL

1. In a large skillet, heat oil over medium-high heat. Sauté onions for 5 minutes or until tender and translucent. Add garlic and sauté for 1 minute. Transfer to slow cooker stoneware.

2. Stir in potatoes, tomatoes with juice, chiles with liquid, black beans, chickpeas, corn, green beans, carrot, chipotle peppers, cumin, broth and lime juice.

3. Cover and cook on Low for 6 to 8 hours or on High for 3 to 4 hours, until soup is bubbling and vegetables are tender.

Variation

Substitute 2 cups (500 mL) diced cooked chicken or turkey for the chickpeas.

4. *Dumplings:* In a bowl, combine flour, cornmeal, baking powder and pepper. In another bowl, whisk together egg, milk and oil. Add to flour mixture; stir with a fork just until combined.

5. Drop 6 to 8 mounds of dumpling dough onto bubbling soup. Cover and cook on Low for about 30 minutes or until a tester inserted in the center of a dumpling comes out clean.

6. Ladle soup into individual serving bowls, making sure each bowl has at least one dumpling.

Make Ahead

This dish can be assembled up to 12 hours in advance. Prepare through step 2, cover and refrigerate overnight. The next day, place stoneware in slow cooker and proceed with step 3.

Creamy Broccoli Soup with Grilled Cheese Croutons

Makes 6 servings

You can serve this flavorful, filling soup at lunch or supper. Be sure to use nice aged Cheddar, as it gives a real lift to this soup.

Tips

You can substitute an equal amount of frozen chopped broccoli.

If you prefer, you can substitute a 12-oz (370 mL) can of evaporated milk for the cream.

- Minimum 4-quart slow cooker

2 tbsp	vegetable oil	30 mL
2	onions, finely chopped	2
8 cups	chopped broccoli	2 L
4 cups	vegetable broth	1 L
1 tbsp	Worcestershire sauce	15 mL
1/2 tsp	ground nutmeg	2 mL
1 1/2 cups	light (5%) cream or half-and-half (10%) cream	375 mL
1 cup	shredded sharp (old) Cheddar cheese	250 mL
2 tbsp	dry sherry (optional)	30 mL
	Salt and freshly ground black pepper	
	Grilled Cheese Croutons (see recipe, opposite)	

1. In a large skillet, heat oil over medium-high heat. Sauté onions for 5 minutes or until tender and translucent. Transfer to slow cooker stoneware. Stir in broccoli, broth, Worcestershire sauce and nutmeg.

2. Cover and cook on Low for 4 to 6 hours or on High for 2 to 3 hours, until soup is bubbling and broccoli is tender.

3. Using an immersion blender, or in a food processor or blender, in batches as necessary, purée soup until smooth. (If using food processor or blender, return purée to stoneware.)

4. Stir in cream, cheese and sherry (if using) until cheese has melted. Season to taste with salt and pepper.

5. Ladle into bowls and garnish with croutons.

> An immersion blender (also called a stick blender, wand blender or hand blender) allows you to blend or purée in almost any container. It is ideal for puréeing soups and emulsifying sauces right in the slow cooker.

Makes about 20 croutons

These miniature sandwich-like cubes are a fun addition to any creamy soup. Try them on tomato soup too!

Grilled Cheese Croutons

¼ cup	butter, softened	60 mL
¼ tsp	dried thyme	1 mL
4	slices sandwich bread	4
4 oz	Cheddar cheese, thinly sliced	125 g

1. Heat a large skillet over medium-high heat. In a small bowl, combine butter and thyme. Spread butter mixture over one side of each bread slice. Place 2 slices in the pan, buttered side down. Top each with half the cheese, then with a remaining bread slice, buttered side up.

2. Cook, turning once, for 3 to 5 minutes per side or until toasted on both sides. Let cool slightly, then cut into 1-inch (2.5 cm) squares.

Adobe Sweet Potato and Chile Soup

Makes 4 to 6 servings

Sweet potato soup, Southwest style. It's not too spicy, but has a nice hint of smokiness from the paprika. Serve with a pan of Southwest Cornbread (see recipe, opposite).

Tip

Smoked paprika is made by grinding peppers that have undergone a smoking process. You can find it in various heat levels (from mild to hot). Be careful how much you use, because smoky seasonings can easily overpower the flavor of a dish.

- **Minimum 4-quart slow cooker**

2 tbsp	butter	30 mL
2	onions, finely chopped	2
2	cloves garlic, minced	2
2	sweet potatoes, peeled and chopped	2
1	jalapeño pepper, seeded and finely chopped	1
1 tsp	smoked paprika	5 mL
4 cups	chicken or vegetable broth	1 L
	Freshly squeezed juice of 2 limes (about $1/4$ cup/60 mL)	
	Salt	
	Sour cream or yogurt	

1. In a large skillet, melt butter over medium-high heat. Sauté onions for 5 minutes or until tender and translucent. Add garlic, sweet potatoes, jalapeño and paprika; sauté for 1 minute. Transfer to slow cooker stoneware. Stir in broth.

2. Cover and cook on Low for 6 to 8 hours or on High for 3 to 4 hours, until soup is bubbling and potatoes are tender.

3. Using an immersion blender, or in a food processor or blender, in batches as necessary, purée soup until smooth. (If using food processor or blender, return purée to stoneware.) Stir in lime juice and season to taste with salt.

4. Ladle into bowls and garnish each with a dollop of sour cream.

*This delicious cornbread
makes the perfect
side dish for any
Southern-inspired meal.*

Tip

Jalapeño peppers contain
volatile oils that can burn
your skin and eyes if they
come into direct contact.
It is best to wear plastic or
rubber gloves when chopping
jalapeños, and take care not
to touch your face or eyes
while you work. If your bare
hands do touch the peppers,
wash your hands and nails
well with hot, soapy water.

Southwest Cornbread

- *Preheat oven to 350°F (180°C)*
- *9-inch (23 cm) square or round metal baking pan, greased*

1/2 cup	all-purpose flour	125 mL
1/2 cup	cornmeal	125 mL
1 tbsp	baking powder	15 mL
2 tsp	packed brown sugar	10 mL
1/2 tsp	salt	2 mL
1 tbsp	vegetable oil	15 mL
1	onion, finely chopped	1
1	small jalapeño pepper, seeded and chopped	1
1/4 cup	diced red bell pepper	60 mL
1/4 cup	diced green bell pepper	60 mL
2	eggs	2
1/2 cup	vegetable oil	125 mL
1 cup	frozen corn kernels, thawed	250 mL
1/4 cup	chopped fresh cilantro	60 mL
1/2 cup	shredded Cheddar cheese	125 mL

1. In a large bowl, combine flour, cornmeal, baking powder, brown sugar and salt; set aside.

2. In a skillet, heat 1 tbsp (15 mL) oil over medium-high heat. Sauté onion, jalapeño, red pepper and green pepper for 3 to 5 minutes or until softened. Transfer to a large bowl and let cool slightly.

3. In a glass measuring cup, whisk together eggs and 1/2 cup (125 mL) oil until well combined. Add to the cooled pepper mixture, along with corn and cilantro. Quickly fold vegetable mixture into flour mixture. Fold in cheese. Spoon into prepared baking pan.

4. Bake in preheated oven for 35 to 40 minutes or until golden and firm on top. Cut into squares or wedges.

Curried Split Pea and Sweet Potato Soup

Makes 6 to 8 servings

There are as many variations on split pea soup as there are cooks, and Curried Split Pea and Sweet Potato Soup is one of my favorites.

Tips

For a smoother consistency, you can purée some of the cooked soup after you remove the pork hock. Use an immersion blender right in the slow cooker for ease, and purée until the desired consistency is reached, or transfer 1½ cups (375 mL) to a blender or food processor and process until smooth, then return purée to slow cooker and continue with recipe.

Dried split peas have been mechanically split along the seam so they will cook faster. It's a good idea to sort them before cooking, to remove any tiny stones or discolored pieces. Then place the peas in a colander and rinse under cold running water until the water is no longer foamy.

Make Ahead

This dish can be assembled up to 12 hours in advance. Prepare through step 2, cover and refrigerate overnight. The next day, place stoneware in slow cooker and proceed with step 3.

- **Minimum 5-quart slow cooker**

1 tsp	vegetable oil	5 mL
1 tsp	cumin seeds	5 mL
1 tsp	fennel seeds	5 mL
1 tsp	grated gingerroot	5 mL
1 tsp	finely minced garlic	5 mL
1	large onion, finely chopped	1
1 lb	dried yellow split peas (about 2 cups/500 mL), sorted, rinsed and drained	500 g
1 lb	smoked pork hock	500 g
1½ cups	coarsely chopped celery	375 mL
3	carrots, coarsely chopped	3
2	sweet potatoes, peeled and coarsely chopped	2
1 tbsp	curry powder	15 mL
1 tbsp	dried marjoram, crushed	15 mL
2	bay leaves	2
¼ tsp	freshly ground black pepper	1 mL

1. In a small skillet, heat oil over medium-high heat. Toast cumin and fennel seeds, stirring constantly, for 10 seconds. (Seeds may or may not begin to pop.) Add ginger, garlic and onion; sauté for about 5 minutes or until onions are tender and translucent and spices are fragrant. Transfer to slow cooker stoneware.

2. Stir in peas, pork hock, celery, carrots, sweet potatoes, curry powder, marjoram, bay leaves and pepper. Stir in 6 cups (1.5 L) water.

3. Cover and cook on Low for 9 to 11 hours or on High for 4½ to 5½ hours, until soup is thick and bubbling and peas are tender.

4. Discard bay leaves. Transfer pork hock to a bowl and let cool slightly. When pork hock is cool enough to handle, remove meat from bone. Discard skin and bone. Coarsely chop meat, return to soup and cook on Low for 20 minutes or until heated through.

Kale and Chickpea Soup

Makes 6 servings

I have often thought that the slow cooker and the bread machine should be combined into one appliance. While this hearty and satisfying dinnertime soup simmers away, make a loaf of homemade bread to serve alongside. If you don't have time, pick up a fresh ciabatta loaf from the supermarket.

Tip

You can substitute other greens, such as collard greens, spinach or escarole, for the kale.

- **Minimum 4-quart slow cooker**

2 tbsp	olive oil	30 mL
1	onion, chopped	1
2	cloves garlic, minced	2
1/2 tsp	salt	2 mL
1/2 tsp	freshly ground black pepper	2 mL
1/4 tsp	crumbled dried sage	1 mL
2	sweet potatoes, peeled and cut into 1-inch (2.5 cm) cubes	2
1	red bell pepper, chopped	1
2 cups	cooked or canned chickpeas (see page 120), drained and rinsed	500 mL
1 1/2 cups	cubed cooked ham or smoked turkey breast	375 mL
3 cups	chicken broth	750 mL
3 cups	chopped kale	750 mL
	Parmesan cheese shavings	

1. In a large saucepan, heat oil over medium-high heat. Sauté onion, garlic, salt, pepper and sage for about 5 minutes or until onion is tender and translucent. Transfer to slow cooker stoneware.

2. Stir in sweet potato, red pepper, chickpeas, ham, broth and 1 cup (250 mL) water.

3. Cover and cook on Low for 6 to 8 hours or on High for 3 to 4 hours, until soup is bubbling and potatoes are tender.

4. Stir in kale. Cover and cook on High for 10 to 15 minutes or until kale is tender.

5. Ladle into bowls and top with Parmesan shavings.

Kale is a nutrient-packed leafy green. It has been cultivated for over 2,000 years and is a member of the *Brassica* family (which also includes cabbage, Brussels sprouts and collard greens, to name a few). Kale leaves are ruffled and are dark to grayish green in color. It is most flavorful during the cold weather months, although it can be found year-round.

Lentil Soup with Italian Sausage and Greens

Makes 6 to 8 servings

Nuggets of sausage give a little meatball action to this hearty, no-fuss soup, chock-full of healthy escarole and lentils.

Tips

If you can't find escarole, curly endive is a good substitute, though it is a little more bitter.

Good-quality salad croutons make a quick substitute for homemade.

Make Ahead

This dish can be assembled up to 12 hours in advance. Cook the sausage completely in step 1 and refrigerate it in its own airtight container. Complete step 2, without adding the lentils, cover and refrigerate overnight. The next day, place stoneware in slow cooker, stir in cooked sausage and lentils and proceed with step 3.

- **Minimum 4-quart slow cooker**

2 tbsp	olive oil, divided	30 mL
1 lb	mild or hot Italian sausage cut into 1-inch (2.5 cm) pieces	500 g
4	cloves garlic, finely chopped	4
2	carrots, diced	2
2	stalks celery, finely chopped	2
1	onion, finely chopped	1
2 tbsp	tomato paste	30 mL
1½ cups	dried red lentils, rinsed and drained	375 mL
1	bay leaf	1
3 cups	chicken broth	750 mL
8 oz	escarole, chopped (about 4 cups/1 L)	250 g
1 to 2 tbsp	red wine vinegar	15 to 30 mL
	Salt and freshly ground black pepper	
	Cumin Croutons (see recipe, opposite)	

1. In a skillet, heat 1 tbsp (15 mL) of the oil over medium-high heat. Cook sausage, stirring, for 8 to 10 minutes or until browned. Using a slotted spoon, transfer sausage to slow cooker stoneware.

2. Add remaining oil to skillet and reduce heat to medium. Add garlic, carrots, celery and onion; sauté for about 5 minutes or until onion is tender and translucent. Stir in tomato paste. Transfer to stoneware. Stir in lentils, bay leaf, broth and 3 cups (750 mL) water.

3. Cover and cook on Low for 8 to 10 hours or on High for 4 to 5 hours, until soup is bubbling and lentils are tender.

4. Stir in escarole. Cover and cook on High for about 3 minutes or until tender. Stir in vinegar to taste and season to taste with salt and pepper. Discard bay leaf.

5. Ladle into bowls and garnish with croutons.

> Escarole might look like a head of romaine, but it is more flavorful, with thicker, more crumpled-looking leaves and a pale yellow center, or "heart." While it is slightly bitter when raw, it gets milder and sweeter when cooked. Escarole is rich in vitamin A and folate and is a good source of fiber.

*Homemade croutons are
extremely addictive — I
often make a pot of soup
just to eat the croutons!
The key is to use a
good-quality bread, such
as ciabatta, whole-grain or
hearty specialty bread.*

Tip

Croutons can be stored in an
airtight container in a cool,
dry place for up to 1 day.

Cumin Croutons

2 tbsp	butter	30 mL
2 tsp	ground cumin	10 mL
2 cups	bread cubes	500 mL

1. In a large skillet, melt butter over medium heat. Stir in cumin.
   Add bread cubes and cook, stirring, for about 5 minutes or
   until croutons are golden brown and crisp. Remove to a plate
   lined with paper towels and let cool completely.

Tex-Mex Tomato Rice Soup

Makes 6 servings

Garnish this kid-friendly soup with minced fresh cilantro, shredded chicken and/or sour cream. Serve with Monterey Jack and Green Pepper Quesadillas (see recipe, opposite).

Tip

You can also serve this soup garnished with Grilled Cheese Croutons (page 71).

• **Minimum 4-quart slow cooker**

2 tbsp	vegetable oil	30 mL
2	cloves garlic, minced	2
1	onion, chopped	1
1	jalapeño pepper, seeded and minced	1
1/2 tsp	ground cumin	2 mL
1/4 tsp	chili powder	1 mL
2	carrots, chopped	2
1 cup	frozen corn kernels, thawed	250 mL
1/4 cup	long-grain white rice	60 mL
1	can (28 oz/796 mL) diced tomatoes, with juice	1
1/4 cup	minced fresh cilantro (optional)	60 mL
1 tbsp	freshly squeezed lime juice	15 mL
	Salt and freshly ground black pepper	

1. In a large skillet, heat oil over medium-high heat. Sauté garlic, onion, jalapeño, cumin and chili powder for about 5 minutes or until onion is tender and translucent. Transfer to slow cooker stoneware. Stir in carrots, corn, rice, tomatoes with juice and 3 cups (750 mL) water.

2. Cover and cook on Low for 6 to 8 hours or on High for 3 to 4 hours, until soup is bubbling and rice is tender. Stir in cilantro (if using) and lime juice. Season to taste with salt and pepper.

Makes 4 to
6 servings as
a sandwich or
12 as an appetizer

Quesadillas sound complicated, but they are really just grilled sandwiches on flour tortillas. I often make them as a tasty accompaniment to a bowl of piping hot soup.

Tip

Jalapeño peppers contain volatile oils that can burn your skin and eyes if they come into direct contact. It is best to wear plastic or rubber gloves when chopping jalapeños, and take care not to touch your face or eyes while you work. If your bare hands do touch the peppers, wash your hands and nails well with hot, soapy water.

Monterey Jack and Green Pepper Quesadillas

- *Preheat oven to 400°F (200°C)*
- *Large rimmed baking sheet*

1 cup	shredded Monterey Jack cheese	250 mL
4	large whole wheat tortillas	4
1/2 cup	finely chopped green bell pepper	125 mL
1 tbsp	minced jalapeño pepper	15 mL
1/4 tsp	dried oregano	1 mL
1/4 tsp	hot pepper flakes	1 mL

1. Sprinkle cheese evenly over half of each tortilla. Sprinkle with green pepper, jalapeño, oregano and hot pepper flakes. Fold other half of tortilla over filling and press edges to seal.

2. Place filled tortillas on baking sheet and bake in preheated oven for about 15 minutes, turning once, until cheese is melted and tortillas are crisp and golden. Cut each tortilla into 3 wedges.

Make Ahead

Complete step 1, then wrap and refrigerate the quesadillas for up to 8 hours before baking.

Greek Lemon and Rice Soup

Makes 4 servings

This classic Greek chicken-egg-lemon soup (known as avgolemono) has been a favorite of children for millennia — it's so cheering on a cold day. A hearty salad and crusty ciabatta bread make this meal complete.

Tip

When cooking rice in the slow cooker, I usually recommend long-grain parboiled (converted) rice; however, for this recipe, short-grain rice, such as Arborio, is recommended. This type of rice softens and absorbs the broth, making the soup thicker. Do not use instant rice.

- **3¹/₂- to 5-quart slow cooker**

4 cups	chicken broth	1 L
¹/₂ cup	short-grain white rice (see tip, at left)	125 mL
3	egg yolks	3
¹/₄ cup	freshly squeezed lemon juice	60 mL
¹/₄ tsp	salt	1 mL
¹/₄ tsp	freshly ground white pepper	1 mL
4	thin slices lemon (optional)	4
2 tbsp	finely chopped fresh parsley	30 mL

1. In slow cooker stoneware, combine broth and rice.

2. Cover and cook on High for 2 to 3 hours or until rice is tender.

3. Reduce heat to Low. In a bowl, whisk together egg yolks and lemon juice. Whisk a large spoonful of the hot broth mixture into the yolk mixture, adding the hot liquid slowly and whisking constantly. (If hot liquid is added too quickly, the yolk mixture will curdle.) When fully blended, whisk into slow cooker stoneware.

4. Cover and cook on Low for 10 minutes. Season to taste with salt and pepper.

5. Ladle into bowls and garnish each with a lemon slice (if using) and parsley.

Cathedral Café Red Bean and Barley Soup

Makes 6 to 8 servings

On a car trip home from Florida one year, we stumbled upon the quaint Cathedral Café in Fayetteville, West Virginia. My daughter ordered this soup and enjoyed it so much that I just had to ask for the recipe.

Tip

To avoid tears when chopping onions, put the onions in the freezer for a few minutes first.

* **Minimum 4-quart slow cooker**

4 cups	cooked or canned red kidney beans (see page 120), drained and rinsed	1 L
1	onion, finely chopped	1
1	green bell pepper, finely chopped	1
1 cup	finely chopped carrots	250 mL
1 cup	finely chopped celery	250 mL
1 cup	pearl barley, rinsed	250 mL
1½ tsp	dried basil	7 mL
¼ tsp	freshly ground black pepper	1 mL
4 cups	vegetable broth	1 L
1	can (19 oz/540 mL) diced tomatoes, with juice	1
1 cup	prepared tomato pasta sauce	250 mL
¼ cup	chopped fresh parsley	60 mL

1. In slow cooker stoneware, combine beans, onion, green pepper, carrots, celery, barley, basil, pepper, broth, tomatoes with juice and pasta sauce.

2. Cover and cook on Low for 6 to 8 hours or on High for 3 to 4 hours, until soup is bubbling and barley is tender.

3. Ladle into bowls and garnish with parsley.

Creamy Tomato Tortellini Soup

Makes 4 to 6 servings

A package of fresh tortellini or other cheese-filled pasta makes this a satisfying soup the whole family will enjoy. Adding the baby spinach at the end gives it a fresh-from-the-garden flavor.

Tip

To ripen tomatoes, place them in a brown paper bag and store at room temperature. Never store tomatoes in the refrigerator, as it destroys their delicate flavor.

Make Ahead

This dish can be assembled up to 12 hours in advance. Prepare through step 1, cover and refrigerate overnight. The next day, place stoneware in slow cooker and proceed with step 2.

- **Minimum 4-quart slow cooker**

1/3 cup	melted butter	75 mL
1/3 cup	all-purpose flour	75 mL
2 cups	chicken broth	500 mL
3	large tomatoes, coarsely chopped	3
3	cloves garlic, minced	3
1	onion, finely chopped	1
1/2 tsp	dried basil	2 mL
1/2 tsp	salt	2 mL
1/4 tsp	dried oregano	1 mL
1/8 tsp	cayenne pepper	0.5 mL
1	package (10 oz/300 g) fresh cheese-filled tortellini	1
1	can (12 oz/370 mL) evaporated milk	1
6 cups	baby spinach leaves or chopped trimmed spinach	1.5 L
	Freshly ground black pepper	
	Freshly grated Parmesan cheese	

1. In slow cooker stoneware, whisk together melted butter and flour until a smooth paste forms. Slowly whisk in broth until combined. Stir in tomatoes, garlic, onion, basil, salt, oregano and cayenne.

2. Cover and cook on Low for 6 to 8 hours or on High for 3 to 4 hours, until soup is thick and vegetables are tender.

3. Using an immersion blender, or in a food processor or blender, purée soup until smooth. (If using food processor or blender, return mixture to stoneware.)

4. In a large pot of boiling salted water, cook tortellini according to package directions. Drain and add to stoneware. Stir in evaporated milk and baby spinach.

5. Cover and cook on High for 5 minutes or until spinach is slightly wilted.

6. Ladle into bowls and sprinkle with black pepper and Parmesan.

Jack's Smashed Potato Soup

Makes 6 to 8 servings

This is my son's favorite recipe from the array I developed for this book. Jack even eats it for breakfast! Potatoes blend with Cheddar cheese, cream and roasted garlic in this chunky good-to-the-last-spoonful soup.

Tips

Spread extra roasted garlic on toasted baguette slices, top with a dollop of softened goat cheese, and serve with the soup.

Leftover roasted garlic can be stored in an airtight container in the refrigerator for up to 3 days. It can be mashed and added to soups, stews or pasta sauces.

- **Minimum 4-quart slow cooker**

3½ lbs	thin-skinned potatoes (about 8 medium), cut into ¾-inch (2 cm) cubes	1.75 kg
½ cup	chopped yellow bell pepper	125 mL
4	cloves roasted garlic	4
½ tsp	freshly ground black pepper	2 mL
4½ cups	chicken broth	1.25 L
1 cup	shredded sharp (old) Cheddar cheese	250 mL
½ cup	light (5%) cream	125 mL
½ cup	thinly sliced green onions	125 mL
	Chopped fresh chives (optional)	

1. In slow cooker stoneware, combine potatoes, yellow pepper, garlic, pepper and broth.

2. Cover and cook on Low for 8 to 10 hours or on High for 4 to 5 hours, until soup is bubbling and potatoes are tender.

3. Using an immersion blender or a potato masher, purée or mash potatoes to make a thick soup. Stir in cheese, cream and green onions.

4. Ladle into bowls and garnish with chives (if using).

Make Ahead

This dish can be assembled up to 12 hours in advance. Prepare through step 1, cover and refrigerate overnight. The next day, place stoneware in slow cooker and proceed with step 2.

To Roast Garlic

Preheat oven to 400°F (200°C). Peel away the outer skins from garlic head, leaving skins of individual cloves intact. With a sharp knife, cut ¼ to ½ inch (0.5 to 1 cm) from the top of the head, exposing individual cloves. Place, base down, on a square of foil or in a garlic baker. Drizzle exposed cloves with oil until well coated; enclose in foil or cover with lid of baker. Bake for 30 to 35 minutes or until cloves feel soft when pressed. Let cool to room temperature, then remove roasted cloves with a cocktail fork or squeeze them out of their skins.

Coastal Fish Chowder

Makes 6 to 8 servings

When you go all-day whale watching off Grand Manan Island in New Brunswick, the captain of the boat serves you a delicious bowl of fish chowder for lunch. It is chock-full of wholesome fish, gently sautéed vegetables and a creamy broth. Make a cozy supper of this soup by serving it with freshly baked biscuits and a salad.

Tips

If using frozen fish in block form, remove packaging and place fish on a microwave-safe plate. Microwave at Medium (50%) power for 5 minutes or until partially thawed. Cut into cubes and let stand for 15 minutes or until completely thawed.

These days, it's a good idea to choose fish from a list of sustainable choices. These fish are well managed, abundant and caught or farmed in an environmentally sustainable way that does not harm the ocean. If you are unsure which fish fit these criteria, ask your fishmonger or check online resources before purchasing. Good North American resources include www.montereybayaquarium.org (click on Seafood Watch) and www.seachoice.org.

- **Minimum 4-quart slow cooker**

¼ cup	butter	60 mL
2	leeks (white and light green parts only), thinly sliced	2
1	large onion, finely chopped	1
½ cup	sliced celery	125 mL
¼ cup	all-purpose flour	60 mL
4 cups	diced peeled potatoes (about 6 small)	1 L
2	carrots, diced	2
1 tsp	dried thyme	5 mL
1 lb	fresh or frozen haddock or halibut fillets (thawed if frozen), bones removed, cut into large bite-size pieces	500 g
1 cup	milk	250 mL
1	can (12 oz/370 mL) evaporated milk or 1½ cups (375 mL) light (5%) cream	1
	Salt and freshly ground black pepper	
	Chopped fresh parsley or chives	
	Paprika	

1. In a skillet, melt butter over medium-high heat. Reduce heat to low and sauté leeks, onion and celery for about 15 minutes or until vegetables are tender and translucent but not browned. Transfer to slow cooker stoneware.

2. Sprinkle flour over vegetables and stir to coat. Gradually add 3 cups (750 mL) water, stirring gently to prevent flour from lumping. Stir in potatoes, carrots and thyme.

3. Cover and cook on Low for 6 to 8 hours or on High for 3 to 4 hours, until chowder is bubbling and vegetables are tender.

4. Stir in fish. Cover and cook on High for 30 to 35 minutes or until fish flakes easily when tested with a fork. Stir in milk and evaporated milk. Cover and cook for 5 minutes or until heated through. Season to taste with salt and pepper.

5. Ladle into bowls and sprinkle with parsley and paprika.

Manhattan Red Clam Chowder

Makes 4 to 6 servings

Tomatoes and their juice make this New York–style chowder stand apart from its creamy New England cousin. To save prep time, skip peeling the potatoes. The skins add a little more nutrient power to this soup.

Variation

Fish Chowder: Omit clams. Increase chicken broth to 4 cups (1 L). Add 12 oz (375 g) cubed fish, such as tilapia or haddock, at the end of cooking. Cover and cook on High for 15 to 20 minutes until fish flakes easily when tested with a fork.

- Minimum 4-quart slow cooker

2	cans (each 5 oz/150 g) baby clams	2
2 tbsp	olive oil	30 mL
1/2 cup	chopped smoked ham	125 mL
2	onions, finely chopped	2
2	cloves garlic, minced	2
2	stalks celery with leaves, diced	2
2	potatoes, peeled and diced	2
1 tsp	dried thyme	5 mL
1/2 tsp	hot pepper flakes	2 mL
1	can (28 oz/796 mL) plum tomatoes, with juice, roughly chopped	1
3 cups	chicken broth	750 mL
	Salt and freshly ground black pepper	
	Chopped fresh parsley	

1. Drain clams, reserving liquid. Place clams in a small bowl; cover and refrigerate.

2. In a skillet, heat oil over medium-high heat. Cook ham, stirring, for 2 minutes. Add onions and garlic; sauté for 5 minutes or until onions are tender and translucent. Transfer to slow cooker stoneware.

3. Stir in celery, potatoes, thyme, hot pepper flakes, tomatoes with juice, broth and reserved clam liquid.

4. Cover and cook on Low for 8 to 10 hours or on High for 4 to 5 hours, until chowder is bubbling and vegetables are tender.

5. Stir in reserved clams. Cover and cook on High for 5 minutes. Season to taste with salt and pepper.

6. Ladle into bowls and garnish with parsley.

Scallop and Corn Chowder

Makes 6 to 8 servings

This thick chowder is all about a melding of pure flavors. The slightly metallic scallops (tasting of butter and salt water), the cool, crisp corn kernels, the salty, crunchy bacon and the tender nuggets of potato all come together in a most satisfying way. Serve this chowder with some crusty bread alongside, because you will want to sop up every golden drop.

Tips

The quality of your scallops is important here, since they dominate the flavor of the chowder. I bought sea scallops, because they looked and smelled the freshest, but I have also successfully made this with bay scallops. For a cost-effective alternative, look for flash-frozen scallops in the seafood department. If using frozen scallops, thaw them before adding them to the soup.

For a lower-fat version, substitute an equal amount of evaporated milk or light (5%) cream for the heavy or whipping (35%) cream.

- **Minimum 4-quart slow cooker**

⅓ cup	butter, divided	75 mL
2	leeks (white and light green parts only), thinly sliced	2
10 oz	pancetta or bacon, chopped	300 g
6	yellow-flesh potatoes, diced	6
5 cups	vegetable broth	1.25 L
2 cups	frozen corn kernels, thawed	500 mL
1 tbsp	minced fresh thyme (or 1 tsp/5 mL dried thyme)	15 mL
¼ cup	all-purpose flour	60 mL
1 lb	sea scallops, quartered	500 g
1 cup	heavy or whipping (35%) cream	250 mL
	Chopped fresh parsley	

1. In a skillet, melt 2 tbsp (30 mL) of the butter over medium-high heat. Add leeks and cook, stirring, for 7 to 8 minutes or until softened. Transfer to slow cooker stoneware.

2. Reduce heat to medium and add pancetta to skillet. Cook, stirring, for 8 to 10 minutes or until lightly browned. Using a slotted spoon, transfer to stoneware. Stir in potatoes, broth, corn and thyme.

3. Cover and cook on Low for 4 to 6 hours or on High for 2 to 3 hours, until chowder is bubbling and potatoes are tender.

4. In a small skillet, melt the remaining butter over medium heat. Whisk in flour to make a thick paste. Add two ladles of hot liquid to the flour mixture, whisking constantly to make a thick sauce. Pour sauce into stoneware and stir until sauce is blended with the broth.

5. Add scallops. Cover and cook on High for about 10 minutes or until scallops are just firm and opaque. Stir in cream.

6. Ladle into bowls and garnish with parsley.

Thai Shrimp and Squash Soup

Makes 6 servings

I am a huge fan of Thai cuisine! The combination of squash, coconut milk and shrimp makes a luscious soup that is a meal in itself. It's not spicy, but it is wonderfully fragrant and flavorful.

Tips

Thai basil can be found in Asian supermarkets. If you can't find it, you can substitute Italian basil.

If you can't find a serrano pepper, you can substitute 1 tsp (5 mL) hot pepper flakes.

- **Minimum 4-quart slow cooker**

1 lb	large shrimp, deveined, shells on	500 g
8 cups	vegetable broth	2 L
1 cup	diced carrots	250 mL
3	stalks lemongrass, crushed	3
4	slices gingerroot	4
4	cloves garlic, crushed	4
1 cup	cubed butternut squash (1-inch/2.5 cm cubes)	250 mL
1½ tbsp	finely chopped fresh Thai basil	22 mL
1½ tbsp	finely chopped fresh mint	22 mL
1½ tbsp	finely chopped fresh cilantro	22 mL
1	serrano chile pepper, seeded and thinly sliced	1
	Freshly squeezed juice of 2 limes	
1	can (14 oz/398 mL) unsweetened coconut milk	1
½ tsp	sambal oelek chili paste	2 mL
6	lime wedges	6

1. Remove shells and tails from shrimp and reserve. Place shrimp in a bowl, cover and refrigerate.

2. In slow cooker stoneware, combine shrimp shells and tails, broth, carrots, lemongrass, ginger and garlic.

3. Cover and cook on Low for 3½ to 4½ hours or on High for 2 to 3 hours, until stock is bubbling. Strain broth and return to slow cooker. (Discard solids.) Stir in squash, basil, mint, cilantro, chile pepper, lime juice, coconut milk and chili paste.

4. Cover and cook on High for 25 to 30 minutes or until squash is tender. Add shrimp and cover and cook for 10 to 15 minutes or until shrimp are pink and opaque.

5. Ladle soup into bowls and garnish with lime wedges.

Sambal oelek is an Indonesian-inspired chili sauce that can be used to "heat up" any food. In many Asian countries, it is commonly offered as a condiment — even by hot dog vendors. You can find it in the Asian section of many supermarkets. Once it is opened, it's a good idea to store it in the refrigerator.

Mexican Chicken Tortilla Soup

Makes 4 servings

This soup is a snap to prepare because it uses a deli-cooked chicken, frozen vegetables and stewed tomatoes with added chili seasonings.

Tips

Using a deli-cooked chicken not only makes the prep go quickly, it adds immense flavor to the broth. Do not add the skin to the broth; be sure to remove it from the chicken first.

For a little extra heat in this recipe, add 1 to 2 sliced, seeded jalapeño peppers to the soup just before serving.

Serving soup in a warm bowl is an excellent way to help it retain heat. To warm your bowls, place them in a clean sink and run hot water over them. When ready to serve, dry them and use them immediately. If your tap water isn't hot enough, use water from a hot kettle. Alternatively, some ovens are equipped with a warming drawer — if you've never used it, here's your chance!

- **Minimum 4-quart slow cooker**

4 cups	chicken broth	1 L
2	cloves garlic, minced	2
1 tsp	ground cumin	5 mL
1 tsp	ground coriander	5 mL
1	can (19 oz/540 mL) chili-style stewed tomatoes, with juice	1
2 cups	shredded cooked chicken	500 mL
2 cups	frozen bell pepper and onion stir-fry vegetables, thawed	500 mL
1/2 cup	frozen corn kernels, thawed	125 mL
1 cup	crushed tortilla chips	250 mL
	Sour cream	
2 tbsp	chopped fresh cilantro	30 mL

1. In slow cooker stoneware, combine broth, garlic, cumin, coriander, tomatoes with juice, chicken, stir-fry vegetables and corn.

2. Cover and cook on Low for 6 to 7 hours or on High for 3 to 3 1/2 hours, until soup is bubbling and vegetables are tender.

3. Ladle soup into warmed bowls and top each with tortilla chips, a dollop of sour cream and a sprinkling of cilantro.

Make Ahead

This dish can be assembled up to 12 hours in advance. Prepare through step 1, cover and refrigerate overnight. The next day, place stoneware in slow cooker and proceed with step 2.

Vietnamese Chicken Pho

Makes 6 to 8 servings

This classic Asian soup, prepared with leftover shredded chicken, packs tons of flavor.

Tip

Hoisin sauce is a thick, reddish brown sauce made from soybeans and used primarily in Thai and Chinese dishes. It can be found in the Asian aisle of the supermarket.

- **Minimum 4-quart slow cooker**

8 cups	chicken broth	2 L
2 cups	shredded cooked chicken (see tip, page 88)	500 mL
8 oz	bean sprouts (about 4 cups/1 L)	250 g
4 oz	dried rice vermicelli noodles	125 g
2 tbsp	chopped fresh Thai basil	30 mL
	Hoisin sauce	
	Lime wedges	

1. In slow cooker stoneware, combine broth and chicken.

2. Cover and cook on Low for 6 to 7 hours or on High for 3 hours, until soup is bubbling.

3. Stir in bean sprouts, noodles and basil. Cover and cook for 10 to 12 minutes or until noodles are soft.

4. Ladle soup into bowls and drizzle with hoisin sauce. Garnish each bowl with a lime wedge.

> Thai basil is used as a condiment in Thai and Vietnamese dishes. It can be found in Asian supermarkets. It has purplish stems and flowers, shiny green leaves and a slight anise, almost citrusy, flavor. If you can't find it, you can substitute Italian basil.

Edamame and Chicken Corn Chowder

Makes 4 to 6 servings

This hearty and nutritious "stoup" is chock-full of goodness.

Tip
Look for edamame in the freezer section of your grocery store. Lima beans are a good alternative if you can't find edamame.

- **4- to 5-quart slow cooker**

3	slices bacon (4 oz/125 g)	3
1 lb	boneless skinless chicken breasts, cut into 1-inch (2.5 cm) pieces	500 g
1	onion, chopped	1
3 cups	chicken broth	750 mL
2	red potatoes, cut into ½-inch (1 cm) cubes	2
1	can (14 oz or 341 mL) cream-style corn	1
2 cups	frozen shelled edamame, thawed	500 mL
1	large red bell pepper, diced	1
1	jalapeño pepper, minced	1
½ tsp	dried oregano	2 mL
2 tbsp	all-purpose flour	30 mL
½ cup	heavy or whipping (35%) cream	125 mL
	Salt and freshly ground black pepper	
	Shredded Monterey Jack cheese	

1. In a large saucepan, cook bacon for 5 to 6 minutes or until browned and crisp. Transfer to paper towels to drain. Pour off all but 1 tbsp (15 mL) fat from pan. Crumble bacon, transfer to an airtight container and refrigerate until ready to use.

2. Add chicken and onion to pan and sauté for 4 to 5 minutes or until onions are tender and translucent. Using a slotted spoon, transfer to slow cooker stoneware. Stir in broth, potatoes, corn, edamame, red pepper, jalapeño and oregano.

3. Cover and cook on Low for 6 to 8 hours or on High for 3 to 4 hours, until chicken is no longer pink inside and vegetables are tender.

4. In a bowl, whisk together flour and cream until smooth. Gently stir into soup. Cover and cook on High for 15 to 20 minutes or until slightly thickened. Season to taste with salt and pepper. Ladle chowder into individual serving bowls and garnish with reserved bacon and cheese.

Smoky Turkey and Black Bean Soup

Makes 6 to 8 servings

This is one of my mother's favorite soups. She likes to put it on to cook before she heads out to the golf course, so it is waiting for her when she gets home. Look for smoked turkey legs in the deli section of your grocery store.

Tips

If you have a small, round slow cooker, use a smoked turkey thigh or chopped smoked turkey sausage (such as turkey kielbasa) instead.

Supermarkets are full of many varieties of canned beans. For this recipe, you can try using kidney or pinto beans.

* **Minimum 5-quart slow cooker**

1 tbsp	vegetable oil	15 mL
1	onion, diced	1
2	cloves garlic, minced	2
1	jalapeño pepper, minced	1
6 cups	chicken broth	1.5 mL
4 cups	cooked or canned black beans (see page 120), drained and rinsed	1 L
1/4 cup	tomato paste	60 mL
1	smoked turkey leg (about 1 1/4 lbs/625 g)	1
2	green bell peppers, diced	2
1	tomato, diced	1
1/4 cup	sour cream	60 mL
1/3 cup	chopped fresh cilantro	75 mL

1. In a nonstick skillet, heat oil over medium-high heat. Sauté onion for 2 to 3 minutes or until tender and translucent. Add garlic and jalapeño; sauté for 1 minute. Transfer to slow cooker stoneware. Stir in broth, black beans and tomato paste. Add turkey leg.

2. Cover and cook on Low for 6 to 8 hours or on High for 3 to 4 hours, until turkey meat is falling off the bone.

3. Using a slotted spoon, transfer turkey leg to a bowl; remove meat from the bone, chop and set aside. (Discard bone.)

4. Using an immersion blender, or in a food processor or blender, in batches as necessary, purée soup until smooth. (If using food processor or blender, return purée to stoneware.)

5. Add green peppers, tomato and chopped turkey to soup; stir to combine. Cover and cook on High for 10 minutes or until vegetables are warmed through.

6. Ladle into bowls and top each with a dollop of sour cream and a sprinkling of cilantro.

Make Ahead

This dish can be assembled up to 12 hours in advance. Prepare through step 1, without adding the smoked turkey leg, cover and refrigerate overnight. The next day, place stoneware in slow cooker, add the turkey leg and proceed with step 2.

Asian Turkey and Rice Soup

Makes 6 servings

Slices of mushroom, slivers of bok choy and chunks of turkey mingle in a soy- and ginger-flavored broth, giving this savory soup all the essence of a stir-fry.

Tip

Grating gingerroot is easiest if you keep a nub of it in the freezer. (Ginger tends to get moldy and soft too quickly when it's stored in the refrigerator.) Use a Microplane-style grater for best results. Microplanes have tiny razor-like edges that make quick and easy tasks of both grating and cleaning. You will find Microplanes in good kitchenware and department stores.

Variation

Substitute boneless skinless chicken thighs for the turkey thighs.

• **Minimum 4-quart slow cooker**

1 lb	turkey thighs, skin removed	500 g
4	cloves garlic, minced	4
2	carrots, cut into thin strips, about 2-inches (5 cm) long	2
2 cups	sliced assorted mushrooms, such as cremini, button and shiitake	500 mL
1/2 cup	chopped onion	125 mL
2 tsp	grated gingerroot	10 mL
3 cups	chicken broth	750 mL
2 tbsp	soy sauce	30 mL
2 cups	cooked brown rice	500 mL
1 1/2 cups	sliced bok choy	375 mL

1. In slow cooker stoneware, combine turkey thighs, garlic, carrots, mushrooms, onion, ginger, broth, soy sauce and 1 1/2 cups (375 mL) water.

2. Cover and cook on Low for 6 to 8 hours or on High for 3 to 4 hours, until turkey is no longer pink inside.

3. Using a slotted spoon, transfer turkey thighs to a cutting board and let cool slightly; remove meat from bones. (Discard bones.) Using two forks, shred meat into bite-size pieces. Return to slow cooker stoneware.

4. Stir in rice and bok choy. Cover and cook on High for 10 to 15 minutes or until rice is warmed through and bok choy is tender.

Bok choy, also known as Chinese cabbage, is one of the most popular Asian greens. It has a large, loose head with crisp white stalks and dark green, flat leaves. The greens have a very mild cabbage flavor when cooked, and the stalks become creamy and tender. The miniature version, called baby bok choy, is equally delicious and is perfect in soup.

Steak and Potato Cowboy Soup

Makes 6 servings

Salsa is the key to the sensational flavors in this soup. Kick up the heat a little by using a hot salsa.

Tip

Broth (or stock) is one of the most indispensable pantry staples. Commercial broth cubes and powders are loaded with salt and just don't deliver the flavor of homemade stock or prepared broth. I like to keep 32-oz (1 L) Tetra Paks on hand, especially the sodium-reduced variety. They come in handy when you're making soups and stews.

- **Minimum 4-quart slow cooker**

1½ lbs	boneless beef shoulder or blade steak, trimmed and cut into 1-inch (2.5 cm) cubes	750 g
2	potatoes, peeled and cut into 1-inch (2.5 cm) cubes	2
1	onion, sliced crosswise and separated into rings	1
2 cups	frozen corn kernels	500 mL
2	cloves garlic, minced	2
1	jar (23 oz/650 mL) mild or hot thick and chunky salsa	1
2 cups	beef broth	500 mL
1 tsp	dried basil	5 mL
	Shredded Monterey Jack cheese or Tex-Mex cheese blend (optional)	

1. In slow cooker stoneware, combine beef, potatoes, onion and corn.

2. In a bowl, stir together garlic, salsa, broth and basil, then pour over beef and vegetables.

3. Cover and cook on Low for 8 to 10 hours or on High for 4 to 5 hours, until soup is bubbling and beef is tender.

4. Ladle into bowls and top with cheese (if using).

Make Ahead

This dish can be assembled up to 12 hours in advance. Prepare through step 2, cover and refrigerate overnight. The next day, place stoneware in slow cooker and proceed with step 3.

Red Curry Beef Noodle Soup

Makes 4 to 6 servings

This beef noodle soup is very popular in Laos and Thailand. In our northern climate, it brings much comfort on a cold winter day. You can pick up most of the ingredients in the Asian section of the supermarket.

Tips

To soak rice noodles, place them in a large heatproof bowl, add enough boiling water to cover and let soak for 10 minutes. Drain; rinse under cold running water, drain again and set aside.

Look for a cut of beef labeled "simmering steak" for this recipe. To yield the best results, it needs to be a cut that can take a long, moist-heat method of cooking.

Thai basil can be found in Asian supermarkets. If you can't find it, you can substitute Italian basil.

- **Minimum 4-quart slow cooker**

2 tbsp	vegetable oil	30 mL
1 lb	boneless beef shoulder or blade steak, cut into 1-inch (2.5 cm) strips	500 g
2 tsp	Thai red curry paste	10 mL
8 oz	green beans, trimmed and cut into 1-inch (2.5 cm) pieces	250 g
4 cups	chicken broth	1 L
1 tbsp	fish sauce (approx.)	15 mL
1 tsp	granulated sugar	5 mL
4	green onions, sliced	4
1/4 cup	slivered fresh Thai basil or basil	60 mL
2 tbsp	rice wine vinegar	30 mL
2 tbsp	soy sauce	30 mL
8 oz	rice stick noodles, soaked (see tip, at left)	250 g
1 cup	bean sprouts	250 mL
1/2 cup	fresh cilantro leaves	125 mL
1/2 cup	unsalted roasted peanuts, coarsely chopped (optional)	125 mL

1. In a skillet, heat 1 tbsp (15 mL) of the oil over medium-high heat. Add beef and cook for 2 to 3 minutes or until browned. Using a slotted spoon, transfer to slow cooker stoneware.

2. Add the remaining oil to the skillet. Add curry paste and cook, stirring, for 1 minute or until fragrant. Add green beans and stir-fry for 1 minute; transfer to stoneware. Stir in broth, fish sauce and sugar.

3. Cover and cook on Low for 7 to 9 hours or on High for 3 1/2 to 4 1/2 hours, until soup is bubbling and beef is tender. Stir in green onions and basil. Taste soup and add more fish sauce, if desired.

4. Meanwhile, in a small bowl, combine vinegar and soy sauce. Divide noodles evenly between individual soup bowls. Ladle soup evenly over noodles. Top with bean sprouts, cilantro and peanuts (if using) , then drizzle with vinegar mixture. Serve immediately.

Fish sauce is the salt of Asia, and one of the most important ingredients in Thai cooking. It is made of fermented, salted anchovies and is used both in cooking and as a condiment on the table.

Nonna's Mini-Meatball Soup

Makes 6 to 8 servings

This soup reminds of the one I'm served when I visit my friend Maria's house. Her mother always has a pot of soup on the stove, or if she doesn't, she will quickly make one for you with whatever ingredients she has on hand.

Tip

If you don't have homemade chicken stock, use ready-to-use chicken broth. I like to keep 32-oz (1 L) Tetra Paks of broth on hand, especially the sodium-reduced variety. They come in handy when you're making soups and stews. Another option is to use three 10-oz (284 mL) cans of broth and add enough water to make 6 cups (1.5 L). Avoid broth cubes and powders, which tend to be salty.

• **Minimum 5-quart slow cooker**

1 lb	lean ground beef	500 g
1 lb	lean ground pork	500 g
1 cup	finely grated Parmesan cheese	250 mL
1 cup	fine dry Italian bread crumbs	250 mL
2	eggs, lightly beaten	2
1	bunch flat-leaf (Italian) parsley, finely chopped (about 1 cup/250 mL)	1
1/2 tsp	salt	2 mL
1/2 tsp	freshly ground black pepper	2 mL
6 cups	chicken broth	1.5 L
2 cups	packed baby spinach, coarsely chopped, or chopped escarole	500 mL
2 cups	cooked small pasta, such as elbows, tubetti, shells or stars	500 mL
	Freshly grated Parmesan cheese (optional)	

1. In a large bowl, combine beef, pork, Parmesan, bread crumbs, eggs, parsley, salt and pepper. Using your hands, roll into 3/4-inch (2 cm) meatballs. Place meatballs in slow cooker stoneware. Gently pour in broth.

2. Cover and cook on Low for 8 to 9 hours or on High for 4 1/2 to 5 hours, until soup is bubbling and meatballs are cooked through.

3. Stir in spinach. Cover and cook on High for 10 to 15 minutes or until greens are wilted, bright green and tender. Stir in cooked pasta.

4. Ladle into bowls and sprinkle with additional Parmesan, if desired.

> Real Parmesan cheese, Parmigiano-Reggiano, is expensive, but its flavor is certainly worth the price. A block keeps for months, well wrapped in the refrigerator, and goes a long way when you freshly grate it as you need it.

Sweet-and-Sour Moroccan Lamb Soup

Makes 4 to 6 servings

There are some nights — particularly cold nights — when soup is what everyone is craving. Be sure to serve plenty of pita bread to go along with this hearty soup. The ingredients are so simple to assemble, it can be put together in a snap before you head out the door in the morning.

Tip

Despite its shape, orzo is not rice, but is pasta made of hard wheat semolina. It was originally made from barley.

Variation

This soup is also very good made with lentils instead of chickpeas.

- Minimum 4-quart slow cooker

2 tbsp	olive oil (approx.)	30 mL
1 lb	boneless lamb shoulder, trimmed and cut into thin strips	500 g
1 tsp	salt	5 mL
1 tsp	ground ginger	5 mL
1 tsp	ground turmeric	5 mL
1/2 tsp	freshly ground black pepper	2 mL
2 cups	cooked or canned chickpeas (see page 120), drained and rinsed	500 mL
1	can (28 oz/796 mL) plum tomatoes, drained	1
1	large onion, chopped	1
1	3-inch (7.5 cm) cinnamon stick	1
2 tbsp	chopped fresh cilantro	30 mL
1 cup	orzo	250 mL
1 cup	dates, finely chopped	250 mL
	Freshly squeezed juice of 1 lemon, divided	
	Chopped fresh cilantro (optional)	

1. In a large nonstick skillet, heat half the oil over medium-high heat. In batches, cook lamb for 3 to 5 minutes or until browned all over, adding oil as necessary between batches. Using a slotted spoon, transfer to slow cooker stoneware.

2. Add salt, ginger, turmeric and pepper; stir to coat lamb evenly. Stir in chickpeas, tomatoes, onion, cinnamon stick, cilantro and 7 cups (1.75 L) water.

3. Cover and cook on Low for 10 to 12 hours or on High for 5 to 6 hours, until soup is bubbling and lamb is tender. Remove cinnamon stick.

4. In a pot of boiling salted water, cook orzo for 6 to 8 minutes or until al dente. Drain.

5. Add orzo, dates and 2 tbsp (30 mL) of the lemon juice to the slow cooker and stir to combine. Taste and adjust the seasoning with more lemon juice, if desired.

6. Ladle into bowls and garnish with additional cilantro, if desired.

Cherry Vanilla Irish Oatmeal (page 21)

Overnight Blueberry French Toast (page 29)

Cranberry Baked Brie (page 42)

Annika's Swedish Meatballs (page 50)

Bloody Mary Dip (page 56)

Thai Shrimp and Squash Soup (page 87)

Smoky Turkey and Black Bean Soup (page 91)

Mixed Vegetable Stew with Herbed Buttermilk Biscuits (page 98)

Stews

Mixed Vegetable Stew with Herbed Buttermilk Biscuits

Makes 6 servings

This is a great vegetarian stew that can be prepared with whatever vegetables are in season. It is not only extremely flavorful, but also economical. Both vegetarians and meat lovers will be satisfied.

Tips

Leeks contain a lot of sand and must be cleaned carefully. Remove most of the green part and halve the white part lengthwise. Rinse thoroughly under cold running water, spreading leaves apart, and drain in a colander, then slice.

If you don't have any buttermilk on hand, here is a quick substitution. Place 1 tbsp (15 mL) lemon juice or white vinegar in a glass measuring cup. Add enough milk to make 1 cup (250 mL). Let stand for 5 minutes before using in the recipe.

- 4- to 6-quart slow cooker

Stew

2 tbsp	vegetable oil	30 mL
1 tbsp	butter	15 mL
3	leeks (white parts only), sliced	3
2	cloves garlic, minced	2
1 tsp	dried thyme	5 mL
1 tbsp	all-purpose flour	15 mL
1½ cups	vegetable broth	375 mL
2	plum tomatoes, seeded and chopped	2
1	carrot, chopped	1
1	small potato, peeled and chopped	1
1	celery root, peeled and chopped	1
1	small white turnip, peeled and chopped	1
1	large parsnip, chopped	1
1	small zucchini, chopped	1
¼ cup	chopped fresh parsley	60 mL
1 tbsp	chopped fresh basil	15 mL
	Salt and freshly ground black pepper	

Herbed Buttermilk Biscuits

2 cups	all-purpose flour	500 mL
1 tsp	dried thyme	5 mL
1 tsp	baking powder	5 mL
½ tsp	baking soda	2 mL
½ tsp	salt	2 mL
6 tbsp	cold butter	90 mL
1 cup	buttermilk	250 mL

1. *Stew:* In a large nonstick skillet, heat oil and butter over medium heat. Sauté leeks for about 10 minutes or until softened. Add garlic and thyme; sauté for 1 minute or until fragrant. Sprinkle with flour and stir to coat vegetables.

2. Gradually stir in broth and bring to a boil, scraping up any brown bits from pan. Transfer to slow cooker stoneware. Stir in tomatoes, carrot, potato, celery root, turnip, parsnip and zucchini.

Variation

Use a combination of carrots, butternut squash, celery, red bell peppers and mushrooms in place of the carrot, potato, celery root, turnip, parsnip and zucchini. The vegetable mixture should measure about 6 cups (1.5 L) total. Replace the thyme with dried rosemary.

3. Cover and cook on Low for 4 to 6 hours or on High for 2 to 3 hours, until vegetables are tender and stew is bubbling. Stir in parsley and basil. Season to taste with salt and pepper.

4. Preheat oven to 425°F (220°C).

5. *Biscuits:* Meanwhile, in a large bowl (or a food processor), combine flour, thyme, baking powder, baking soda and salt.

6. Using two knives or your fingertips, cut in butter until mixture resembles coarse crumbs. (Or pulse briefly in food processor, then transfer to a bowl.)

7. Add buttermilk to flour mixture and toss lightly with a fork to make a soft dough.

8. Drop spoonfuls of dough onto bubbling stew. Transfer slow cooker stoneware to preheated oven and bake, uncovered, for 15 to 20 minutes or until biscuits are lightly browned and a tester inserted in the center of a biscuit comes out clean.

Golden Lentil Stew

Makes 6 to 8 servings

This slightly sweet Moroccan lentil and chickpea stew is brightened by mixing a combination of sweet and savory spices in the stew and adding a twist of lemon at the end.

Tips

Broth (or stock) is one of the most indispensable pantry staples. Commercial broth cubes and powders are loaded with salt and just don't deliver the flavor of homemade stock or prepared broth. I like to keep 32-oz (1 L) Tetra Paks on hand, especially the sodium-reduced variety. They come in handy when you're making soups and stews.

Tomato paste is now available in tubes in many supermarkets and delis. It keeps for months in the refrigerator.

Orzo is a small, rice-shaped pasta. You can substitute any small pasta for the orzo or break spaghetti noodles into short pieces.

- Minimum 4-quart slow cooker

1 tbsp	olive oil	15 mL
1	onion, finely chopped	1
3	cloves garlic, minced	3
½ tsp	sweet paprika	2 mL
½ tsp	ground turmeric	2 mL
½ tsp	ground ginger	2 mL
½ tsp	ground coriander	2 mL
¼ tsp	ground nutmeg	1 mL
4	stalks celery, finely chopped	4
1	can (19 oz/540 mL) diced tomatoes, with juice	1
2 cups	vegetable broth	500 mL
2 cups	cooked or canned chickpeas (see page 120), drained and rinsed	500 mL
1 cup	dried red lentils, rinsed	250 mL
1 tbsp	tomato paste	15 mL
3	whole cloves	3
1	3-inch (7.5 cm) cinnamon stick	1
¼ tsp	freshly ground black pepper	1 mL
½ cup	cooked orzo or other small pasta	125 mL
½ cup	chopped pitted dates	125 mL
2 tbsp	coarsely chopped fresh parsley	30 mL
2 tbsp	finely chopped fresh cilantro	30 mL
1 tbsp	freshly squeezed lemon juice	15 mL
1	lemon, cut into wedges	1

1. In a large nonstick skillet, heat oil over medium-high heat. Sauté onion for 3 to 5 minutes or until tender and translucent. Add garlic, paprika, turmeric, ginger, coriander and nutmeg; sauté for 1 minute or until fragrant. Transfer to slow cooker stoneware.

2. Stir in celery, tomatoes with juice, broth, chickpeas, lentils, tomato paste, cloves, cinnamon stick and pepper.

3. Cover and cook on Low for 8 to 10 hours or on High for 4 to 5 hours, until stew is bubbling.

If you have any leftovers, this stew stores very well in the refrigerator for up to 5 days. Store in an airtight container and reheat as necessary, adding a little water if the stew is too thick.

4. Stir in orzo and dates. Cover and cook on High for 10 to 15 minutes or until heated through. Discard cinnamon stick. Stir in parsley, cilantro and lemon juice. Serve garnished with lemon wedges.

Make Ahead

This dish can be assembled up to 12 hours in advance. Prepare through step 2, but don't add the lentils. Cover and refrigerate overnight. The next day, stir in lentils, place stoneware in slow cooker and proceed with step 3.

Keep the Lid On!

When something is cooking in the slow cooker, resist the temptation to lift the lid. The domed lid allows condensation to run into the stoneware, forming a water seal. This seal keeps in the heat; if you remove the lid, the seal is broken and the heat escapes. It takes the cooker a long time to restore the heat level. Slow cooker recipes shouldn't need stirring, but if you need to add ingredients, do so and replace the lid quickly. If you lift the lid without being instructed to do so, add about 20 more minutes to the cooking time.

Italian Chicken Stew with Crisp Polenta

Makes 4 to 6 servings

This rustic, country-style Italian stew cooks in a rich tomato-mushroom sauce. You can serve it over mashed potatoes, but picking up a package of ready-made polenta is much faster and easier. If you have two slow cookers, serve the stew over Pecorino and Parsley Polenta (page 297).

Tips

Bone-in thighs cook a little more slowly than boneless, so they are ideal for this dish. If you can't find skinless bone-in chicken thighs, purchase them with the skin on. It is easy to remove and discard the skin yourself.

To prepare mushrooms, wipe them with a damp paper towel. Don't rinse or soak them, or they'll absorb water and turn mushy when cooked.

- **Minimum 4-quart slow cooker**
- *Rimmed baking sheet*

Italian Chicken Stew

2 tbsp	all-purpose flour	30 mL
1 tsp	salt	5 mL
1/2 tsp	freshly ground black pepper	2 mL
8 to 12	skinless bone-in chicken thighs (about 3 lbs/1.5 kg)	8 to 12
2 tbsp	olive oil (approx.)	30 mL
1 lb	mushrooms, quartered	500 g
2	onions, sliced	2
4	cloves garlic, sliced	4
1/2 cup	dry white wine	125 mL
1	can (19 oz/540 mL) tomatoes, with juice	1
1 tsp	dried Italian seasoning	5 mL
1/3 cup	pitted green olives, halved	75 mL
	Chopped fresh parsley	

Crisp Polenta

1	tube (1 lb/500 g) plain prepared polenta, cut into 12 slices	1
1 tbsp	olive oil	15 mL
	Salt and freshly ground black pepper	

1. *Stew:* In a bowl, combine flour, salt and pepper. Dredge chicken in flour mixture to coat. (Reserve remaining flour.)

2. In a large nonstick skillet, heat half the oil over medium-high heat. Cook chicken in batches, adding more oil as needed, for 2 to 3 minutes per side or until browned all over. Using a slotted spoon, transfer to slow cooker stoneware. Add mushrooms.

3. Return skillet to medium-high heat. Add onions to remaining drippings in pan, adding more oil if pan is dry, and sauté for 3 to 5 minutes or until tender and translucent. Add garlic and sauté for 1 minute. Sprinkle with reserved flour mixture and stir until onion mixture is coated. Pour in wine, stirring until blended.

4. Pour onion mixture over chicken and mushrooms. Stir in tomatoes with juice and Italian seasoning, using a wooden spoon to break up tomatoes slightly.

5. Cover and cook on Low for 8 to 10 hours or on High for 4 to 6 hours, until juices run clear when chicken is pierced. Sprinkle with olives, cover and cook for about 5 minutes.

6. *Polenta:* Meanwhile, preheat broiler, with rack positioned 6 to 8 inches (15 to 20 cm) from the heat. Brush both sides of each polenta slice with oil and place on baking sheet. Season to taste with salt and pepper. Broil, without turning, for 10 to 15 minutes or until deep golden brown.

7. Arrange polenta on individual plates or bowls, spoon stew over top and garnish with parsley.

Spanish Chicken with Chickpeas

Makes 4 to 6 servings

On a trip to Spain with our Swiss friends Patrizia and Thomas, my husband and I whiled away the afternoon in a cozy restaurant in the small mountain village of Ronda. The owner made a version of this fragrant dish, and we soaked up the remnants of it with slices of warm, crusty bread while sipping glasses of local red wine. I thought I was in heaven.

Tip

Chorizo, a flavorful pork sausage, gets its distinctive smokiness and deep color from the smoked paprika used to make it. It can be found fresh or cured, but I prefer the cured, smoked European variety for this recipe. You can find it in the deli section of well-stocked supermarkets or in specialty stores that sell Spanish sausage.

- **4- to 6-quart slow cooker**

¼ cup	all-purpose flour	60 mL
1 tsp	salt	5 mL
½ tsp	freshly ground black pepper	2 mL
2 lbs	boneless skinless chicken thighs (8 to 10)	1 kg
8 oz	cured chorizo sausage, cut into ½-inch (1 cm) pieces	250 g
2 cups	cooked or canned chickpeas (see page 120), drained and rinsed	500 mL
3	large cloves garlic, smashed	3
1 tsp	dried oregano	5 mL
1	can (14 oz/398 mL) diced tomatoes, with juice	1
2 tsp	sherry vinegar	10 mL
Pinch	saffron threads	Pinch

1. In a bowl, combine flour, salt and pepper. Dredge chicken in flour mixture to coat and shake off any excess. Arrange chicken in slow cooker stoneware. Sprinkle with sausage, chickpeas, garlic and oregano. Discard any excess flour mixture.

2. In a blender or food processor, purée tomatoes with juice, ½ cup (125 mL) water, vinegar and saffron. Pour over chicken mixture.

3. Cover and cook on Low for 8 to 10 hours or on High for 4 to 6 hours, until juices run clear when chicken is pierced. Remove garlic cloves, if desired. Season to taste with salt and pepper.

North African Chicken Stew

Makes 4 servings

With this stew, you can enjoy the flavors of North African cuisine without having to go to an exotic grocery store to buy the ingredients. Ladle it over couscous and serve it with some warm flatbread to soak up the savory sauce.

Tips

You can add a little more heat to this recipe by increasing the amount of cayenne pepper. Or you can add some hot sauce at the end of the cooking time, if you prefer to taste the level of heat before adding extra spice.

Look for precut fresh squash in the produce department of your supermarket. It will save a lot of preparation time, since the peel and seeds have already been removed. Simply cut it into 1-inch (2.5 cm) cubes.

- **Minimum 4-quart slow cooker**

1½ lbs	boneless skinless chicken thighs, cut into 2-inch (5 cm) pieces	750 g
1½ tbsp	freshly squeezed lemon juice	22 mL
1 tsp	ground cumin	5 mL
½ tsp	ground allspice	2 mL
½ tsp	cayenne pepper	2 mL
2	cloves garlic, minced	2
1	red onion, chopped	1
1	butternut or other winter squash, peeled and cubed (about 6 cups/1.5 L)	1
2 cups	cooked or canned chickpeas (see page 120), drained and rinsed	500 mL
½ cup	chicken broth	125 mL
	Salt and freshly ground black pepper	
4	green onions, chopped	4
	Hot cooked couscous	
	Chopped fresh cilantro or parsley	
4	lemon slices	4

1. Place chicken in slow cooker stoneware. Drizzle with lemon juice and toss chicken to coat.

2. In a small bowl, combine cumin, allspice and cayenne. Sprinkle over chicken. Arrange garlic, red onion, squash and chickpeas on top. Pour in broth.

3. Cover and cook on Low for 5 to 7 hours or on High for 2½ to 4 hours, until chicken is no longer pink inside. Season to taste with salt and black pepper.

4. Add green onions. Cover and cook on High for 10 minutes.

5. Ladle over couscous and garnish each serving with cilantro and lemon slices.

Tex-Mex Beef Stew

Makes 6 to 8 servings

The blend of spices gives this stew the most wonderful flavor. At the end of the long cooking time, and before adding the dumpling batter, add an extra pinch of chili powder and cinnamon to brighten the flavors.

Tips

Here's a foolproof way to chop an onion: Peel the onion and halve it from top to base. Place each half cut side down on a cutting board. Slice horizontally across each half. Holding the slices together, slice vertically.

Jalapeño peppers contain volatile oils that can burn your skin and eyes if they come into direct contact. It is best to wear plastic or rubber gloves when chopping jalapeños, and take care not to touch your face or eyes while you work. If your bare hands do touch the peppers, wash your hands and nails well with hot, soapy water.

Most recipes use large eggs. If a recipe doesn't specify a size, assume you need large.

When browning meat in hot oil, avoid overfilling the skillet. If the pan is too full, the meat will steam rather than brown. Turn the meat frequently and cook it as quickly as possible, then use a slotted spoon to remove it.

- **4- to 6-quart slow cooker**

Stew

4	slices smoked bacon, diced	4
3 lbs	boneless stewing beef, cut into 1-inch (2.5 cm) cubes	1.5 kg
	Vegetable oil	
1/2 cup	dark beer	125 mL
1	can (28 oz/796 mL) tomatoes, with juice	1
4	cloves garlic, minced	4
2	onions, diced	2
1	red onion, diced	1
1	yellow bell pepper, diced	1
1	jalapeño pepper, seeded and chopped	1
1 tbsp	ancho chile powder	15 mL
2 tsp	dried oregano	10 mL
1/2 tsp	ground cinnamon	2 mL

Cornmeal Dumplings

1/2 cup	all-purpose flour	125 mL
2 tbsp	cornmeal	30 mL
1/2 tsp	salt	2 mL
1	egg, lightly beaten	1
1/3 cup	milk	75 mL
1 tbsp	butter, melted	15 mL
	Lime wedges	

1. **Stew:** In a large nonstick skillet, cook bacon over medium-high heat, stirring, for 5 to 7 minutes or until crisp. Using a slotted spoon, transfer to a plate lined with paper towels to drain, reserving drippings in pan.

2. Return skillet to medium-high heat. Cook beef in batches, adding more oil as needed, for 5 minutes or until browned all over. Using a slotted spoon, transfer to slow cooker stoneware.

3. Add beer to pan and bring to a boil, scraping up any brown bits from pan. Transfer to stoneware. Stir in bacon, tomatoes with juice, garlic, onions, red onion, yellow pepper, jalapeño, chile powder, oregano and cinnamon.

4. Cover and cook on Low for 8 to 10 hours or on High for
4 to 6 hours, until beef and vegetables are tender and stew is
bubbling.

5. *Dumplings:* In a bowl, combine flour, cornmeal and salt. In a
separate bowl, whisk together egg, milk and butter. Stir into
flour mixture just until combined.

6. Drop spoonfuls of dumpling batter onto bubbling stew. Cover
and cook on High for 20 to 25 minutes or until tester inserted
into center of dumplings comes out clean. Serve garnished
with lime wedges.

Make Ahead

This dish can be assembled up to 12 hours in advance, as long
as the beef is left out. Cook the bacon in step 1 and refrigerate
it in its own airtight container. Skip over step 2 and complete
step 3. Cover and refrigerate overnight. The next day, brown
the beef in 2 tbsp (25 mL) vegetable oil. Place stoneware in
slow cooker, add beef and bacon and proceed with step 4.

Ancho chile powder, also called ground ancho chile pepper, is
the most commonly used chile powder in Mexican cooking. It is
ground from dried ancho (poblano) peppers and has a smoky
flavor and mild to medium heat. If you can't find ancho chile
powder, you can substitute regular chili powder.

Country Italian Beef Stew

Makes 6 to 8 servings

This stew features the wonderful flavors of the Mediterranean — fennel, basil and rosemary. Fennel has a distinctive mild licorice flavor, but even if you are not a licorice fan, you will enjoy the bold flavors of this beef stew.

Tip

Crush dried rosemary between your thumb and fingers before adding it to a dish. This helps release the full aromatic flavor of the herb.

- Minimum 4-quart slow cooker

3 tbsp	all-purpose flour	45 mL
1 tsp	salt	5 mL
1 tsp	freshly ground black pepper, divided	5 mL
2 lbs	stewing beef, cut into 1-inch (2.5 cm) cubes	1 kg
2 tbsp	vegetable oil (approx.)	30 mL
6	tiny new potatoes, halved or quartered	6
2	parsnips, cut into 1- to 2-inch (2.5 to 5 cm) pieces	2
1	fennel bulb, trimmed and cut into 1/2-inch (1 cm) wedges	1
1 cup	chopped onion	250 mL
1 cup	beef broth	250 mL
1/2 cup	dry red wine	125 mL
1	can (7 1/2 oz/213 mL) pizza sauce	1
4	cloves garlic, minced	4
1 tsp	dried rosemary, crumbled	5 mL
1 cup	fresh baby spinach leaves	250 mL

1. In a heavy plastic bag, combine flour, salt and 1/2 tsp (2 mL) of the pepper. In batches, add beef to bag and toss to coat with flour mixture. Discard excess flour mixture.

2. In a large nonstick skillet, heat half the oil over medium-high heat. Cook beef in batches, adding more oil as needed, for 5 minutes or until browned all over. Using a slotted spoon, transfer to slow cooker stoneware. Stir in potatoes, parsnips, fennel and onion.

3. In a 2-cup (500 mL) measuring cup, combine broth, wine, pizza sauce, garlic, rosemary and the remaining pepper. Pour over beef mixture.

4. Cover and cook on Low for 8 to 10 hours or on High for 4 to 5 hours, until bubbling. Just before serving, stir in spinach until wilted.

Lemony Veal Milanese

Makes 6 to 8 servings

This hearty dish is as much of a hit with young children as it is with sophisticated adults. Serve the stew atop egg noodles, to sop up the rich sauce. The noodles take no time to cook after a long day at work.

Tips

To get the most juice from a lemon, let it warm to room temperature, then roll it on the counter, pressing down with the palm of your hand, before squeezing it.

When browning meat in hot oil, avoid overfilling the skillet. If the pan is too full, the meat will steam rather than brown. Turn the meat frequently and cook it as quickly as possible, then use a slotted spoon to remove it.

- **Minimum 4-quart slow cooker**

1/2 cup	all-purpose flour	125 mL
3/4 tsp	freshly ground black pepper	3 mL
2 1/2 lbs	boneless stewing veal, cut into 1-inch (2.5 cm) cubes	1.25 kg
1/4 cup	olive oil	60 mL
1/2 cup	dry white wine	125 mL
1 1/2 cups	chicken broth	375 mL
6	stalks celery, chopped	6
4	carrots, chopped	4
4	cloves garlic, minced	4
2	leeks (white and light green parts only), sliced	2
2	small onions, chopped	2
1	can (19 oz/540 mL) diced tomatoes, with juice	1
2 tsp	dried basil	10 mL
2 tsp	dried rosemary	10 mL
2 tsp	dried Italian seasoning	10 mL
1/4 cup	chopped fresh parsley	60 mL
1 tsp	grated lemon zest	5 mL
2 tbsp	freshly squeezed lemon juice	30 mL
1 tsp	salt	5 mL

1. In a heavy plastic bag, combine flour and pepper. In batches, add veal to bag and toss to coat with flour mixture. Discard excess flour mixture.

2. In a large nonstick skillet, heat 2 tbsp (25 mL) of the oil over medium-high heat. Cook veal in batches, adding more oil as needed, for 5 minutes or until browned all over. Using a slotted spoon, transfer to slow cooker stoneware.

3. Add wine to skillet and boil, scraping up any brown bits from pan, for 2 to 3 minutes or until reduced by half. Add broth and simmer for 1 minute. Pour over veal. Stir in celery, carrots, garlic, leeks, onions, tomatoes with juice, basil, rosemary and Italian seasoning.

4. Cover and cook on Low for 6 to 7 hours or on High for 3 to 3 1/2 hours, until stew is bubbling. Stir in parsley, lemon zest, lemon juice and salt.

Pesto Meatball Stew

Makes 4 to 6 servings

Sometimes we just want a quick, throw-it-together meal the whole family will enjoy. My friend Christopher taste-tested this one with his family, and it has since become a staple meal in their busy household.

Tip

Keeping a box of premade cooked meatballs in the freezer makes for really quick dinner prep. You can use beef, pork, turkey or chicken meatballs for this recipe — they will all taste great in the stew.

- **Minimum 4-quart slow cooker**

2	carrots, finely chopped	2
2	stalks celery, finely chopped	2
1	red bell pepper, finely chopped	1
1	box (2 lbs/1 kg) frozen cooked Italian-style meatballs, thawed	1
1	can (28 oz/796 mL) Italian-style stewed tomatoes, with juice	1
2 cups	cooked or canned white kidney beans (see page 120), drained and rinsed	500 mL
1/4 cup	basil pesto	60 mL
2 cups	cooked short pasta, such as rotini or penne	500 mL
1/2 cup	finely shredded Parmesan cheese	125 mL

1. In slow cooker stoneware, combine carrots, celery, red pepper, meatballs, tomatoes with juice, beans, pesto and 1/2 cup (125 mL) water.

2. Cover and cook on Low for 5 to 7 hours or on High for 2 1/2 to 3 1/2 hours, until vegetables are tender and stew is bubbling.

3. Stir in pasta. Cover and cook for 15 to 20 minutes or until heated through. Serve sprinkled with cheese.

> Pesto is a dark green, fragrant spread that originated in Italy. In Italian, *pesto* means "pounded," and the spread got its name because the herb and garlic were originally pounded together (likely using a pestle, a tool whose name comes from the same root).

Pork Paprikash

**Makes 4 to
6 servings**

*While old-school Hungarian
cooks would use lard
instead of oil, and probably
double the amount of sour
cream, this lighter version
of traditional paprikash
is equally delicious. My
taste testers gave this
recipe a Triple-A rating,
and recommended serving
it over hot, buttered egg
noodles.*

Tip

Broth (or stock) is one of
the most indispensable
pantry staples. Commercial
broth cubes and powders
are loaded with salt and
just don't deliver the flavor
of homemade stock or
prepared broth. I like to
keep 32-oz (1 L) Tetra Paks
on hand, especially the
sodium-reduced variety.

- **4- to 5-quart slow cooker**

2 lbs	boneless pork shoulder blade (butt), trimmed and cut into 1-inch (2.5 cm) cubes	1 kg
2 tbsp	sweet paprika	30 mL
1/2 tsp	dried marjoram	2 mL
1	onion, chopped	1
1	can (19 oz/540 mL) tomatoes, drained	1
1/2 cup	chicken broth	125 mL
1	green bell pepper, coarsely chopped (optional)	1
8 oz	egg noodles	250 g
1 tbsp	butter, cut into pieces	15 mL
	Chopped fresh parsley	
1/2 cup	sour cream	2 mL
	Salt and freshly ground black pepper	

1. In slow cooker stoneware, toss together pork, paprika and marjoram. Stir in onion, tomatoes and broth.

2. Cover and cook on Low for 7 to 8 hours or on High for 3 1/2 to 4 hours, until pork is tender.

3. Stir in green pepper (if using). Cover and cook on High for 15 to 20 minutes or until pepper is bright green and tender-crisp.

4. Meanwhile, in a pot of boiling salted water, cook noodles according to package directions. Drain and toss with butter and parsley.

5. Stir sour cream into paprikash. Season to taste with salt and pepper. Divide noodles among individual serving bowls and ladle paprikash over top. Garnish with additional parsley.

Although paprika is made from ground chiles and looks pretty, it doesn't taste like much. But when it's heated, this spice comes to life, exuding a sweet flavor with rich, earthy undertones and varying heat levels. Try to purchase Hungarian or Spanish paprika (found in colorful tins) rather than the generic paprika found in the spice aisle of the supermarket.

Cinderella Stew

*I came across a recipe
with this name and
couldn't resist it, since
Cinderella is my daughter
Darcy's all-time favorite
princess movie! In fact,
we nicknamed her "Darc-
arella" when she was little,
because it was the only
movie she would watch.
If you have time, you can
carve out a pumpkin and
fill it with this stew for a
unique presentation. All the
princes and princesses in
your family will love it!*

Tips

To avoid tears when
chopping onions, put the
onions in the freezer for a
few minutes first.

You can make your own
pumpkin pie spice using
1 tbsp (15 mL) ground
cinnamon and ¼ tsp (1 mL)
each ground ginger, nutmeg
and cloves.

- **Minimum 4-quart slow cooker**

2	large sweet onions, chopped	2
2	cloves garlic, minced	2
¼ cup	all-purpose flour	60 mL
1 tsp	salt	5 mL
¼ tsp	freshly ground black pepper	1 mL
3 lbs	boneless pork shoulder blade (butt), trimmed and cut into 1-inch (2.5 cm) cubes	1.5 kg
2 tbsp	vegetable oil (approx.)	30 mL
1 tbsp	butter	15 mL
1	can (19 oz/540 mL) tomatoes, with juice	1
1	sweet potato, chopped	1
1	Granny Smith or other tart apple, chopped	1
3 tbsp	dried currants	45 mL
½ tsp	pumpkin pie spice	2 mL
¼ tsp	ground cumin	1 mL
1	bay leaf	1

Topping

1½ cups	plain yogurt	375 mL
½ cup	chopped green onions	125 mL

1. Layer onions and garlic in slow cooker stoneware.

2. In a heavy plastic bag, combine flour, salt and pepper. In batches, add pork to bag and toss to coat with flour mixture. Discard excess flour mixture.

3. In a large nonstick skillet, heat half the oil and the butter over medium-high heat. Cook pork in batches, adding oil as needed, for about 4 minutes or until browned all over. Using a slotted spoon, transfer to stoneware.

4. Stir in tomatoes with juice, sweet potato, apple, currants, pumpkin pie spice, cumin and bay leaf.

5. Cover and cook on Low for 8 to 10 hours or on High for 4 to 5 hours, until pork is tender. Discard bay leaf.

6. In a bowl, combine yogurt and green onions. Ladle stew into individual serving bowls and top each with a dollop of yogurt mixture.

Cooking times can vary a great deal between slow cooker manufacturers. Always let your food cook for the minimum amount of time before testing for doneness.

Make Ahead

This dish can be assembled up to 12 hours in advance, as long as the pork is left out. Complete step 1, skip over steps 2 and 3, then complete step 4. Cover and refrigerate overnight. The next day, dredge and brown the pork as directed in steps 2 and 3. Place stoneware in slow cooker, add pork and proceed with step 4.

There are several varieties of sweet onions, including Vidalia, Walla Walla, Maui and Sweetie Sweet. Although all onions have natural sugars, sweet onions have a lower sulfur content and higher water content, which emphasizes their sweetness and makes them less pungent.

Indonesian Pork Satay Stew

Makes 4 to 6 servings

Satay is an Indonesian specialty of spicy marinated meat that is skewered, then broiled or grilled. Here I've taken all the great flavors of a pork satay and created a lively stew.

Tips

Grating gingerroot is easiest if you keep a nub of it in the freezer. (Ginger tends to get moldy and soft too quickly when it's stored in the refrigerator.) Use a Microplane-style grater for best results. Microplanes have tiny razor-like edges that make quick and easy tasks of both grating and cleaning. You will find Microplanes in good kitchenware and department stores.

To store gingerroot, peel it and place it in a jar with a tight-fitting lid. Add enough sherry to cover. The sherry will saturate and preserve the ginger. Refrigerate for up to 1 month. Use the infused wine to flavor other chicken dishes, or check out the recipe for Mary's Australian Ginger Beer (page 33).

- **4- to 6-quart slow cooker**

2 tbsp	all-purpose flour	30 mL
½ tsp	salt	2 mL
½ tsp	freshly ground black pepper	2 mL
2 lbs	boneless pork shoulder blade (butt), cut into 1-inch (2.5 cm) cubes	1 kg
2 tbsp	vegetable oil (approx.)	30 mL
2	red or green bell peppers, cut into 1-inch (2.5 cm) pieces	2
1	large red onion, cut into wedges	1
1 cup	thick and chunky salsa (mild or hot)	250 mL
½ cup	creamy peanut butter	125 mL
1 tbsp	soy sauce	15 mL
1 tbsp	freshly squeezed lime juice	15 mL
1½ tsp	grated gingerroot	7 mL
½ tsp	ground turmeric	2 mL
½ tsp	ground coriander	2 mL
½ cup	light (5%) cream or evaporated milk	125 mL
1 tbsp	cornstarch	15 mL
3 cups	hot cooked white or brown rice	750 mL
⅓ cup	chopped dry-roasted peanuts	75 mL
2	green onions, sliced	2

1. In a heavy plastic bag, combine flour, salt and pepper. In batches, add pork to bag and toss to coat with flour mixture. Discard excess flour mixture.

2. In a large nonstick skillet, heat half the oil over medium-high heat. Cook pork in batches, adding more oil as needed, for about 4 minutes or until browned all over. Using a slotted spoon, transfer to slow cooker stoneware.

3. Stir in bell peppers, red onion, salsa, peanut butter, soy sauce, lime juice, ginger, turmeric and coriander.

4. Cover and cook on Low for 8 to 10 hours or on High for 4 to 6 hours, until pork is tender.

5. In a jar with a tight-fitting lid, combine cream and cornstarch; shake until blended. Stir into stew. Cover and cook on High for 10 to 15 minutes or until sauce has thickened.

6. Divide rice among bowls and ladle stew over top. Garnish with peanuts and green onions.

Make Ahead

Combine the ingredients in step 3 in the stone cooker stoneware. Cover and refrigerate overnight. The next day, dredge and brown the pork as directed in steps 1 and 2. Place stoneware in slow cooker, add pork and proceed with step 4.

Chili Verde

Makes 4 servings

This warm, hearty stew is based on an authentic Mexican recipe in which chunks of pork are slow-cooked in a green chili sauce made with tomatillos, garlic and jalapeños. It is wonderful on its own, served over rice with some tortilla chips for scooping up extra sauce, or as a filling for a burrito or taco, with toppings such as shredded lettuce and avocado.

Tips

You can use cubed trimmed boneless pork shoulder blade (butt) instead of the tenderloin, but increase the cooking time to 8 to 10 hours on Low or 4 to 5 hours on High.

Browning the pork before it is placed in the slow cooker gives the dish an extra-rich flavor and eliminates some of the fat. If you are pressed for time, however, you can place the pork directly into the slow cooker stoneware without browning it first.

- **Minimum 4-quart slow cooker**

1 tbsp	vegetable oil	15 mL
1	pork tenderloin (about 12 oz/375 g), trimmed and cut into 1-inch (2.5 cm) cubes	1
1	large onion, thinly sliced	1
6	cloves garlic, sliced	6
1	can (14 oz/400 mL) tomatillos, drained, rinsed and coarsely chopped (or 1 lb/500 g fresh tomatillos, husked, rinsed and coarsely chopped)	1
1	can (4½ oz/127 mL) diced mild green chiles	1
2 cups	cooked or canned great Northern or white kidney beans (see page 120), drained and rinsed	500 mL
1½ cups	chicken broth	375 mL
1 tsp	ground cumin	5 mL
	Salt and freshly ground black pepper	
½ cup	lightly packed fresh cilantro, chopped	125 mL
1	jalapeño pepper, sliced (optional)	1

1. In a large nonstick skillet, heat oil over medium-high heat. Cook pork for about 4 minutes or until browned all over. Using a slotted spoon, transfer to slow cooker stoneware. Stir in onion, garlic, tomatillos, green chiles, beans, broth and cumin.

2. Cover and cook on Low for 5 to 7 hours or on High for 2½ to 3 hours, until pork is tender.

3. Season to taste with salt and pepper. Stir in cilantro. Cover and cook on Low for 10 minutes. Serve garnished with jalapeño (if using).

The tomatillo, a staple in Mexican cooking, is a relative of the tomato. It is about the size of a table tennis ball and has a light brown, papery husk around the outside. Although tomatillos are available year-round, they aren't always available fresh. But you can substitute canned tomatillos in any recipe that calls for fresh.

Sausage, Spinach and White Bean Stew

Makes 4 servings

This wonderful stew is a variation on a classic Italian bean soup. My family loved the flavor, and the spinach gives the stew an authentic rustic quality. Don't forget to add the croutons at the end, for some added crunch.

Tips

You can use chopped Swiss chard, escarole or arugula in place of the spinach.

Use a hearty bread, such as ciabatta, to make the bread cubes.

- **Minimum 4-quart slow cooker**

Stew

1 tbsp	olive oil	15 mL
1	onion, chopped	1
1 lb	hot Italian sausage, bulk or casings removed	500 g
2	cloves garlic, minced	2
4 cups	cooked or canned white kidney beans (see page 120), drained and rinsed	1 L
1 cup	chicken broth	250 mL
2 cups	packed baby spinach leaves	500 mL
1½ tsp	red wine vinegar (approx.)	7 mL
	Salt	
¼ cup	freshly grated Parmesan cheese	60 mL

Rustic Croutons

2 tbsp	olive oil	30 mL
2 cups	lightly packed bread cubes	500 mL
	Salt	

1. **Stew:** In a heavy skillet, heat oil over medium heat. Sauté onion for 5 to 6 minutes or until tender and translucent. Add sausage, increase heat to medium-high and cook, stirring and breaking up sausage with a spoon, for 8 to 10 minutes or until lightly browned and no longer pink inside. Using a slotted spoon, transfer to slow cooker stoneware. Stir in garlic, beans and broth.

2. Cover and cook on Low for 6 to 7 hours or on High for 3 to 4 hours, until stew is bubbling.

3. Stir in spinach and vinegar. Cover and cook on High for 8 to 10 minutes or just until spinach is wilted. Season to taste with salt.

4. **Croutons:** Meanwhile, in a nonstick skillet, heat oil over medium-high heat. Add bread cubes, stirring to coat and seasoning to taste with salt. Cook, stirring, for 2 to 4 minutes or until crisp and browned all over.

5. Ladle stew into bowls, sprinkle with Parmesan and garnish with croutons.

Provençal Lamb Stew

Makes 4 servings

This stew is full of flavors from the south of France, and is one of those dishes that tastes even better the day after it is made. Serve it over a heaping mound of garlic mashed potatoes, with a simple steamed green vegetable, such as fresh green beans.

Tips

If you are not a lamb fan, you can substitute cubes of lean pork shoulder blade (butt) or stewing beef.

The best cuts for lamb stew come from the shoulder or shank. Avoid using lamb loin — it can be very expensive and will overcook quickly.

Make Ahead

In slow cooker stoneware, combine onions, garlic, carrot, celery, wine, tomatoes, beans, broth, rosemary and bay leaf. Cover and refrigerate overnight. The next day, dredge and brown the lamb as directed in steps 1 and 2. Place stoneware in slow cooker, add lamb and proceed with step 4.

- **Minimum 4-quart slow cooker**

2 tbsp	all-purpose flour	30 mL
1/2 tsp	salt	2 mL
1/4 tsp	freshly ground black pepper	1 mL
1 1/2 lbs	boneless lamb shoulder, trimmed and cut into 1-inch (2.5 cm) cubes	750 g
2 tbsp	olive oil (approx.)	30 mL
2	onions, chopped	2
2	cloves garlic, minced	2
1	carrot, chopped	1
1	stalk celery, chopped	1
1/2 cup	dry white wine	125 mL
1	can (19 oz/540 mL) tomatoes, drained and chopped	1
2 cups	cooked or canned white kidney beans (see page 120), drained and rinsed	500 mL
1/2 cup	chicken broth	125 mL
1 tbsp	chopped fresh rosemary	15 mL
1	bay leaf	1
	Chopped fresh parsley	

1. In a heavy plastic bag, combine flour, salt and pepper. In batches, add lamb to bag and toss to coat with flour mixture. Discard excess flour mixture.

2. In a large nonstick skillet, heat half the oil over medium-high heat. Cook lamb in batches, adding more oil as needed, for 5 minutes or until browned all over. Using a slotted spoon, transfer to slow cooker stoneware. Sprinkle with onions, garlic, carrot and celery.

3. Add wine to the skillet and bring to a boil, scraping up any brown bits from pan. Pour over lamb mixture. Stir in tomatoes, beans, broth, rosemary and bay leaf.

4. Cover and cook on Low for 8 to 10 hours or on High for 4 to 5 hours, until lamb and vegetables are tender and stew is bubbling. Discard bay leaf. Season to taste with salt and pepper. Serve garnished with parsley.

Chilis and Beans

Basic Beans

The slow cooker is very useful for cooking dried beans, peas and lentils, which can be tiresome to prepare using other methods. This is great news for anyone who wants to avoid the salt and preservatives added to precooked canned beans — and you'll save money if you buy dried beans in bulk.

Many of the legume recipes in this book call for cooked beans by volume, so that you can use your own cooked beans instead of relying on canned beans — but whether to use cooked or canned is entirely up to you. (Some recipes call for dried beans; in those recipes, the beans are cooked right in the method, and canned beans cannot be substituted.) It is important to remember that dried beans will more than double in size after cooking. One pound (500 g), or about 2 cups (500 mL), of dried beans yields 4 to 5 cups (1 to 1.25 L) of cooked beans.

Transforming dried legumes into tender, edible beans, peas and lentils requires a three-step process: sorting, soaking and cooking. The cooking time depends on the type of slow cooker used, the variety, age and quality of the bean, your altitude and whether you use hard or soft water for cooking. The best way to test for doneness is to taste them. Cooked beans are free of any raw, starchy taste, and are tender.

Step 1: Sorting

To prepare dried beans for cooking, start by sorting and discarding any damaged, broken or cracked beans and foreign material. Then place in a colander and give them a thorough rinse under cold water.

Step 2: Soaking

Soaking the beans is an important step in the preparation process, helping to replace the water that was removed in the drying process, shortening the cooking time and improving the flavor, texture, appearance and digestibility of the beans. Most dried beans (the exception is lentils) must be soaked for several hours before they are cooked. The most time-efficient strategy is to soak your beans overnight, then start the cooking process in the morning. Never let beans sit in water for more than 18 hours.

I have provided instructions for both a long soak (the best option for making beans more digestible) and a quick soak (which may be more convenient if you're short on time). Once the soak is finished, drain the beans, discarding the soaking liquid, and rinse well.

1. *Long Soak:* Place the beans in your slow cooker or a large bowl and add 10 cups (2.5 L) boiling water. Cover and let soak for 12 hours or overnight. Drain and rinse thoroughly under cold running water. The beans are now ready to cook.

2. *Quick Soak:* Place the beans in a large saucepan or stockpot (be sure pot is large enough to allow beans to expand to two and a half times the size). Add 10 cups (2.5 L) water and bring to a boil over high heat. Reduce heat and simmer for 3 minutes. Remove from heat, cover and let soak for 1 hour. Drain and rinse thoroughly under cold running water. The beans are now ready to cook.

Step 3: Cooking

Place drained presoaked beans in the slow cooker stoneware. Add enough fresh cold water to completely cover beans with three times their volume of water. For additional flavor, you can add seasonings, such as a bay leaf, garlic or a bouquet garni (made from your favorite herbs tied together in a cheesecloth bag), to the cooking liquid. Beans must be completely cooked before they are combined with salt, sugar or acidic foods such as molasses or tomatoes (all of which prevent beans from softening).

Cover and cook on Low for 4 to 6 hours. Don't worry if the beans have not absorbed all of the water. They should be tender, but not mushy. Drain and rinse thoroughly under cold running water. The beans are now fully cooked and ready for use in your favorite recipe.

Storing Cooked Beans

Once beans are completely cool, divide them into 1- or 2-cup (250 or 500 mL) portions and pack into storage containers or freezer bags and label the portion size. This makes it convenient for recipe preparation, since this is the amount usually called for in recipes. The beans will store nicely in the refrigerator for up to 1 week or in the freezer for up to 1 month, so while you're going to the trouble of preparing cooked beans, you might as well make enough for several meals. Thaw beans first before adding to any recipe. This is to ensure the cooking process is not slowed down.

Canned Beans

Canned beans are a quick and easy substitute for cooked dried beans. Although can sizes vary, the difference won't affect the results of most cooked recipes. A standard 19-oz (540 mL) can of beans yields about 2 cups (500 mL) drained and rinsed beans. If you have smaller or larger cans, you can use the volume called for or just add the amount from your can (unless otherwise specified in the recipe). Drain canned beans in a colander and rinse thoroughly under cold running water before adding them to your recipe.

Holy Mole Chili

**Makes 4 to
6 servings**

*With its notes of cumin,
cinnamon and chocolate
playing off the gentle
spices, this meatless
chili combines the best
of a mole sauce and a
Cincinnati-style chili. Its rich
body makes it a seriously
satisfying dinner any night
of the week.*

Tip
If you can't find mole paste,
substitute 1 tbsp (15 mL)
unsweetened cocoa powder
and ½ tsp (2 mL) ground
cinnamon.

- **Minimum 4-quart slow cooker**

4	cloves garlic, minced	4
1	large green bell pepper, diced	1
1	onion, finely chopped	1
1	can (19 oz/540 mL) diced tomatoes, with juice	1
1	can (14 oz/398 mL) baked beans in tomato sauce	1
2 cups	cooked or canned romano or pinto beans (see page 120), drained and rinsed	500 mL
2 cups	cooked or canned black beans (see page 120), drained and rinsed	500 mL
1 tbsp	chili powder	15 mL
2 tsp	ground cumin	10 mL
2 tsp	ground coriander	10 mL
¼ cup	mole paste (see tip, at left)	60 mL
½ cup	vegetable or chicken broth	125 mL
	Crushed tortilla chips, chopped fresh cilantro, shredded Cheddar cheese (optional)	

1. In slow cooker stoneware, combine garlic, green pepper, onion, tomatoes with juice, beans in tomato sauce, romano beans, black beans, chili powder, cumin and coriander.

2. In a bowl, combine mole paste and broth. Using a fork, gently stir together into a thin sauce. Stir into bean mixture.

3. Cover and cook on Low for 5 to 6 hours or on High for 2½ to 3 hours, until vegetables are tender and chili is bubbling. Serve topped with tortilla chips, cilantro and cheese (if using).

Make Ahead

This dish can be assembled up to 12 hours in advance. Prepare through step 2, cover and refrigerate overnight. The next day, place stoneware in slow cooker and proceed with step 3.

Mole paste is a rich, dark, reddish brown sauce used in many Mexican poultry dishes. It is a smooth cooked blend of onions, garlic, several varieties of chiles, ground seeds (such as pumpkin or sesame) and a small amount of Mexican chocolate, which adds richness without being overly sweet. You can find mole paste in the Mexican foods section of the supermarket or in specialty stores.

White Bean and Toasted Cumin Chili with Lime Cream

Makes 4 to 6 servings

Toasting the cumin seeds intensifies their flavor, giving this chili a rich, nutty taste.

Tips

To toast cumin seeds, place in a dry nonstick skillet over low heat. Cook, stirring often, for about 8 minutes or until fragrant. Remove from heat and let cool.

Once opened, transfer canned chipotle peppers and their sauce to a glass jar with a tight-fitting lid and store in the refrigerator for up to 10 days. For longer storage, transfer the peppers and sauce to a freezer bag and gently press out the air, then seal the bag. Manipulate the bag to separate the peppers, so it will be easy to break off a frozen section of pepper and sauce without thawing the whole package.

- **Minimum 4-quart slow cooker**

3	cloves garlic, minced	3
1	onion, finely chopped	1
1	canned chipotle pepper in adobo sauce, chopped	1
1	can (28 oz/796 mL) tomatoes, with juice, chopped	1
1	bottle (12 oz/341 mL) dark beer	1
4 cups	cooked or canned white kidney beans (see page 120), drained and rinsed	1 L
1½ cups	diced winter squash	375 mL
1 tbsp	cumin seeds, toasted (see tip, at left)	15 mL
1 tsp	granulated sugar	5 mL
½ cup	sour cream	125 mL
2 tbsp	freshly squeezed lime juice	30 mL
1 tbsp	snipped fresh chives	15 mL

1. In slow cooker stoneware, combine garlic, onion, chipotle, tomatoes with juice, beer, beans, squash, cumin seeds and sugar.

2. Cover and cook on Low for 8 to 10 hours or on High for 4 to 5 hours, until bubbling.

3. In a small bowl, combine sour cream, lime juice and chives. Spoon chili into bowls and top with sour cream mixture.

Make Ahead

This dish can be assembled up to 12 hours in advance. Prepare through step 1, cover and refrigerate overnight. The next day, place stoneware in slow cooker and proceed with step 2.

Greek Chicken Chili

Makes 6 to 8 servings

Greek chili? My assistant, Leslie, came up with this recipe to please her teenage daughter, who only eats poultry. It's certainly not something you would be served in Greece, but this chili uses some of the flavors and seasonings found in Greek dishes.

Tip

For this recipe, I used the bottled sun-dried tomatoes packed in olive oil, but you can also use the packaged dried ones found in the produce section of the supermarket. To rehydrate the packaged tomatoes, simply cover them with boiling water and let soak for 30 minutes or until soft and pliable.

- 4- to 6-quart slow cooker

2 tsp	olive oil	10 mL
8	boneless skinless chicken thighs (about 1½ lbs/750 g), cut into 1-inch (2.5 cm) pieces	8
3	cloves garlic, minced	3
1	zucchini, diced	1
1	red bell pepper, diced	1
1 cup	chopped red onion	250 mL
2 tbsp	chili powder	30 mL
1 tbsp	packed brown sugar	15 mL
1 tsp	freshly ground black pepper	5 mL
1 tsp	ground cumin	5 mL
1 tsp	dried oregano	5 mL
1	can (19 oz/540 mL) diced tomatoes, with juice	1
2 cups	cooked or canned chickpeas (see page 120), drained and rinsed	500 mL
1½ cups	tomato pasta sauce	375 mL
¼ cup	diced drained oil-packed sun-dried tomatoes (see tip, at left)	60 mL
2 tbsp	chopped fresh cilantro	30 mL
⅓ cup	crumbed feta cheese	75 mL

1. In a large nonstick skillet, heat oil over medium-high heat. Add chicken and cook for 3 to 5 minutes or until browned all over. Using a slotted spoon, transfer to slow cooker stoneware.

2. Stir in garlic, zucchini, red pepper, onion, chili powder, brown sugar, pepper, cumin, oregano, tomatoes with juice, chickpeas, pasta sauce and sun-dried tomatoes.

3. Cover and cook on Low for 5 to 7 hours or on High for 2½ to 3½ hours, until juices run clear when chicken is pierced. Stir in cilantro. Serve sprinkled with cheese.

Make Ahead

The ingredients in step 2 can be assembled in the stoneware up to 12 hours in advance. Cover and refrigerate overnight. The next day, brown the chicken as directed in step 1. Place stoneware in slow cooker, stir in chicken and proceed with step 3.

Red and White Chili

Makes 6 servings

*This robust chili is a
satisfying change from the
traditional, heavier beef
chilis. Leftovers can be
served in a warmed pita
the next day, or reheated
as a nacho dip.*

Tips

Mild green chiles are found
in the Mexican foods section
of the supermarket. They are
sold whole or chopped.

Whole turkey thighs are a
perfect addition to this chili.
There is a lot of meat on
thighs, so 2 are plenty. If you
have difficulty finding turkey
thighs, you can substitute
approximately 4 turkey
drumsticks or 9 bone-in
chicken thighs.

- **4- to 6-quart slow cooker**

2	cloves garlic, finely chopped	2
1	onion, chopped	1
2	cans (each 4$\frac{1}{2}$ oz/127 mL) chopped mild green chiles	2
3$\frac{1}{2}$ cups	chicken broth	875 mL
2 cups	cooked or canned white kidney beans (see page 120), drained and rinsed	500 mL
2 cups	cooked or canned red kidney beans (see page 120), drained and rinsed	500 mL
2 tsp	ground cumin	10 mL
$\frac{1}{8}$ tsp	cayenne pepper	0.5 mL
2 lbs	turkey thighs (about 2), skin removed	1 kg
1 cup	frozen corn kernels, thawed	250 mL
2 tbsp	all-purpose flour	30 mL
1	lime, cut into wedges (optional)	1

1. In slow cooker stoneware, combine garlic, onion, chiles, broth, white beans, red beans, cumin and cayenne. Place turkey thighs on top.

2. Cover and cook on Low for 8 to 10 hours or on High for 4 to 5 hours, until bubbling.

3. Transfer turkey to a cutting board. Remove meat from bones and cut into bite-size pieces. (Discard bones.) Return turkey to slow cooker, along with corn; stir to combine.

4. In a small bowl, combine flour and $\frac{1}{4}$ cup (60 mL) water. Stir into turkey mixture. Cover and cook on High for 20 to 30 minutes or until heated through and slightly thickened. If desired, serve garnished with lime wedges to squeeze over chili.

Make Ahead

This dish can be partially assembled up to 12 hours in advance. Prepare through step 1, without adding the turkey thighs. Cover and refrigerate vegetable mixture overnight. The next day, place stoneware in slow cooker, add turkey thighs and proceed with step 2.

Canadian Maple Turkey Chili

Makes 6 to 8 servings

Hats off! It's time to make a pot of this chili and sing Canada's national anthem! This chili is slightly sweet, but has lots of meat. It's sure to become a family favorite.

Tips

While ground turkey is a wonderful substitute for other ground meats in various popular dishes, it has a much milder flavor than beef or pork. Don't be afraid to increase the seasoning, adding at least twice what you would when using other ground meats.

It's important to fully cook ground meat before adding it to the slow cooker. Cook ground meat until no longer pink inside. Use the back of a wooden spoon to break up the meat as it cooks; otherwise, you will end up with large chunks of meat.

Make Ahead

This dish can be assembled up to 24 hours in advance. Prepare through step 2, keeping turkey mixture and bean mixture separate. Cover each and refrigerate overnight. The next day, combine turkey and bean mixtures in stoneware, place in slow cooker and proceed with step 3.

- Minimum 4-quart slow cooker

1 tsp	vegetable oil	5 mL
6	slices bacon, chopped	6
1	onion, finely chopped	1
1 lb	lean ground turkey (see tips, at left)	500 g
10	mushrooms, sliced	10
2	stalks celery, finely chopped	2
1	large tomato, chopped	1
1/2	green bell pepper, finely chopped	1/2
1/2	red bell pepper, finely chopped	1/2
1	can (10 oz/284 mL) sodium-reduced condensed tomato soup	1
1	can (14 oz/398 mL) baked beans in tomato sauce	1
2 cups	cooked or canned mixed beans (see page 120), drained and rinsed	500 mL
1 cup	chopped carrots	250 mL
2 tbsp	pure maple syrup	30 mL
1 tbsp	chili powder	15 mL
1 tbsp	ground cumin	15 mL
1/2 tsp	salt	2 mL
1/2 tsp	freshly ground black pepper	2 mL
1/8 tsp	cayenne pepper	0.5 mL
1 cup	frozen corn kernels, thawed	250 mL

1. In a large skillet, heat oil over medium-high heat. Add bacon and cook, stirring, for 3 to 5 minutes or until slightly crisp. Drain all but 1 tbsp (15 mL) fat from pan. (Discard drained fat.)

2. Add onion and sauté for 3 to 5 minutes or until tender and translucent. Add turkey and cook, breaking up with the back of a wooden spoon, for 5 to 7 minutes or until no longer pink inside. Transfer to slow cooker stoneware.

3. Stir in mushrooms, celery, tomato, green pepper, red pepper, soup, baked beans in tomato sauce, mixed beans, carrots, maple syrup, chili powder, cumin, salt, pepper and cayenne.

4. Cover and cook on Low for 8 to 10 hours or on High for 4 to 5 hours, until bubbling. Stir in corn and cook for 20 minutes.

East-West Fruit and Nut Chili

Makes 6 to 8 servings

This chili melds curry from the East with chili and chocolate from the West, for an interesting version that is surprisingly good. Make sure you serve it with some crusty rolls or naan bread and, of course, a beer or two for the adults!

Tip

A good chili is dependent on the quality of the chili powder used. Most chili powders are a blend of ground chiles and cumin, oregano, garlic and salt. Don't confuse chili powder with cayenne pepper or hot pepper flakes, which are much hotter.

- **Minimum 4-quart slow cooker**

1¹⁄₂ lbs	lean ground beef	750 g
3	cloves garlic, minced	3
2	large onions, finely chopped	2
3 tbsp	chili powder	45 mL
2 tbsp	unsweetened cocoa powder	30 mL
1 tbsp	curry powder	15 mL
1	red bell pepper, chopped	1
1	tart apple, such as Granny Smith, chopped	1
2	cans (each 4¹⁄₂ oz/127 mL) diced mild green chiles, drained	2
1	can (28 oz/796 mL) diced tomatoes, with juice	1
1	can (14 oz/398 mL) tomato sauce	1
2 cups	cooked or canned red kidney beans (see page 120), drained and rinsed	500 mL
1 cup	chicken broth	250 mL
1 tsp	ground cinnamon	5 mL
²⁄₃ cup	toasted slivered almonds	150 mL
²⁄₃ cup	raisins	150 mL
	Plain yogurt (optional)	

1. In a large nonstick skillet, cook beef, garlic and onions over medium-high heat, breaking up beef with the back of a spoon, until vegetables are tender and beef is no longer pink. Add chili powder, cocoa powder and curry powder and cook for 1 minute. Using a slotted spoon, transfer beef mixture to slow cooker stoneware, draining off any excess fat and liquid.

2. Stir in red pepper, apple, chiles, tomatoes with juice, tomato sauce, beans, broth and cinnamon.

3. Cover and cook on Low for 8 to 10 hours or on High for 4 to 5 hours, until bubbling.

4. Just before serving, stir in almonds and raisins. Ladle into bowls and top each with a dollop of yogurt (if using).

Make Ahead

This chili can be assembled up to 12 hours in advance. Prepare through step 2, keeping beef mixture and bean mixture separate. Cover each and refrigerate overnight. The next day, combine beef and bean mixtures in slow cooker stoneware, place in slow cooker and proceed with step 3.

Touchdown Beer Chili and Nachos

Makes 6 to 8 servings

Watching football makes people hungry. All the rooting and cheering really stirs up an appetite. Game day is a good time to take advantage of the ease a slow cooker delivers. This simple, hearty chili with nacho chips will keep everyone satisfied, charged up and focused on the game.

Tip

It is always best to brown ground meat thoroughly before adding it to the slow cooker. This ensures that the meat reaches the recommended cooked temperature of 160°F (71°C), or 165°F (74°C) for ground poultry. If you have a good nonstick skillet, you will not need to add cooking oil unless you are browning ground turkey or chicken, which is generally very lean.

- **Minimum 4-quart slow cooker**
- *Preheat oven to 350°F (180°C)*
- *Rimmed baking sheet*

1½ lbs	lean ground beef	750 g
4	cloves garlic, finely chopped	4
1	large sweet onion, finely chopped	1
1	can (19 oz/540 mL) diced tomatoes, with juice	1
1	can (4½ oz/127 mL) diced mild green chiles	1
1	bottle (12 oz/341 mL) dark beer	1
2 cups	cooked or canned red kidney beans (see page 120), drained and rinsed	500 mL
1 cup	frozen corn kernels, thawed	250 mL
3 tbsp	chili powder	45 mL
2 tbsp	liquid honey	30 mL
1 tbsp	hot pepper sauce	15 mL
1 tsp	curry powder	5 mL
1	bag (8 oz/225 g) multigrain or blue corn tortilla chips	1
2 cups	shredded Cheddar cheese or Monterey Jack cheese	500 mL
1	can (8 oz/220 mL) sliced jalapeño peppers, drained	1
	Sour cream (optional)	

1. In a large nonstick skillet, cook beef, garlic and onion over medium-high heat, breaking up beef with the back of a wooden spoon, until vegetables are tender and beef is no longer pink. Using a slotted spoon, transfer beef to slow cooker stoneware, draining excess fat and liquid from the pan.

2. Stir in tomatoes with juice, chiles, beer, beans, corn, chili powder, honey, hot pepper sauce and curry powder.

3. Cover and cook on Low for 6 to 8 hours or on High for 3 to 4 hours, until bubbling.

In a pinch, it's not difficult to make your own tortilla chips. Using a pizza cutter, cut 10-inch (25 cm) flour tortillas into 6 or 8 pieces each, depending on the size of chips you want. Lightly brush both sides of each piece with vegetable oil and season lightly with salt and freshly ground black pepper. Bake in a preheated 450°F (230°C) oven, turning once, for 10 to 12 minutes or until golden brown.

4. Meanwhile, spread tortilla chips over baking sheet. Top with cheese and jalapeños. Bake in preheated oven for 10 to 15 minutes or until Cheddar has melted but is not browned. Transfer to a serving bowl.

5. Ladle chili into bowls and top each with a dollop of sour cream (if using). Serve tortilla chips alongside.

Make Ahead

This chili can be assembled up to 12 hours in advance. Prepare through step 2, keeping beef mixture and bean mixture separate. Cover each and refrigerate overnight. The next day, combine beef and bean mixtures in slow cooker stoneware, place in slow cooker and proceed with step 3.

White Bean Salad with Sun-Dried Tomatoes

Makes 4 to 6 servings

This bean salad can be eaten as a side dish with grilled chicken or pork. It is also a light, tasty salad on its own.

Tips

To zest a lemon, use the fine side of a box cheese grater, making sure not to grate the white pith underneath. Or use a zester to remove the zest, then finely chop it. Zesters are inexpensive and widely available at specialty kitchenware shops.

To extract the most juice from a lemon, let it warm to room temperature, then roll it on the counter, pressing down with the palm of your hand, before squeezing it. Or microwave a whole lemon on High for 30 seconds, then roll it. The juice can be frozen in ice cube trays, then the frozen cubes stored in sealable plastic bags for later use. Lemon zest can also be wrapped and frozen for later use.

- **4- to 5-quart slow cooker**

1 lb	dried great Northern beans or white kidney beans (about 2 cups/500 mL), sorted, rinsed and soaked (see page 120)	500 g
3	cloves garlic, finely chopped	3
1½ tsp	dried basil	7 mL
¼ tsp	freshly ground black pepper	1 mL
¾ cup	finely chopped drained oil-packed sun-dried tomatoes	175 mL
2 tbsp	oil from sun-dried tomatoes	30 mL
	Grated zest and freshly squeezed juice of 2 lemons	
3	green onions, finely chopped	3
2	stalks celery, finely chopped	2
1½ cups	sliced black olives	375 mL
¼ cup	chopped fresh flat-leaf (Italian) parsley	60 mL
½ cup	crumbled feta cheese	125 mL
	Salt	

1. In a large saucepan, combine beans and enough water to cover beans by three times their volume. Bring mixture to a boil; reduce heat and simmer for 3 minutes. Remove from heat, cover and stand for 1 hour. Drain and rinse beans.

2. In slow cooker stoneware, combine soaked beans, garlic, basil, pepper and 6 cups (1.5 L) water.

3. Cover and cook on Low for 4 to 6 hours or until beans are tender.

4. Drain beans and transfer to a bowl. Stir in sun-dried tomatoes, oil, lemon zest and lemon juice. Add green onions, celery, olives, parsley and cheese to beans; toss to combine. Season to taste with salt and pepper. Serve warm or at room temperature.

Make Ahead

The salad can be prepared through step 3, covered and refrigerated for up to 1 day. To serve, let beans warm to room temperature and proceed with step 4.

Italian Baked Beans

Makes 6 servings

These beans bear no resemblance to their traditional cousins from Boston. This dish is packed with the robust flavors of good spaghetti. All you need is a crusty loaf of bread and a salad of lettuce, tomatoes and cucumbers to make this a hearty meal for a cold winter night.

Tips

To make fresh bread crumbs, lightly pulse a few slices of bread in your food processor until processed to a light, fluffy crumb mixture.

Tomato paste is now available in tubes in many supermarkets and delis. It keeps for months in the refrigerator.

- **4- to 6-quart slow cooker**

2	carrots, coarsely chopped	2
2	stalks celery, coarsely chopped	2
2	cloves garlic, minced	2
1	onion, finely chopped	1
1	green bell pepper, finely chopped	1
1	can (28 oz/796 mL) diced tomatoes with Italian seasonings, with juice	1
2 cups	cooked or canned white kidney beans (see page 120), drained and rinsed	500 mL
2 cups	cooked or canned chickpeas (see page 120), drained and rinsed	500 mL
2 cups	cubed mozzarella cheese	500 mL
2 tbsp	tomato paste	30 mL
2 tsp	dried Italian seasoning	10 mL
Pinch	hot pepper flakes	Pinch
Pinch	granulated sugar	Pinch
1 cup	fresh bread crumbs (see tip, at left)	250 mL
2 tbsp	freshly grated Parmesan cheese	30 mL
2 tbsp	finely chopped fresh flat-leaf (Italian) parsley	30 mL
2 tbsp	butter, melted	30 mL

1. In slow cooker stoneware, combine carrots, celery, garlic, onion, green pepper, tomatoes, kidney beans, chickpeas, mozzarella, tomato paste, Italian seasoning, hot pepper flakes and sugar.

2. Cover and cook on Low for 7 to 9 hours or on High for 3 to 4 hours, until bubbling and vegetables are tender.

3. In a bowl, combine bread crumbs, Parmesan and parsley. Stir in butter. Sprinkle evenly over beans and cook for 1 hour.

Maple Mochaccino Beans

Makes 4 to 6 servings

This may look like an odd combination of ingredients, but trust me, it is fantastic! The recipe was passed along to me by a good friend, who takes these beans to family parties all the time and earns rave reviews. The ground coffee gives the beans a dark, rich brown color, and the maple syrup lends a touch of sweetness.

Tip

By baked beans in tomato sauce, I mean the canned "pork and beans" style. They are available with additional flavorings, such as maple syrup or chipotle seasonings. Be adventurous and give these a try.

- 4- to 6-quart slow cooker

6	slices bacon, chopped	6
1	large red onion, very thinly sliced	1
3	cans (each 14 oz/398 mL) baked beans in tomato sauce	2
2 tbsp	finely ground coffee or espresso	60 mL
1 tsp	dry mustard	5 mL
½ cup	pure maple syrup	125 mL

1. In a large nonstick skillet, cook bacon over medium-high heat, stirring, for 4 to 5 minutes or until lightly browned but not crisp. Using a slotted spoon, transfer to a plate lined with paper towels, leaving drippings in pan.

2. Return pan to medium-high heat. Sauté onion for 4 to 6 minutes or until tender and translucent. Remove from heat.

3. Sprinkle half the bacon over bottom of slow cooker stoneware. Cover with half the onions, then with 1 can of beans. Repeat layers. Sprinkle ground coffee evenly over top.

4. In a bowl, combine mustard and maple syrup; pour over bean mixture.

5. Cover and cook on Low for 7 to 9 hours or on High for 3 to 4 hours, until bubbling and sauce has thickened.

Make Ahead

This dish can be assembled up to 12 hours in advance. Prepare through step 3, cover and refrigerate overnight. The next day, place stoneware in slow cooker and proceed with step 4.

Hot Curried Beans

Makes 6 servings

This bean dish — perfect as a side dish or on its own for a potluck — is a real hit with my vegetarian daughter, Darcy, who loves the combination of beans, crunchy apples and sweet raisins. She is not a cilantro fan, but my husband and I enjoy a sprinkling of cilantro on top. The chutney lends some sweetness, with a little heat, while the nuts add a nice crunch.

Tip

To toast almonds, spread nuts in a single layer in a shallow baking pan or rimmed baking sheet. Bake in a 350°F (180°C) oven, stirring or shaking once or twice, for 5 to 10 minutes or until golden brown and fragrant.

- **4- to 6-quart slow cooker**

1 lb	dried red kidney beans (about 2 cups/500 mL), sorted, rinsed and soaked (see page 120)	500 g
1	onion, sliced	1
8 oz	button mushrooms, sliced	250 g
1/2 cup	golden raisins	125 mL
1 tbsp	curry powder	15 mL
1/2 tsp	freshly ground black pepper	2 mL
1 1/2 cups	vegetable or chicken broth	375 mL
1	large red or green apple, chopped	1
	Hot cooked couscous	
	Mango chutney	
	Chopped toasted almonds (see tip, at left)	

1. In slow cooker stoneware, combine soaked beans, onion, mushrooms, raisins, curry powder, pepper, broth and 3/4 cup (175 mL) water.

2. Cover and cook on Low for 4 to 6 hours or until beans are tender. Stir in apples and cook for 15 minutes.

3. Spoon beans over couscous, top each serving with a dollop of chutney and sprinkle with almonds.

Christmas Cake Beans and Couscous

Makes 6 servings

Don't worry: there aren't actually any bits of Christmas cake in this recipe. But the golden raisins and dried fruit, which add sweetness to this delicious combination of beans and couscous, remind me of the flavors of my favorite holiday treat. Loaded with fiber and protein, this dish is wonderful with a salad at the end of a long day at any time of year.

Tip

Dried candied fruit are the type used to make old-fashioned Christmas fruit cake. Do not use larger dried fruit, such as apricots, apples and prunes.

- **4- to 6-quart slow cooker**

2 cups	cooked or canned pinto beans (see page 120), drained and rinsed	500 mL
2 cups	frozen shelled edamame, thawed	500 mL
1 cup	golden raisins	250 mL
1 cup	chopped candied fruit	250 mL
2 tsp	grated gingerroot	10 mL
1/2 tsp	salt	2 mL
1/4 tsp	hot pepper flakes	1 mL
1 cup	vegetable broth	250 mL
1 3/4 cups	unsweetened orange or pineapple juice	425 mL
1/2 cup	couscous	125 mL
1 tbsp	olive oil	15 mL
1/2 cup	sliced toasted almonds (see tip, page 133)	125 mL
	Sliced green onion	

1. In slow cooker stoneware, combine beans, edamame, raisins, dried fruit, ginger, salt, hot pepper flakes, broth and orange juice.

2. Cover and cook on Low for 6 to 7 hours or on High for 3 to 3 1/2 hours, until bubbling.

3. Turn off heat and stir in couscous and oil. Cover and let stand for 5 to 10 minutes or until couscous is tender. Fluff mixture with a fork. Serve garnished with almonds and green onion.

Edamame are sweet, green soybeans commonly used in Japanese cooking. They are rich in proteins and vitamins A, B and C, making them a nutrition powerhouse. In the supermarket, they are generally found frozen in the health food section or with the frozen vegetables.

Carolyn's Boozy Baked Beans

Makes 8 to 10 servings

This recipe was passed along to me by my friend Carolyn Culp. She is always the hit of the family reunion when she turns up with this. You can omit the rum, if you want, but it really adds spirit to this dish.

Tip

If using fresh pineapple, substitute 1½ cups (375 mL) fresh pineapple chunks and ½ cup (125 mL) unsweetened apple juice for the pineapple juice.

- **4- to 5-quart slow cooker**

1 lb	dried white pea beans (about 2 cups/500 mL), rinsed and sorted	500 g
1	can (14 oz/398 mL) pineapple chunks, with juice	1
4 oz	salt pork	125 g
½ cup	amber or dark rum	125 mL
¼ cup	light (fancy) molasses	60 mL
¼ cup	packed dark brown sugar	60 mL
2 tsp	dry mustard	10 mL
1 tsp	salt	5 mL

1. In a large saucepan, combine beans and 10 cups (2.5 L) water; bring to a boil over high heat. Reduce heat and simmer for 3 minutes. Remove from heat, cover and let soak for 1 hour. Drain and rinse, reserving 1 cup (250 mL) of the soaking liquid.

2. In slow cooker stoneware, combine reserved soaking liquid, pineapple with juice, salt pork, rum, molasses, brown sugar and mustard. Stir in beans.

3. Cover and cook on Low for 8 hours or until bubbling. Season with salt.

> White pea beans, also known as navy beans or *alubias chicas*, are the type of cooked bean you will find in canned baked beans in tomato sauce (aka pork and beans). The term "navy bean" was adopted during the Second World War, when pork and beans was regularly fed to the troops.

Chipotle Baked Beans and Kielbasa

Makes 4 to 6 servings

My neighbor taste-tested this recipe. I passed him the slow cooker, and he ate the entire pot by himself. You control the flavor and spice in these simple baked beans by choosing your favorite bottled barbecue sauce. Canned beans make this dish a breeze to prepare. For an extra kick, toss some sliced jalapeño peppers or hot pepper flakes into the sauce while it's cooking.

Tip

Chipotle chile powder can be found in the spice aisle of the supermarket. Use it to add smoky flavor and a little heat. If you have difficulty finding it, use 2 tsp (10 mL) regular chili powder and 1 tsp (5 mL) chipotle hot pepper sauce.

Variation

For a vegetarian version, simply omit the turkey kielbasa.

* **4- to 6-quart slow cooker**

1	large onion, finely chopped	1
2 cups	cooked or canned great Northern, pinto or white pea beans (see page 120), drained and rinsed	500 mL
2 cups	cooked or canned black beans (see page 120), drained and rinsed	500 mL
1 1/4 cups	tangy barbecue sauce	300 mL
1/4 cup	packed brown sugar or pure maple syrup	60 mL
1 tbsp	dry mustard	15 mL
1 tbsp	Worcestershire sauce	15 mL
2 tsp	chipotle chile powder (see tip, at left) or chili powder	10 mL
1 lb	fully cooked turkey kielbasa sausage (one large piece)	500 g

1. In slow cooker stoneware, combine onion, great Northern beans, black beans, barbecue sauce, brown sugar, mustard, Worcestershire sauce and chipotle powder. Place sausage on top.

2. Cover and cook on Low for 5 to 6 hours or on High for 2 1/2 to 3 hours, until bubbling.

3. Transfer sausage to a cutting board and slice diagonally. Serve with beans.

Make Ahead

This dish can be assembled up to 12 hours in advance. Prepare through step 1, cover and refrigerate overnight. The next day, place stoneware in slow cooker and proceed with step 2.

Vegetarian Mains

Eggplant Parmesan

Makes 6 to 8 servings

This version of the classic Italian recipe is made with breaded and roasted eggplant slices. It takes a little preparation, but it's worth every bit of effort. The trick is to drain the eggplant of excess moisture before cooking. You'll want to use an oval slow cooker, to make sure all the slices fit.

Tips

Eggplants are very perishable and become bitter with age. They should be stored in a cool, dry place and used within a day or two. If you plan to cook eggplant the same day you buy it, store it at room temperature. If you store it in the refrigerator, place it in a sealed plastic bag.

Salting improves the taste of eggplant by drawing out bitter juices. It also collapses the air pockets in the flesh, making the eggplant less likely to soak up excess fat when cooking.

- **Minimum 5-quart oval slow cooker**
- *Baking sheet, lined with parchment paper*

2	large firm eggplants	2
	Coarse salt	
3	egg whites	3
1¼ cups	fine dry bread crumbs	300 mL
1 cup	freshly grated Parmesan cheese, divided	250 mL
1	jar (28 oz/796 mL) tomato pasta sauce	1
1 lb	fresh bocconcini, sliced into ¼-inch (0.5 cm) rounds	500 g
¼ cup	packed fresh basil leaves, slivered	60 mL

1. Using a sharp knife, remove the stem end and bottom from each eggplant. Slice eggplant crosswise into ½-inch (1 cm) rounds. Arrange a single layer in a large colander set in the sink and sprinkle with salt. Continue layering and salting until all of the eggplant is in the colander. Place a couple of plates on the eggplant to weight it down and let drain for 30 to 60 minutes or until moisture is released. Pat drained slices dry with paper towels.

2. Preheat oven to 350°F (180°C). In a shallow dish, whisk together egg whites and 3 tbsp (45 mL) water until frothy. In another shallow dish, combine bread crumbs and ¼ cup (60 mL) of the Parmesan. Dip eggplant slices in egg mixture, then in bread crumb mixture, coating evenly. Arrange in a single layer on prepared baking sheet. Bake for 30 minutes, turning halfway through, until crisp and golden.

3. Spread half the pasta sauce over bottom of slow cooker stoneware. Arrange one-third of the eggplant slices, overlapping slightly, on sauce. Top with half the bocconcini and sprinkle with one-third of the remaining Parmesan and half the basil. Repeat the layers twice, using half of the remaining pasta sauce, eggplant slices, bocconcini and basil each time.

Bocconcini is also known as fresh baby mozzarella. It is quite different from the drier, slightly aged brick kind we use on pizza. It comes packed in water and tastes much like milk, only with a little tang. It should never be rubbery or stringy.

4. Cover and cook on Low for 4 to 5 hours or until bubbling and browned around the edges. Turn off heat and let cool for 10 minutes before serving.

Make Ahead

This dish can be assembled up to 24 hours in advance. Prepare through step 3, cover and refrigerate overnight. The next day, place stoneware in slow cooker and proceed with step 4.

An eggplant is actually a giant berry and comes from the same family as tomatoes and potatoes. There are many varieties, but the globe eggplant is the most common. It has dark purple skin and a creamy white, spongy center. It tends to be larger than other varieties, so you can get good-size slices for a dish like this.

Garlicky Mushroom Ragoût with Polenta

Makes 4 to 6 servings

Portobello mushrooms give this versatile dish a rich, robust flavor and an almost meaty texture. It's a popular main course even among diehard meat eaters.

Tips

Store mushrooms in a paper bag, with the top loosely folded over once or twice, or place them in a glass container and cover it with a tea towel or moist paper towel. Be sure to allow air circulation. Store in the refrigerator (but not in the crisper) and use within a few days — or a week, if they are packaged and unopened.

To prepare mushrooms, first trim off the bottoms of the stems, then wipe off the mushrooms. Don't rinse or soak the mushrooms, or they'll absorb water and turn mushy when you cook them.

- 4- to 5-quart slow cooker
- *Baking sheet, lined with parchment paper*

2 tbsp	olive oil	30 mL
1	onion, finely chopped	1
2	cloves garlic, finely chopped	2
1 lb	white or cremini mushrooms, sliced	500 g
8 oz	portobello mushroom caps, thinly sliced	250 g
1/2 tsp	dried rosemary or tarragon	2 mL
Pinch	hot pepper flakes	Pinch
1/2 cup	vegetable broth	125 mL
1 tbsp	balsamic vinegar	15 mL
	Salt and freshly ground black pepper	
1/4 cup	chopped fresh parsley	60 mL
	Crumbled goat cheese	

Grilled Polenta

1	tube (1 lb/500 g) plain prepared polenta	1
	Olive oil	
	Salt and freshly ground black pepper	

1. In a nonstick skillet, heat oil over medium-high heat. Sauté onion for 3 to 4 minutes or until tender and translucent. Add garlic and sauté for 1 minute. Transfer to slow cooker stoneware.

2. Stir in white mushrooms, portobello mushrooms, rosemary, hot pepper flakes and broth.

3. Cover and cook on Low for 6 to 8 hours or on High for 3 to 4 hours, until mushrooms are tender. Stir in balsamic vinegar. Season to taste with salt and black pepper.

4. *Polenta:* Meanwhile, preheat broiler. Using a sharp knife, cut polenta into 1/2-inch (1 cm) slices. Place on prepared baking sheet and brush tops with oil. Broil 6 to 8 inches (15 to 20 cm) from heat, without turning, for 10 to 15 minutes or until golden and just starting to brown. Season to taste with salt and pepper. Arrange on a serving plate.

Variation

The mushroom mixture could also be served over hot cooked rice or pasta or in individual baked puff pastry shells.

5. Ladle mushroom mixture over polenta and garnish with parsley and goat cheese.

Make Ahead

This dish can be assembled up to 24 hours in advance. Prepare through step 2, cover and refrigerate overnight. The next day, place stoneware in slow cooker and proceed with step 3.

Polenta is the name given to both the popular Italian dish of cornmeal mush and the cornmeal used to make the dish.

Chunky Vegetable Paella

Makes 6 servings

This vegetable-rich recipe calls for saffron, an exotic herb that is worth the extra pennies. By adding beans to this rice dish, you get the nutritional benefit of a complete protein and a delicious, well-balanced meal. If you have meat lovers in your house, serve this as a side dish with grilled chicken or fish.

Tips

I really like the canned tomatoes labeled "fire-roasted," which have been roasted slowly over an open fire for a great, smoky Southwestern flavor. If you can't find them, use canned diced tomatoes with chili seasonings added. If you have difficulty finding either of those, a can of plain diced tomatoes is just fine, too.

Cajun seasoning is mixture of dried herbs and seasonings available in the packaged-spice section of the supermarket. But it's easy to make your own: In a small bowl, combine 1 tbsp (15 mL) each paprika and dried parsley, 1½ tsp (7 mL) each garlic powder and dried thyme, ¼ tsp (1 mL) salt and ⅛ tsp (0.5 mL) cayenne pepper.

- Minimum 4-quart slow cooker

½ tsp	saffron threads	2 mL
2 tbsp	hot water	30 mL
2 tsp	olive oil	10 mL
2	cloves garlic, minced	2
1	onion, finely chopped	1
4	stalks celery, thickly sliced	4
1	large red bell pepper, cut into ¾-inch (2 cm) pieces	1
1	large zucchini, quartered lengthwise and cut into ¾-inch (2 cm) pieces	1
1	can (19 oz/540 mL) fire-roasted tomatoes (see tip, at left), drained	1
2 cups	cooked or canned white kidney beans (see page 120), drained and rinsed	500 mL
1 cup	long-grain brown parboiled (converted) rice	250 mL
1 tsp	dried oregano	5 mL
1 tsp	Cajun seasoning (see tip, at left)	5 mL
½ tsp	salt	2 mL
2 cups	vegetable broth	500 mL
½ cup	frozen peas, thawed	125 mL

1. In a small bowl, combine saffron and hot water. Let steep for 10 to 15 minutes.

2. In a large nonstick skillet, heat oil over medium-high heat. Sauté garlic and onion and for about 5 minutes or until tender and translucent. Transfer to slow cooker stoneware.

3. Stir in saffron with steeping water, celery, red pepper, zucchini, tomatoes, beans, rice, oregano, Cajun seasoning, salt and broth.

4. Cover and cook on Low for 6 to 8 hours or on High for 3 to 4 hours, until liquid is absorbed and rice is fluffy.

5. Stir in peas. Cover and cook on High for 10 to 15 minutes or until heated through.

Very Veggie Vindaloo

Makes 6 to 8 servings

Vindaloo is a common dish in southern India, and it usually features meat. A vegetarian vindaloo has sweet summer vegetables cooked in a rich, tart sauce. You can substitute various in-season vegetables, as long as the substitutes are sweet and firm, not sour and leafy. Serve vindaloo with plain rice and raita (see tip, below).

Tips

Look for precut vegetables, such as carrots and squash, in the produce section of the supermarket. They make the preparation of this recipe go very quickly.

Raita is an Indian yogurt condiment seasoned with cilantro, cumin, mint and chile peppers. Like its Greek cousin, tzatziki, raita has a soothing effect on the palate, so it often accompanies spicy dishes.

- Minimum 4-quart slow cooker

3	cloves garlic, minced	3
1	eggplant, peeled and cut into $\frac{1}{2}$-inch (1 cm) cubes	1
1	large tomato, coarsely chopped	1
2 cups	cooked or canned chickpeas (see page 120), drained and rinsed	500 mL
2 cups	coarsely chopped zucchini (about 2)	500 mL
1 cup	coarsely chopped carrots	250 mL
1 cup	diced butternut squash	250 mL
1 cup	chopped onion	250 mL
1	can (5$\frac{1}{2}$ oz/156 mL) tomato paste	1
1 tsp	dried basil	5 mL
$\frac{1}{2}$ tsp	ground cinnamon	2 mL
$\frac{1}{2}$ tsp	salt	2 mL
$\frac{1}{4}$ tsp	paprika	1 mL
$\frac{1}{4}$ tsp	ground ginger	1 mL
1$\frac{1}{2}$ cups	vegetable broth	375 mL
2 tbsp	liquid honey	30 mL
1 tsp	olive oil	5 mL
	Salt and freshly ground black pepper	
	Plain yogurt	

1. In slow cooker stoneware, combine garlic, eggplant, tomato, chickpeas, zucchini, carrots, squash and onion.

2. In a large glass measuring cup, whisk together tomato paste, basil, cinnamon, salt, paprika, ginger, broth, honey and oil. Pour evenly over vegetable mixture and stir gently to coat vegetables.

3. Cover and cook on Low for 7 to 8 hours or on High for 4 hours, until bubbling and vegetables are tender. Season to taste with salt and pepper.

4. Spoon into individual serving bowls and top each with a dollop of yogurt.

Make Ahead

This dish can be assembled up to 24 hours in advance. Prepare through step 2, cover and refrigerate overnight. The next day, place stoneware in slow cooker and proceed with step 3.

Candlestick's Creamy Vegetarian Burritos

Makes 8 servings

My husband is a huge sports fan. Anytime we visit a city that boasts an NFL team or a Major League Baseball park, we must take in a game. I had a delicious vegetarian burrito at Candlestick Park in San Francisco, and the 49ers won that day, too! The creaminess comes from the delicious guacamole served on this all-star wrap.

Tip

To help avoid drips, roll foil or parchment paper around the burritos, folding the bottom edge up and leaving them open at the top.

- **4- to 6-quart slow cooker**

1	can (19 oz/540 mL) fire-roasted or chili-style diced tomatoes (see tip, page 142), drained	1
2 cups	cooked or canned black beans (see page 120), drained and rinsed	500 mL
1 cup	long-grain parboiled (converted) white rice	250 mL
1/2 cup	frozen corn kernels, thawed	125 mL
1	package (1 oz/35 g) taco seasoning mix	1
2 cups	vegetable broth	500 mL
8	10-inch (25 cm) whole wheat flour tortillas, warmed (see tip, page 149)	8
1 cup	guacamole (see recipe, below)	250 mL
1 cup	shredded Monterey Jack cheese (optional)	250 mL

1. In slow cooker stoneware, combine tomatoes, beans, rice, corn, taco seasoning and broth.

2. Cover and cook on Low for 6 to 8 hours or on High for 3 to 4 hours, until flavors are blended, rice is tender and liquid is absorbed.

3. Lay tortillas flat on a work surface. Evenly divide guacamole, cheese (if using) and rice mixture on each tortilla. Fold right side of tortilla over filling. Fold bottom of tortilla up, then fold left side over and continue rolling until the filling is enclosed.

Makes 1/2 cup (125 mL)

It's almost impossible to eat Mexican-inspired food without a little guacamole. This recipe is easy to put together. You can easily double the recipe and serve it alongside some crispy tortilla chips.

Guacamole

1	large avocado, peeled and pitted	1
2	cloves garlic, finely minced	2
1	serrano pepper, seeded and chopped	1
1/4 cup	finely chopped red onion	60 mL
2 tbsp	chopped fresh cilantro	30 mL
2 tsp	freshly squeezed lime juice	10 mL
1/4 tsp	salt	1 mL

1. In a bowl, mash avocado with a fork. Add garlic, serrano pepper, red onion, cilantro, lime juice and salt; mash together until blended.

Turkish Lentils and Couscous Salad

Makes 6 to 8 servings

Making the lentils for this salad in the slow cooker is a great way to keep your kitchen cool in the summer. Serve this alongside grilled lamb kebabs on a bed of rice.

Tip

To grease stoneware, use a nonstick vegetable spray or use the cake pan grease available in specialty cake decorating shops or bulk food stores.

- **4- to 6-quart slow cooker, stoneware greased**

1½ cups	dried brown lentils, sorted and rinsed	375 mL
2½ cups	vegetable broth	625 mL
¼ cup	white wine vinegar, divided	60 mL
	Salt and freshly ground black pepper	
1 cup	couscous	250 mL
¼ cup	olive oil, divided	60 mL
2	large cloves garlic, minced	2
2 cups	trimmed and chopped arugula leaves	250 mL
2 cups	cherry tomatoes, halved	500 mL
1 cup	crumbled feta cheese	250 mL
½ cup	finely chopped fresh mint leaves	125 mL

1. In prepared slow cooker stoneware, combine lentils and broth. Cover and cook on Low for 4 to 5 hours or on High for 3½ to 4 hours, until lentils are tender.

2. Drain any excess liquid and transfer hot lentils to a bowl. Stir in 2 tbsp (30 mL) of the vinegar. Season to taste with salt and pepper. Let cool completely, stirring occasionally.

3. Meanwhile, in a saucepan, bring 1¼ cups (300 mL) water to a boil. Add couscous and ½ tsp (2 mL) salt. Remove from heat, cover and let stand for 5 minutes. Fluff with a fork and transfer to a large bowl. Stir in 1 tbsp (15 mL) of the oil. Let cool completely, stirring occasionally.

4. In a small bowl, whisk together garlic, the remaining vinegar and the remaining oil. Season to taste with salt and pepper. Stir into couscous, along with lentils.

5. Just before serving, toss in arugula, tomatoes, feta and mint. Season to taste with salt and pepper.

Make Ahead

This dish can be partially prepared 24 hours in advance. Prepare through step 2, cover and refrigerate lentils overnight. The next day, proceed with step 3.

Black Bean Tostadas with Corn Relish

Makes 4 to 8 servings

This entrée shows off a rainbow of vegetables. The black beans and cheese ensure that meat won't be missed.

Tips

To get the most juice from a lime, let it warm to room temperature, then roll it on the counter, pressing down with the palm of your hand, before squeezing it. Or microwave a whole lime on High for 30 seconds, then roll, cut and squeeze it. Juice can be frozen in ice cube trays, then kept in the freezer in sealable plastic bags for later use. Zest can also be wrapped and frozen for later use.

Jalapeño peppers contain volatile oils that can burn your skin and eyes if they come into direct contact. It is best to wear plastic or rubber gloves when chopping jalapeños, and take care not to touch your face or eyes while you work. If your bare hands do touch the peppers, wash your hands and nails well with hot, soapy water.

- **4- to 6-quart slow cooker**

Corn Relish

2	green onions, thinly sliced	2
1 cup	frozen corn kernels, thawed	250 mL
1 tbsp	olive oil	15 mL
	Freshly squeezed juice of 2 limes	
	Salt and freshly ground black pepper	

Black Bean Tostadas

1½ cups	dried black beans, sorted and rinsed	375 mL
4	cloves garlic, minced	4
3	jalapeño peppers, seeded and finely chopped, divided	3
1	large onion, chopped	1
2	bay leaves	2
2 tsp	ground cumin	10 mL
2 tsp	lime zest	10 mL
¼ tsp	freshly ground black pepper	1 mL
1½ cups	chicken broth	375 mL
½ tsp	salt	2 mL
2 cups	grape tomatoes, halved	500 mL
8	10-inch (25 cm) flour tortillas	8
2 tbsp	olive oil	30 mL
1 cup	shredded Monterey Jack cheese	250 mL
1	avocado, peeled, pitted and chopped	1
	Sour cream (optional)	

1. *Relish:* In a bowl, combine green onions, corn, oil and lime juice. Season to taste with salt and pepper. Cover and refrigerate until ready to use.

2. *Tostadas:* In a large saucepan, combine beans and 4 cups (1 L) water; bring to a boil over medium-high heat. Reduce heat and simmer for 3 minutes. Remove from heat and let soak for 1 hour. Drain and rinse.

3. In slow cooker stoneware, combine beans, garlic, two-thirds of the jalapeños, onion, bay leaves, cumin, lime zest, pepper and broth.

4. Cover and cook on Low for 4 to 6 hours or on High for 2 to 3 hours, until beans are tender. Discard bay leaves. Drain beans and transfer to a bowl or return to stoneware. Mash slightly, stir in salt and set aside.

5. In a bowl, combine the remaining jalapeños and tomatoes.

6. Preheat oven to 475°F (240°C). Brush both sides of tortillas with oil. Arrange 4 of the tortillas on two baking sheets. Spread half the bean mixture evenly over tortillas. Top with half the tomato mixture and half the cheese. Bake for about 10 minutes, switching and rotating pans halfway through, until golden and crisp. Transfer tostadas to individual serving plates and keep warm. Repeat with the remaining tortillas, bean mixture, tomato mixture and cheese.

7. Top each tortilla with avocado, relish and sour cream (if using).

Avocados should be purchased a few days before they are needed, and ripened at home. To speed up ripening, wrap them in newspaper or a paper bag. They are at their peak when they yield to gentle pressure, but be sure not to bruise them by squeezing too hard. Since avocado flesh darkens when exposed to air, peel and mash the avocado just before use. To help keep the color bright, stir in a few drops of freshly squeezed lime juice, then cover the avocado with plastic wrap until use.

Susan's Mediterranean Barley Salad

Makes 6 servings as an entrée or 10 as a side salad

A friend of mine gave me this salad from her great recipe collection, and I've adapted it to the slow cooker. This chilled whole-grain salad is wonderful with grilled chicken, but it's also flavorful enough to enjoy on its own for lunch. My daughter likes to take it in her lunch bag to school, and I pack her some crackers and hummus to eat alongside.

Tips

For this recipe, I used the bottled sun-dried tomatoes packed in olive oil, but you can also use the packaged dried ones found in the produce section of the supermarket. To rehydrate the packaged tomatoes, simply cover them with boiling water and let soak for 30 minutes or until soft and pliable.

For added protein, add 2 cups (500 mL) cooked or canned chickpeas, white kidney beans or navy beans (see page 120), drained and rinsed, with the vegetables.

- **4- to 6-quart slow cooker**

1 cup	pot barley	250 mL
2 cups	vegetable broth	500 mL
3	green onions, chopped	3
½	red bell pepper, finely chopped	½
½	yellow bell pepper, finely chopped	½
½ cup	drained oil-packed sun-dried tomatoes (see tip, at left), finely chopped	125 mL
1 tsp	dried oregano	5 mL
½ cup	finely chopped fresh parsley	125 mL
½ cup	crumbled feta cheese	125 mL
¼ cup	pine nuts, toasted	60 mL
¼ cup	olive oil	60 mL
¼ cup	balsamic vinegar	60 mL
	Salt and freshly ground black pepper	

1. In slow cooker stoneware, combine barley and broth. Cover and cook on Low for 6 to 8 hours or on High for 3 to 4 hours, until barley is tender. Fluff with a fork and let cool slightly.

2. Stir in green onions, red pepper, yellow pepper, sun-dried tomatoes, oregano, parsley, feta and pine nuts.

3. In a jar with a tight-fitting lid, combine oil and vinegar; cover and shake well. Pour over salad and toss to coat. Season to taste with salt and pepper. Serve warm, cover and refrigerate until chilled, about 2 hours, or store in an airtight container in the refrigerator for up to 5 days.

> Barley, an important cereal grain, has had the inedible hulls removed. Pot barley is husked and coarsely ground. It is polished like pearl barley, but to a lesser extent, so the kernels are less refined and retain more of the bran layer than the pearl variety. Since pot barley kernels are not as small those of pearl barley, they take a little longer to cook. In the grocery store, you'll likely find pot barley near dried peas, lentils and beans.

Springtime Bean and Barley Wraps

Makes 4 to 5 servings

This delicious bean and barley mixture makes a great vegetarian wrap. Top with a little salsa and sour cream. The filling is also tasty spooned into a hollowed-out fresh tomato for a quick, easy salad.

Tip

To warm tortillas, stack them, wrap the stack in foil and heat in a 350°F (180°C) oven for 15 to 20 minutes.

Make Ahead

This dish can be assembled up to 24 hours in advance. Prepare through step 1, cover and refrigerate overnight. The next day, place stoneware in slow cooker and proceed with step 2.

- 3- to 4-quart slow cooker

2	cloves garlic, minced	2
1	red bell pepper, finely chopped	1
2 cups	cooked or canned black beans (see page 120), drained and rinsed	500 mL
½ cup	pot barley	125 mL
½ cup	frozen corn kernels, thawed	125 mL
½ cup	finely chopped carrot	125 mL
1 tsp	dried Italian seasoning	5 mL
½ tsp	salt	2 mL
¼ tsp	freshly ground black pepper	1 mL
1½ cups	vegetable broth	375 mL
1	small zucchini, finely chopped	1
1	green onion, finely chopped	1
1 tbsp	freshly squeezed lemon juice	15 mL
8 to 10	10-inch (25 cm) flour tortillas, warmed (see tip, at left)	8 to 10
½ cup	shredded Cheddar cheese	125 mL
	Salsa (optional)	
	Sour cream (optional)	

1. In slow cooker stoneware, combine garlic, red pepper, beans, barley, corn, carrot, Italian seasoning, salt and pepper. Stir in broth.

2. Cover and cook on Low for 7 to 8 hours or on High for 3½ to 4 hours, until bubbling and barley is tender.

3. Stir in zucchini, green onion and lemon juice. Cover and cook on Low for 20 to 30 minutes or until vegetables are tender and heated through.

4. Lay tortillas flat on a work surface. Spoon bean mixture down the center of each tortilla, dividing evenly. Top with cheese, salsa (if using) and sour cream (if using). Fold right side of tortilla over filling. Fold bottom of tortilla up, then fold left side over and continue rolling until the filling is enclosed.

Pesto Beans and Pasta

Makes 6 servings

You honestly won't miss the meat in this hearty, rich bean-vegetable mixture. I use whole wheat pasta to give it an extra nutritional boost, and the red and green peppers give it a lively appearance.

Tips

A generous amount of salt in the cooking water seasons the pasta internally as it absorbs the water and swells. The claim that salted water cooks food faster (because the salt increases the boiling temperature) is exaggerated: you're not adding enough salt to raise the boiling temperature by more than about 1°F (1°C).

To prevent soft, mushy pasta, do not allow it to be in the water any longer than necessary. Add it only when the water is at a full boil, and keep it at a steady boil while it cooks.

- **4- to 6-quart slow cooker**

4	cloves garlic, minced	4
1	green bell pepper, chopped	1
1	red bell pepper, chopped	1
1	onion, chopped	1
1	can (14 oz/398 mL) Italian-style stewed tomatoes, with juice	1
4 cups	cooked or canned white kidney beans (see page 120), drained and rinsed	1 L
2 tsp	dried Italian seasoning, crushed	10 mL
1/2 tsp	freshly ground black pepper	1 mL
1/2 cup	vegetable broth	125 mL
1/2 cup	dry white wine or vegetable broth	125 mL
1/4 cup	pesto (see recipe, opposite)	60 mL
2 cups	whole wheat penne pasta	500 mL
1/2 cup	finely grated Parmesan or Romano cheese	125 mL
	Chopped fresh basil	

1. In slow cooker stoneware, combine garlic, green pepper, red pepper, onion, tomatoes, beans, Italian seasoning, pepper, broth and wine.

2. Cover and cook on Low for 7 to 9 hours or on High for 3 1/2 to 4 1/2 hours, until bubbling. Stir in pesto.

3. Meanwhile, in a large pot of boiling salted water, cook penne according to package directions. Drain and stir into bean mixture.

4. Ladle into individual serving bowls and sprinkle with Parmesan and basil.

**Makes about
½ cup (125 mL)**

Pesto is readily available in the supermarket, but it is also simple to make your own if you have an abundance of fresh basil in your garden.

Variation
Parsley Pesto: Substitute parsley for the basil and walnuts for the pine nuts.

Homemade Pesto

1	clove garlic, minced	1
⅓ cup	packed fresh basil leaves	75 mL
¼ cup	extra virgin olive oil	60 mL
1 tbsp	toasted pine nuts	15 mL
¼ tsp	salt	1 mL
¼ tsp	freshly ground black pepper	1 mL

1. In a food processor, combine garlic, basil, oil, pine nuts, salt and pepper. Process until smooth. Transfer to an airtight container and store in the refrigerator for up to 2 days.

Pesto originated in northern Italy. It gets its name from the Italian word *pestare*, meaning "to pound," which describes the traditional method of making this garlic-herb mixture: pounding the basil with a mortar and pestle.

Pumpkin and Spinach Lasagna

Makes 6 to 8 servings

This one-dish casserole is to die for. It is perfect to serve at a holiday meal if you have any vegetarians in the group — even the non-vegetarians will love it. The walnuts are optional, but they add a nice change of texture in the dish. Feel free to substitute another nut, such as pecans or hazelnuts.

Tips

To grease stoneware, use a nonstick vegetable spray or use the cake pan grease available in specialty cake decorating shops or bulk food stores.

Make sure you use pure pumpkin purée, not pumpkin pie filling, for this lasagna. Pie filling has been seasoned with spices and sugar. If your can is larger than 14 oz (398 mL), measure out 1½ cups (375 mL) and reserve the remainder for another use.

- Minimum 4-quart slow cooker, stoneware greased

Pumpkin Filling

3 tbsp	butter	45 mL
3	cloves garlic, minced	3
1	onion, finely chopped	1
2 tbsp	finely chopped fresh sage	30 mL
1	can (14 oz/398 mL) pure pumpkin purée (not pie filling)	1
½ cup	chopped walnuts (optional)	125 mL

Cheese Sauce

3 tbsp	butter	45 mL
⅓ cup	all-purpose flour	75 mL
3 cups	milk	750 mL
4 oz	goat cheese or chèvre	125 g
¼ tsp	ground nutmeg	1 mL
1 tsp	salt	5 mL
½ tsp	freshly ground black pepper	2 mL
1	package (12 oz/340 g) fresh whole wheat lasagna sheets (see tip, at right)	1
1	package (10 oz/300 g) frozen chopped spinach, thawed and well drained	1
½ cup	freshly grated Parmesan cheese	125 mL

1. *Filling:* In a large skillet, melt butter over medium heat. Sauté garlic and onion for 5 to 7 minutes or until translucent and golden. Add sage and sauté for about 1 minute or until fragrant. Stir in pumpkin purée and walnuts (if using). Remove from heat and set aside.

2. *Sauce:* In a saucepan, melt butter over medium heat. Cook flour, stirring, for 1 minute. Gradually add milk, whisking continuously until well blended; bring to a boil, whisking. Reduce heat and simmer, stirring, for about 5 minutes or until slightly thickened. Remove from heat and stir in goat cheese, nutmeg, salt and pepper until cheese is melted.

Use the fresh pasta sheets found refrigerated in the supermarket. They do not require any preboiling, making the preparation of this dish a snap. They fit easily into the slow cooker with minimal trimming. If you can't find them, use 9 to 12 "no-boil" or "oven-ready" dry lasagna noodles instead.

3. Spoon $\frac{1}{2}$ cup (125 mL) of the sauce over bottom of prepared slow cooker stoneware. Lay one-third of the lasagna sheets over sauce to cover, cutting to fit into stoneware where necessary. Top with half the filling and half the spinach. Spread with $\frac{1}{2}$ cup (125 mL) of the sauce. Repeat layers once. Top with the remaining lasagna sheets and spread the remaining sauce over top. Sprinkle with Parmesan.

4. Cover and cook on Low for 6 to 8 hours or on High for 3 to 4 hours, until bubbling and noodles are tender. Let stand for 10 minutes before cutting.

Chèvre is a light, often fluffy, mild-flavored cheese. Many people simply call it soft goat cheese. It is usually sold in logs or discs, and is often rolled in or flavored with chopped herbs or cracked peppercorns. Check the best-before date on the wrapping and, once opened, rewrap the cheese and refrigerate for up to 1 week or until the best-before date.

Ricotta-Stuffed Shells Florentine

Makes 4 to 6 servings

These plump shells with their flavorful filling are easy to prepare — the kids can even help with the stuffing. Serve with a tossed green salad and some hot garlic bread on the side.

Tips

If using a smaller (4-quart) slow cooker, pour ¼ cup (60 mL) of the pasta sauce in bottom of stoneware. Arrange a layer of filled shells snugly, open side up, over sauce. Top with ¼ cup (60 mL) sauce. Repeat layers, using the remaining filled shells and remaining sauce. Sprinkle with mozzarella and drizzle with oil. Cook as directed.

You can use fresh spinach in place of the frozen. Choose crisp, bright leaves with a light, fresh aroma. (If it smells like cabbage, it's too old.) Wash well, then remove and discard the stems. Use 2 lbs (1 kg) or 1 package (10 oz/300 g).

- **5- to 6-quart oval slow cooker**

1	package (12 oz/340 g) jumbo pasta shells	1
1	package (10 oz/300 g) frozen chopped spinach, thawed and well drained	1
1	egg, lightly beaten	1
1	tub (1 lb/500 g) ricotta cheese	1
1 cup	crumbled feta cheese	250 mL
½ cup	grated Parmesan cheese	125 mL
1	clove garlic, minced	1
½ tsp	salt	2 mL
⅛ tsp	ground nutmeg	0.5 mL
1	jar (28 oz/796 mL) marinara pasta sauce	1
½ cup	shredded mozzarella cheese	125 mL
1 tsp	olive oil	15 mL

1. In a pot of boiling salted water, cook pasta shells according to package directions until tender but firm (al dente), making sure not to overcook them. Drain, rinse under cold running water and place on a damp tea towel. Set aside.

2. In a large bowl, combine spinach, egg, ricotta, feta, Parmesan, garlic, salt and nutmeg.

3. Pour half the pasta sauce into bottom of slow cooker stoneware. Spoon 1 heaping tbsp (15 mL) of the spinach mixture into each pasta shell. Arrange snugly, open side up, over pasta sauce. Top with the remaining pasta sauce and sprinkle with mozzarella. Drizzle with oil.

4. Cover and cook on Low for 6 to 8 hours or on High for 3 to 4 hours, until mozzarella has melted and sauce is bubbling.

Make Ahead

This dish can be assembled up to 12 hours in advance. Prepare through step 3, cover and refrigerate overnight. The next day, place stoneware in slow cooker and proceed with step 4.

Wheat and Beet Risotto

Makes 6 to 8 servings

Of course, this isn't a true risotto, since it's not made with rice, but the result is much like a risotto. Wheat berries — minimally processed grains of whole wheat with a nutty, chewy texture — are sometimes labeled "hard wheat." They need to cook slowly to tenderize, so cooking them in the slow cooker is a great way to soften them up.

Tip

To speed up the cooking time by a couple of hours, you can soak the wheat berries for 1 hour in water to cover, then drain before cooking. However, in the slow cooker, the berries tenderize nicely without presoaking.

- **4- to 6-quart slow cooker**

1 tbsp	butter	15 mL
1 tsp	olive oil	5 mL
1	onion, finely chopped	1
2	cloves garlic, minced	2
1 tsp	dried oregano	5 mL
3	beets, peeled and diced	3
2 cups	wheat berries (whole wheat kernels)	500 mL
3 cups	vegetable broth	750 mL
½ cup	dry white wine	125 mL
4 oz	goat cheese or chèvre	125 g
1 tbsp	freshly squeezed lemon juice	15 mL
	Chopped fresh oregano (optional)	

1. In a nonstick skillet, heat butter and oil over medium-high heat. Sauté onion for 3 to 4 minutes or until tender and translucent. Add garlic and oregano; sauté for 1 minute. Transfer to slow cooker stoneware. Stir in beets, wheat berries, broth and wine.

2. Cover and cook on Low for 6 to 8 hours or on High for 3 to 4 hours, until wheat berries are tender and most of the liquid is absorbed.

3. Crumble three-quarters of the goat cheese into stoneware and stir to combine. Cover and cook for about 10 minutes or until cheese is melted. Stir in lemon juice. Ladle onto individual serving plates and garnish with the remaining goat cheese and oregano (if using).

Barbecue Tofu Sandwiches

Makes 4 to 6 servings

A friend of mine said that barbecue sauce is the one thing she misses now that she is a vegetarian, since it's typically eaten with steak or chicken. I decided to try to satisfy her craving by creating a tasty barbecue tofu dish made in the slow cooker. She loved the recipe and has added it to her slow cooker repertoire. Use extra-firm tofu in the slow cooker, so it will retain its texture. You won't believe your taste buds.

Tips

Because tofu has a sponge-like consistency, it absorbs the flavors of any sauce in which it is marinated.

Smoked paprika is made by grinding peppers that have undergone a smoking process. You can find it in various heat levels (from mild to hot). Be careful how much you use, because smoky seasonings can easily overpower the flavor of a dish.

- **4- to 6-quart slow cooker, stoneware greased**

2	packages (each 14 oz/420 g) extra-firm or dry-style tofu	2
2	cloves garlic, minced	2
1/4 cup	firmly packed brown sugar	60 mL
1 tbsp	chili powder	15 mL
1 tsp	paprika or smoked paprika	5 mL
1	can (7 1/2 oz/213 mL) tomato sauce	1
1 cup	ketchup	250 mL
2 tbsp	soy sauce	30 mL
2 tbsp	freshly squeezed lemon juice	30 mL
2 tbsp	Dijon mustard	30 mL
4 to 6	panini rolls or ciabatta buns	4 to 6
	Baby arugula or shredded lettuce	
	Sautéed onion slices	

1. If using extra-firm tofu, slice each block into four 3/4-inch (2 cm) slabs. Line a baking sheet with a triple layer of paper towels. Arrange tofu slabs in a single layer on top. Cover tofu with another triple layer of paper towels, then place another baking sheet on top and weigh it down with unopened canned goods. Let stand for 15 minutes to 1 hour to press out extra liquid. (If using dry-style tofu, no pressing is necessary.)

2. In a large bowl, combine garlic, brown sugar, chili powder, paprika, tomato sauce, ketchup, soy sauce, lemon juice and mustard.

3. Cut tofu into cubes and place in prepared slow cooker stoneware. Pour sauce over tofu and toss gently to coat.

4. Cover and cook on High for 2 to 3 hours or on Low for 4 to 6 hours, until hot and fragrant.

5. Split rolls in half lengthwise. Pile arugula on bottom halves and spoon tofu mixture over arugula. Top with onion slices and cover with top halves. Serve immediately.

There are many types of tofu available, but the type that works best for this recipe is labeled "extra-firm" or "super-firm." Much of the liquid has already been pressed out of it, but you need to press out the rest or your tofu will just melt into the sauce. I prefer to use "dry-style tofu," which doesn't require the pressing step; look for it in Asian supermarkets.

Seafood

Asian Steamed Sea Bass with Ginger

Makes 4 servings

This simple fish dish pairs succulent steamed cod with ginger-soy flavors. Serve it with a helping of steamed brown rice for a complete, protein-packed meal.

Tips

Julienned vegetables are also known as matchstick vegetables because of the size and shape of the cut pieces. You can purchase a small kitchen tool called a julienne slicer (it looks like a vegetable peeler) to julienne your vegetables for you, but it is just as easy to do it with a sharp knife.

An oval slow cooker is the ideal shape for this dish because the fillets will fit in a single layer.

Before purchasing fish, always learn what you can about sustainability and fishing practices. Ask your fishmonger or check online resources.

- **Minimum 4-quart slow cooker, preferably oval**

1	fennel bulb with fronds	1
2 tbsp	minced gingerroot	30 mL
2 tbsp	rice vinegar	30 mL
2 tbsp	vegetable oil	30 mL
1 tsp	granulated sugar	5 mL
1/4 tsp	hot pepper flakes	1 mL
3	large leeks (white and light green parts only), thinly sliced	3
2	large carrots, julienned (see tip, at left)	2
6	pieces sea bass, halibut or other firm-fleshed fish fillet (each about 6 oz/170 g)	6
	Salt and freshly ground black pepper	

1. Remove and reserve green fronds from fennel bulb and cut bulb and the remaining stalks into 1/2-inch (1 cm) slices. Set aside.

2. In a small bowl, combine ginger, vinegar, oil, sugar and hot pepper flakes. Set aside.

3. Arrange half the fennel slices, half the leeks and half the carrots on bottom of slow cooker stoneware. Place fish fillets on top. Drizzle vinegar mixture over fish. Season to taste with salt and black pepper. Top with the remaining fennel slices, leeks and carrots.

4. Cover and cook on Low for 2 to 3 hours or on High for 1 to 1 1/2 hours, until fish flakes easily when tested with a fork.

5. Spoon fish and vegetables onto a serving plate and garnish with reserved fennel fronds.

Salmon and Potato Strata

Makes 4 to 6 servings

Potato slices replace the usual bread in this homey, economical main dish. Serve with buttered green peas and a little chili sauce on the side.

Tips

If you are a fan of smoked salmon, you can add about 1/4 cup (60 mL) chopped smoked salmon along with the canned salmon. Be careful not to overdo it, though, or the flavor of the smoked salmon will overpower the flavor of the potatoes.

I like to use Yukon Gold or other yellow-flesh potatoes for their buttery flavor and yellow color when cooked. You can use russet potatoes in this dish, but the color won't be as yellow.

- **Minimum 5-quart slow cooker, stoneware greased**

2 tbsp	butter	30 mL
1 cup	thinly sliced leeks (white and light green parts only)	250 mL
2 tbsp	all-purpose flour	30 mL
3 cups	half-and-half (10%) cream or evaporated milk	750 mL
1 cup	shredded Gruyère or Swiss cheese	250 mL
2 tbsp	chopped fresh dill	30 mL
1/2 tsp	salt	2 mL
1/4 tsp	freshly ground black pepper	1 mL
8 cups	thinly sliced peeled yellow-flesh potatoes (8 to 10)	2 L
2	cans (each 7 1/2 oz/213 g) red sockeye salmon, drained and skin removed, broken into pieces	2
1 cup	dry bread crumbs	250 mL
3 tbsp	butter, melted	45 mL

1. In a skillet, melt 2 tbsp (30 mL) butter over medium-high heat. Sauté leeks for about 5 minutes or until softened. Sprinkle flour over leeks and stir to coat. Gradually add cream, whisking constantly, and bring to a boil. Remove from heat and stir in Gruyère, dill, salt and pepper until cheese has melted.

2. Spoon 1 cup (250 mL) of the leek mixture into prepared slow cooker stoneware. Spread one-third of the potatoes over the leeks. Spread salmon over potatoes. Arrange the remaining potatoes on top. Pour the remaining leek mixture over potatoes.

3. In a medium bowl, combine bread crumbs and melted butter. Sprinkle over mixture in stoneware.

4. Cover and cook on Low for 6 to 8 hours or on High for 3 to 4 hours, until strata is heated through and potatoes are tender.

Make Ahead

This dish can be assembled up to 12 hours in advance. Prepare through step 2, cover and refrigerate overnight. The next day, place stoneware in slow cooker and proceed with step 3.

Salmon Cobb Salad with Creamy Buttermilk Dressing

Makes 4 servings as an entrée or 8 as a side salad

This simple recipe takes the traditional Cobb salad to a new level. The salmon is poached in the slow cooker, then tossed with the greens. A creamy buttermilk dressing adds the finishing touch to this salad, which can be served as a meal or on the side.

Tips

An oval slow cooker works best for shallow steam poaching.

The naturally high fat content of salmon makes this fish forgiving if it's slightly overcooked.

If you don't have any buttermilk on hand, here is a quick substitution. Place 1¹/₂ tsp (7 mL) lemon juice or white vinegar in a glass measuring cup. Add enough milk to make ¹/₂ cup (125 mL). Let stand for 5 minutes before using in the recipe.

* **Minimum 4-quart slow cooker, preferably oval**

1	lemon, thinly sliced	1
1	large shallot, minced	1
1	carrot, quartered lengthwise	1
4	sprigs fresh flat-leaf (Italian) parsley	4
1	piece (about 2 lbs/1 kg) skinless center-cut salmon fillet	1
	Salt and freshly ground black pepper	
¹/₂ cup	dry white wine or chicken broth	125 mL

Creamy Buttermilk Dressing

¹/₂ cup	buttermilk	125 mL
¹/₂ cup	regular or light mayonnaise	125 mL
¹/₄ cup	minced shallots (about 2)	60 mL
3 tbsp	chopped fresh dill	45 mL
1 tbsp	freshly squeezed lemon juice	15 mL
¹/₂ tsp	salt	2 mL
Pinch	freshly ground black pepper	Pinch

Salad

10	slices lean bacon (about 8 oz/250 g)	10
1	head Boston or Bibb lettuce, leaves torn into 3-inch (7.5 cm) pieces	1
3	hard-cooked eggs (see box, opposite), quartered lengthwise and halved crosswise	3
1	avocado, peeled and diced	1
	Freshly ground black pepper	

1. Place lemon slices on bottom of slow cooker stoneware and sprinkle with shallot. Arrange carrot and parsley on top. Place salmon on top. Season salmon to taste with salt and pepper.

2. In a small saucepan, combine wine and ¹/₂ cup (125 mL) water; bring to a boil over high heat. Add to stoneware, pouring around salmon (not directly onto fish).

3. Cover and cook on Low for 2 to 3 hours or on High for 1 to 1¹/₂ hours, until fish flakes easily when tested with a fork. Remove stoneware from slow cooker and let fish cool for 20 minutes. Use at room temperature or cover and refrigerate overnight.

Hard-cooked eggs can be kept in the refrigerator for up to a week. They make a delicious snack or quick sandwich, so prepare a few extra.

4. *Dressing:* Meanwhile, in a bowl, whisk together buttermilk, mayonnaise, shallots, dill, lemon juice, salt and pepper. Cover and refrigerate for at least 30 minutes, until chilled, or for up to 1 day.

5. *Salad:* In a large nonstick skillet, in batches as necessary, cook a single layer of bacon over medium heat, turning occasionally, for 8 to 10 minutes or until crisp. Transfer to a plate lined with paper towels and let cool. Crumble into bite-size pieces.

6. Discard vegetables and liquid from salmon. Break salmon into bite-size chunks. Arrange lettuce on a platter. Top with salmon, bacon, eggs and avocado. Drizzle with half the dressing. Season to taste with pepper. Serve the remaining dressing on the side.

Perfect Hard-Cooked Eggs

Place a single layer of eggs in a saucepan. Add enough water to cover eggs by at least 1 inch (2.5 cm). Cover and bring to a boil over high heat (with the lid on or off). Immediately remove saucepan from heat and let stand for 18 to 20 minutes — the eggs will continue to cook in the boiled water. Rinse under cold running water, then immerse in ice water and let cool completely. Crackle each shell by gently tapping on a hard surface, then roll the egg between your palms to loosen the shell, and peel it off.

Tuna and Broccoli Frittata

Makes 4 servings

I was a firm believer that it didn't work very well to cook eggs in the slow cooker — until I decided to experiment a little. Playing with some recipes, I came up with this dish. The key to good results is not to overcook the dish, so the eggs don't become too firm.

Tip

I like to blanch the broccoli before adding it to this dish. Blanching helps to preserve the color and keep the broccoli tender-crisp. To blanch, bring a pot of salted water to a boil. Meanwhile, fill a bowl with ice-cold water. In batches, add broccoli to boiling water and blanch for about 30 seconds or just until color turns bright green. Using a slotted spoon, immediately transfer broccoli to the bowl of cold water to stop the cooking process. Let cool and drain well.

- **4- to 6-quart slow cooker, stoneware greased**

6	eggs	6
1	can (12 oz or 370 mL) evaporated milk	1
$\frac{1}{2}$ tsp	salt	2 mL
$\frac{1}{4}$ tsp	freshly ground black pepper	1 mL
2	cans (each $6\frac{1}{2}$ oz/184 g) tuna, drained (see tip, page 163)	2
2	green onions, chopped	2
2 cups	chopped fresh broccoli, blanched (see tip, at left)	500 mL
$\frac{1}{2}$ cup	shredded Cheddar cheese	125 mL
$\frac{1}{4}$ cup	raw sunflower seeds	60 mL
2 tbsp	chopped fresh flat-leaf (Italian) parsley	30 mL
1 tsp	paprika	5 mL

1. In a bowl, whisk together eggs, evaporated milk, salt and pepper until blended. Pour into prepared slow cooker stoneware. Gently stir in tuna, green onions, broccoli, Cheddar, sunflower seeds and parsley. Sprinkle with paprika.

2. Cover and cook on Low for 3 to 4 hours or until eggs are set and edges are browned. (Do not overcook, or eggs will become too firm.) Let stand for 5 minutes before serving.

Mediterranean Tuna Noodle Casserole

Makes 6 to 8 servings

This version of the popular comfort food is a new take on the traditional tuna casseroles we grew up with. Rotini pasta, chunks of red pepper and artichoke hearts update the cozy dinnertime favorite. It's delicious with a dollop of Carolyn's Fiery Red Pepper Jelly (page 63). All it needs is a simple tossed green salad served alongside.

Tips

For this dish, I like to use tuna that has been packed in olive oil rather than water. Even after it is drained, the tuna will taste moister and richer, thanks to the oil.

When adding cooked pasta to a slow cooker dish, it's important to slightly undercook the pasta in the boiling water, since it will continue to cook in the slow cooker. For firm, tender pasta in the finished dish, boil it for about 2 minutes less than recommended by the package directions.

- **4- to 6-quart slow cooker, stoneware greased**

3 cups	rotini pasta	750 mL
1/4 cup	olive oil	60 mL
2	red bell peppers, thinly sliced lengthwise	2
1	red onion, thinly sliced	1
1/2 tsp	salt	2 mL
1/4 tsp	freshly ground black pepper	1 mL
1/2 cup	all-purpose flour	125 mL
5 cups	whole milk	1.25 L
2	cans (each 6 1/2 oz/184 g) tuna packed in olive oil, drained	2
1	can (14 oz/398 mL) artichoke hearts, drained and thickly sliced	1
1/2 cup	freshly grated Parmesan cheese	125 mL

1. In a large pot of boiling salted water, cook rotini for about 6 minutes, or 2 minutes less than recommended by package directions, until almost tender. Drain and rinse under cold running water. Set aside.

2. In a large, heavy saucepan, heat oil over medium heat. Sauté red peppers and red onion for 3 to 4 minutes or until just tender. Season with salt and pepper. Add flour and cook, stirring, for 1 minute. Gradually add milk and cook, stirring, until smooth. Bring mixture to a simmer, stirring occasionally.

3. Remove from heat and stir in reserved rotini, tuna and artichokes. Transfer to prepared slow cooker stoneware. Sprinkle with Parmesan.

4. Cover and cook on Low for 5 to 6 hours or on High for 2 1/2 hours, until bubbling.

Brazilian Fish Stew

Makes 6 to 8 servings

This contemporary seafood stew blends the savory flavors of coconut milk, cilantro and garlic with the sweetness of yams and bananas. Serve over steamed basmati rice.

Tips

Any firm white fish will work well in this stew.

Thaw frozen scallops in cold water, but keep them in a sealed plastic bag so you don't rinse out their flavorful juices.

To ripen tomatoes, place them in a brown paper bag and store at room temperature. Never store tomatoes in the refrigerator, as it destroys their delicate flavor.

Canned coconut milk is made from grated soaked coconut pulp — it's not the liquid found inside the coconut. It can be found in the Asian food section of the supermarket or in Asian food stores. Be sure you don't buy coconut cream, often used to make tropical drinks such as piña coladas.

- **4- to 6-quart slow cooker**

1 lb	skinless firm white fish fillets, such as haddock or tilapia (see tip, at left), cut into 1½-inch (4 cm) chunks	500 g
1 lb	large sea scallops	500 g
1	lime	1
2 tbsp	olive oil	30 mL
3	cloves garlic, minced	3
1	large onion, finely chopped	1
2	large tomatoes, chopped	2
1	yellow bell pepper, chopped	1
1 tsp	salt	5 mL
½ tsp	freshly ground black pepper	2 mL
½ tsp	hot pepper flakes	2 mL
2	large bananas, diagonally cut into ½-inch (1 cm) slices	2
1	large sweet potato, peeled and cut diagonally into very thin slices	1
1	can (14 oz/398 mL) unsweetened coconut milk	1
	Chopped fresh cilantro or parsley	
¼ cup	toasted shredded coconut	60 mL

1. In a bowl, combine fish and scallops. Grate zest from lime and set aside. Cut lime into 4 wedges and squeeze juice from each over fish mixture. Add wedges to fish mixture and toss gently. Cover with plastic wrap and let marinate in the refrigerator for 30 minutes.

2. Meanwhile, in a large skillet, heat oil over medium-high heat. Sauté garlic and onion for about 3 minutes or until onion is tender and translucent. Add tomatoes, yellow pepper, salt, black pepper and hot pepper flakes; sauté for 3 to 5 minutes or until tomatoes begin to release juice and yellow pepper starts to soften.

3. Transfer vegetable mixture to slow cooker stoneware. Discard lime wedges from fish mixture. Arrange fish mixture on top of vegetable mixture, gently pushing fish and scallops into vegetables. Arrange banana slices on top, overlapping as necessary. Arrange sweet potato slices over bananas, overlapping as necessary. Pour coconut milk evenly over top.

Scallops toughen easily, so always take care not to overcook them. As soon as they lose their translucency and become opaque, they are done.

4. Cover and cook on Low for 4 to $4\frac{1}{2}$ hours or on High for 2 to $2\frac{1}{2}$ hours, until fish flakes easily when tested with a fork, scallops are opaque throughout (see tip, at left) and banana and sweet potato slices are tender.

5. Ladle into individual serving bowls and sprinkle with reserved lime zest, cilantro and coconut.

These days, it's a good idea to choose fish from a list of sustainable choices. These fish are well managed, abundant and caught or farmed in an environmentally sustainable way that does not harm the ocean. If you are unsure which fish fit these criteria, ask your fishmonger or check online resources before purchasing. Good North American resources include www.montereybayaquarium.org (click on Seafood Watch) and www.seachoice.org.

Indian Fish Curry

Makes 6 to 8 servings

This curry has intense color from the turmeric and bold flavors from the medley of added spices, but it is not spicy-hot. Since the fish and seafood take very little time to cook, the sauce is simmered in advance, allowing the flavors to develop before the fish and seafood are added.

Tips

Here's a foolproof way to chop an onion: Peel the onion and halve it from top to base. Place each half cut side down on a cutting board. Slice horizontally across each half. Holding the slices together, slice vertically.

When handling hot peppers, wear rubber gloves and make sure you keep your hands away from your face and eyes. Wash hands and utensils afterwards.

If using frozen seafood and fish fillets for this recipe, thaw them first. You may wish to stir 1 tbsp (15 mL) cornstarch into the coconut milk before adding it. The cornstarch will help thicken the extra liquid from the thawed seafood and fish.

- **4- to 6-quart slow cooker**

1/3 cup	vegetable oil	75 mL
1	onion, chopped	1
2	cloves garlic, minced	2
2	hot green chile peppers, such as Anaheim or jalapeño, seeded and chopped	2
2 tsp	ground cumin	10 mL
1 tsp	ground coriander	5 mL
1 tsp	ground turmeric	5 mL
1 tsp	minced gingerroot	5 mL
2	tomatoes, chopped	2
1 tbsp	granulated sugar	15 mL
1 tsp	salt	5 mL
1 1/2 to 2 lbs	mixed seafood, such as shrimp and scallops, and firm skinless white fish fillets, such as tilapia	750 g to 1 kg
1 cup	unsweetened coconut milk	250 mL
	Chopped fresh cilantro	

1. In a large skillet, heat oil over medium-high heat. Sauté onion for 3 to 5 minutes or until tender and translucent. Stir in garlic, chiles, cumin, coriander, turmeric and ginger; sauté for about 1 minute or until spices are fragrant and evenly coat onion. Add tomatoes, sugar and salt; cook, stirring, for about 5 minutes or until tomatoes begin to release juice.

2. Add 1 cup (250 mL) water to vegetable mixture in skillet and bring to a boil, scraping up any brown bits from pan. Transfer to slow cooker stoneware.

3. Cover and cook on Low for 6 to 8 hours or on High for 3 to 4 hours, until bubbling.

4. Gently stir in seafood, fish and coconut milk until coated with sauce. Cover and cook on High for 25 to 30 minutes or until seafood is opaque throughout, fish flakes easily when tested with a fork and sauce has thickened. (Check sauce halfway through cooking time; if it's thickening too much, stir in water, about 1/4 cup/60 mL at a time, until desired consistency is reached.)

5. Ladle into individual serving bowls and sprinkle with cilantro.

Tip

Cooking times can vary a great deal between slow cooker manufacturers. Always let your food cook for the minimum amount of time before testing for doneness.

Make Ahead

This dish can be assembled up to 12 hours in advance. Prepare through step 2, cover and refrigerate overnight. The next day, place stoneware in slow cooker and proceed with step 3.

Named after the California city, Anaheim chile peppers are among the most commonly used varieties in the United States. They are medium green in color, have a long, slender shape and are only mildly hot.

Seafood Chowder Pot Pie

A pot pie is usually a meal in itself, and this one is no exception. A flaky puff pastry crust tops a rich mixture of vegetables, shrimp and crabmeat. It is full of bubbly warm goodness! Feel free to experiment with other seafood favorites, such as lobster and scallops. This pot pie is great for brunch or dinner, served with a salad of crisp bitter greens tossed in a citrus vinaigrette.

Tip

Puff pastry package sizes vary between brands, ranging from 14 to 18 oz (397 to 511 g). If your package is slightly larger or smaller, half a package will still work just fine for this recipe.

- **5- to 6-quart slow cooker, stoneware greased**
- *Large baking sheet*

2 cups	diced peeled potatoes	500 mL
4	slices bacon, cut in half	4
1	onion, finely chopped	1
1/2 cup	all-purpose flour	125 mL
2	bottles (each 8 oz/236 mL) clam juice	2
1/4 cup	heavy or whipping (35%) cream or evaporated milk	60 mL
1 cup	frozen mixed peas and carrots, thawed	250 mL
1 cup	frozen corn kernels, thawed	250 mL
1 tsp	dried thyme	5 mL
1 cup	cooked shrimp, peeled and deveined	250 mL
1	can (6 oz/170 g) crabmeat, drained and flaked	1
1	sheet frozen puff pastry (half a 14 oz/397 g package), thawed (see tip, at left)	1
1	egg	1

1. In a large pot of boiling salted water, cook potatoes for 5 to 7 minutes or until just tender. Drain and set aside.

2. In a heavy saucepan, cook bacon over medium heat, turning occasionally, for 5 to 7 minutes or until crisp. Using tongs, transfer to a plate lined with paper towels and let cool. Crumble and set aside.

3. Return pan with bacon drippings to medium heat and sauté onion for 3 to 4 minutes or until tender and translucent. Sprinkle with flour and stir to coat. Gradually whisk in clam juice and cream (mixture will be very thick). Stir in potatoes, reserved bacon, peas and carrots, corn and thyme. Transfer to prepared slow cooker stoneware.

4. Cover and cook on Low for $3\frac{1}{2}$ to $4\frac{1}{2}$ hours or on High for $1\frac{1}{2}$ to 2 hours, until bubbling. Stir in shrimp and crabmeat.

For a decorative finish, cut shell or fish shapes out of the puff pastry dough instead of squares or circles.

5. Preheat oven to 375°F (190°C). On a lightly floured surface, roll out pastry to a 15- by 10-inch (38 by 25 cm) rectangle. Cut into 6 squares (or use a large, round cookie cutter to cut circles) and place at least $\frac{1}{2}$ inch (1 cm) apart on baking sheet.

6. Bake pastry pieces for 15 to 20 minutes or until puffed and golden brown. Ladle chowder into serving bowls and top each with a pastry crust. Serve immediately.

Most slow cooker stoneware is designed to be both microwave-safe and oven-safe, so you can take it out of the metal casing, cover it with pastry and place it in the oven. To avoid cracking it, make sure your stoneware is warm when you place it in the oven.

Cioppino

This classic, slow-simmered seafood stew shares its name with the famous Cioppino's restaurant in San Francisco, which I visited with my husband on our 20th wedding anniversary. At the turn of the 20th century, fishermen in boats moored along the wharf would toss seafood and various vegetables and herbs into a bucket for the makings of a communal stew. "Chip In! Chip In!" was the cry that prompted each contribution. Of course, said with an Italian accent, this American slang had to end with a vowel. And the "in" was, of course, "een." So "chio-peen-o" was born.

Tips

Haddock and tilapia are also great additions to this stew. If using frozen fillets, make sure you thaw them first. Before purchasing fish, always learn what you can about sustainability and fishing practices. Ask your fishmonger or check online resources.

Serve this dish with plenty of sourdough bread to sop up every last drop of the wonderful broth. If you want to be adventurous, purchase small sourdough breads, hollow out the center of each and serve the stew right in these edible bowls.

- **Minimum 5-quart slow cooker**

5	cloves garlic, finely chopped	5
2	large onions, chopped	2
2	stalks celery, finely chopped	2
1	can (28 oz/796 mL) diced tomatoes, with juice	1
1	bottle (8 oz/236 mL) clam juice	1
1	can (5½ oz/156 mL) tomato paste	1
¾ cup	dry white wine or water	175 mL
1 tbsp	red wine vinegar	15 mL
1 tbsp	olive oil or vegetable oil	15 mL
2½ tsp	dried Italian seasoning	12 mL
¼ tsp	granulated sugar	1 mL
¼ tsp	hot pepper flakes	1 mL
1	bay leaf	1
1 lb	skinless firm white fish fillets, such as red snapper or mahi mahi (see tip, at left), cut into 1-inch (2.5 cm) pieces	500 g
12 oz	shrimp, peeled and deveined	375 g
1	can (5 oz/142 g) chopped clams, with juice	1
1	can (6 oz/170 g) crabmeat, drained	1
¼ to ½ tsp	hot pepper sauce (optional)	1 to 2 mL
	Salt and freshly ground black pepper	
¼ cup	chopped fresh parsley	60 mL

1. In slow cooker stoneware, combine garlic, onions, celery, tomatoes with juice, clam juice, tomato paste, wine, vinegar, oil, Italian seasoning, sugar, hot pepper flakes and bay leaf.

2. Cover and cook on Low for 6 to 8 hours or on High for 3 to 4 hours, until bubbling. Discard bay leaf.

3. Stir in fish and shrimp. Cover and cook on Low for 25 to 30 minutes or until fish flakes easily when tested with a fork and shrimp are pink and opaque.

4. Add clams with juice and crabmeat. Cover and cook for 10 minutes or until warmed through. Stir in hot pepper sauce to taste (if using) and season to taste with salt and black pepper.

5. Ladle into individual serving bowls and sprinkle with parsley. Serve immediately.

Creole Seafood and Pasta Gratin

Makes 6 to 8 servings

This super, kicked-up version of macaroni and cheese is a fantastic one-dish meal. It's so rich, creamy and cheesy, all you'll need is a simple green salad to serve alongside. If you really want to make it luxurious, make sure the seafood mix includes lobster.

Tip

Look for Cajun seasoning in the spice aisle of the supermarket. If you can't find it, combine 2 tbsp (30 mL) each paprika and dried parsley, 1 tbsp (15 mL) each garlic powder, oregano and thyme, $\frac{1}{2}$ tsp (2 mL) salt and $\frac{1}{4}$ tsp (1 mL) cayenne pepper. Store in an airtight container for up to 1 month. It's also a good rub for pork, chicken or beef.

Make Ahead

This dish can be assembled up to 12 hours in advance. Prepare through step 3, cover and refrigerate overnight. The next day, place stoneware in slow cooker and proceed with step 4.

- **Minimum 4-quart slow cooker**

4 cups	elbow macaroni pasta	1 L
$\frac{1}{4}$ cup	butter	60 mL
1	onion, finely chopped	1
1	clove garlic, minced	1
$\frac{1}{3}$ cup	all-purpose flour	75 mL
3 cups	whole or evaporated milk	750 mL
1 tsp	salt	5 mL
$\frac{1}{2}$ tsp	finely ground black pepper	2 mL
$\frac{1}{4}$ tsp	ground nutmeg	1 mL
1 lb	cooked seafood, such as shrimp, crab and/or lobster, coarsely chopped	500 g
3 cups	shredded Italian 4-cheese blend (Parmesan, Cheddar, Swiss and fontina)	750 mL
$\frac{1}{2}$ cup	dry bread crumbs	125 mL
$\frac{1}{2}$ tsp	Cajun seasoning	2 mL
2 tbsp	melted butter	30 mL

1. In a large pot of boiling salted water, cook macaroni for about 6 minutes, or 2 minutes less than recommended by package directions, until almost tender. Drain and rinse under cold running water. Set aside.

2. In a large saucepan, melt $\frac{1}{4}$ cup (60 mL) butter over medium heat. Sauté onion and garlic for 3 to 5 minutes or until onion is tender and translucent. Add flour and cook, stirring, for 1 minute. Slowly whisk in milk until smooth; bring to a boil. Reduce heat and simmer, stirring, for 2 to 3 minutes or until thickened. Season with salt, pepper and nutmeg.

3. Remove pan from heat and fold in macaroni, seafood and cheese blend. Transfer to prepared slow cooker stoneware.

4. In a bowl, toss together bread crumbs, Cajun seasoning and melted butter. Sprinkle over mixture in stoneware.

5. Cover and cook on Low for 3 to 4 hours or on High for $1\frac{1}{2}$ to 2 hours, until bubbling.

Linguine with Seafood Puttanesca Sauce

Makes 4 to 6 servings

The name "puttanesca" comes from the Italian word puttana, *meaning "lady of the evening." Legend says these working girls would put their sauce on to cook while they took care of their clients. If they'd had this slow cooker version, they would have had to work overtime!*

Tips

Anchovy paste is readily available, in small tubes, in many supermarkets and specialty stores.

A generous amount of salt in the cooking water seasons the pasta internally as it absorbs the water and swells. The claim that salted water cooks food faster (because the salt increases the boiling temperature) is exaggerated: you're not adding enough salt to raise the boiling temperature by more than about 1°F (1°C).

- 3- to 4-quart slow cooker

2	cloves garlic, minced	2
1	onion, finely diced	1
1	can (28 oz/796 mL) diced tomatoes, with juice	1
2 tbsp	tomato paste	30 mL
1 tsp	granulated sugar	5 mL
1 tsp	dried basil	5 mL
1 tsp	dried thyme	5 mL
1 tsp	dried oregano	5 mL
1/2 tsp	anchovy paste	2 mL
1/2 tsp	salt	2 mL
1/4 tsp	freshly ground black pepper	1 mL
20	jumbo shrimp (21–25 size), peeled and deveined	20
20	sea scallops	20
2 tbsp	chopped oil-cured black olives	30 mL
1 tbsp	capers, drained	15 mL
1 lb	whole wheat linguine pasta	500 g
1/4 cup	freshly grated Parmesan cheese	60 mL

1. In slow cooker stoneware, combine garlic, onion, tomatoes with juice, tomato paste, sugar, basil, thyme, oregano, anchovy paste, salt and pepper.

2. Cover and cook on Low for 5 to 6 hours or on High for 2$\frac{1}{2}$ to 3 hours, until bubbling.

3. Stir in shrimp, scallops, olives and capers. Cover and cook on High for 15 to 20 minutes or until seafood is opaque.

4. Meanwhile, in a pot of boiling salted water, cook linguine according to package directions until tender but firm (al dente). Drain well.

5. Divide pasta evenly among serving plates, top evenly with sauce and sprinkle with Parmesan.

Anchovy paste is made from ground anchovy fillets. Since it is highly concentrated, a small amount can have an immense impact in soups, sauces and sandwiches. It has a very distinctive salty, fishy flavor, with a hint of sweetness.

Spicy Mussels and Chorizo

Makes 4 servings

This is one of my favorite meals to order in a restaurant. I decided to experiment to see if I could get a hot, spicy broth in the slow cooker. That way, at the end of the day, I could just add the mussels and let them steam open. It worked, and with great results. Serve this dish with lots of garlic toast to mop up all the savory broth.

Tips

Wild mussels must be thoroughly cleaned and rinsed before cooking. Scrub them with a stiff brush to remove any barnacles, sand or grit. Their beards must also be removed. Give each beard a forceful tug with your fingers and pull it away, or cut it off with a small sharp knife or kitchen shears. Rinse mussels several times, but do not let them sit in water (fresh water will kill them).

Farmed mussels (generally found fresh in the seafood department of the supermarket) will have been prepared for cooking, so they just need a quick rinse under cold running water. Remove any beards.

- **4- to 6-quart slow cooker**

1 tbsp	olive oil	15 mL
1	large shallot, minced	1
2	cloves garlic, thinly sliced	2
1/4 tsp	hot pepper flakes	1 mL
2 cups	dry white wine	500 mL
1	can (28 oz/796 mL) crushed tomatoes, with juice	1
8 oz	cured hot chorizo sausage, cut diagonally into 1/4-inch (0.5 cm) slices	250 g
2 lbs	mussels, scrubbed and debearded (see tips, at left)	1 kg
	Freshly ground black pepper	
	Kosher salt	
1/3 cup	coarsely chopped flat-leaf (Italian) parsley	75 mL

1. In a large skillet, heat oil over medium-high heat. Sauté shallot for about 3 minutes or until softened. Add garlic and hot pepper flakes; sauté for 1 minute. Add wine and bring to a boil. Stir in tomatoes with juice and sausage. Transfer to slow cooker stoneware.

2. Cover and cook on Low for 6 to 8 hours or on High for 3 to 4 hours, until bubbling.

3. Add mussels and toss to coat with sauce. Cover and cook on High for 15 to 20 minutes or until mussels open. (Discard any mussels that do not open.) Using a slotted spoon, transfer mussels to individual serving bowls.

4. Stir black pepper to taste into the sauce. Taste and add salt, if necessary. Pour sauce over mussels and sprinkle with parsley.

Make Ahead

This dish can be assembled up to 24 hours in advance. Prepare through step 1, cover and refrigerate overnight. The next day, place stoneware in slow cooker and proceed with step 2.

Shrimp and Penne Arrabbiata

Makes 4 to 6 servings

This is one of the dishes my daughter likes to order when we visit our favorite neighborhood Italian bistro. The versatile tomato sauce gets its name from the addition of dried hot pepper flakes. Arrabbiata is Italian for "angry," but don't worry that you are going to taste a really hot sauce; it just has a little kick, without being too "mad."

Tip

Select shrimp that are moist and firm, have translucent flesh and smell fresh. Unless you go to a fishmonger to purchase your seafood, most of the shrimp available today will have been frozen. If you purchase frozen shrimp, make sure it is frozen solid and has no signs of freezer burn. Thaw under cold running water or overnight in the refrigerator; rinse and drain well before peeling.

Make Ahead

This dish can be assembled up to 24 hours in advance. Prepare through step 1, cover and refrigerate overnight. The next day, place stoneware in slow cooker and proceed with step 2.

- **4- to 6-quart slow cooker**

1 tbsp	olive oil	15 mL
1	onion, finely chopped	1
4	cloves garlic, minced	4
½ tsp	hot pepper flakes	2 mL
½ tsp	dried Italian seasoning	2 mL
½ tsp	dried oregano	2 mL
1	can (28 oz/796 mL) crushed tomatoes	1
¼ cup	red wine	60 mL
2 tbsp	tomato paste	30 mL
1 tsp	freshly squeezed lemon juice or balsamic vinegar	5 mL
½ tsp	salt	2 mL
	Freshly ground black pepper	
1 lb	jumbo shrimp (21–25 size), peeled and deveined	500 g
1 lb	penne pasta	500 g
⅓ cup	chopped fresh basil	75 mL
	Freshly grated Parmesan cheese (optional)	

1. In a large nonstick skillet, heat oil over medium-high heat. Sauté onion for 3 to 5 minutes or until tender and translucent. Stir in garlic, hot pepper flakes, Italian seasoning and oregano; sauté for 1 minute or until fragrant. Transfer to slow cooker stoneware. Stir in tomatoes, wine, tomato paste and lemon juice.

2. Cover and cook on Low for 5 to 6 hours or on High for 2½ to 3 hours, until bubbling. Season with salt and black pepper to taste.

3. Add shrimp. Cover and cook on High for 15 minutes or until shrimp are pink and opaque.

4. Meanwhile, in a pot of boiling salted water, cook penne according to package directions until tender but firm (al dente). Drain well.

5. Divide penne evenly among individual serving bowls, ladle sauce over top and sprinkle with basil and Parmesan (if using). Serve immediately.

Spanish Paella-Style Shrimp and Rice

Makes 4 to 6 servings

This no-meat version of a popular Spanish dish cooks up very well in the slow cooker, provided you use the right rice. This dish must be made with long-grain converted rice, which is ideally suited to the slow cooker. Pass hot pepper sauce at the table, in case diners want to spice their portion up.

Tip

To avoid tears when chopping onions, put the onions in the freezer for a few minutes first.

- 4- to 6-quart slow cooker

4 tbsp	olive oil, divided	60 mL
1	large onion, finely chopped	1
4	cloves garlic, minced	4
1	red bell pepper, finely chopped	1
1 cup	chopped tomato	250 mL
1½ cups	long-grain parboiled (converted) white rice	375 mL
2½ cups	chicken broth	625 mL
⅓ cup	dry white wine	75 mL
1 tsp	salt	5 mL
½ tsp	saffron threads	2 mL
⅛ tsp	hot pepper flakes	0.5 mL
1	bay leaf	1
	Freshly ground black pepper	
1 lb	jumbo shrimp (21–25 size), peeled and deveined	500 g
1 cup	frozen peas, thawed	250 mL

1. In a nonstick skillet, heat 3 tbsp (45 mL) of the oil over medium-high heat. Sauté onion for 3 to 5 minutes or until tender and translucent. Add garlic and sauté for 1 minute. Add red pepper and tomato; sauté for about 2 minutes or until heated through. Add rice and stir until well coated. Stir in broth, wine, salt, saffron, hot pepper flakes and bay leaf. Transfer to slow cooker stoneware.

2. Cover and cook on Low for 4 to 5 hours or on High for 2 to 3 hours, until liquid is absorbed and rice is tender.

3. Toss shrimp in the remaining oil and season to taste with salt and black pepper. Stir shrimp and peas into stoneware. Cover and cook on High for 20 minutes or until shrimp are pink and opaque and peas are heated through. Discard bay leaf.

Saffron threads are the stigmas of a particular kind of crocus, and they must be picked by hand. It takes about 75,000 stigmas to produce 1 lb (500 g) of saffron, which is why it is so expensive. Some recipes replace saffron with turmeric to save money; the finished dish may look similar, but the flavor is very different.

Sweet-and-Sour Thai Shrimp Stew

Makes 4 to 6 servings

Thai cuisine balances hot, sour, salty and sweet for a symphony of flavors. Serve this stew over hot cooked brown rice or steamed rice noodles, to soak up extra sauce.

Tips

Do not add raw shrimp to the slow cooker until the last 20 to 35 minutes of cooking time; otherwise, you will overcook them and they will toughen.

- **4- to 5-quart slow cooker**

4	large cloves garlic, minced	4
2	large red bell peppers, sliced into thin 1½-inch (4 cm) long strips	2
2	onions, thinly sliced	2
1	can (19 oz/540 mL) diced tomatoes, with juice	1
½ cup	sweet Thai chili sauce	125 mL
2 lbs	jumbo shrimp (21–25 size), peeled and deveined	1 kg
½ tsp	coarse salt	2 mL
1	can (14 oz/398 mL) unsweetened coconut milk	1
2 tbsp	freshly squeezed lime juice	30 mL
½ cup	chopped fresh cilantro	125 mL

1. In slow cooker stoneware, combine garlic, red peppers, onions, tomatoes with juice and chili sauce.

2. Cover and cook on Low for 4 to 5 hours or on High for 2 to 2½ hours, until bubbling.

3. In a large bowl, combine shrimp and salt, tossing to coat. Cover and refrigerate while stew is cooking.

4. Drain any liquid from shrimp. Add shrimp and coconut milk to stoneware, stirring to coat shrimp with sauce. Cover and cook on High for 20 to 25 minutes or until shrimp are pink and opaque. Stir in lime juice. Serve sprinkled with cilantro.

Make Ahead

This dish can be partially assembled up to 12 hours in advance. Prepare through step 1, cover and refrigerate overnight. The next day, place stoneware in slow cooker and proceed with step 2.

Sweet Thai chili sauce can be found in supermarkets and Asian grocery stores. The taste is mildly spicy and sweet. Its pinkish red color and confetti-like specks of chile flakes make it a visually appealing condiment. It is wonderful with fish.

Poultry

Buffalo Chicken and Potatoes

Makes 6 servings

This fun dish reminds me of my favorite bar food: chicken wings. Team it up with a plate of celery and carrot sticks and lots of cold beer, and you have a guaranteed party!

Tips

Look for precut raw chicken tenders in your local supermarket, so you can save chopping time when making this recipe.

Traditional Buffalo-style chicken wing sauce is composed of two ingredients: butter and a vinegar-based cayenne pepper hot sauce. It is readily available in the sauce and condiment aisle of the supermarket.

- **4- to 5-quart slow cooker, stoneware greased**

1 ¼ lbs	boneless skinless chicken breasts (about 2 large), cut into 1-inch (2.5 cm) strips	625 g
⅓ cup	Buffalo wing sauce	75 mL
1	can (10 oz/284 mL) condensed cream of celery soup	1
6 cups	frozen hash brown potatoes, thawed	1.5 L
1 cup	ranch or blue cheese salad dressing	250 mL
½ cup	shredded Cheddar cheese	125 mL
½ cup	fine dry bread crumbs or crushed corn flakes cereal	125 mL
2 tbsp	butter, melted	30 mL
3	green onions, chopped	3

1. In a bowl, combine chicken and Buffalo wing sauce, stirring to coat chicken. Place on bottom of prepared slow cooker stoneware.

2. In a large bowl, combine soup, potatoes, dressing and cheese. Spoon over chicken.

3. In a small bowl, stir together bread crumbs and butter. Sprinkle evenly over chicken mixture.

4. Cover and cook on Low for 6 to 8 hours or on High for 3 to 4 hours, until potatoes are tender and chicken is no longer pink inside. Serve sprinkled with green onions.

Creamy Chicken Artichoke Casserole

Makes 6 servings

I love recipes that let me use some ready-made ingredients to make a simple, tasty dish. The crushed salad croutons on the casserole give it a crunchy topping. Serve with rice and a crisp green salad to finish this dish nicely.

Tip

You can substitute light Alfredo sauce and mayonnaise for the regular versions called for in this recipe.

- **4- to 6-quart slow cooker, stoneware greased**

1	red bell pepper, chopped	1
3 cups	chopped cooked chicken	750 mL
1 cup	shredded Asiago cheese	250 mL
1/4 cup	chopped green onions	60 mL
1	can (14 oz/398 mL) artichoke hearts, drained and chopped	1
1	container (10 oz/300 mL) Alfredo sauce	1
1/2 cup	mayonnaise	125 mL
1 1/2 cups	croutons, coarsely crushed	375 mL
	Sliced green onions (optional)	

1. In a large bowl, combine red pepper, chicken, Asiago, green onions, artichokes, Alfredo sauce and mayonnaise. Transfer to prepared slow cooker stoneware. Sprinkle with croutons.

2. Cover and cook on Low for 5 to 6 hours or on High for 2 1/2 to 3 hours, until bubbling. If desired, sprinkle with sliced green onions.

Braised Chicken in Riesling

Makes 6 servings

Traditionally, this dish is made with red wine, but when you use white wine, such as Riesling, it is lighter and equally delicious. You can also substitute an equal amount of chicken broth or apple juice, if you prefer not to use wine. Serve over cooked brown rice.

Tip

Tomato paste is now available in tubes in many supermarkets and delis. It keeps for months in the refrigerator.

- **Minimum 4-quart slow cooker**

6	skinless bone-in chicken thighs, trimmed	6
1/2 tsp	salt	2 mL
1/4 tsp	freshly ground black pepper	1 mL
1 tbsp	olive oil	15 mL
1	onion, thinly sliced	1
1 1/2 cups	finely shredded green cabbage	375 mL
1 cup	chopped baby carrots	250 mL
3	cloves garlic, minced	3
3/4 cup	Riesling or other dry white wine	175 mL
3/4 cup	chicken broth	175 mL
2 tbsp	tomato paste	30 mL
2 tbsp	all-purpose flour	30 mL

1. Sprinkle chicken with salt and pepper. In a large nonstick skillet, heat oil over medium-high heat. Cook chicken for 2 to 3 minutes per side or until browned all over. Using a slotted spoon, transfer to slow cooker stoneware.

2. Add onion and cabbage to skillet. Reduce heat to medium and sauté for about 5 minutes or until onion is tender and translucent and cabbage is softened. Stir into chicken and top with carrots and garlic.

3. In a glass measuring cup, whisk together wine, broth and tomato paste. Pour over chicken mixture.

4. Cover and cook on Low for 5 to 6 hours or on High for 3 to 4 hours, until juices run clear when chicken is pierced. Using a slotted spoon, transfer chicken and vegetables to a platter and keep warm.

5. In a bowl, whisk together flour and 1/3 cup (75 mL) water until smooth. Whisk in about 1/4 cup (60 mL) hot liquid from stoneware until blended. Stir flour mixture into stoneware. Cover and cook on High for about 15 minutes or until liquid has thickened. Season to taste with salt and pepper. Spoon over chicken and vegetables.

Chicken with Sourdough Mushroom Stuffing

Makes 4 to 6 servings

Since I first made Thanksgiving stuffing in the slow cooker more than 10 years ago, I have maintained that this is the best way to ensure that this side dish is moist and delicious. Now I have combined the stuffing with chicken and vegetables to make a complete one-dish meal.

Tips

To zest a lemon, use the fine side of a box cheese grater, making sure not to grate the white pith underneath. Or use a zester to remove the zest, then finely chop it. Zesters are inexpensive and widely available at specialty kitchenware shops.

Sourdough bread is a little heavier than regular French bread, making it a great choice for the slow cooker, but if you wish to use a French loaf, you can.

- Minimum 4-quart slow cooker, stoneware greased

2 tbsp	grated lemon zest, divided	30 mL
1 tbsp	dried sage	15 mL
1 tsp	salt	5 mL
1 tsp	freshly ground black pepper	5 mL
8	skinless bone-in chicken drumsticks or thighs (about 2 lbs/1 kg)	8
1/4 cup	butter	60 mL
2	cloves garlic, minced	2
1	onion, finely chopped	1
4 cups	quartered assorted mushrooms, such as cremini, portobello, shiitake or button	1 L
8 cups	cubed sourdough bread (1 inch/2.5 cm cubes)	2 L
1 cup	coarsely shredded carrots	250 mL
1/2 cup	dried cranberries (optional)	125 mL
1 cup	chicken broth	250 mL
1/4 cup	finely chopped fresh parsley	60 mL

1. Set aside 1 tsp (5 mL) of the lemon zest. In a small bowl, combine the remaining zest, sage, salt and pepper. Sprinkle over chicken and rub all over. Place chicken in prepared slow cooker stoneware.

2. Meanwhile, in a skillet, melt butter over medium-high heat. Sauté garlic, onion and mushrooms for 3 to 5 minutes or until mushrooms are tender.

3. In a large bowl, combine bread cubes, carrots and cranberries (if using). Add mushroom mixture. Drizzle with broth and toss gently to combine. Lightly pack over chicken in stoneware.

4. Cover and cook on High for 4 to 5 hours or on Low for 8 to 10 hours, until juices run clear when chicken is pierced. Using a slotted spoon, transfer stuffing and chicken to a warmed platter. (Discard juices in stoneware.)

5. In a small bowl, combine parsley and the reserved lemon zest. Sprinkle over chicken and stuffing.

Fennel and Pear Chicken Thighs

Makes 6 servings

If you can't find dried pears, this dish is equally delicious with dried apples. And fennel? Well, I just can't say enough wonderful things about it. I love the flavor it gives this or any other recipe.

Tips

Store mushrooms in a paper bag, with the top loosely folded over once or twice, or place them in a glass container and cover it with a tea towel or moist paper towel. Be sure to allow air circulation. Store in the refrigerator (but not in the crisper) and use within a few days — or a week, if they are packaged and unopened.

To prepare mushrooms, first trim off the bottoms of the stems, then wipe off the mushrooms. Don't rinse or soak the mushrooms, or they'll absorb water and turn mushy when you cook them.

Look for dried pears and apples in the produce, baking or bulk departments of the supermarket.

- **4- to 6-quart slow cooker**

1	fennel bulb with fronds	1
8 oz	mushrooms, sliced	250 g
½ cup	chopped dried pears or apples	125 mL
2½ lbs	boneless skinless chicken thighs (about 12)	1.25 kg
¾ tsp	salt	3 mL
½ tsp	freshly ground black pepper	2 mL
½ tsp	dried thyme	2 mL
1 cup	unsweetened pear nectar or apple juice	250 mL
	Hot cooked couscous	
2 tbsp	cornstarch	30 mL
2 tbsp	cold water	30 mL

1. Remove and reserve green fronds from fennel bulb and cut bulb and the remaining stalks into ½-inch (1 cm) slices.

2. In slow cooker stoneware, combine fennel slices, mushrooms and pears. Arrange chicken on top and sprinkle with salt, pepper and thyme. Pour pear nectar over chicken.

3. Cover and cook on Low for 7 to 8 hours or on High for 3½ to 4 hours, until juices run clear when chicken is pierced.

4. Spoon hot couscous onto a warmed platter. Using a slotted spoon, arrange chicken and vegetables on top and keep warm.

5. In a small bowl, whisk together cornstarch and water. Whisk into liquid in stoneware. Cover and cook on High for 10 to 15 minutes or until sauce is thickened. Spoon over chicken and vegetables. Garnish with reserved fennel fronds.

Salsa Cinnamon Chicken

Makes 6 servings

You might think the combination of peanut sauce (Asian) and salsa (Mexican) is an unlikely fusion. However, these two ingredients, along with the fresh basil, are a wonderful complement to the chicken.

Tips

Feel free to substitute red kidney beans for the black beans in this dish.

If using a combination of chicken breasts, drumsticks and thighs, place the breasts on top to prevent them from getting overcooked.

Peanut sauce is commonly used in Thai cuisine, where it is served with satays, spring rolls and raw vegetables. It is generally a mixture of ground peanuts, chile peppers and oil, with seasonings such as ginger, garlic and lemongrass. I used a store-bought version for this recipe, but if you have a recipe for homemade, so much the better!

- **4- to 6-quart slow cooker, stoneware greased**

2 cups	cooked or canned black beans (see page 120), drained and rinsed	1
1 cup	corn kernels, thawed if frozen	250 mL
1 cup	medium or hot salsa, divided	250 mL
3 lbs	bone-in chicken pieces (skin-on breasts, skinless drumsticks and/or thighs)	1.5 kg
1/4 cup	chopped fresh basil, divided	60 mL
1 tsp	ground cinnamon	5 mL
3/4 cup	peanut sauce	175 mL

1. In prepared slow cooker stoneware, combine beans and corn. Pour half the salsa over bean mixture. Layer chicken on top (see tip, at left).

2. In a bowl, combine 2 tbsp (30 mL) of the basil, cinnamon, peanut sauce and the remaining salsa. Pour over chicken.

3. Cover and cook on Low for 5 to 6 hours or on High for 2 1/2 to 3 hours, until breasts are no longer pink inside and/or juices run clear when drumsticks and thighs are pierced. Serve sprinkled with the remaining basil.

Make Ahead

This dish can be assembled up to 12 hours in advance. Prepare through step 2, cover and refrigerate overnight. The next day, place stoneware in slow cooker and proceed with step 3.

Jamaican Chicken Casserole

Makes 4 servings

Create an easy one-dish dinner by baking chicken in a Caribbean-inspired rub. The flavors give the dish a delightful warmth that makes it a perfect meal for a cold night.

Tip

If your liquid honey has crystallized (or if you are using solid creamed honey instead), place the jar (or as much as you need in a small heatproof bowl) in a saucepan of hot water and let warm until the crystals dissolve and the honey is melted. Or heat in the microwave on Medium-High (70%) for about 1 minute, stirring after 30 seconds, until melted.

- Minimum 4-quart slow cooker, stoneware greased

1 tsp	salt	5 mL
3/4 tsp	ground allspice	3 mL
3/4 tsp	dried thyme	3 mL
1/2 tsp	pumpkin pie spice	2 mL
1/4 tsp	cayenne pepper	1 mL
8	boneless skinless chicken thighs	8
2 tbsp	vegetable oil (approx.)	30 mL
1	large sweet potato, peeled and cubed (about 3 cups/750 mL)	1
2 cups	cooked or canned black beans (see page 120), drained and rinsed	500 mL
1/4 cup	liquid honey	60 mL
1/4 cup	freshly squeezed lime juice	60 mL
2 tbsp	cornstarch	30 mL
1 tbsp	cold water	15 mL
2	green onions, chopped	2

1. In a bowl, combine salt, allspice, thyme, pumpkin pie spice and cayenne. Add chicken and rub all over with spices.

2. In a large nonstick skillet, heat half the oil over medium-high heat. Cook chicken in batches, adding more oil as needed, for 2 to 3 minutes per side or until browned all over. Set aside.

3. In prepared slow cooker stoneware, combine sweet potato and beans. Top with chicken.

4. In a small saucepan, combine honey and lime juice. Bring to a boil and cook, stirring, for 1 minute. Pour over chicken.

5. Cover and cook on Low for 4 to 6 hours or on High for 2 1/2 to 3 hours, until juices run clear when chicken is pierced. Using a slotted spoon, transfer chicken and vegetables to a platter and keep warm.

6. In a small bowl, whisk together cornstarch and water. Whisk into liquid in stoneware. Cover and cook on High for 10 to 15 minutes or until sauce has thickened. Spoon over chicken and vegetables. Garnish with green onions.

Easy Chicken Rarebit

Makes 4 to 6 servings

This dish is reminiscent of Welsh rarebit, also known as "rabbit" in Great Britain, where it originated. Rarebit is toasted bread topped with savory sauce made from melted cheese and seasonings. The addition of chicken makes it a satisfying meal on its own, but serve it with a crisp kosher dill pickle on the side.

Tips

This recipe uses boneless skinless chicken breasts, which require a very short cooking time. If you want to cook this recipe for longer, use boneless skinless chicken thighs, cut into strips, instead, to ensure that you don't overcook the chicken. Increase the cooking time to 6 to 8 hours on Low or 3 to 4 hours on High, until juices run clear when chicken is pierced.

If you can, purchase single cans of specialty beer at the liquor store. This recipe uses dark beer, but a good ale is also acceptable.

- 4- to 6-quart slow cooker

1	large onion, halved crosswise and thinly sliced	1
2 lbs	boneless skinless chicken breasts, cut diagonally into ½-inch (1 cm) thick slices	1 kg
2 tbsp	butter	30 mL
2 tbsp	all-purpose flour	30 mL
1 tsp	Dijon mustard	5 mL
1 tsp	Worcestershire sauce	5 mL
½ tsp	salt	2 mL
½ tsp	freshly ground black pepper	2 mL
½ cup	dark beer, such as porter or stout	125 mL
¾ cup	heavy or whipping (35%) cream	175 mL
1½ cups	shredded Cheddar cheese	375 mL
Dash	hot pepper sauce	Dash
6	pumpernickel or rye buns, split and toasted	6
4	slices bacon, cooked crisp and crumbled (optional)	4
1	tomato, chopped (optional)	1

1. Arrange onion on bottom of slow cooker stoneware and lay chicken on top.

2. In a saucepan, melt butter over medium-high heat. Cook flour, whisking constantly and being careful not to let it brown, for 2 minutes. Whisk in mustard, Worcestershire sauce, salt and pepper until smooth. Whisk in beer until combined. Add cream and cook, stirring, until smooth. Pour over chicken.

3. Cover and cook on Low for 4 to 5 hours or on High for 2 to 2½ hours, until chicken is no longer pink inside. Using a slotted spoon, transfer chicken to a plate and keep warm.

4. Stir Cheddar and hot pepper sauce into liquid in stoneware. Cover and cook on High for 10 minutes or until cheese has melted.

5. Arrange chicken evenly on bottom halves of buns and ladle cheese mixture on top. Sprinkle with bacon and tomato (if using). Cover with top halves of buns.

Spanish Paella with Chicken and Garden Vegetables

Makes 6 to 8 servings

This dish is traditionally made with a variety of meats, seafood and vegetables. This simple slow cooker version uses chicken, sausage and vegetables, and it's absolutely delicious.

Tip

For an easier version, substitute 2 cups (500 mL) thawed frozen mixed vegetables for the red pepper, zucchini and peas. Stir in about 20 minutes before the end of cooking.

- **Minimum 4-quart slow cooker**

1 tbsp	olive oil	15 mL
6	boneless skinless chicken thighs	6
1	onion, chopped	1
1	clove garlic, minced	1
1	can (19 oz/540 mL) tomatoes, with juice	1
1 lb	smoked hot sausage, sliced into rounds	500 g
3 cups	chicken broth	750 mL
1 cup	long-grain parboiled (converted) white rice	250 mL
1 tsp	dried thyme	5 mL
Pinch	saffron threads	Pinch
1	red or yellow bell pepper, chopped	1
1	zucchini, chopped	1
½ cup	frozen peas, thawed	125 mL

1. In a large nonstick skillet, heat oil over medium-high heat. Cook chicken for 2 to 3 minutes per side or until browned all over. Using a slotted spoon, transfer to slow cooker stoneware.

2. Add onion to skillet and sauté for 3 to 4 minutes or until tender and translucent. Stir in garlic, tomatoes with juice, sausage, broth, rice, thyme and saffron; cook for 5 minutes. Spoon over chicken.

3. Cover and cook on Low for 6 to 8 hours or on High for 3 to 4 hours, until juices run clear when chicken is pierced and rice is tender. About 20 minutes before the end of cooking, stir in red pepper, zucchini and peas.

Slow Roast Chicken with Peas and Prosciutto

Makes 6 servings

Don't be daunted by the fusion of French and Italian flavors in this recipe; it works well with the mild flavor of the chicken.

Tips

If a whole chicken is too large to fit into your slow cooker, cut it into pieces with a sharp knife, placing the breast portion on top in the stoneware.

Herbes de Provence is a blend of dried basil, fennel seed, lavender, marjoram, rosemary, sage, summer savory and thyme. Look for it in the spice aisle of the supermarket.

- Minimum 5-quart slow cooker

1	whole roasting chicken (about 2½ lbs/1.25 kg)	1
1 tbsp	herbes de Provence	15 mL
1 tsp	lemon pepper	5 mL
½ tsp	salt	2 mL
1 tsp	olive oil	5 mL
1	onion, finely chopped	1
5 oz	prosciutto, chopped	150 g
½ cup	dry white wine	125 mL
1 cup	frozen green peas, thawed	250 mL
½ cup	evaporated milk or heavy or whipping (35%) cream	125 mL
3 tbsp	cornstarch	45 mL
2 tbsp	cold water	30 mL
	Hot cooked linguine pasta	

1. Rinse chicken, inside and out, under cold running water and pat dry with paper towels. (Discard any giblets, but reserve chicken neck for another use, if desired).

2. In a bowl, combine herbes de Provence, lemon pepper and salt. Rub oil over skin of chicken and sprinkle with herb mixture. Place chicken, breast side up, in slow cooker stoneware. Arrange onion and prosciutto evenly around chicken. Pour wine over top.

3. Cover and cook on Low for 8 to 10 hours or until a meat thermometer inserted in the thickest part of a thigh registers 170°F (77°C). About 30 minutes before the end of cooking, add peas and evaporated milk to cooking liquid.

4. With two large spoons or pancake flippers, carefully transfer chicken to a plate and let stand for 15 minutes before carving.

5. Meanwhile, in a small bowl, whisk together cornstarch and cold water. Whisk into liquid in stoneware. Cover and cook on High for 10 to 15 minutes or until sauce is thickened.

6. Carve chicken. Divide cooked pasta evenly among individual serving plates. Arrange chicken on pasta and ladle sauce over top.

Italian Lemon Chicken with Gremolata

Makes 6 to 8 servings

Everyone loves chicken, and this is an easy dish you can serve to company. Serve it with steamed rice and a salad of Italian greens tossed in a light vinaigrette.

Tips

The gremolata can be prepared in advance and refrigerated for up to 4 hours.

Pearl onions are easy to prepare. Simply cut an X into the base of each onion. Bring a pot of water to a boil over medium-high heat. Drop onions into pot and boil for 1 minute. Drain and immediately immerse in ice-cold water. Let cool, then squeeze the onions out of their skins.

- **4- to 6-quart slow cooker**

2 lbs	skinless bone-in chicken thighs and drumsticks	1 kg
1 tsp	salt	5 mL
½ tsp	freshly ground black pepper	2 mL
2	cans (each 14 oz/398 mL) artichoke hearts, drained and quartered	2
2 cups	pearl onions, skins removed (see tip, at left)	500 mL
2 cups	baby carrots	500 mL
1 tsp	crumbled dried rosemary	5 mL
½ cup	chicken broth	125 mL
¼ cup	dry vermouth or white wine	60 mL
1 tbsp	freshly squeezed lemon juice	15 mL

Gremolata

2	cloves garlic, minced	2
3 tbsp	chopped fresh parsley	45 mL
1 tbsp	coarsely chopped lemon zest	15 mL

1. Arrange chicken in slow cooker stoneware. Sprinkle with salt and pepper. Arrange artichokes, onions and carrots around chicken. Sprinkle chicken and vegetables with rosemary.

2. In a bowl, combine broth, vermouth and lemon juice. Pour over chicken and vegetables.

3. Cover and cook on Low for 6 to 8 hours or on High for 3 to 4 hours, until juices run clear when chicken is pierced.

4. *Gremolata:* In a bowl, combine garlic, parsley and lemon zest. Sprinkle over chicken and vegetables before serving.

Chicken and Pepperoni Bake

Makes 4 servings

If you love the flavors of pizza, this recipe will be a favorite. The pepperoni slices add a great dimension to the sauce. I've even used small pepperettes in this recipe, as I seem to always have some in the refrigerator for my son, Jack. Serve this with noodles and a cooked green vegetable, for a complete meal.

Tip

To extract the most juice from a lemon, let it warm to room temperature, then roll it on the counter, pressing down with the palm of your hand, before squeezing it. Or microwave a whole lemon on High for 30 seconds, then roll it. The juice can be frozen in ice cube trays, then the frozen cubes stored in sealable plastic bags for later use. Lemon zest can also be wrapped and frozen for later use.

- **4- to 6-quart slow cooker**

1/2 cup	all-purpose flour	125 mL
1 tbsp	dried thyme	15 mL
1/2 tsp	salt	2 mL
3 lbs	skinless bone-in chicken thighs and drumsticks	1.5 kg
4	cloves garlic, minced	4
2	onions, finely chopped	2
1	can (28 oz/796 mL) tomatoes, drained	1
1 cup	thinly sliced pepperoni	250 mL
1/4 tsp	hot pepper flakes	1 mL
1/2 cup	dry red wine	125 mL
2 tbsp	tomato paste	30 mL
3/4 cup	sliced kalamata olives	175 mL
2 tbsp	chopped fresh oregano	30 mL
2 tsp	freshly squeezed lemon juice	10 mL

1. In a heavy plastic bag, combine flour, thyme and salt. In batches, add chicken to bag and toss to coat with flour mixture. Transfer chicken to slow cooker stoneware. Reserve the remaining flour mixture.

2. Add garlic, onions, tomatoes, pepperoni and hot pepper flakes to stoneware.

3. In a bowl, combine wine and tomato paste. Pour over chicken and vegetables.

4. Cover and cook on Low for 5 to 6 hours or on High for 2 1/2 to 3 hours, until juices run clear when chicken is pierced. Using a slotted spoon, transfer chicken to a platter and keep warm.

5. In a bowl, combine the reserved flour mixture and 2 tbsp (30 mL) water. Whisk into liquid in stoneware. Cover and cook on High for 10 to 15 minutes or until sauce is thickened. Stir in olives, oregano and lemon juice. Season to taste with salt. Spoon sauce over chicken.

Braised Chicken Marbella-Style

This recipe is inspired by one of my favorites from The Silver Palate Cookbook. The chicken is marinated overnight for moistness and flavor, then braised with dried fruit. All you need alongside is a crisp green salad and some rice to soak up the juices.

Tips

If using a combination of chicken breasts, drumsticks and thighs, place the breasts on top to prevent them from getting overcooked.

Cooking times for poultry may be longer for larger slow cookers and/or where there is a relatively high proportion of dark to white meat. For predominantly white meat dishes, be sure to avoid overcooking. It is best to check doneness at the earliest time suggested in the recipe.

- **4- to 6-quart slow cooker**

3	cloves garlic, minced	3
1	bay leaf	1
2 tbsp	packed brown sugar	30 mL
1 tsp	dried oregano	5 mL
1 tsp	salt	5 mL
1/2 tsp	freshly ground black pepper	2 mL
1/2 cup	dry white wine	125 mL
2 tbsp	red wine vinegar	30 mL
3 lbs	bone-in chicken pieces (skin-on breasts, skinless drumsticks and/or thighs)	1.5 kg
1/2 cup	pitted prunes, chopped	125 mL
1/2 cup	dried figs, chopped	125 mL
1/4 cup	whole pitted Spanish green olives	60 mL
2 tbsp	capers, drained	30 mL
2 tbsp	chopped fresh parsley	30 mL

1. In a glass measuring cup, combine garlic, bay leaf, brown sugar, oregano, salt, pepper, wine and vinegar. Place chicken in a sealable plastic bag and pour in garlic mixture. Seal bag and massage marinade around the meat. Refrigerate overnight.

2. Transfer chicken and marinade to slow cooker stoneware (see tip, at left). Add prunes and figs.

3. Cover and cook on Low for 5 to 6 hours or on High for 2 1/2 to 3 hours, until breasts are no longer pink inside and/or juices run clear when drumsticks and thighs are pierced. About 10 minutes before the end of cooking, stir in olives and capers. Discard bay leaf. Serve sprinkled with parsley.

Capers are the flower buds of a bush native to the Mediterranean. Once picked, the buds are sun-dried, then pickled in a vinegar brine. They can be found in various sizes, from petite to small (about the size of your little fingertip). If desired, rinse capers before using to remove excess salt.

Moroccan Chicken

Makes 4 to 6 servings

I have acquired a taste for Middle Eastern cuisine in the past few years. While you're cooking this exotic dish, the pungent aromas of curry and lemon will emanate throughout the house.

Tips

Preserved lemons are a key ingredient in many Moroccan dishes. Their flavor is mildly tart and intensely lemony. You can find them in gourmet food shops. If you can't find one, simply omit it.

If using a combination of chicken breasts, drumsticks and thighs, place the breasts on top to prevent them from getting overcooked.

Cooking times for poultry may be longer for larger slow cookers and/or where there is a relatively high proportion of dark to white meat. For predominantly white meat dishes, be sure to avoid overcooking. It is best to check doneness at the earliest time suggested in the recipe.

- **4- to 6-quart slow cooker**

1/2 cup	all-purpose flour	125 mL
1 tbsp	garam masala or curry powder	15 mL
1 tsp	salt	5 mL
1/2 tsp	freshly ground black pepper	2 mL
3 lbs	bone-in chicken pieces (skin-on breasts, skinless drumsticks and/or thighs)	1.5 kg
2 tbsp	olive oil (approx.)	30 mL
2	onions, chopped	2
2	cloves garlic, minced	2
1/2 cup	dry white wine	125 mL
1/2 cup	chicken broth	125 mL
	Finely grated zest and freshly squeezed juice of 1 lemon	
1	preserved lemon (see tip, at left), finely chopped	1
1/2 cup	pitted ripe kalamata olives	125 mL
1/4 cup	chopped fresh cilantro	60 mL

1. In a heavy plastic bag, combine flour, garam masala, salt and pepper. In batches, add chicken to bag and toss to coat with flour mixture. (Once all the chicken is coated, reserve the remaining flour mixture.)

2. In a large skillet, heat half the oil over medium-high heat. Cook chicken in batches, adding more oil as needed, for 2 to 3 minutes per side or until browned all over. Using a slotted spoon, transfer to slow cooker stoneware (see tip, at left).

3. Add onions to skillet, reduce heat to medium and sauté for about 2 minutes or until tender and translucent. Add garlic and reserved flour mixture; cook, stirring, for about 3 minutes or until flour is toasted. Add wine and broth; cook, stirring, until thickened. Remove from heat and stir in 1/2 tsp (2 mL) of the lemon zest. Pour over chicken. Scatter preserved lemon on top.

4. Cover and cook on Low for 5 to 6 hours or on High for 2 1/2 to 3 hours, until breasts are no longer pink inside and/or juices run clear when drumsticks and thighs are pierced.

5. Using a slotted spoon, transfer chicken to a platter. Stir remaining lemon zest, lemon juice, olives and cilantro into sauce. Spoon over chicken.

Bollywood Chicken Loaf with Chutney Glaze

Makes 4 to 6 servings

In this dish, ground chicken is spiced with tandoori curry paste for a zesty change from the usual meatloaf. Serve with roasted potatoes, and cauliflower seasoned with curry powder. A little yogurt sauce on the side cools down the taste buds (although this is not a particularly spicy dish).

Tip
You can also line the stoneware with cheesecloth, using a large enough piece to drape over the rim, and use it to lift out the cooked meatloaf.

Variation
Substitute 2 lbs (1 kg) lean ground beef or turkey for the ground chicken, or combine 1 lb (500 g) ground beef with 1 lb (500 g) ground turkey or chicken.

- **Minimum 4-quart slow cooker**

2 lbs	lean ground chicken	1 kg
2	cloves garlic, minced	2
1	egg, lightly beaten	1
1/3 cup	crushed pappadams or fine dry bread crumbs	75 mL
2 tbsp	tandoori curry paste	30 mL
2 tsp	garam masala or curry powder	10 mL
Pinch	salt	Pinch
1/4 tsp	freshly ground black pepper	1 mL
1/4 cup	mango chutney	60 mL

Spiced Yogurt Sauce

1/2 cup	plain nonfat yogurt	125 mL
1/2 tsp	minced fresh garlic	2 mL
1/2 tsp	ground coriander	2 mL
1/4 tsp	ground cumin	1 mL

1. Cut a 2-foot (60 cm) length of foil in half lengthwise to make 2 strips. Fold each strip in half lengthwise. Crisscross the strips on the bottom of the slow cooker stoneware, bringing the ends up the sides and over the rim.

2. In a large bowl, combine chicken, garlic, egg, pappadams, curry paste, garam masala, salt and pepper. Using your hands, blend well. Mound into a loaf shape and place in prepared stoneware. Spread chutney over top.

3. Tucking strip ends under lid, cover and cook on Low for 4 to 6 hours or on High for 2 1/2 to 3 hours, until a meat thermometer inserted in the center of the loaf registers 170°F (77°C). Remove lid and grasp strip ends to lift out meatloaf. Transfer to a platter.

4. *Sauce:* Meanwhile, in a bowl, combine yogurt, garlic, coriander and cumin. Refrigerate until ready to serve. Serve on the side.

Garam masala is a blend of spices used in Indian cooking. *Garam* means "warm" or "hot" in Hindi and *masala* means "mixture," so as you might expect, this blend adds a pleasant heat to dishes. If you can't find garam masala, an equal amount of curry powder will work almost as well.

North African Chicken Stew (page 105)

Cinderella Stew (page 112)

Canadian Maple Turkey Chili (page 126)

Turkish Lentils and Couscous Salad (page 145)

Wheat and Beet Risotto (page 155)

Salmon and Potato Strata (page 159)

Brazilian Fish Stew (page 164)

Chicken with Sourdough Mushroom Stuffing (page 181)

Sweet Butter Chicken

Makes 4 to 6 servings

Here's one of my favorite menu offerings at an Indian restaurant. The smooth sauce and tender chicken melt in your mouth — like butter! It's perfect served over cooked basmati rice, with a crisp cucumber salad and savory pappadams (crisp Indian flatbreads) on the side.

Tips

The most flavorful paprika comes from Hungary. Types range from mild to hot. Use the type that suits your taste.

Evaporated milk holds up extremely well in the slow cooker and will not curdle when it is cooked over a long period of time. Don't confuse evaporated milk with the sweetened condensed milk used in desserts and candies.

Toasting cashews brings out their sweet, buttery flavor. Spread nuts in a single layer on a rimmed baking sheet and toast in a 350°F (180°C) oven for about 10 minutes or until golden and fragrant.

- **4- to 6-quart slow cooker**

2 tbsp	melted butter, divided	30 mL
2 tbsp	tandoori curry paste or tikka curry paste, divided	30 mL
1 tbsp	minced gingerroot	15 mL
1 tsp	ground cumin	5 mL
1 tsp	paprika	5 mL
1	can (12 oz/370 mL) evaporated milk	1
1	can (5½ oz/156 mL) tomato paste	1
1 tbsp	packed brown sugar	15 mL
8	boneless skinless chicken thighs	8
½ cup	plain yogurt	125 mL
2 tbsp	freshly squeezed lime juice	30 mL
	Hot cooked basmati rice	
2 tbsp	chopped fresh cilantro	30 mL
2 tbsp	chopped toasted cashews	30 mL

1. In a saucepan, cook 1 tbsp (15 mL) of the butter until just beginning to brown. Add 1 tbsp (15 mL) of the curry paste, ginger, cumin and paprika; cook, stirring, for about 2 minutes or until fragrant. Stir in evaporated milk, tomato paste and brown sugar; bring to a boil. Reduce heat and simmer, stirring often, for about 10 minutes or until thickened.

2. Add the remaining butter to slow cooker stoneware and swirl to coat bottom and sides.

3. In a bowl, combine chicken, yogurt and the remaining curry paste. Arrange in stoneware and pour sauce evenly over top.

4. Cover and cook on Low for 5 to 6 hours or on High for 3 hours, until juices run clear when chicken is pierced. Stir in lime juice.

5. Serve over rice, sprinkled with cilantro and cashews.

Tandoori and tikka curry pastes are complex blends of freshly ground spices and herbs, preserved in vegetable oil to seal in freshness. Both are mild blends and can be mixed with broth, yogurt or canned tomatoes to create a delicious sauce for meat, poultry, seafood or vegetables. Once opened, curry paste can be stored in the refrigerator for up to 6 months.

Sweet Thai Chili Chicken

Makes 5 to
6 servings

This Thai chicken dish is so good that everyone will want seconds. It blends all of the great flavor profiles found in Thai cooking — sweet, salty, spicy and sour. Serve over hot cooked rice noodles, with Ginger Snow Peas and Peppers (see recipe, below) on the side.

- **4- to 6-quart slow cooker**

10 to 12	boneless skinless chicken thighs	10 to 12
2	cloves garlic, minced	2
2 tsp	paprika	10 mL
1/4 tsp	Chinese five-spice powder	1 mL
1/2 cup	sweet Thai chili sauce	125 mL
1/4 cup	ketchup	60 mL
2 tbsp	fish sauce	30 mL

1. Place chicken thighs in slow cooker stoneware. In a bowl, combine garlic, paprika, five-spice powder, chili sauce, ketchup, fish sauce and 2 tbsp (30 mL) water. Pour evenly over chicken.

2. Cover and cook on Low for 5 to 6 hours or on High for 2$\frac{1}{2}$ to 3 hours, until juices run clear when chicken is pierced.

> If you want to make your own Chinese five-spice powder, you'll need equal amounts of ground cinnamon, cloves, star anise, fennel seeds and Szechuan peppercorns. (You can substitute freshly ground black pepper for the Szechuan peppercorns.) Use a clean coffee grinder or a mortar and pestle to finely grind the spices together.

Makes 6 servings

This quick, easy side dish is an excellent accompaniment to an Asian entrée.

Ginger Snow Peas and Peppers

8 oz	snow peas, trimmed	250 mL
2	bell peppers (any color), cut into 3/4-inch (2 cm) strips	2
2 tbsp	rice vinegar	30 mL
1 tbsp	vegetable oil	15 mL
1 tsp	grated gingerroot	5 mL
	Salt and freshly ground black pepper	

1. Place a steamer basket in a saucepan filled with 1 inch (2.5 cm) water. Bring to a gentle boil. Add snow peas and bell peppers. Cover and cook for 2 to 4 minutes or until tender-crisp.

2. In a serving bowl, whisk together vinegar, oil and ginger. Add snow peas and peppers and toss to coat. Season to taste with salt and pepper. Serve immediately.

Chicken Sausage and Bean Casserole

Makes 6 to 8 servings

Makes 6 to 8 servings

Warm up a cold winter night with this rustic, sage-infused sausage and bean casserole. It's especially good served with a crisp green salad, a crusty baguette and white wine.

Tips

Any white bean can be used in this recipe. If you're not a fan of chickpeas, try white kidney beans. For some added color, use red kidney beans.

For the wine, try a Sauvignon Blanc or Chardonnay.

- **4- to 6-quart slow cooker, stoneware greased**
- *Food processor*

½	crusty baguette, torn into pieces	½
¼ cup	olive oil, divided	60 mL
	Kosher salt and freshly ground black pepper	
⅓ cup	fresh sage leaves (about 25)	75 mL
4	cloves garlic, minced	4
1	large onion, finely chopped	1
1 lb	chicken or turkey sausage, casings removed	500 g
4 cups	canned or cooked chickpeas (see page 120), drained and rinsed	1 L
½ cup	dry white wine	125 mL

1. In food processor, pulse baguette pieces to very coarse crumbs. Add 2 tbsp (30 mL) of the oil and pulse briefly to moisten crumbs. Season with salt and pepper; set aside.

2. In a skillet, heat the remaining oil over medium-high heat. Sauté sage for 2 to 3 minutes or until crisp. Using a slotted spoon, transfer sage to a plate lined with paper towels and set aside.

3. Add garlic and onion to skillet; sauté for 5 to 7 minutes or until onion is tender and translucent. Add sausage and cook, breaking up sausage with the back of a wooden spoon, for 3 to 5 minutes or until no longer pink inside. Stir in chickpeas and wine. Transfer to prepared slow cooker stoneware. Sprinkle with reserved bread crumbs.

4. Cover and cook on Low for 6 to 8 hours or on High for 3 to 5 hours, until bubbling. Season to taste with salt and pepper. Before serving, crumble reserved sage leaves over top.

Chicken in Orange Sesame Sauce

Makes 4 servings

This recipe is a fusion of two classic dishes, orange chicken and sesame chicken. Serve it with a crisp green vegetable, such as broccoli, on the side.

Tip

Broth (or stock) is one of the most indispensable pantry staples. Commercial broth cubes and powders are loaded with salt and just don't deliver the flavor of homemade stock or prepared broth. I like to keep 32-oz (1 L) Tetra Paks on hand, especially the sodium-reduced variety. They come in handy when you're making soups and stews.

The simplest way to toast sesame seeds is in a small dry skillet over medium heat. Cook, shaking the pan constantly, until the seeds are fragrant, about 3 minutes.

- **4- to 6-quart slow cooker**

2	oranges	2
1 tbsp	ground coriander	15 mL
1/2 tsp	cayenne pepper	2 mL
	Salt and freshly ground black pepper	
3 lbs	skinless bone-in chicken thighs or drumsticks	1.5 kg
2 tbsp	vegetable oil (approx.)	30 mL
1 tsp	sesame oil	5 mL
3	cloves garlic, minced	3
1 tbsp	minced gingerroot	15 mL
1/4 tsp	hot pepper flakes	1 mL
1/2 cup	chicken broth	125 mL
3 tbsp	tamari or dark soy sauce	45 mL
2 tbsp	cornstarch	30 mL
2 tbsp	cold water	30 mL
3	green onions, thinly sliced	3
1/2	red bell pepper, thinly sliced	1/2
1 cup	snow peas, trimmed	250 mL
	Hot cooked rice noodles or steamed rice	
2 tbsp	toasted sesame seeds	30 mL

1. Grate zest from oranges and set aside. Using a paring knife, remove peel and all of the pith from each orange, discarding peel and pith. Cut each orange into 1/4-inch (0.5 cm) slices and set aside.

2. In a bowl, combine coriander, cayenne, 1/2 tsp (2 mL) salt and 1/4 tsp (1 mL) black pepper. Rub all over chicken.

3. In a large nonstick skillet, heat half the vegetable oil and the sesame oil over medium-high heat. Cook chicken in batches, adding more oil as needed, for 2 to 3 minutes per side or until browned all over. Using a slotted spoon, transfer to slow cooker stoneware.

4. Add garlic, ginger and hot pepper flakes to skillet; sauté for 1 to 2 minutes. Stir in broth and tamari; increase heat to high and cook for 1 minute. Pour over chicken. Sprinkle with 1 tsp (5 mL) of the reserved orange zest and arrange orange slices on top.

Cooking times can vary a great deal between slow cooker manufacturers. Always let your food cook for the minimum amount of time before testing for doneness.

5. Cover and cook on Low for 5 to 6 hours or on High for $2\frac{1}{2}$ to 3 hours, until juices run clear when chicken is pierced.

6. In a small bowl, whisk together cornstarch and cold water. Stir into stoneware, along with green onions, red pepper and snow peas. Cover and cook on High for 10 to 15 minutes or until sauce is thickened. Season to taste with salt and pepper.

7. Arrange noodles on a platter. Place chicken on noodles and spoon vegetables and sauce over top. Sprinkle with the remaining orange zest and sesame seeds.

Tamari is similar to soy sauce, but is thicker in consistency and darker in color. It has a distinctly mellow flavor and is often used as a condiment or dipping sauce. It can be found in the Asian foods aisle of the supermarket or in an Asian market.

Santa Fe Turkey Breast

Makes 8 servings

This simple turkey roast evokes the flavors of the American Southwest. The chipotle pepper gives the salsa a nice smoky taste. It is best to use a chunky salsa, to thicken the sauce. For an authentic flair, serve with Mexican Corn (see recipe, below) on the side.

- Minimum 4-quart slow cooker

1	bone-in skin-on turkey breast (about 4 lbs/2 kg)	1
1 cup	thick and chunky salsa	250 mL
2 tbsp	liquid honey	30 mL
1 tbsp	chopped chipotle pepper in adobo sauce	15 mL
2 tbsp	cornstarch	30 mL
2 tbsp	cold water	30 mL

1. Place turkey, bone side down, in prepared slow cooker stoneware. In a small bowl, combine salsa, honey and chipotle pepper. Pour over turkey.

2. Cover and cook on Low for 6 to 8 hours or until a meat thermometer inserted in the thickest part of the breast registers 170°F (77°C). Using tongs, remove turkey from stoneware and let stand for 10 minutes before carving.

3. Meanwhile, in a small bowl, whisk together cornstarch and cold water. Stir into liquid in stoneware. Cover and cook on High for 10 to 15 minutes or until liquid is thickened.

4. Remove skin from turkey and discard. Slice turkey and arrange on a heated platter. Drizzle some of the gravy over turkey and serve the rest in a warmed gravy boat.

Makes 4 to 6 servings

This colorful side dish exhibits bold Southwestern flavors. It is delicious served hot, but makes a great picnic or barbecue side dish served at room temperature.

Mexican Corn

2 tbsp	butter	30 mL
1	onion, finely chopped	1
1	red bell pepper, finely chopped	1
1	jalapeño pepper, seeded and finely chopped	1
2 cups	frozen corn kernels, thawed	500 mL
	Salt and freshly ground black pepper	
1 tbsp	chopped fresh cilantro (optional)	15 mL

1. In a skillet, melt butter over medium-low heat. Sauté onion, red pepper, jalapeño and corn for 6 to 8 minutes or until vegetables are tender. Season to taste with salt and pepper. Serve garnished with cilantro (if using).

Turkey Bolognese with Spaghetti Squash

Makes 6 to 8 servings

Now here's a twist: a mildly flavored Bolognese sauce served over spaghetti squash instead of pasta. Of course, you can still serve it over pasta, but spaghetti squash is a healthier option. Sprinkle it with a little freshly grated Parmesan cheese, and add a tossed green salad on the side.

Tips

Choose a squash that is heavy for its size and has a hard, firm, deep-colored rind free of any blemishes or moldy spots.

To cook squash, halve it lengthwise and scoop out the seeds. Place cut side down on a rimmed baking sheet and bake in a 350°F (180°C) oven for 55 to 60 minutes or until strands of flesh separate easily when raked with a fork. Let cool slightly, then use a fork to rake the flesh into spaghetti-like strands.

To save time getting this meal on the table, cook the squash the day before and refrigerate the whole halves until ready to use. Reheat it gently in the microwave on Medium (50%) power for 2 minutes or in a 350°F (180°C) oven for 10 to 12 minutes or until warmed through. Rake into strands before serving.

- 4- to 5-quart slow cooker

2 tbsp	butter	30 mL
2 tbsp	olive oil	30 mL
1	onion, finely chopped	1
1	small carrot, finely chopped	1
1	stalk celery, finely chopped	1
1½ lbs	lean ground turkey	750 g
4 oz	thickly sliced pancetta, finely chopped	125 g
	Salt and freshly ground black pepper	
½ cup	dry white wine	125 mL
1	can (28 oz/796 mL) crushed tomatoes	1
½ cup	chicken broth	125 mL
¼ cup	hot evaporated milk or heavy or whipping (35%) cream	60 mL
	Salt and freshly ground black pepper	
1	spaghetti squash (2 to 3 lbs/1 to 1.5 kg), cooked (see tips, at left)	1

1. In a large skillet, heat butter and oil over medium-high heat. Sauté onion, carrot and celery for 5 to 7 minutes or until onion is tender and translucent. Add turkey and pancetta; cook, breaking up turkey with the back of a wooden spoon, for 3 to 5 minutes or until turkey is no longer pink. Add wine and cook, stirring, for 3 to 5 minutes or until wine has almost evaporated. Transfer to slow cooker stoneware. Stir in tomatoes and broth.

2. Cover and cook on Low for 6 to 8 hours or on High for 3 to 4 hours, until bubbling. Just before serving, stir in evaporated milk. Season to taste with salt and pepper. Serve over spaghetti squash.

Pancetta is an Italian bacon that is cured with salt and spices but is not smoked. It is sold in a sausage-like roll in the deli department of the supermarket. Tightly wrapped, it can be stored in the refrigerator for up to 3 weeks or frozen for up to 6 months.

Turkey Osso Buco

Makes 6 servings

Although classic Italian osso buco is made with veal shanks, this slow cooker version is tasty proof that turkey thighs can be a first-rate substitute.

Tips

This comforting meal could also be served over mashed potatoes instead of pasta.

Look for turkey parts after holidays, such as Thanksgiving and Christmas, when they can be purchased more economically. Freeze them to have on hand for dishes like this one.

- **Minimum 5-quart slow cooker**

2 tbsp	all-purpose flour	30 mL
1/2 tsp	salt	2 mL
1/4 tsp	freshly ground black pepper	1 mL
3 lbs	turkey thighs, skin removed	1.5 kg
2 tbsp	olive oil (approx.)	30 mL
6	cloves garlic, minced	6
3	carrots, chopped	3
3	stalks celery, chopped	3
1	onion, finely chopped	1
1	can (7 1/2 oz/213 mL) tomato sauce	1
1/2 cup	dry white wine	125 mL
1/4 cup	chicken broth	60 mL
1 tsp	grated lemon zest	5 mL
1 tsp	dried thyme	5 mL
3 cups	hot cooked pasta, such as penne or farfalle	750 mL

1. In a bowl, combine flour, salt and pepper. Sprinkle over turkey, coating evenly.

2. In a large skillet, heat half the oil over medium-high heat. Cook turkey in batches, adding more oil as needed, for 3 to 4 minutes per side or until browned all over. Remove from heat.

3. In slow cooker stoneware, combine garlic, carrots, celery and onion. Arrange turkey on top.

4. In a bowl, combine tomato sauce, wine, broth, lemon zest and thyme. Pour over turkey.

5. Cover and cook on Low for 6 to 8 hours or on High for 3 to 4 hours, until meat is falling off the bones. Using a slotted spoon, transfer turkey to a cutting board. Remove meat from bones and cut into large chunks. (Discard bones.)

6. Stir pasta into liquid in stoneware. Using a slotted spoon, spoon pasta onto individual serving plates and top with turkey. Ladle sauce over top.

Turkey and Couscous Stuffed Peppers

Makes 4 servings

Do you like stuffed peppers? Get a head start on dinner with this fresh take on a slow-simmered meal. Make a batch when peppers are in season. If there are just two of you, cook all 4 peppers, and you'll have a second meal ready to go — these peppers reheat surprisingly well.

Tip

Use an apple corer to cut a small hole in the bottom of each pepper. This will allow moisture and steam to penetrate, promoting even cooking.

- **4- to 5-quart slow cooker**

4	large red or green bell peppers	4
8 oz	lean ground turkey	250 g
1/2 cup	chopped onion	125 mL
1	clove garlic, finely chopped	1
1	can (14 oz/398 mL) tomato sauce	1
1/2 tsp	ground cumin	2 mL
1/4 tsp	ground cinnamon	1 mL
1/4 tsp	salt	1 mL
1/8 tsp	cayenne pepper	0.5 mL
2/3 cup	couscous	150 mL
	Crumbled feta or goat cheese (optional)	
	Pine nuts (optional)	
	Chopped fresh cilantro (optional)	

1. Cut around stem on each bell pepper to remove stem. Scoop out seeds and membranes. Rinse peppers.

2. In a nonstick skillet, cook turkey, onion and garlic over medium-high heat, breaking up turkey with the back of a wooden spoon, for about 5 minutes or until turkey is no longer pink. Drain off any liquid. Stir in tomato sauce, cumin, cinnamon, salt and cayenne. Stir in couscous.

3. Spoon turkey mixture into peppers, dividing evenly. Pour 1/2 cup (125 mL) water into slow cooker stoneware. Set peppers upright in water.

4. Cover and cook on Low for 5 to 7 hours or until peppers are tender. Using a spatula or a large serving spoon, gently remove peppers to a serving dish. Discard cooking liquid.

5. Serve stuffed peppers sprinkled with cheese, pine nuts and cilantro (if using).

Turkey and Cranberry Cobbler

Makes 6 to 8 servings

Some dishes evoke the feeling of home. This old-fashioned favorite has been given an updated twist with the addition of dried cranberries.

Tips

To prepare mushrooms, wipe them with a damp paper towel. Don't rinse or soak them, or they'll absorb water and turn mushy when cooked.

Puff pastry package sizes vary between brands, ranging from 14 to 18 oz (397 to 511 g). If your package is slightly larger or smaller, half a package will still work just fine for this recipe.

It's so easy to use frozen puff pastry dough, and it looks decadently impressive on top of this stew, but you can also serve this stew in puff pastry shells. Bake shells according to package directions and serve stew mixture spooned into shells.

- **4- to 6-quart slow cooker**
- *Large baking sheet*

⅓ cup	all-purpose flour	75 mL
1 tsp	ground dried sage	5 mL
1 tsp	salt	5 mL
¼ tsp	freshly ground black pepper	1 mL
2½ lbs	boneless skinless turkey thighs, cut into 1-inch (2.5 cm) cubes	1.25 kg
2 tbsp	vegetable oil (approx.)	30 mL
8	mushrooms, quartered	8
2	onions, chopped	2
2	carrots, diced	2
2	stalks celery, finely chopped	2
1 tsp	dried thyme	5 mL
1½ cups	chicken broth	375 mL
⅓ cup	dried cranberries	75 mL
1 cup	frozen peas, thawed	250 mL
1	sheet frozen puff pastry (half a 14 oz/397 g package), thawed (see tips, at left)	1

1. In a bowl or a heavy plastic bag, combine flour, sage, salt and pepper. In batches, dredge turkey in flour mixture, shaking off any excess. (Once all the turkey is coated, reserve the remaining flour mixture.)

2. In a large skillet, heat half the oil over medium-high heat. Cook turkey in batches, adding more oil as needed, for 2 to 3 minutes or until browned all over. Using a slotted spoon, transfer to slow cooker stoneware.

3. Add mushrooms, onions, carrots, celery and thyme to skillet; sauté for 5 minutes or until vegetables are tender. Stir in reserved flour mixture until vegetables are coated. Reduce heat to medium. Stir in broth and bring to a boil, stirring and scraping up any brown bits from pan. Pour over turkey. Stir in cranberries.

4. Cover and cook on Low for 6 to 8 hours or on High for 3 to 4 hours, until turkey is tender.

5. Stir in peas. Cover and cook on High for 10 to 15 minutes or until heated through.

Slow cooker stoneware inserts are heatproof, so you can top any hot stew made in the slow cooker with a pastry crust or biscuit dough and put it in a preheated oven — it won't suffer a temperature shock and crack.

6. Meanwhile, preheat oven to 375°F (190°C). On a lightly floured surface, roll out pastry to a 15- by 10-inch (38 by 25 cm) rectangle. Cut into 6 or 8 squares (or use a large, round cookie cutter to cut circles) and place at least $\frac{1}{2}$ inch (1 cm) apart on baking sheet.

7. Bake pastry pieces for 15 to 20 minutes or until puffed and golden brown.

8. Ladle cobbler into serving bowls and top each with a pastry crust. Serve immediately.

Turkey, Bacon and Avocado Wraps

Makes 8 wraps

My friend Lisa Gray, who lived in New Zealand for many years, says this is one of the country's most popular sandwich choices. They like to call it a BLAT. In this version, the turkey is cooked slowly in the slow cooker, then shredded and topped with bacon and avocado. Yum! This mixture makes an excellent panini as well.

Tip

If time is a concern, you can place the turkey in the stoneware without browning it first. Cook the bacon separately and layer it on each tortilla just before serving.

- **4- to 6-quart slow cooker**

4	slices bacon, cut into ½-inch (1 cm) pieces	4
2 lbs	turkey drumsticks or thighs, skin removed	1 kg
¾ cup	barbecue sauce	175 mL
2 tbsp	taco seasoning mix	30 mL
8	10-inch (25 cm) flour tortillas	8
1	ripe avocado, mashed	1
2 cups	shredded lettuce	500 mL
½ cup	roasted red bell peppers, drained and chopped	125 mL

1. In a nonstick skillet, cook bacon over medium heat, stirring occasionally, for 4 to 6 minutes or until almost crisp. Add turkey and cook for 3 to 4 minutes per side or until browned all over. Using a slotted spoon or tongs, transfer turkey and bacon to slow cooker stoneware. Discard fat from pan.

2. In a glass measuring cup, combine barbecue sauce and taco seasoning. Pour over turkey and bacon.

3. Cover and cook on Low for 6 to 8 hours or on High for 3 to 4 hours, until turkey is falling off the bones.

4. Using a slotted spoon, transfer turkey to a cutting board. Using two forks, pull meat off bones in shreds and discard bones. Return meat to sauce in slow cooker to keep warm. (Turkey mixture will hold on Low, with occasional stirring, for up to 2 hours.)

5. Preheat oven to 350°F (180°C). Wrap a stack of tortillas in foil and heat for 10 minutes.

6. Spread each tortilla with avocado. Layer lettuce, turkey mixture and peppers on top. Drizzle with sauce, if desired. Fold right side of tortilla over filling. Fold bottom of tortilla up, then fold left side over and continue rolling until the filling is enclosed.

Turkey and Pepper Cheese Steak Heroes

Makes 6 servings

Here's an easy-to-make sandwich the whole family will enjoy. Add a tossed Caesar salad and your dinner is done!

Tip
Any prepared oil and vinegar salad dressing can be used in this recipe. For extra flavor, try Greek dressing or sun-dried tomato dressing.

- **3- to 5-quart slow cooker**

3 lbs	turkey thighs, skin removed	1.5 kg
1/3 cup	Italian salad dressing	75 mL
1 tbsp	vegetable oil	15 mL
1	red bell pepper, cut into thin strips	1
1	yellow bell pepper, cut into thin strips	1
1	onion, sliced	1
6	kaiser rolls, split	6
1/2 cup	herb and garlic spreadable cream cheese	125 mL

1. Place turkey in slow cooker stoneware. Pour dressing over turkey.

2. Cover and cook on Low for 6 to 8 hours or on High for 3 to 4 hours, until turkey is falling off the bones.

3. Using a slotted spoon, transfer turkey to a cutting board. Using two forks, pull meat off bones in shreds and discard bones. Return meat to sauce in slow cooker to keep warm. (Turkey mixture will hold on Low, with occasional stirring, for up to 2 hours.)

4. In a skillet, heat oil over medium-high heat. Sauté red pepper, yellow pepper and onion for 6 to 8 minutes or until softened.

5. Spread bottom half of each roll with 1 tbsp (15 mL) of the cream cheese, then top with turkey mixture and pepper mixture. Cover with top half.

Low and Slow Turkey Joes

Makes 4 to 6 servings

Everyone will love this easy turkey version of sloppy Joes.

Tips

Because ground turkey has such a mild flavor, I often find I need to add extra seasoning to it.

Leftover turkey mixture can be used to top baked potatoes or nachos, for a second-day supper rescue!

• **4- to 5-quart slow cooker**

1 tbsp	vegetable oil	15 mL
1½ lbs	lean ground turkey	750 g
1	small onion, finely chopped	1
1	stalk celery, finely chopped	1
1	can (14 oz/398 mL) diced tomatoes	1
2 tbsp	packed brown sugar	30 mL
1½ tsp	ground cumin	7 mL
1 tsp	chili powder	5 mL
½ tsp	salt	2 mL
3 tbsp	Worcestershire sauce	45 mL
6	whole wheat hamburger buns, split and toasted	6
1 cup	shredded mozzarella or provolone cheese	250 mL
1 cup	shredded carrots	250 mL

1. In a large nonstick skillet, heat oil over medium-high heat. Cook turkey, breaking up with the back of a wooden spoon, for 5 minutes or until no longer pink. Using a slotted spoon, transfer to slow cooker stoneware.

2. Stir in onion, celery, tomatoes, brown sugar, cumin, chili powder, salt and Worcestershire sauce.

3. Cover and cook on Low for 6 to 8 hours or on High for 3 to 4 hours, until bubbling.

4. Spoon turkey mixture over bottom halves of buns. Top with mozzarella and carrot. Cover with top halves.

Beef and Veal

Braised Pot Roast with Caramelized Vegetables

Makes 6 to 8 servings

Use a full-bodied red wine, such as a Shiraz or Bordeaux, to bring out the richest flavor of the gravy in this pot roast. The red wine permeates the meat, adding a robust flavor. You can vary the vegetables, choosing seasonal produce from your local farmer's market. Think about the cooking time, and select vegetables that require the same amount of cooking, so they can all go into the oven at the same time.

Tips

Once the roast is in the slow cooker, it's a good idea to turn it halfway through the cooking time. That way, both sides will evenly braise in the cooking liquid.

You can substitute 1 sprig of fresh rosemary for the dried.

- **Minimum 4-quart slow cooker**
- *Rimmed baking sheet, lined with parchment paper*

3	carrots	3
⅓ cup	all-purpose flour	75 mL
	Salt and freshly ground black pepper	
1	boneless beef cross rib, blade, chuck or shoulder pot roast (about 4 lbs/2 kg)	1
3 tbsp	olive oil, divided	45 mL
1 cup	red wine	250 mL
1 cup	beef broth	250 mL
2 tbsp	tomato paste	30 mL
1 tsp	dried rosemary	5 mL
1	bay leaf	1
8	cloves garlic, smashed	8
2	parsnips, cut into 1-inch (2.5 cm) chunks	2
2	sweet potatoes, cut into 1-inch (2.5 cm) chunks	2
1	celery root, peeled and cut into 1-inch (2.5 cm) chunks	1
1	onion, cut into wedges	1
1	stalk celery, chopped	1
2 tbsp	cold water	25 mL

1. Chop 1 of the carrots into 3 pieces and place in slow cooker stoneware. Cut the remaining carrots into 1-inch (2.5 cm) chunks and set aside.

2. In a bowl, combine flour, 1 tsp (5 mL) salt and ½ tsp (2 mL) pepper. Pat roast dry with paper towels and coat all over with flour mixture. Reserve the remaining flour mixture.

3. In a large skillet, heat 2 tbsp (30 mL) of the oil over medium-high heat. Cook roast, turning with two wooden spoons, for 7 to 10 minutes or until browned all over. Transfer to stoneware.

4. Add wine to skillet and bring to a boil, scraping up any brown bits from pan. Stir in broth, tomato paste, rosemary and bay leaf. Pour into stoneware.

5. Cover and cook on Low for 8 to 12 hours or on High for 4 to 6 hours, until roast is fork-tender.

Variation

This is a perfect autumn dish. Feel free to use your favorite fall vegetable combination. Be inspired by your local farmer's market, your garden or what you have at home. Other choices could include cubed zucchini, halved small red new potatoes, cubed acorn or butternut squash and sweet Vidalia or red onions.

6. During the last hour of cooking time, preheat oven to 425°F (220°C). On prepared baking sheet, combine reserved carrot chunks, garlic, parsnips, sweet potatoes, celery root, onion and celery. Toss with the remaining oil and season to taste with salt and pepper; spread into a single layer. Roast for 40 minutes, turning once, until vegetables are tender.

7. Transfer beef to a cutting board and tent with foil to keep warm. Strain braising liquid from stoneware into a saucepan. Discard solids.

8. In a bowl, whisk together reserved flour mixture and cold water until a smooth paste forms. Whisk into braising liquid and bring to a boil over medium-high heat. Reduce heat and simmer, stirring often, for about 10 minutes or until liquid is thickened.

9. Slice beef across the grain into $\frac{1}{2}$-inch (1 cm) slices. Arrange on a warmed platter, with roasted vegetables alongside. Drizzle beef with some of the gravy and serve the rest in a warmed gravy boat.

Slow Cooker Caramelized Onions

In the stoneware of a 4- to 6-quart slow cooker, toss together 4 large onions, thinly sliced, and 2 tbsp (30 mL) olive oil. Cover and cook on High for 6 to 8 hours, stirring occasionally. Store in an airtight container in the refrigerator for up to 2 weeks.

Pot Roast with Dill Sauce

Makes 4 to 6 servings

Beef pot roast is a versatile and economical dish. Thanks to the addition of a creamy dill sauce, this version has a Danish influence. Serve it with egg noodles, which pair well with the dill sauce. If you like, sprinkle the finished dish with minced fresh dill.

Tips

Homemade beef broth is best, but a 10-oz (284 mL) can of condensed beef broth, plus a can of water, will make enough broth for this recipe. Ready-to-use broth in convenient Tetra-Paks is also a handy ingredient and doesn't need to be diluted. Avoid using cubes and powders, which tend to be very salty.

A well-marbled beef cross rib or chuck pot roast is a good choice. The marbling produces a very tender result.

- **Minimum 4-quart slow cooker**

4 tbsp	all-purpose flour, divided	60 mL
1 tsp	salt	5 mL
¼ tsp	freshly ground white pepper	1 mL
1	boneless beef cross rib, blade, chuck or shoulder pot roast (about 2 lbs/1 kg)	1
2 tbsp	vegetable oil	30 mL
4	cloves garlic, finely chopped	4
½ tsp	dried dillweed	2 mL
1 cup	beef broth	250 mL
1 tbsp	Dijon mustard	15 mL
4	Yukon Gold potatoes, cut into 1-inch (2.5 cm) cubes	4
1	large onion, cut into 12 wedges	1
1	bag (12 oz/340 g) baby carrots	1
½ tsp	lemon pepper	2 mL
1 tsp	dried dillweed (or 1 tbsp/15 mL fresh dill)	5 mL
1 cup	regular or light sour cream	250 mL

1. In a bowl or a large sealable plastic bag, combine 2 tbsp (30 mL) of the flour, salt and white pepper. Dredge roast in flour mixture, turning to coat evenly. Discard any excess flour mixture.

2. In a large skillet, heat oil over medium heat. Cook roast, turning with two wooden spoons, for 7 to 10 minutes or until browned all over. Transfer to slow cooker stoneware.

3. In a small bowl, combine garlic, dill, broth and mustard. Pour over roast. Arrange potatoes, onion and carrots around roast. Sprinkle with lemon pepper.

4. Cover and cook on Low for 8 to 10 hours or on High for 4 to 6 hours, until roast and vegetables are fork-tender. Transfer roast to a cutting board and vegetables to a warmed platter and cover to keep warm.

5. In a small bowl, whisk together the remaining flour, dill and 2 tbsp (30 mL) water until smooth. Spoon off any fat from liquid in slow cooker. Pour liquid into a saucepan and bring to a boil over medium-high heat. Stir in flour mixture and cook, stirring constantly, for 2 to 3 minutes or until thickened. Remove from heat and stir in sour cream.

6. Slice meat across the grain and pour sauce over beef and vegetables.

Sheila's Mother's Coffee Pot Roast

Makes 8 to 10 servings

This recipe came to me from my friend Sheila McKee-Protopapas, who is a biology professor. She inherited the recipe from her mother, and it's a perfect example of how a recipe evolves, created with pride and joy by one generation after another. Sheila's family has made it for years. She says the flavor is out of this world, and I have to agree!

Tips

Adding vinegar, apple juice or wine to a pot roast helps tenderize the meat while it simmers.

Slow cooking helps tenderize less expensive cuts of meat. Pot roast benefits from long, slow cooking on Low, but if you are short of time you can use the High setting — you'll still create fork-tender meat.

- **Minimum 4-quart slow cooker**

1	boneless beef cross rib, blade, chuck or shoulder pot roast (about 4 lbs/2 kg)	1
1	head garlic, cloves separated (or 1 onion, cut into wedges)	1
1 cup	white or cider vinegar	250 mL
2 tbsp	vegetable oil	30 mL
2 cups	strong brewed coffee	500 mL
2 tbsp	gin or whisky (optional)	30 mL

1. Using the tip of a sharp knife, slit roast all over and insert garlic cloves (or onion wedges). Place roast in a bowl or a large sealable plastic bag and pour vinegar into slits. Cover bowl or seal bag and refrigerate for at least 24 hours or up to 48 hours. Drain off vinegar and discard.

2. In a large skillet, heat oil over medium-high heat. Cook roast, turning with two wooden spoons, for 7 to 10 minutes or until browned all over. Transfer to slow cooker stoneware.

3. Add coffee, gin (if using) and 2 cups (500 mL) water to skillet and stir to scrape up any brown bits from pan. Pour into stoneware.

4. Cover and cook on Low for 8 to 10 hours or on High for 4 to 6 hours, until roast is fork-tender. Transfer roast to a cutting board, tent with foil and let stand for 10 minutes.

5. Skim fat from pan juices. Slice meat across the grain and serve drizzled with juices.

BBQ Pot Roast Sandwiches

Makes 4 to 6 servings

This recipe, featuring the popular sweet and spicy flavor combination, makes the perfect dish for a potluck. Cook the meat in advance, then shred it, return it to the slow cooker and let people help themselves. I recommend it served on thick kaiser rolls, along with flavored mayonnaise.

Tip

To make a flavored mayonnaise for these sandwiches, combine ½ cup (125 mL) mayonnaise and 1 tbsp (15 mL) Dijon mustard or horseradish. You can raid your pantry for other ingredients, such as curry powder, mango chutney, paprika or freshly chopped garlic, to make your own flavor combinations. Double or triple the amounts as needed.

- **Minimum 4-quart slow cooker**

2	cloves garlic, minced	2
1 tbsp	grated gingerroot	15 mL
1 tbsp	chili powder	15 mL
½ tsp	ground cumin	2 mL
¼ tsp	hot pepper flakes	1 mL
¾ cup	root beer	175 mL
⅓ cup	hickory-flavored barbecue sauce	75 mL
2 tbsp	tomato paste	30 mL
1 tbsp	freshly squeezed lemon juice	15 mL
2 tsp	Worcestershire sauce	10 mL
1	beef sirloin tip roast (3 to 3½ lbs/ 1.5 to 1.75 kg)	1
	Salt and freshly ground black pepper	
2 tsp	olive oil	10 mL
1	onion, cut into wedges	1
2 tbsp	cornstarch	30 mL
2 tbsp	cold water	30 mL
4 to 6	crusty kaiser rolls, split and warmed	4 to 6

1. In a saucepan, whisk together garlic, ginger, chili powder, cumin, hot pepper flakes, root beer, barbecue sauce, tomato paste, lemon juice and Worcestershire sauce. Bring to a boil over medium-high heat. Reduce heat and simmer gently, stirring, for 5 minutes. Remove from heat.

2. Pat roast dry with paper towels and sprinkle lightly with salt and pepper. In a large skillet, heat oil over medium-high heat. Cook roast, turning with two wooden spoons, for 7 to 10 minutes or until browned all over. Transfer to slow cooker stoneware. Arrange onion around roast. Pour sauce over top.

3. Cover and cook on Low for 8 to 10 hours or on High for 4 to 6 hours, until roast is fork-tender. Transfer roast to a cutting board and, using a slotted spoon, transfer onion to a bowl.

4. Pour cooking liquid from stoneware into a saucepan and skim off as much fat as possible. In a small bowl, whisk together cornstarch and water until smooth. Whisk into saucepan and bring to a boil over high heat, whisking constantly, until liquid is slightly thickened.

5. Thinly slice roast across the grain (it may be so tender that it falls apart). Top warm kaisers with sliced meat and reserved onions; spoon sauce over top.

Braised Brisket with Cranberries

Makes 6 to 8 servings

This festive dish is perfect for the holidays. The brilliant cranberries stand out like jewels, and there is plenty of juice to spoon over creamy mashed potatoes. Make sure you buy fresh brisket (not corned beef). An inside round roast would also work well.

Tips

If you prefer thicker gravy, keep the cooked brisket warm and pour the cooking liquid into a saucepan. Measure 2 tbsp (30 mL) all-purpose flour into a small bowl and add ¼ cup (60 mL) of the cooking liquid, 2 tbsp (30 mL) at a time, stirring to blend thoroughly after each addition. Stir flour mixture into saucepan and cook over medium heat, stirring, until thickened.

If you only have a smaller (4-quart) slow cooker, cut the brisket in half and lay one half on top of the other. It is a good idea to flip the two pieces halfway through the cooking time to ensure even braising in the cooking liquid.

- **Minimum 4-quart slow cooker**

1	double beef brisket (4 to 5 lbs/2 to 2.5 kg), trimmed	1
3 tbsp	all-purpose flour	45 mL
	Salt and freshly ground black pepper	
1 cup	beef broth	250 mL
1 cup	dry red wine, such as Cabernet Sauvignon	250 mL
2 tbsp	light (fancy) molasses	30 mL
24	pearl onions, peeled (see tip, page 188)	24
2 cups	fresh or frozen cranberries, thawed if frozen	500 mL
1	bay leaf	1

1. Rub brisket all over with flour and season with salt and pepper. Place in slow cooker stoneware.

2. In a bowl, combine broth, wine, molasses and ½ cup (125 mL) water. Pour over brisket. Add onions, cranberries and bay leaf.

3. Cover and cook on Low for 10 to 12 hours or on High for 5 to 6 hours, until brisket is very fork-tender. Transfer brisket to a cutting board, tent with foil and let stand for 10 minutes.

4. Slice brisket very thinly across the grain and arrange on a warmed platter. Remove bay leaf from sauce and skim off as much fat as possible. Pour sauce over brisket or serve separately in a gravy boat.

Mexican Brisket

Makes 6 to 8 servings

The brisket is a large, fatty cut of meat from the front of the steer. The slow cooker is the ideal way to cook it, leading to very tender meat. Mexican flavors add heat and give traditional brisket a new twist. Serve with mashed potatoes sprinkled with shredded Cheddar and minced green onions for a Tex-Mex meal.

Tips

If you have leftovers, shred the meat to use for taco filling. Serve it with the traditional taco condiments: salsa, sour cream, shredded cheese and guacamole. You've got two meals!

If you halve this recipe, reduce the cooking time to about 6 hours on Low or 3 hours on High.

Variation

Replace the brisket with a boneless cross rib, blade, chuck or shoulder pot roast (2½ to 3 lbs/1.25 to 1.5 kg). Prepare as directed at right. Cook on Low for 8 to 12 hours or on High for 4 to 6 hours, until fork-tender.

- Minimum 5-quart slow cooker

1	double beef brisket (4 to 5 lbs/ 2 to 2.5 kg), trimmed	1
	Freshly ground black pepper	
1 tbsp	vegetable oil	15 mL
4	cloves garlic, minced	4
1	onion, thinly sliced	1
1	can (28 oz/796 mL) diced tomatoes	1
1 tbsp	dried oregano	15 mL
1 tbsp	chili powder	15 mL
1 tbsp	packed brown sugar	15 mL
1 tsp	ground cumin	5 mL
1 tsp	dried thyme	5 mL
1 tbsp	red wine vinegar	15 mL
2 tsp	finely chopped chipotle pepper in adobo sauce	10 mL
2 tbsp	cornstarch	30 mL
2 tbsp	cold water	30 mL
2	green onions, sliced	2

1. If necessary, cut brisket in half to fit slow cooker stoneware. Generously sprinkle pepper all over brisket. In a large skillet, heat oil over medium-high heat. Cook brisket, one piece at a time if necessary, turning with two wooden spoons, for 7 to 10 minutes or until browned all over. Transfer to stoneware.

2. In a bowl, combine garlic, onion, tomatoes, oregano, chili powder, brown sugar, cumin, thyme, vinegar and chipotle pepper. Pour over brisket.

3. Cover and cook on Low for 10 to 12 hours or on High for 5 to 6 hours, until brisket is fork-tender. Transfer brisket to a cutting board, tent with foil and let stand for 10 minutes.

4. Skim off as much fat as possible from cooking liquid and transfer to a saucepan. In a small bowl, whisk together cornstarch and water. Add to saucepan and bring to a boil over high heat, whisking constantly, until liquid is slightly thickened.

5. Slice brisket very thinly across the grain. Spoon some of the sauce onto a warmed platter. Arrange meat on top. Sprinkle with green onions and drizzle with the remaining sauce.

Slow Cooker Steak with Creamy Red Wine Gravy

Makes 4 to 6 servings

For best results in this recipe, use a 4- to 6-quart oval slow cooker to ensure that the steak is completely covered with sauce. Serve it with steamed broccoli and lots of crusty baguette slices to soak up the gravy. The next day, you can use leftovers to make open-faced sandwiches. Toast bread or baguette slices, then butter them, pile with steak and drizzle with gravy.

Tips

You will need a large oval slow cooker to cook the steak in one piece. When placed in the stoneware, the meat may extend up the sides, but it will shrink as it cooks. If you are using a smaller slow cooker, cut the steak in half.

You can also use portobello mushrooms in this recipe. You'll need enough to cover the steak; 3 larger mushrooms may be enough.

• **Minimum 4-quart slow cooker (preferably oval)**

1	beef flank steak (1½ to 2 lbs/ 750 g to 1 kg), trimmed	1
	Salt and freshly ground black pepper	
2 tbsp	all-purpose flour	30 mL
12	brown mushrooms, such as cremini or shiitake, stems removed	12
6	green onions, white parts only, thinly sliced	6
4	cloves garlic, minced	4
1 tsp	dried Italian seasoning	5 mL
¼ cup	red wine	60 mL
1	can (10 oz/284 mL) condensed cream of mushroom soup (preferably reduced-sodium)	1

1. Season steak with salt and pepper and coat each side evenly with flour. Transfer to slow cooker stoneware. Arrange mushrooms and green onions on top. Sprinkle with garlic, Italian seasoning and 1 tsp (5 mL) pepper.

2. In a bowl, combine wine, soup and 2 tbsp (30 mL) water. Pour over steak and vegetables.

3. Cover and cook on Low for 8 to 10 hours or on High for 4 to 5 hours, until steak is fork-tender. Transfer steak to a cutting board and mushrooms to a warmed deep platter. Tent steak with foil and let stand for 10 minutes.

4. Slice steak very thinly across the grain and arrange on platter with mushrooms. Season gravy in stoneware with salt and pepper. Pour over steak and mushrooms.

Steak with Mushrooms and Mustard

Makes 4 servings

Steak and mushrooms share a natural affinity. I've given this pairing a contemporary touch by using wild mushrooms. This dish tastes great with polenta or fresh egg noodles.

Tips

Feel free to use your favorite variety of Dijon mustard, such as Provençal, red wine or peppercorn.

Slow cooking helps tenderize less expensive cuts of meat. Braising steak benefits from long, slow cooking on Low, but if you are short of time, count on 6 hours on High to produce fork-tender meat.

Make Ahead

This dish can be assembled up to 24 hours in advance. Prepare through step 2, cover and refrigerate. The next day, place stoneware in slow cooker and proceed with step 3.

- **4- to 6-quart slow cooker**

1	boneless beef blade, shoulder or inside round steak (about 1½ lbs/750 g)	1
1 tbsp	all-purpose flour	15 mL
4 oz	cremini or portobello mushroom caps, coarsely chopped	125 g
4	shallots or small onions, halved	4
3	cloves garlic, thinly sliced, divided	3
1	bay leaf	1
½ tsp	dried thyme	2 mL
1 cup	beef broth	250 mL
3 tbsp	Dijon mustard	45 mL
2 tbsp	brandy or beef broth	30 mL
2 tbsp	butter	30 mL
4 oz	oyster or button mushrooms, sliced	125 g
4 oz	shiitake mushroom caps, sliced	125 g
	Salt and freshly ground black pepper	
¼ cup	crumbled goat cheese (optional)	60 mL

1. Trim steak and cut into 4 pieces. Coat both sides of each piece with flour and place in slow cooker stoneware. Sprinkle cremini mushrooms, shallots, two-thirds of the garlic, bay leaf and thyme over beef.

2. In a bowl, whisk together broth, mustard and brandy. Pour over beef and vegetables.

3. Cover and cook on Low for 8 to 10 hours or on High for 4 to 5 hours, until steak is fork-tender.

4. Just before serving, in a large nonstick skillet, melt butter over medium-high heat. Sauté oyster mushrooms, shiitake mushrooms, the remaining garlic and salt and pepper to taste for 3 to 5 minutes or until mushrooms are softened.

5. Using a slotted spoon, transfer steak and vegetables to a warmed platter. Discard bay leaf. If using goat cheese, stir into cooking liquid until melted. Season sauce to taste with salt and pepper, then spoon over steak. Top with sautéed mushrooms.

Ranchero Steak and Beans

Makes 4 servings

A cowboy steak is a cut of beef that is usually less expensive and less popular, and one that needs marinating or slow cooking to taste good. This blade steak is cut up, layered with potatoes, onions and baked beans and cooked until the meat is flavorful and very tender. This is a simple and pleasing meal, and it's very economical.

Tips

I like to use baked beans in barbecue sauce, but you can substitute maple-flavored baked beans or beans in tomato sauce.

Save and freeze leftovers from this tasty meal in small plastic containers for a healthy, microwave-ready lunch box filler.

- **Minimum 4-quart slow cooker**

1	boneless beef blade, shoulder or inside round steak (about 2 lbs/1 kg)	1
4	potatoes, cut into 1-inch (2.5 cm) cubes	4
1	onion, chopped	1
1 tsp	salt	5 mL
¼ tsp	freshly ground black pepper	1 mL
1	can (28 oz/796 mL) baked beans in barbecue sauce	1

1. Trim steak and cut into 4 pieces. Place in slow cooker stoneware.

2. Arrange potatoes and onion over beef and sprinkle with salt and pepper. Spread beans over beef mixture.

3. Cover and cook on Low for 8 to 10 hours or on High for 4 to 5 hours, until steak and potatoes are tender and liquid is bubbling.

> Cut from under the blade or shoulder roast, blade or shoulder steak is a tough piece of meat that is not tender enough to grill, broil or pan-fry, but is very flavorful when slow-cooked or braised.

Steak Fajitas with Tomato Corn Relish

Makes 6 servings

This is a good meal for a casual get-together with friends. Have everything ready and let your guests assemble the fajitas themselves. Make it a Mexican party and throw together some lime margaritas!

Tips

If you like heat, add a minced jalapeño to the relish.

How to fill and fold tortillas: Spoon filling along the center of the warm tortilla. Fold the right side of the tortilla over the filling, then fold up the bottom. Fold the left side over the filling and wrap it around to form a tight roll. To prevent drips, wrap a small piece of foil, waxed paper or parchment paper around the bottom of the fajita.

- Minimum 4-quart slow cooker

1	beef flank steak (about 2 lbs/1 kg), trimmed	1
2	onions, thinly sliced	2
2	cloves garlic, finely chopped	2
1 cup	thick and chunky salsa	250 mL
1½ tsp	smoked paprika	7 mL
1 tsp	salt, divided	5 mL
½ tsp	ground cumin	2 mL
1	red bell pepper, cut into strips	1
1	yellow bell pepper, cut into strips	1
12	10-inch (25 cm) cheese-flavored flour tortillas	12
½ cup	sour cream	125 mL
2 cups	shredded Monterey Jack cheese	500 mL
1	large tomato, diced	1
1	can (14 oz/398 mL) corn kernels, drained	1
3 tbsp	finely chopped fresh cilantro	45 mL
1 tbsp	freshly squeezed lime juice	15 mL
¼ tsp	freshly ground black pepper	1 mL

1. Place steak in slow cooker stoneware. Spread onions on top.

2. In a bowl, combine garlic, salsa, paprika, ½ tsp (2 mL) of the salt and cumin. Pour over steak and onions.

3. Cover and cook on Low for 6 to 8 hours or on High for 3 to 4 hours, until steak is tender. Transfer steak to a cutting board or bowl and, using two forks, shred meat. Return to stoneware.

4. Stir in red and yellow bell peppers. Cover and cook on High for 30 to 45 minutes or until peppers are tender-crisp.

5. Meanwhile, in a bowl, combine tomato, corn, cilantro, lime juice, the remaining salt and pepper. Let stand at room temperature for 20 to 30 minutes before serving.

6. Just before serving, preheat oven to 350°F (180°C). Wrap a stack of tortillas in foil and heat in oven for 10 minutes.

7. Spoon about ½ cup (125 mL) of the steak mixture along the center of each tortilla. Top with relish, sour cream and cheese. Fold tortilla around filling (see tip, at left).

Beer-Braised Beef

Makes 6 servings

This recipe is a tribute to one of the national dishes of Belgium: brisket à la carbonnade. Instead of cooking a brisket, this version uses stewing beef but holds onto the beer and lots of onions. It is important to use dark ale, as its deep flavor enhances and adds richness to this dish.

Tips

To prepare mushrooms, first trim off the bottoms of the stems, then wipe off the mushrooms. Don't rinse or soak the mushrooms, or they'll absorb water and turn mushy when you cook them.

Resist the urge to lift the lid and taste or smell whatever is inside the slow cooker as it's cooking. Every peek will increase the cooking time by 20 minutes.

Serve this stew over cooked egg noodles tossed with melted butter and minced fresh dill.

- **Minimum 4-quart slow cooker**

3 tbsp	all-purpose flour	45 mL
	Salt and freshly ground black pepper	
3 lbs	stewing beef, trimmed and cut into 1-inch (2.5 cm) cubes	1.5 kg
3 to 4 tbsp	vegetable oil	45 to 60 mL
4	carrots, quartered lengthwise and cut into ½-inch (1 cm) pieces	4
6	onions, sliced	6
4	cloves garlic, minced	4
8 oz	small mushrooms, trimmed	250 g
1 tsp	dried thyme	5 mL
1	bottle (12 oz/341 mL) dark ale, such as Guinness or stout	1
½ cup	beef broth, divided	125 mL
1 tbsp	packed brown sugar	15 mL
1 tbsp	red wine vinegar	15 mL
2	bay leaves	2

1. In a heavy plastic bag, combine flour, 1 tsp (5 mL) salt and ½ tsp (2 mL) pepper. In batches, add beef to bag and toss to coat with flour mixture. Reserve the remaining flour mixture.

2. In a large nonstick skillet, heat half the oil over medium-high heat. Cook beef in batches, adding more oil as needed, for 5 minutes or until browned all over. Using a slotted spoon, transfer to slow cooker stoneware. Stir in carrots.

3. Reduce heat to medium. Add onions to skillet and sauté for 3 to 4 minutes or until tender and translucent. Add garlic, mushrooms, thyme, ½ tsp (2 mL) pepper and the reserved flour mixture; sauté for 1 minute. Stir in ale, broth, brown sugar and vinegar; cook, stirring, for 1 minute or until thickened. Pour over beef mixture. Add bay leaves.

4. Cover and cook on Low for 8 to 10 hours or on High for 4 to 6 hours, until vegetables are tender and stew is bubbling. Discard bay leaves. Season to taste with salt and pepper.

Madras Beef

Makes 6 servings

This is a simple, delicious recipe cooked in an easy sauce that's full of Indian flavorings. Using a can of tomato soup speeds up the preparation time. Serve over steamed basmati rice, with steamed green beans and warm naan (an Indian flatbread). Garnish the beef with minced fresh cilantro, if you like.

Tip

When browning meat in hot oil, avoid overfilling the skillet. If the pan is too full, the meat will steam rather than brown. Turn the meat frequently and cook it as quickly as possible, then use a slotted spoon to remove it.

- **4- to 6-quart slow cooker**

2 tbsp	vegetable oil (approx.)	30 mL
2 lbs	stewing beef, trimmed and cut into 1-inch (2.5 cm) cubes	1 kg
2	onions, thinly sliced	2
1	can (10 oz/284 mL) condensed tomato soup	1
2 tbsp	Madras curry paste	30 mL
½ tsp	garam masala or curry powder	2 mL
½ tsp	paprika	2 mL
½ cup	plain yogurt	125 mL

1. In a large nonstick skillet, heat half the oil over medium-high heat. Cook beef in batches, adding more oil as needed, for 5 minutes or until browned all over. Using a slotted spoon, transfer to slow cooker stoneware.

2. Reduce heat to medium. Add onions to skillet and sauté for 3 to 4 minutes or until tender and translucent. Spoon over beef.

3. In a bowl, combine soup, curry paste, garam masala and paprika. Stir into beef mixture.

4. Cover and cook on Low for 8 to 10 hours or on High for 4 to 5 hours, until beef is tender. Stir in yogurt.

Garam masala is a blend of ground spices commonly used in Indian and other South Asian cuisines. It is not necessarily hot, but it adds intense flavor. Good commercial brands of garam masala are now widely available in supermarkets.

Hoisin Slivered Slow Cooker Beef

Makes 4 to 6 servings

There's no need to order Chinese takeout! This Asian-inspired dish uses some unusual ingredients, but they're all available at the supermarket. Steamed rice or cooked vermicelli noodles, along with steamed chopped baby bok choy, will complete the meal. Garnish with thinly sliced green onions and chopped peanuts, if you like. If you have extra sauce left over, toss it with noodles for a quick lunch the next day.

Tip

You can also serve this dish with rice and green beans.

- 3- to 5-quart slow cooker

1 tbsp	vegetable oil (approx.)	15 mL
1 tsp	sesame oil (optional)	5 mL
1½ lbs	boneless beef outside round, blade or shoulder steak, trimmed and cut into 1-inch (2.5 cm) cubes	750 g
3	cloves garlic, minced	3
2 tsp	grated gingerroot	10 mL
¼ cup	soy sauce	60 mL
2 tbsp	fish sauce	30 mL
2 tbsp	sweet Thai chili sauce	30 mL
2 tbsp	hoisin sauce	30 mL
1 tbsp	rice vinegar	15 mL
½ tsp	sambal oelek (optional)	2 mL

1. In a large nonstick skillet, heat half the vegetable oil and the sesame oil (if using) over medium-high heat. Cook beef in batches, adding more oil as needed, for 5 minutes or until browned all over. Using a slotted spoon, transfer to slow cooker stoneware.

2. Stir in garlic, ginger, soy sauce, fish sauce, chili sauce, hoisin sauce, vinegar and sambal oelek (if using).

3. Cover and cook on Low for 6 to 8 hours or on High for 3 to 4 hours, until beef is fork-tender.

> Sambal oelek is an Indonesian-inspired chili sauce. Even a small spoonful adds heat and character to a dish. It can be found with the Asian foods in the grocery store or in Asian supermarkets.

Italian Pot Pie with Parmesan Mashed Potatoes

Makes 6 to 8 servings

Warm, traditional comfort food takes on an Italian twist. If you have leftover mashed potatoes, this recipe is a great way to use them up.

Tips

Store mushrooms in a paper bag, with the top loosely folded over once or twice, or place them in a glass container and cover it with a tea towel or moist paper towel. Be sure to allow air circulation. Store in the refrigerator (but not in the crisper) and use within a few days — or a week, if they are packaged and unopened.

To prepare mushrooms, first trim off the bottoms of the stems, then wipe off the mushrooms. Don't rinse or soak the mushrooms, or they'll absorb water and turn mushy when you cook them.

Authentic Italian Parmesan cheese (Parmigiano-Reggiano) is expensive, but its flavor is certainly worth the price. Well-wrapped in the refrigerator, a block keeps for months, and it goes a long way when you freshly grate it as you need it.

- **4- to 6-quart slow cooker**

2 tbsp	vegetable oil (approx.)	30 mL
2 lbs	stewing beef, trimmed and cut into 1-inch (2.5 cm) cubes	1 kg
1	onion, chopped	1
1	clove garlic, minced	1
2	carrots, cut into 1-inch (2.5 cm) chunks	2
1½ cups	sliced mushrooms	375 mL
½ tsp	dried basil	2 mL
½ tsp	dried oregano	2 mL
¼ tsp	freshly ground black pepper	1 mL
1	jar (28 oz/796 mL) tomato pasta sauce	1

Parmesan Mashed Potatoes

1½ lbs	baking potatoes (3 or 4 large), peeled and quartered	750 g
1	egg, lightly beaten	1
1 cup	freshly grated Parmesan cheese, divided	250 mL
	Salt and freshly ground black pepper	
2 tbsp	chopped fresh parsley	30 mL

1. In a large nonstick skillet, heat half the oil over medium-high heat. Cook beef in batches, adding more oil as needed, for 5 minutes or until browned all over. Using a slotted spoon, transfer to slow cooker stoneware.

2. Reduce heat to medium. Add onion and garlic to skillet and sauté for about 5 minutes or until onion is tender and translucent. Add carrots, mushrooms, basil, oregano and pepper; sauté for about 5 minutes or until mushrooms are softened. Pour over beef mixture, along with pasta sauce, stirring to combine.

3. Cover and cook on Low for 6 to 8 hours or on High for 3 to 4 hours, until beef is almost tender and stew is bubbling.

4. *Potatoes:* Meanwhile, place potatoes in a large pot. Add enough cold water to cover and bring to a boil over medium-high heat. Reduce heat and boil gently for 20 minutes or until tender. Drain well and mash until smooth. Stir in egg and ¾ cup (175 mL) of the cheese. Season to taste with salt and pepper. Stir in parsley.

5. Spoon potatoes evenly over beef in stoneware and sprinkle with the remaining cheese. Cover and cook on Low for 1 to 2 hours or until potatoes are light golden brown.

Make Ahead

You can make the mashed potato topping up to 12 hours before preparing this dish. Transfer to an airtight container and refrigerate until ready to use.

Step 2 can be completed up to 2 days in advance. Transfer the sautéed vegetable mixture to an airtight container, stir in the pasta sauce and refrigerate. When you are ready to cook, complete step 1, add the vegetable mixture and proceed with step 3.

The fluffiness of your mash depends on the type of potatoes used. The creamy yellow Yukon gold variety has a wonderful buttery flavor and makes delicious mashed potatoes. Russet potatoes (baking potatoes) also work well. Regular white potatoes, while not as flavorful, still mash well. In fact, the only type that don't really fluff up is new potatoes, as they don't have a very high starch content.

Philly Cheese and Beef Casserole

Makes 4 to 6 servings

The taste of this casserole is reminiscent of a good Philadelphia cheese steak. Even though it breaks my normal condiment rules, ketchup is a must alongside. This dish is not exactly low in fat, but then, neither is its namesake.

Tip

Always use a large, deep pot to boil pasta. You need at least 1 quart (1 L) water per 3¹/₂ oz (100 g) dry pasta. And always salt the water, because this seasons the pasta internally as it absorbs the liquid and swells. You'll need about 1 tbsp (15 mL) salt for a large pot of boiling water. Chefs prefer to use sea salt or kosher salt because it is easier to control the amount you add and it dissolves faster than table salt.

- **4- to 6-quart slow cooker, stoneware greased**

3 cups	short pasta, such as penne, rigatoni or rotini	750 mL
1 lb	lean ground beef	500 g
2	onions, finely chopped	2
2	cloves garlic, minced	2
1	small green bell pepper, finely chopped	1
8 oz	mushrooms, chopped	250 g
¹/₂ tsp	dried thyme	2 mL
1	can (12 oz/370 mL) evaporated milk	1
8 oz	herb and garlic spreadable cream cheese	250 g
1 tbsp	Dijon mustard	15 mL
2 cups	shredded sharp (old) Cheddar cheese	500 mL

Topping

1 cup	dry bread crumbs	250 mL
3 tbsp	melted butter	45 mL
¹/₂ cup	shredded sharp (old) Cheddar cheese	125 mL

1. In a large pot of boiling salted water, cook pasta for about 8 minutes or until tender but firm (al dente). Drain and place in prepared slow cooker stoneware.

2. In a large nonstick skillet, cook beef over medium-high heat, breaking it up with the back of a wooden spoon, for 7 minutes or until no longer pink. Using a slotted spoon, transfer to stoneware.

3. Reduce heat to medium. Add onions, garlic, green pepper, mushrooms and thyme to skillet and sauté for 3 to 4 minutes or until softened. Transfer to stoneware.

4. Add milk, cream cheese and mustard to skillet and cook, stirring gently, for 3 to 4 minutes or until thickened. Stir into pasta mixture, along with cheese.

5. Cover and cook on Low for 8 hours or on High for 4 hours, until bubbling.

6. *Topping:* In a bowl, toss together bread crumbs, butter and cheese. Sprinkle over pasta mixture. Cover and cook on High for 20 minutes or until cheese is melted.

Moroccan Chicken (page 191)

Turkey Bolognese with Spaghetti Squash (page 199)

Steak Fajitas with Tomato Corn Relish (page 218)

Veal and Leek Ragoût in Herbed Popovers (page 236)

Pork and Potato Poutine (page 254)

Jerk Pork Ribs and Sweet Potatoes (page 272)

Edamame Succotash (page 286)

Multigrain Asian Pilaf (page 303)

Family-Style Chili Mac and Cheese

Makes 4 to 6 servings

An old family favorite takes a new turn with the addition of tomatoes. This dish is exceptionally easy and fast by slow cooker standards! My son likes the cheesy version, but you can also make it without cheese. This is a great weeknight supper for those busy months that are filled with lots of after-school activities. It's calming to know that dinner will be ready when you get home.

Tip

To avoid tears when chopping onions, put the onions in the freezer for a few minutes first.

- 3- to 5-quart slow cooker

1 lb	lean ground beef or turkey	500 g
1	onion, finely chopped	1
2	cloves garlic, minced	2
1	can (14 oz/398 mL) diced tomatoes, drained	1
1	can (8 oz/227 mL) tomato sauce	1
2 tbsp	chili powder	30 mL
1/2 tsp	ground cumin	2 mL
1/4 tsp	hot pepper flakes	1 mL
1/4 tsp	freshly ground black pepper	1 mL
1 cup	elbow macaroni	250 mL
1 cup	shredded Cheddar cheese	250 mL

1. In a large nonstick skillet, cook beef, onion and garlic over medium-high heat, breaking up beef with the back of a wooden spoon, for about 7 minutes or until beef is no longer pink. Using a slotted spoon, transfer to slow cooker stoneware.

2. Stir in tomatoes, tomato sauce, chili powder, cumin, hot pepper flakes and black pepper.

3. Cover and cook on Low for 4 hours or on High for 2 hours, until bubbling.

4. In a pot of boiling salted water, cook macaroni for 7 to 8 minutes or until tender but firm (al dente). Drain and stir into beef mixture, along with cheese. Cover and cook on Low for 1 hour.

Make Ahead

This dish can be assembled up to 12 hours in advance. Prepare through step 2, cover and refrigerate overnight. The next day, place stoneware in slow cooker and proceed with step 3.

Fiesta Tamale Pie

Makes 4 to 6 servings

The entire family will enjoy this economical and tasty main course pie. You can serve leftovers as a dip with nacho chips or use them to fill tortillas for quick burritos!

Tips

Buy ground beef when it's on special. Divide it into 1-lb (500 g) portions, flatten each into a thin disc and seal tightly in a freezer bag, then freeze to have on hand for spur-of-the-moment casseroles. A thin disc thaws much more easily, right in a skillet, than a thick clump.

It is always best to brown ground meat thoroughly before adding it to the slow cooker. This ensures that the meat reaches the recommended cooked temperature of 160°F (71°C), or 165°F (74°C) for ground poultry. If you have a good nonstick skillet, you will not need to add cooking oil unless you are browning ground turkey or chicken, which is generally very lean.

- **4- to 6-quart slow cooker**

1 tbsp	vegetable oil	15 mL
1 lb	lean ground beef	500 g
1	onion, chopped	1
1 tbsp	chili powder	15 mL
1 tbsp	dried oregano	15 mL
1 tsp	ground cumin	5 mL
1	can (10 oz/284 mL) enchilada sauce	1
2 cups	cooked or canned red kidney beans (see page 120), drained and rinsed	500 mL
1	package (6 1/2 oz/184 g) cornbread and muffin mix	1
1	egg, lightly beaten	1
1/3 cup	milk	75 mL
2 tbsp	butter, melted	30 mL
1/2 cup	shredded Monterey Jack cheese	125 mL
1	can (4 1/2 oz/127 mL) chopped mild green chiles, with juice	1
1/4 cup	sour cream	60 mL
4	green onions, chopped	4

1. In a large nonstick skillet, heat oil over medium-high heat. Cook ground beef and onion, breaking up beef with the back of a wooden spoon, for about 7 minutes or until beef is no longer pink. Add chili powder, oregano and cumin; sauté for 1 to 2 minutes or until fragrant. Using a slotted spoon, transfer to slow cooker stoneware. Stir in enchilada sauce and beans.

2. Place cornbread mix in a bowl and make a well in the center. Pour egg, milk and butter into well and stir just until blended (the batter will be lumpy). Stir in cheese and chiles with juice. Spread cornbread mixture evenly over beef mixture.

3. Place two clean, dry tea towels over top of stoneware, then place lid on top of towels (this will allow the topping to rise without getting soggy). Cook on Low for 6 to 8 hours or on High for 3 to 4 hours, until cornbread mixture has risen and is crusty and meat mixture is bubbling.

4. Top each serving with a dollop of sour cream and sprinkle with green onions.

Diner Red Brick

Makes 4 to 6 servings

There has been a recent rebirth of comfort food, and meatloaf is making a comeback! It not only transports us back to many a childhood supper, it's a satisfying and economical meal. In the days of the diner, a meatloaf was called a "red brick" on the menu. This updated version uses lean ground beef, with turkey and pork for extra flavor. Serve with steamed green beans and mashed potatoes.

Tips

You can add a little heat to this meatloaf by using hot salsa instead of mild.

When making your mashed potatoes, substitute buttermilk for milk or cream, to add a bit of tang. Once you try it, you will use buttermilk every time.

- **4- to 6-quart slow cooker**

1 lb	lean ground beef	500 g
8 oz	ground turkey	250 g
8 oz	lean ground pork	250 g
2	eggs, lightly beaten	2
1 cup	fine dry bread crumbs	250 mL
1½ cups	mild salsa, divided	375 mL
1 tbsp	Worcestershire sauce	15 mL
1 tsp	dry mustard	5 mL
½ tsp	salt	2 mL
¼ tsp	freshly ground black pepper	1 mL

1. Cut a 2-foot (60 cm) length of foil in half lengthwise to make two strips. Fold each strip in half lengthwise. Crisscross the strips on the bottom of the slow cooker stoneware, bringing the ends up the sides and over the rim.

2. In a large bowl, using your hands, combine beef, turkey, pork, eggs, bread crumbs, 1 cup (250 mL) of the salsa, Worcestershire sauce, mustard, salt and pepper. Press evenly into prepared stoneware.

3. Tucking strip ends under lid, cover and cook on Low for 8 to 10 hours or on High for 4 to 6 hours, until a meat thermometer inserted into center of meatloaf registers 170°F (77°C). Spread the remaining salsa over meatloaf. Cover and cook on High for 10 minutes.

4. Remove lid and grasp strip ends to lift out meatloaf, draining off any accumulated fat from top. Transfer to a cutting board and let cool for 10 minutes before slicing.

Curried Beef with Mashed Sweet Potatoes

Makes 4 to 6 servings

Mashed sweet potatoes add both sweetness and color to the curried beef. It's a nice alternative to mashed potatoes or rice.

Tips

It's important to fully cook ground meat before adding it to the slow cooker. Cook ground meat until no longer pink inside. Use the back of a wooden spoon to break up the meat as it cooks; otherwise, you will end up with large chunks of meat.

Broth (or stock) is one of the most indispensable pantry staples. Commercial broth cubes and powders are loaded with salt and just don't deliver the flavor of homemade stock or prepared broth. I like to keep 32-oz (1 L) Tetra Paks on hand, especially the sodium-reduced variety.

Tomato paste is now available in tubes in many supermarkets and delis. It keeps for months in the refrigerator.

- **3- to 5-quart slow cooker**

5	cloves garlic, finely chopped	5
1	onion, coarsely chopped	1
1	2-inch (5 cm) piece gingerroot, roughly chopped	1
2 tbsp	vegetable oil	30 mL
1½ lbs	lean ground beef or lamb	750 g
1 tbsp	curry powder	15 mL
1 tsp	ground cumin	5 mL
1 tsp	ground coriander	5 mL
½ tsp	cayenne pepper	2 mL
2 cups	beef broth	500 mL
2 tbsp	tomato paste	30 mL
4	large sweet potatoes	4
2 tbsp	butter	30 mL
	Salt and freshly ground black pepper	
1 tbsp	chopped fresh parsley	15 mL
1 cup	frozen peas, thawed	250 mL
⅓ cup	slivered almonds	75 mL
⅓ cup	raisins	75 mL
1 tbsp	chopped fresh cilantro	15 mL
	Chopped cashews	

1. In a food processor, process garlic, onion and ginger into paste (or finely chop by hand).

2. In a large nonstick skillet, heat oil over medium heat. Sauté garlic mixture for 5 minutes or until fragrant and starting to turn golden. Add beef and cook, breaking up beef with the back of a wooden spoon, for about 7 minutes or until beef is no longer pink. Stir in curry powder, cumin, coriander and cayenne; sauté for 1 to 2 minutes or until fragrant. Using a slotted spoon, transfer to slow cooker stoneware. Stir in broth and tomato paste.

3. Cover and cook on Low for 6 to 8 hours or on High for 3 to 4 hours, until bubbling.

4. Meanwhile, preheat oven to 400°F (200°C). Using a fork, pierce sweet potatoes several times. Bake for about 1 hour or until tender. Let cool slightly, then peel off skins. In a bowl, mash with butter, 1 tsp (5 mL) salt and $\frac{1}{2}$ tsp (2 mL) black pepper. Stir in parsley. Keep warm.

5. Stir peas, almonds and raisins into stoneware. Cover and cook on High for 10 to 15 minutes. Season to taste with salt and black pepper.

6. Spoon sweet potato mixture onto a warmed platter. Make a well in the center and spoon in curried beef. Sprinkle with cilantro and cashews.

Make Ahead

The mashed sweet potatoes can be prepared as directed in step 4, then covered and refrigerated for up to 1 day or frozen for up to 2 months. Let thaw in the refrigerator, if necessary, then let stand at room temperature for 30 minutes before reheating.

The curried beef can be assembled up to 2 days in advance. Prepare through step 2, cool immediately, then cover and refrigerate. When ready to cook, place stoneware in slow cooker and proceed with step 3.

Pizza Meatloaf

Makes 4 servings

This is any kid's favorite! Serve it with linguine tossed with butter and grated Parmesan cheese. Instead of using ground beef, chicken or turkey, you can use a combination of the three, or use some ground pork or veal. Look for a combination package of ground beef, veal and pork at the grocery store or ask your butcher for a portion of each.

Tip

Make your own bread crumbs: In a food processor, process leftover bread to fine crumbs. Transfer to a ziplock bag, date it and freeze for up to 3 months. To dry or toast, spread bread crumbs on a large rimmed baking sheet and toast in a 350°F (180°C) oven, stirring occasionally, for 10 to 12 minutes or until golden brown.

Variation

Add ½ cup (125 mL) sliced pepperoni to the ground beef mixture.

- **Minimum 4-quart slow cooker**

1 lb	lean ground beef, chicken or turkey	500 g
1	egg, lightly beaten	1
1	clove garlic, minced	1
1½ cups	shredded mozzarella or Cheddar cheese, divided	375 mL
⅔ cup	tomato pasta sauce, divided	150 mL
¼ cup	dry bread crumbs	60 mL
1 tsp	dried basil	5 mL
½ tsp	salt	2 mL
¼ tsp	dried oregano	1 mL
¼ tsp	freshly ground black pepper	1 mL

1. Cut a 2-foot (60 cm) length of foil in half lengthwise to make two strips. Fold each strip in half lengthwise. Crisscross the strips on the bottom of the slow cooker stoneware, bringing the ends up the sides and over the rim.

2. In a large bowl, using your hands, combine beef, egg, garlic, half the cheese, half the pasta sauce, bread crumbs, basil, salt, oregano and pepper. Press evenly into prepared stoneware.

3. Tucking strip ends under lid, cover and cook on Low for 8 to 10 hours or on High for 4 to 6 hours, until a meat thermometer inserted into center of meatloaf registers 170°F (77°C). Spread the remaining pasta sauce over meatloaf and sprinkle with the remaining cheese. Cover and cook on Low for 20 minutes or until cheese has melted.

4. Remove lid and grasp strip ends to lift out meatloaf, draining off any accumulated fat from top. Transfer to a cutting board and let cool for 10 minutes before slicing.

Stuffed Mediterranean Meatloaf

Makes 6 to 8 servings

This flavorful filled loaf is delicious served with rice and a chunky Greek salad. Slice any leftover meatloaf and stuff it into a pocket pita for lunch. Add shredded lettuce and slices of tomato and cucumber, and sprinkle with crumbled feta cheese. Wrap the pita and take it to school or work. It sure beats the traditional sandwich.

Tips

If using a large, oval slow cooker, press beef mixture into an oval shape, ensuring that each layer is at least 1 inch (2.5 cm) thick. Thinner layers will cook too quickly.

Ground pork adds flavor to the meatloaf, but you can replace it with ground chicken or more ground beef.

- **Minimum 4-quart slow cooker**

1½ lbs	lean ground beef	750 g
8 oz	lean ground pork	250 g
2	cloves garlic, minced	2
1	egg, lightly beaten	1
¼ cup	fine dry bread crumbs	60 mL
1 tsp	dried oregano	5 mL
¼ tsp	freshly ground black pepper	1 mL
	Chopped fresh parsley	

Stuffing

½ cup	crumbled feta cheese	125 mL
¼ cup	chopped drained oil-packed sun-dried tomatoes	60 mL
½ tsp	dried oregano	2 mL
1	clove garlic, minced	1

1. Cut a 2-foot (60 cm) length of foil in half lengthwise to make two strips. Fold each strip in half lengthwise. Crisscross the strips on the bottom of the slow cooker stoneware, bringing the ends up the sides and over the rim.

2. In a large bowl, using your hands, combine beef, pork, garlic, egg, bread crumbs, oregano and pepper. Set aside.

3. *Stuffing:* In a small bowl, combine cheese, sun-dried tomatoes, oregano and garlic. Press half the beef mixture evenly into slow cooker stoneware. Spread cheese mixture over beef mixture, leaving a border on all sides so stuffing doesn't ooze out. Top with the remaining beef mixture and press edges together.

4. Tucking strip ends under lid, cover and cook on Low for 8 to 10 hours or on High for 4 to 6 hours, until a meat thermometer inserted into center of meatloaf registers 170°F (77°C).

5. Remove lid and grasp strip ends to lift out meatloaf, draining off any accumulated fat from top. Transfer to a cutting board and let cool for 10 minutes before slicing. Serve sprinkled with parsley.

Spicy Meatball Sandwiches with Coleslaw

Makes 4 to 6 servings

These fun, easy sandwiches are great at a casual get-together with friends, a football party or a meal with the family. The tangy coleslaw offsets the heat of the spicy meatballs. These sandwiches combine crunch (the bun), tang (the coleslaw) and heat (the meatballs) in every bite!

Tips

When rolling the meat mixture into meatballs, don't overmix. Meatballs should be springy and firm enough to hold their shape, yet still tender. In other words, don't handle the meat too much or pack it too densely.

To keep my hands from getting sticky when rolling meatballs, I moisten my hands with water or give them a light coating of oil or flour.

The ideal meatball for soups and sandwiches is just one or two bites in diameter: about 1 inch (2.5 cm). Keep your eye on your work as you roll — meatballs tend to get bigger as your mind wanders!

- **4- to 6-quart slow cooker**

Meatballs

1½ lbs	lean ground beef	750 g
2	cloves garlic, minced	2
2 tsp	celery seeds	10 mL
½ tsp	salt	2 mL
¼ tsp	freshly ground black pepper	1 mL
2 tbsp	vegetable oil (approx.)	30 mL

Spicy Tomato Sauce

6	thin lemon slices	6
¼ cup	packed brown sugar	60 mL
1 cup	ketchup	250 mL
⅔ cup	chili sauce	150 mL
2 tbsp	Worcestershire sauce	30 mL
2 tbsp	spicy mustard	30 mL
6 to 8	small submarine rolls or hot dog buns	6 to 8
12 to 16	thin red or white onion slices	12 to 16
1 lb	coleslaw or broccoli slaw mix	500 g
½ cup	coleslaw dressing	125 mL

1. *Meatballs:* In a bowl, using your hands, combine beef, garlic, celery seeds, salt and pepper. Form mixture into 1-inch (2.5 cm) meatballs.

2. In a skillet, heat half the oil over medium-high heat. Cook meatballs in batches, adding more oil as needed, for about 3 minutes or until browned all over. Using a slotted spoon, transfer to slow cooker stoneware.

3. *Sauce:* Reduce heat to medium. Add lemon slices, brown sugar, ketchup, chili sauce, Worcestershire sauce, mustard and ½ cup (125 mL) water to skillet and bring to a boil, stirring. Pour sauce over meatballs.

4. Cover and cook on Low for 8 hours or on High for 4 hours, until meatballs are no longer pink inside. Discard lemon slices.

You can also use kaiser buns or lightly toasted baguette slices to hold the meatballs.

5. Split rolls in half horizontally and hollow out some of the bread from each half, leaving them about $\frac{1}{2}$ inch (1 cm) thick around the edges. Separate red onion slices into rings. Set aside. In a bowl, combine coleslaw and dressing.

6. Place 2 or 3 meatballs on bottom half of each roll. Evenly divide onion rings and coleslaw over top and drizzle with sauce, if desired.

Make Ahead

Split and hollow out the buns in advance, then store them in a plastic bag until you're ready to assemble the sandwiches. Dress the coleslaw and refrigerate it at the beginning of the day to let the raw vegetables absorb the dressing and become slightly more tender.

Short Ribs Barolo

Makes 4 to 6 servings

Settle in for meltingly tender ribs that are long on flavor but short on effort. Look for small, thick bone-in short ribs, which are meatier than flanken-style ribs (cut long and thin). Each rib weighs about 4 oz (125 g). Before serving, pull out the bones, if you like. This dish is fantastic served with Pecorino and Parsley Polenta (page 297) and steamed broccoli.

Tips

You can use an 8-oz (227 mL) can of tomato sauce instead of the 1 cup (250 mL).

If you can't find pancetta, use thickly sliced bacon. Even sodium-reduced side bacon will work well.

- **4- to 6-quart slow cooker**

2 tbsp	vegetable oil (approx.)	30 mL
2 lbs	beef short ribs or braising ribs, cut into 3-inch (7.5 cm) sections	1 kg
	Salt and freshly ground black pepper	
2	Spanish onions, diced	2
2	stalks celery, cut into ½-inch (1 cm) slices	2
1	carrot, cut into ½-inch (1 cm) rounds	1
4 oz	pancetta, diced	125 g
1 cup	Barolo wine or other hearty red wine	250 mL
1 cup	tomato sauce	250 mL

1. In a large Dutch oven, heat half the oil over high heat until smoking. Generously season beef with salt and pepper. Cook beef in batches, adding more oil as needed, for 4 to 5 minutes per side or until browned all over. Using a slotted spoon, transfer to slow cooker stoneware.

2. Pour any excess oil out of the pot. Reduce heat to medium-high. Add onions, celery, carrot and pancetta; sauté for about 8 minutes or until vegetables are lightly browned and starting to soften. Transfer to stoneware, arranging around beef.

3. In a bowl, combine wine and tomato sauce. Pour over beef and vegetable mixture.

4. Cover and cook on Low for 8 to 12 hours or on High for 4 to 6 hours, until beef is falling off the bones and vegetables are tender. Using a slotted spoon, transfer beef to a platter and keep warm.

5. Strain cooking liquid through a fine-mesh sieve into a saucepan. Discard solids. Bring to a boil over medium-high heat. Reduce heat and simmer, stirring often, for 10 to 12 minutes or until slightly thickened and reduced to about 2½ cups (625 mL). Season to taste with salt and pepper. Pour over beef. Serve immediately.

Make Ahead

Making this dish a day ahead and reheating it enhances the flavors. Prepare through step 5, adding the beef to the sauce, let cool slightly, then cover and refrigerate for up to 1 day. For best results, reheat in a covered ovenproof casserole dish at 350°F (180°C) for about 30 minutes or until heated through.

Veal Shanks with Spicy Black Bean Sauce

Makes 6 to 8 servings

Veal shanks traditionally get an Italian treatment. I have given them a Chinese twist instead, using bottled black bean sauce. Serve them with steamed rice and sautéed Chinese greens, such as baby bok choy or snow peas. Toss any leftover sauce with noodles the next day for lunch.

Tips

Veal shanks are readily available at supermarkets and butcher shops. They have a piece of connective tissue around the outer edge that helps keep the meat connected to the bone. During long, slow cooking, this tissue can be broken down, causing the meat to come away from the bone and fall apart in the stew, so it's important to secure shanks with butcher's twine. Before browning, wrap a piece of twine around the circumference of the meat and tie it with a tight knot. You can also ask the butcher to do this for you.

If you can't find an Anaheim chile pepper, you can substitute a jalapeño pepper.

- **4- to 6-quart slow cooker**

2 tbsp	vegetable oil (approx.)	30 mL
6 to 8	veal shanks (each about 12 oz/375 g), tied (see tip, at left)	6 to 8
4	green onions, sliced, white and light green parts separated	4
1	red Anaheim chile pepper, minced	1
½ cup	black bean sauce with garlic	125 mL
1 tsp	minced gingerroot	5 mL
½ tsp	freshly ground black pepper	2 mL
	Grated zest and juice of 1 orange	

1. In a large skillet, heat half the oil over medium heat. Cook veal in batches, adding more oil as needed, for 4 minutes or until lightly browned on all sides. Transfer to slow cooker stoneware.

2. In a bowl, combine white parts of green onions, chile pepper, black bean sauce, ginger, pepper, half the orange zest and the orange juice. Pour over veal and stir to combine.

3. Cover and cook on Low for 10 hours or on High for 6 hours, until veal is very tender. Serve garnished with the remaining green onions and orange zest.

Veal and Leek Ragoût in Herbed Popovers

Makes 6 servings

This simple stew reminds me of Sunday dinners at my Nanna McClaren's house. She came from fine English stock, so roast beef with Yorkshire pudding was the standard fare. I have used veal, leeks and mushrooms, but the dish has that same rich taste.

Tips

Leeks contain a lot of sand and must be cleaned carefully. Remove most of the green part and halve the white part lengthwise. Rinse thoroughly under cold running water, spreading leaves apart, and drain in a colander, then slice.

Store mushrooms in a paper bag, with the top loosely folded over once or twice, or place them in a glass container and cover it with a tea towel or moist paper towel. Be sure to allow air circulation. Store in the refrigerator (but not in the crisper) and use within a few days — or a week, if they are packaged and unopened.

- **4- to 6-quart slow cooker**
- *12-cup muffin tin, well greased*

2 tbsp	vegetable oil (approx.)	30 mL
2 lbs	stewing veal, cut into 1-inch (2.5 cm) cubes	1 kg
4	leeks (white and light green parts only), thickly sliced	4
8 oz	mushrooms, chopped	250 g
2 tbsp	all-purpose flour	30 mL
	Salt and freshly ground black pepper	
2 cups	veal or chicken broth	500 mL
2 tbsp	white balsamic vinegar or cider vinegar	30 mL
1 tsp	dried thyme	5 mL
½ cup	heavy or whipping (35%) cream	125 mL

Herbed Popovers

2	eggs	2
1 cup	all-purpose flour	250 mL
1 cup	milk	250 mL
1 tbsp	snipped fresh chives	15 mL
1 tbsp	chopped fresh parsley	15 mL
½ tsp	dried rosemary	2 mL
½ tsp	salt	2 mL

1. In a large skillet, heat half the oil over medium-high heat. Cook veal in batches, adding more oil as needed, for about 4 minutes or until browned all over. Using a slotted spoon, transfer to slow cooker stoneware.

2. Add leeks and mushrooms to skillet and sauté for 5 to 10 minutes or until softened. Sprinkle with flour, 1 tsp (5 mL) salt and ½ tsp (2 mL) pepper; stir to coat. Stir in broth, vinegar, thyme and ½ cup (125 mL) water; bring to a boil, scraping up any brown bits from pan. Pour over veal.

3. Cover and cook on Low for 8 hours or on High for 4 hours, until veal is tender. Stir in cream and season to taste with salt and pepper.

Tip

When browning meat in hot oil, avoid overfilling the skillet. If the pan is too full, the meat will steam rather than brown. Turn the meat frequently and cook it as quickly as possible, then use a slotted spoon to remove it.

4. *Popovers:* Meanwhile, in a large bowl, beat eggs until frothy. Stir in flour, milk, chives, parsley, rosemary and salt until just blended. (Leave a few lumps and don't overmix.) Divide batter evenly among prepared muffin cups.

5. Place muffin tin in cold oven. Set oven temperature to 450°F (230°C) and bake for 25 minutes. Using the tip of a sharp knife, prick each popover to let steam escape. Bake for 5 to 10 minutes or until golden brown and puffed.

6. Split open popovers, place in serving bowls and ladle stew over top.

Make Ahead

The popovers can be baked, removed from muffin cups and placed on a baking sheet, covered with a clean tea towel and set aside at room temperature for up to 8 hours. Reheat in a 350°F (180°C) oven for 5 to 10 minutes.

Veal Marengo

Makes 6 servings

I love this simple but rustic veal dish. When my Swiss friend Thomas heads to his vacation home in the Piedmont area of Italy, he likes to go truffle hunting with his neighbor, then he cooks up a dish similar to this one. I have substituted regular mushrooms for the truffles, but you can finish with a drizzle of truffle oil before serving, for an authentic twist.

Tips

Pearl onions come in red, white and golden varieties. They are found in the produce section of the supermarket, loose or in small mesh bags. If you purchase a bag of onions, there are about 24 inside.

For ease of preparation, you can use frozen pearl onions. But if you can't find them, it is quite easy to prepare fresh onions. Simply cut an X into the base of each onion. Bring a pot of water to a boil over high heat. Drop onions (with skins) into boiling water and cook for 1 minute. Drain and immediately immerse in ice-cold water. Let cool, then squeeze onions out of their skins.

- **4- to 6-quart slow cooker**

3 tbsp	all-purpose flour	45 mL
1 tsp	salt	5 mL
½ tsp	freshly ground black pepper	2 mL
2 lbs	stewing veal, cut into 1-inch (2.5 cm) cubes	1 kg
2 tbsp	vegetable oil (approx.)	30 mL
2	cloves garlic, minced	2
1	onion, finely chopped	1
1 cup	diced tomatoes	250 mL
2 tbsp	tomato paste	30 mL
⅔ cup	dry white wine	150 mL
1 cup	veal or chicken broth	250 mL
8 oz	small mushrooms	250 g
24	pearl onions, peeled (see tips, at left)	24
12 to 15	kalamata olives	12 to 15
	Hot cooked farfalle or penne pasta	
	Chopped fresh parsley (optional)	
	White truffle oil (optional)	

1. In a heavy plastic bag, combine flour, salt and pepper. In batches, add veal to bag and toss to coat with flour mixture.

2. In a large nonstick skillet, heat half the oil over medium-high heat. Cook veal in batches, adding more oil as needed, for about 4 minutes or until browned all over. Using a slotted spoon, transfer to slow cooker stoneware.

3. Add garlic, chopped onion, tomatoes and tomato paste to skillet; stir to combine. Add wine and boil until sauce is reduced by half. Add to stoneware, along with broth, mushrooms and pearl onions; stir to combine.

4. Cover and cook on Low for 6 to 8 hours or on High for 3 to 4 hours, until meat is tender.

5. Stir in olives. Cover and cook on High for 15 minutes or until heated through.

6. Divide farfalle among serving bowls and spoon stew over top. Sprinkle with parsley (if using) and drizzle with truffle oil (if using).

Pork and Lamb

Roast Pork Loin with Port and Fig Sauce

Makes 4 to 6 servings

Pork is enhanced by many kinds of fruit, but the subtle sweetness of fresh figs with port wine makes an especially seductive combination.

Tip

If your liquid honey has crystallized (or if you are using solid creamed honey instead), place the jar (or as much as you need in a small heatproof bowl) in a saucepan of hot water and let warm until the crystals dissolve and the honey is melted. Or heat in the microwave on Medium-High (70%) for about 1 minute, stirring after 30 seconds, until melted.

- **Minimum 4-quart slow cooker**

1	boneless pork loin rib roast (about 2½ lbs/1.25 kg), trimmed	1
1 tbsp	olive oil	15 mL
1 tsp	dried rosemary	5 mL
½ tsp	freshly ground black pepper	2 mL
¾ cup	chopped dried Mission figs	175 mL
1	shallot, diced	1
1 cup	port wine	250 mL
½ cup	chicken broth	125 mL
1 tbsp	liquid honey	15 mL
2	3-inch (7.5 cm) cinnamon sticks	2
2 tbsp	butter	30 mL

1. Place pork in slow cooker stoneware. Brush with oil and sprinkle with rosemary and pepper. Arrange figs around pork.

2. In a bowl, stir together shallot, port, broth and honey. Pour around pork. Immerse cinnamon sticks in port mixture.

3. Cover and cook on Low for 4 to 6 hours or until pork is fork-tender. Transfer pork to a warmed platter and tent loosely with foil.

4. Remove cinnamon sticks from cooking liquid. Using an immersion blender, or in a food processor or blender, purée cooking liquid until smooth. Stir in butter until melted.

5. Slice pork across the grain and serve sauce in a gravy boat on the side.

Make Ahead

This dish can be assembled up to 12 hours in advance. Prepare through step 2, cover and refrigerate overnight. The next day, place stoneware in slow cooker and proceed with step 3.

Mission figs are small black figs grown in California. Dried Mission figs have a complex smoky flavor, which makes them a good ingredient for savory stews.

Saucy Pepper Pork

- **4- to 6-quart slow cooker**

2 tbsp	all-purpose flour	30 mL
1/2 tsp	dried thyme	2 mL
1/2 tsp	paprika	2 mL
1/2 tsp	salt	2 mL
1/4 tsp	freshly ground black pepper	1 mL
4 to 6	pork loin rib chops (about 1 inch/ 2.5 cm thick), trimmed	4 to 6
2 tbsp	vegetable oil (approx.)	30 mL
1 cup	chicken broth	250 mL
2	red bell peppers, thinly sliced	2
2	cloves garlic, minced	2
1	onion, thinly sliced	1
2 tbsp	chopped fresh parsley	30 mL

1. On a plate, combine flour, thyme, paprika, salt and pepper. Gently coat both sides of each pork chop with flour mixture. Discard excess flour mixture.

2. In a large nonstick skillet, heat half the oil over medium-high heat. Cook pork chops in batches, adding more oil as needed, for about 3 minutes per side or until browned on both sides. Transfer to slow cooker stoneware.

3. Add broth to skillet and cook, scraping up any brown bits from pan. Add to stoneware, along with red peppers, garlic and onion.

4. Cover and cook on Low for 4 to 5 hours or on High for 2 to 2 1/2 hours, until pork chops are fork-tender and sauce is bubbling.

5. Place pork chops on plates and spoon sauce over top. Sprinkle with parsley.

Italian Pork Roast Braised with Beans

Makes 6 to 8 servings

As it cooks, this Italian-inspired pork roast fills the house with the scent of garlic, rosemary and sage. The pork roast is coated with a dry rub, then braised in a tangy tomato sauce.

Tips

Crush dried rosemary between your thumb and fingers before adding it to a dish. This helps release the full aromatic flavor of the herb.

There are three types of pork loin roast: sirloin, rib and center-cut. I prefer the rib roast for slow cooking because it has a little more marbling, which suits the long, moist heat of the slow cooker.

While this recipe calls for a boneless roast, you can also use a bone-in rib roast, which slices easily into individual portions.

- **Minimum 4-quart slow cooker**
- *Food processor*

1	clove garlic, minced	1
1 tsp	dried sage	5 mL
1 tsp	dried rosemary	5 mL
2 tbsp	olive oil, divided	30 mL
1	boneless pork loin roast (2½ to 3 lbs/1.25 to 1.5 kg), trimmed	1
	Salt and freshly ground black pepper	
1	onion, finely chopped	1
1	can (14 oz/398 mL) tomato sauce	1
4 cups	cooked or canned white kidney beans (see page 120), drained and rinsed	1 L
¼ cup	dry white wine	60 mL
1	clove garlic	1
¼ cup	chopped fresh sage	60 mL
¼ cup	chopped fresh flat-leaf (Italian) parsley	60 mL
1 tsp	chopped fresh rosemary	5 mL
2 tbsp	toasted pine nuts (see tip, page 246)	30 mL

1. In a bowl, combine minced garlic, dried sage, dried rosemary and 1 tbsp (15 mL) of the oil. Rub all over pork and season to taste with salt and pepper. Place pork in slow cooker stoneware.

2. In a bowl, combine onion, tomato sauce, beans and wine. Set aside.

3. In food processor, process garlic clove, fresh sage, fresh parsley and fresh rosemary until finely chopped. Add the remaining oil and pine nuts; process until well combined. Stir half the fresh herb mixture into the reserved bean mixture and pour around pork. Cover and refrigerate the remaining fresh herb mixture.

4. Cover and cook on Low for 5 to 6 hours or until pork is fork-tender. Transfer pork to a warmed platter and tent loosely with foil.

Resist the urge to lift the lid and taste or smell whatever is inside the slow cooker as it's cooking. Every peek will increase the cooking time by 20 minutes.

5. Transfer bean mixture to a saucepan and bring to a boil over medium-high heat. Reduce heat and simmer for 5 minutes or until slightly thickened. Stir in the reserved fresh herb mixture.

6. Slice pork across the grain and spoon bean mixture around pork.

Make Ahead

This dish can be assembled up to 12 hours in advance. Prepare through step 2, cover and refrigerate overnight. The next day, place stoneware in slow cooker and proceed with step 3.

Pork Chop, Bean and Potato Bake

Makes 4 servings

This all-in-one dinner makes life so much easier. I love hash browns, especially the casserole version that seems to show up at every potluck. For smaller households, this recipe can easily be cut in half.

Tip

You can use pork shoulder blade (butt) chops in this recipe, but you will need to increase the cooking time to 6 to 8 hours on Low or 3 to 4 hours on High.

- **4- to 6-quart slow cooker**

2 cups	fresh or frozen lima beans, thawed if frozen	500 mL
1	onion, finely chopped	1
1 tbsp	dried parsley	15 mL
1 tbsp	packed brown sugar	15 mL
1 tsp	dry mustard	15 mL
2 tbsp	vegetable oil (approx.)	30 mL
4	pork loin rib chops (about 1 inch/2.5 cm thick)	4
3 cups	frozen hash brown potatoes, thawed	750 mL
1 cup	shredded Cheddar cheese, divided	250 mL
½ cup	sour cream	125 mL
	Chopped fresh parsley (optional)	

1. In a pot of boiling salted water, cook beans for about 5 minutes or until slightly tender. Drain, reserving ½ cup (125 mL) of the cooking water. Transfer beans to slow cooker stoneware.

2. In a bowl, stir together the reserved cooking water, onion, dried parsley, brown sugar and mustard. Pour over beans.

3. In a large nonstick skillet, heat half the oil over medium-high heat. Cook pork chops in batches, adding more oil as needed, for about 3 minutes per side or until browned on both sides. Place over beans.

4. In a bowl, combine hash browns, half the cheese and sour cream. Spoon over pork chops.

5. Cover and cook on Low for 4 to 5 hours or on High for 2 to 2½ hours, until pork chops are fork-tender.

6. Sprinkle the remaining cheese over the hash brown mixture. Cover and cook on High for 10 minutes or until cheese is melted. Garnish with fresh parsley, if desired.

Make Ahead

This dish can be partially assembled up to 2 days in advance. Prepare through step 2, cover and refrigerate. When ready to cook, place stoneware in slow cooker and proceed with step 3.

Pizza Mia Pork Chops

Makes 6 servings

The simplest recipes are sometimes the best. This dish was named after my friend and assistant, Leslie Huber. Her youngest daughter, Mia, is a huge pizza fan. (Are there any kids that aren't?) I like to use ready-made pasta or pizza sauce, since all of the seasoning has been added. You can serve these chops over any shape of pasta, but orzo soaks up some of the extra sauce.

Tips

Be as creative as you wish with your toppings. Imagine the pork chops as your pizza crust and garnish with your favorite pizza toppings, such as pepperoni, pineapple, hot peppers or olives.

You can use pork shoulder blade (butt) chops, instead of the pork loin chops, but you will need to increase the cooking time to 6 to 8 hours on Low or 3 to 4 hours on High.

- **4- to 6-quart slow cooker (preferably oval)**

6	pork loin rib chops (about 1 inch/2.5 cm thick)	6
1/2 tsp	salt	2 mL
1/4 tsp	freshly ground black pepper	1 mL
2 tbsp	vegetable oil (approx.)	30 mL
1	onion, chopped	1
1	green bell pepper, chopped	1
1 cup	sliced mushrooms	250 mL
2 cups	pizza sauce	500 mL
1 cup	shredded mozzarella cheese	250 mL
4 cups	hot cooked orzo	1 L

1. Season both sides of pork chops with salt and pepper. In a large nonstick skillet, heat half the oil over medium-high heat. Cook pork chops in batches, adding more oil as needed, for about 3 minutes per side or until browned on both sides. Transfer to slow cooker stoneware.

2. Arrange onion, green pepper and mushrooms over pork chops. Pour pizza sauce over top.

3. Cover and cook on Low for 4 to 5 hours or on High for 2 to 2 1/2 hours, until pork chops are fork-tender.

4. Sprinkle cheese over top, cover and cook for 10 minutes or until cheese is melted.

5. Divide orzo evenly among individual serving plates. Top each with a pork chop and sauce.

Pork Marrakesh

Makes 4 servings

These pork chops are succulent and full of flavor. The aromatic dried and fresh herbs, combined with the fruit, stimulate your senses, inviting you to indulge. Serve over hot couscous.

Tips

Browning the pork before placing it in the stoneware gives the dish an extra-rich flavor and eliminates some of the fat. But if you're pressed for time, you can season the meat and add it directly to the slow cooker without browning it first.

To toast pine nuts, place the nuts in a dry nonstick skillet over low heat and toast, stirring gently, for 2 to 3 minutes or until fragrant and light golden brown. Be careful: they can burn in an instant!

- **4- to 6-quart slow cooker**

4	pork loin rib chops (about 1 inch/2.5 cm thick), trimmed	4
½ tsp	salt	2 mL
¼ tsp	freshly ground black pepper	1 mL
2 tbsp	olive oil (approx.), divided	30 mL
1	large red onion, thinly sliced	1
12	dried apricots, sliced	12
¾ cup	unsweetened apple juice	175 mL
2 tsp	minced gingerroot	10 mL
½ tsp	dried thyme	2 mL
1	3-inch (7.5 cm) cinnamon stick	1
¼ cup	chopped fresh cilantro	60 mL
	Toasted pine nuts (see tip, at left)	

1. Season both sides of pork chops with salt and pepper. In a large nonstick skillet, heat 1 tbsp (15 mL) of the oil over medium-high heat. Cook pork chops in batches, adding more oil as needed, for about 3 minutes per side or until browned on both sides. Transfer to a plate.

2. Reduce heat to medium and add the remaining 1 tbsp (15 mL) oil to skillet. Sauté red onion for about 3 minutes or until tender and translucent.

3. Arrange half the onion and half the apricots in slow cooker stoneware. Place pork chops on top. Spread the remaining onion and apricots on top. Add apple juice, ginger, thyme and cinnamon stick.

4. Cover and cook on Low for 4 to 5 hours or on High for 2 to 2½ hours, until pork chops are fork-tender. Discard cinnamon stick. Sprinkle with cilantro and pine nuts.

Pork Chops with Horseradish Apples

Makes 4 servings

This home-style dish delivers the wonderful flavors of fall. Granny Smith apples add their special tartness, and the horseradish ups the ante.

Tips

When choosing pork chops for slow cooking, select chops that are at least 1 inch (2.5 cm) thick. Chops that are too thin will overcook and dry out, making them tough and tasteless. I find that shoulder blade (butt) chops, sirloin chops or rib chops give the best results.

You can use pork loin rib chops in this recipe, but you will need to reduce the cooking time to 4 to 5 hours on Low or 2 to 2½ hours on High.

A flour and liquid combination added to a dish to thicken it is called a slurry. To prevent lumps in soups and stews when adding a slurry, combine the liquid and flour in a jar with a tight-fitting lid, then shake well until blended and smooth before pouring it into hot cooking liquid or sauce.

- **4- to 6-quart slow cooker**

4	pork shoulder blade (butt) chops (about 1 inch/2.5 cm thick), trimmed	4
1 tbsp	paprika	15 mL
1 tsp	dried thyme	5 mL
1 tsp	salt	5 mL
½ tsp	freshly ground black pepper	2 mL
2 tbsp	vegetable oil (approx.)	30 mL
2	Granny Smith apples, peeled and cut into ½-inch (1 cm) wedges	2
1	onion, thinly sliced	1
⅓ cup	dry white wine	75 mL
⅓ cup	chicken broth	75 mL
½ cup	heavy or whipping (35%) cream	125 mL
2 tbsp	all-purpose flour	30 mL
2 tbsp	creamed horseradish (approx.)	30 mL
1 tbsp	Dijon mustard	15 mL
2 tbsp	snipped fresh chives (optional)	30 mL

1. Season both sides of pork chops with paprika, thyme, salt and pepper. In a large nonstick skillet, heat half the oil over medium-high heat. Cook pork chops in batches, adding more oil as needed, for about 3 minutes per side or until browned on both sides. Transfer to a plate lined with paper towels and let drain. Transfer to slow cooker stoneware. Arrange apples and onion over pork chops. Pour in wine and broth.

2. Cover and cook on Low for 6 to 8 hours or on High for 3 to 4 hours, until pork chops are fork-tender. Using a slotted spoon, transfer pork chops to a warmed platter and tent loosely with foil.

3. In a jar with a tight-fitting lid, combine cream and flour, shaking until well combined. Stir into liquid in stoneware, along with horseradish and mustard.

4. Cover and cook on High for 15 to 20 minutes or until liquid is slightly thickened. Pour over pork chops. Garnish with chives (if using).

Vietnamese Sticky Pork Chops

Makes 4 to 6 servings

These chops are cooked slowly with spices and a little bit of sugar to create a dish that is sweet, with a hint of heat.

Tips

Rice stick noodles can be prepared in a number of different ways. For this dish, the easiest way is to cook them in boiling water until they are wilted, then drain and rinse. Don't let them boil for too long (only about 2 or 3 minutes) or they will turn to mush.

You can substitute boneless pork shoulder blade (butt) chops for the pork loin rib chops, but you will need to increase the cooking time to 6 to 8 hours on Low or 3 to 4 hours on High.

Hoisin sauce is a thick, reddish brown sauce made from soybeans and used primarily in Thai and Chinese dishes. It can be found in the Asian aisle of the supermarket.

- **4- to 5-quart slow cooker**

2 tbsp	vegetable oil (approx.)	30 mL
4 to 6	pork loin rib chops (about 1 inch/2.5 cm thick), trimmed	4 to 6
3	cloves garlic, minced	3
3	star anise pods (or 1 tsp/5 mL Chinese five-spice powder)	3
1 tbsp	minced gingerroot	15 mL
1 tbsp	granulated sugar	15 mL
1/4 tsp	freshly ground black pepper	1 mL
1/2 cup	hoisin or black bean sauce	125 mL
2 tbsp	rice vinegar	30 mL
1 tbsp	Sriracha chili sauce	15 mL
4	carrots, cut into 1-inch (2.5 cm) pieces	4
1 tbsp	cornstarch	15 mL
2 tbsp	cold water	30 mL
1	green onion, finely chopped	1
	Cooked rice stick noodles	
2 tbsp	chopped fresh cilantro	30 mL
	Toasted sesame seeds (optional)	

1. In a large nonstick skillet, heat half the oil over medium-high heat. Cook pork chops in batches, adding more oil as needed, for about 3 minutes per side or until browned on both sides. Transfer to a plate.

2. In a bowl, combine garlic, star anise, ginger, sugar, pepper, hoisin sauce, vinegar and chili sauce.

3. Arrange carrots in slow cooker stoneware. Place pork chops on carrots. Pour garlic mixture over pork chops.

4. Cover and cook on Low for 4 to 5 hours or on High for 2 to 2 1/2 hours, until pork chops are fork-tender. Using a slotted spoon, transfer pork chops and carrots to a plate. Cover to keep warm.

5. Pour cooking liquid into a saucepan and bring to a boil over medium-high heat. In a bowl, whisk together cornstarch and water. Stir into saucepan and return to a boil. Reduce heat and boil gently, stirring, until sauce is thickened. Stir in green onion.

6. Place noodles on a platter and arrange pork chops on top. Drizzle with sauce and serve additional sauce on the side, if desired. Sprinkle with cilantro and sesame seeds (if using).

Sriracha chili sauce is a purée of chiles, sugar, vinegar, garlic and salt. It is to Thai cuisine what ketchup is to North American cuisine. It is used in cooking and as a condiment to add heat to a dish. You can find it in Asian grocery stores and at many well-stocked supermarkets.

Pulled Pork Taco Supper

Makes 6 to 8 servings

I couldn't choose, so this dish has the makings of a taco with the seasonings of a fajita. It's easy on the cook and on the budget.

Tips

To warm hard taco shells, place on a baking sheet in a 350°F (180°C) oven for 5 minutes. If using soft tortillas, wrap in foil and warm in a 350°F (180°C) oven for 15 to 20 minutes.

To avoid tears when chopping onions, put them in the freezer for a few minutes beforehand.

- **Minimum 4-quart slow cooker**

1	boneless pork shoulder blade (butt) roast (about 3½ lbs/1.75 kg), trimmed	1
½ tsp	salt	2 mL
½ tsp	freshly ground black pepper	2 mL
6	cloves garlic, minced	6
2	onions, finely chopped	2
1 cup	chicken broth	250 mL
1 tbsp	chili powder	15 mL
1 cup	frozen corn kernels, thawed	250 mL
1 cup	salsa	250 mL
2 tbsp	tomato paste	30 mL
¼ cup	finely chopped fresh cilantro or parsley	60 mL
16	hard or soft taco shells, warmed (see tip, at left)	16
2 cups	chopped iceberg lettuce	500 mL
1 cup	chopped tomatoes	250 mL
1 cup	shredded Cheddar cheese	250 mL
¼ cup	light sour cream	60 mL

1. Place pork in slow cooker stoneware and sprinkle with salt and pepper. Add garlic, onions, broth and chili powder.

2. Cover and cook on Low for 8 to 10 hours or on High for 4 to 5 hours, until pork is fork-tender. Transfer pork to a cutting board and let cool slightly.

3. Remove any butcher's string holding the roast together. Using two forks, shred pork.

4. Skim fat from cooking liquid in stoneware. Return pork to cooking liquid. Stir in corn, salsa and tomato paste. Cover and cook on High for 15 minutes or until pork is heated through and sauce is thickened. Stir in cilantro.

5. Ladle into a bowl and serve alongside taco shells, with lettuce, tomatoes, cheese and sour cream for toppings.

Make Ahead

This dish can be assembled up to 2 days in advance. Prepare through step 1, cover and refrigerate. When ready to cook, place stoneware in slow cooker and proceed with step 2.

Liki Tiki Pork

Makes 6 servings

This delicious sweet-and-sour pork evokes thoughts of warm tropical breezes, swaying palm trees and the smell of sand and surf. It is elegant enough to serve on festive occasions or whenever you want to make something special for your family. Serve over rice.

Tip

Hoisin sauce has a sweet, tangy flavor and is available in the Asian foods section of the supermarket.

- **3- to 4-quart slow cooker**

2 tbsp	vegetable oil (approx.)	30 mL
1	boneless pork shoulder blade (butt) roast (about 2 lbs/1 kg), trimmed and cut into 1-inch (2.5 cm) cubes	1
2	stalks celery, chopped	2
1	onion, finely chopped	1
2 tbsp	white wine vinegar	30 mL
1 tbsp	Dijon mustard	15 mL
1 tbsp	hoisin sauce	15 mL
1 tsp	salt	5 mL
1/2 tsp	freshly ground black pepper	2 mL
1	can (8 oz/227 mL) pineapple chunks, drained, reserving juice	1
2 tbsp	cornstarch	30 mL
2 tbsp	cold water	30 mL
1	ripe mango, cut into chunks (see box, page 273)	1
1 cup	macadamia nuts or blanched almonds	250 mL
1/2 cup	unsweetened shredded coconut	125 mL

1. In a large nonstick skillet, heat half the oil over medium-high heat. Cook pork in batches, adding more oil as needed, for about 4 minutes or until browned all over. Using a slotted spoon, transfer to slow cooker stoneware. Stir in celery and onion.

2. In a bowl, combine vinegar, mustard, hoisin sauce, salt, pepper and pineapple juice. Stir into stoneware.

3. Cover and cook on Low for 6 to 8 hours or on High for 3 to 4 hours, until pork is fork-tender and stew is bubbling. Using a slotted spoon, transfer pork to a bowl.

4. In a small bowl, whisk together cornstarch and water. Stir into cooking liquid in stoneware. Cover and cook on High for 10 to 15 minutes or until thickened.

5. Return pork to stoneware, along with pineapple chunks, mango, macadamia nuts and coconut. Stir until warmed through.

BBQ Pork Sandwiches with Five-Vegetable Slaw

Makes 4 to 6 servings

Start the ingredients in the slow cooker in the morning, so dinner simmers during the day. Spicy roast pork and crisp coleslaw add up to down-home sandwiches with uptown taste.

Tips

The most flavorful paprika comes from Hungary. Types range from mild to hot. Use the type that suits your taste.

Tomato paste is now available in tubes in many supermarkets and delis. It keeps for months in the refrigerator.

Molasses is the syrup left over after the sugar crystals have been extracted from the juice of the sugarcane. Light molasses (also called fancy molasses) is sweet, while dark molasses (also called cooking molasses) is thicker, more robust in flavor and less sweet. Blackstrap molasses is bittersweet and very thick. Light and dark molasses can be used interchangeably in most recipes. Try to use unsulfured molasses, which has a purer flavor than sulfured.

- **Minimum 4-quart slow cooker**

4	large garlic cloves, minced	4
1 tsp	ground cumin	5 mL
½ tsp	paprika	2 mL
½ tsp	ground coriander	2 mL
½ tsp	salt	2 mL
¼ tsp	freshly ground black pepper	1 mL
¼ tsp	cayenne pepper	1 mL
⅓ cup	dark (cooking) molasses	75 mL
⅓ cup	cider vinegar	75 mL
¼ cup	tomato paste	60 mL
1	boneless pork shoulder blade (butt) roast (about 2 lbs/1 kg), trimmed	1
2	bay leaves	2
4 to 6	crusty kaiser rolls, split	4 to 6

Five-Vegetable Slaw

4 cups	coleslaw or broccoli slaw mix	1 L
½ cup	thinly sliced red bell pepper	125 mL
½ cup	thinly sliced green bell pepper	125 mL
½	cucumber, peeled, halved lengthwise, seeded and thinly sliced	½
3	green onions, thinly sliced on the diagonal	3
⅓ cup	mayonnaise	75 mL
1 tbsp	cider vinegar	15 mL
¼ tsp	salt	1 mL
¼ tsp	freshly ground black pepper	1 mL

1. In a bowl, whisk together garlic, cumin, paprika, coriander, salt, black pepper, cayenne, molasses, vinegar and tomato paste.

2. Arrange pork and bay leaves in slow cooker stoneware. Stir in molasses mixture until pork is coated.

3. Cover and cook on Low for 8 to 10 hours or on High for 4 to 5 hours, until pork is fork-tender. Transfer pork to a cutting board and let cool slightly.

4. Remove any butcher's string holding the roast together. Using two forks, shred pork.

Resist the urge to lift the lid and taste or smell whatever is inside the slow cooker as it's cooking. Every peek will increase the cooking time by 20 minutes.

5. Skim fat from cooking liquid in stoneware. Discard bay leaves. Return pork to cooking liquid.

6. *Slaw:* In a large bowl, toss together coleslaw mix, red pepper, green pepper, cucumber and green onions. Add mayonnaise, vinegar, salt and pepper; toss to coat.

7. Heap pork mixture on bottom halves of rolls, place a heaping serving of slaw on top and cover with tops of rolls. Serve immediately.

Make Ahead

You can make the vegetable slaw up to 2 days in advance. Cover and refrigerate until ready to use.

This dish can be assembled up to 2 days in advance. Prepare through step 2, cover and refrigerate. When ready to cook, place stoneware in slow cooker and proceed with step 3.

Pork and Potato Poutine

Makes 6 to 8 servings

What teenager doesn't like poutine? This version uses roasted fingerling potatoes, rather than deep-fried french fries, and traditional cheese curds. If you can't find the curds, replace them with shredded white Cheddar or mozzarella cheese.

Tips

While many pork dishes use chicken broth to make the gravy, I like to use beef broth for this one, to add richness. For a lighter-flavored gravy, you can use chicken or veal broth.

Broth (or stock) is one of the most indispensable pantry staples. Commercial broth cubes and powders are loaded with salt and just don't deliver the flavor of homemade stock or prepared broth. I like to keep 32-oz (1 L) Tetra Paks on hand, especially the sodium-reduced variety.

- 4- to 5-quart slow cooker
- Rimmed baking sheet, lined with parchment paper

6	slices bacon, chopped	6
1	boneless pork shoulder blade (butt) roast (about 3 lbs/1.5 kg), trimmed and cut into 1-inch (2.5 cm) cubes	1
1 tbsp	vegetable oil (optional)	15 mL
3	cloves garlic, minced	3
2	carrots, diced	2
2	stalks celery, diced	2
1	large onion, chopped	1
1 tbsp	dried thyme	15 mL
1 tbsp	dried parsley	15 mL
1 tsp	paprika	5 mL
1/2 tsp	salt	2 mL
1/4 tsp	freshly ground black pepper	1 mL
1 1/2 cups	beef broth (see tips, at left)	375 mL
1	bay leaf	1
2 tbsp	cornstarch	30 mL
2 tbsp	cold water	30 mL

Potato Poutine

3 lbs	fingerling potatoes, halved lengthwise	1.5 kg
3 tbsp	olive oil	45 mL
2 tsp	kosher salt	10 mL
1/4 tsp	freshly ground black pepper	1 mL
8 oz	fresh white cheese curds	250 g
	Chopped fresh parsley	

1. In a large nonstick skillet, cook bacon over medium-high heat, stirring, for about 5 minutes or until crisp. Transfer to a plate lined with paper towels. Set aside.

2. In batches, add pork to skillet and cook, adding oil if needed, for about 4 minutes or until browned all over. Using a slotted spoon, transfer to slow cooker stoneware.

3. Add garlic, carrots, celery, onion, thyme, parsley, paprika, salt and pepper to skillet and sauté for about 5 minutes or until fragrant. Add onion mixture and bacon to stoneware.

Variations

This recipe also works well with beef. Use a braising roast, such as a blade, cross rib, chuck or shoulder, and cut it into 1-inch (2.5 cm) cubes.

Reduce the beef broth to 1 cup (250 mL) and add ½ cup (125 mL) dry red wine.

For an upscale version of the poutine, use a soft melting cheese, such as Brie, cut into chunks.

4. Add broth to skillet, bring to a boil and cook for about 5 minutes, scraping up any brown bits from pan. Pour over pork mixture. Add bay leaf.

5. Cover and cook on Low for 8 to 10 hours or on High for 4 to 5 hours, until pork is fork-tender.

6. *Poutine:* Meanwhile, preheat oven to 400°F (200°C). In a large bowl, toss potatoes with oil, salt and pepper. Spread in a single layer on prepared baking sheet. Bake for 40 to 50 minutes, stirring once or twice, until browned and tender.

7. In a bowl, whisk together cornstarch and water. Stir into stoneware. Cover and cook on High for 10 minutes or until gravy is thickened. Discard bay leaf.

8. Divide potatoes evenly among individual serving plates. Ladle pork mixture on top and top with cheese curds and parsley. Serve immediately.

Make Ahead

This dish can be assembled up to 2 days in advance, as long as the pork is left out. Complete steps 1, 3 and 4. Cover and refrigerate. When ready to cook, add vegetable oil to the skillet and brown the pork as directed in step 2. Place stoneware in slow cooker, add pork and proceed with step 5.

Mexican Fiesta Pork

Makes 4 to 6 servings

It's hard to believe this dish could taste so great with so few ingredients. But that's its appeal! Use mild, medium or hot salsa depending on the level of heat you like.

Tips

To save yourself the work, ask the butcher to cut a roast into cubes for you. If that's not possible, trim and cube a piece of pork shoulder for this dish. If the pork shoulder is bone-in, be sure to buy enough to yield 2 lbs (1 kg) once the bone is removed.

Many independent butchers sell pork stew meat, which is fine to use in this recipe.

- **Minimum 4-quart slow cooker**

1	boneless pork shoulder blade (butt) roast (about 2 lbs/1 kg), trimmed and cut into 1-inch (2.5 cm) cubes	1
1	can (4½ oz/127 mL) chopped mild green chiles, drained	1
4½ cups	thick and chunky salsa	1.125 L
2 cups	cooked or canned black beans (see page 120), drained and rinsed	500 mL
	Mexican Rice (see recipe, opposite) or flour tortillas, warmed	
1 cup	shredded Monterey Jack cheese	250 mL
	Guacamole or sour cream (optional)	

1. In slow cooker stoneware, combine pork, chiles and salsa.

2. Cover and cook on Low for 6 to 8 hours or until fork-tender.

3. Stir in beans. Cover and cook on Low for 5 to 10 minutes or until beans are heated through.

4. Spoon pork mixture over Mexican Rice or into warm tortillas. Sprinkle with cheese. Top each portion with a dollop of guacamole (if using).

Make Ahead

This dish can be assembled up to 12 hours in advance. Prepare through step 1, cover and refrigerate overnight. The next day, place stoneware in slow cooker and proceed with step 2.

Tip

Jalapeño peppers contain volatile oils that can burn your skin and eyes if they come into direct contact. It is best to wear plastic or rubber gloves when chopping jalapeños, and take care not to touch your face or eyes while you work. If your bare hands do touch the peppers, wash your hands and nails well with hot, soapy water.

Mexican Rice

- *Preheat oven to 350°F (180°C)*
- *Large ovenproof skillet, with lid*

1	white onion, finely chopped	1
1	can (19 oz/540 mL) diced tomatoes, with juice	1
2 cups	long-grain white rice	500 mL
1/3 cup	vegetable oil	75 mL
4	cloves garlic, minced	4
3	jalapeño peppers, seeded and minced, divided	3
2 cups	chicken broth	500 mL
1 1/2 tsp	salt	7 mL
1/2 cup	finely chopped fresh cilantro	125 mL
1	lime, cut into wedges	1

1. In a bowl, combine onion and tomatoes with juice. Set aside.

2. In a fine-mesh strainer, rinse rice under cold running water until water runs clear. Drain well.

3. In ovenproof skillet, heat oil over medium-high heat for about 2 minutes. (Add a few grains of rice; if they sizzle, the oil is hot enough.) Stir-fry rice for 6 to 8 minutes or until light golden and translucent.

4. Reduce heat to medium. Add garlic and two-thirds of the jalapeños to skillet and sauté for about 1 1/2 minutes or until fragrant. Stir in reserved onion mixture, broth and salt. Increase heat to high and bring to a boil.

5. Cover and bake in preheated oven for 30 to 35 minutes, stirring once halfway through, until liquid is absorbed and rice is tender. Stir in cilantro and the remaining jalapeño to taste. Serve with lime wedges on the side.

Pork Curry with Apples and Chinese Noodles

Makes 6 servings

This tasty curry looks as good as it tastes. Offer a dish of mango chutney alongside, to complement the flavors of the fruit. You can also serve this curry over hot cooked rice.

Tips

It's easy to grate gingerroot if you keep an unpeeled nub of it in the freezer, wrapped in a plastic freezer bag. (Ginger tends to quickly get moldy and soft when it's stored in the fridge.) Use a Microplane-style rasp grater, available at good kitchenware and department stores, for best results. These have tiny razor-like edges that make quick and easy tasks of grating and cleaning.

It is best to use lo mein noodles for this dish since they can be cooked in boiling water, which is easier than frying the noodles to serve with the curry. If Chinese egg noodles aren't available, thin Italian pasta, such as fettuccini or linguini, makes a handy substitute.

- **3½- to 5-quart slow cooker**

2 tbsp	vegetable oil (approx.)	30 mL
1	boneless pork shoulder blade (butt) roast (about 2 lbs/1 kg), trimmed and cut into 1-inch (2.5 cm) cubes	1
1	large onion, sliced	1
2	cloves garlic, minced	2
1 tbsp	grated gingerroot	15 mL
1	3-inch (7.5 cm) cinnamon stick	1
1 tsp	ground coriander	5 mL
1 tsp	ground cumin	5 mL
1 tsp	ground turmeric	5 mL
½ tsp	hot pepper flakes	2 mL
½ tsp	fennel seeds	2 mL
½ tsp	salt	2 mL
¼ tsp	freshly ground black pepper	1 mL
½ cup	chicken broth	125 mL
1 tbsp	all-purpose flour	15 mL
1 cup	plain yogurt (not fat-free)	250 mL
1 tbsp	liquid honey	15 mL
2	red-skinned apples, cut into cubes	2
1	package (12 oz/350 g) fresh lo mein noodles	1
⅓ cup	chopped fresh cilantro or parsley	75 mL
¼ cup	raisins	60 mL
¼ cup	chopped roasted peanuts	60 mL

1. In a large nonstick skillet, heat half the oil over medium-high heat. Cook pork in batches, adding more oil as needed, for about 4 minutes or until browned all over. Using a slotted spoon, transfer to slow cooker stoneware.

2. Reduce heat to medium. Add onion to skillet and sauté until tender and translucent. Add garlic, ginger, cinnamon stick, coriander, cumin, turmeric, hot pepper flakes, fennel seeds, salt and black pepper; sauté for about 3 minutes or until fragrant. Stir in broth. Pour into stoneware.

3. Cover and cook on Low for 8 to 10 hours or on High for 4 to 5 hours, until pork is fork-tender.

Cooking times can vary a great deal between slow cooker manufacturers. Always let your food cook for the minimum amount of time before testing for doneness.

4. In a bowl, stir together flour, yogurt and honey. Stir into stoneware, along with apples. Cover and cook on High for 20 minutes or until pork mixture is thickened and apples are warmed through and slightly softened. Discard cinnamon stick.

5. Meanwhile, in a large pot of boiling salted water, cook noodles for 3 to 4 minutes or until tender. Drain and toss into pork mixture. Transfer to a large platter and sprinkle with cilantro, raisins and peanuts.

In Chinese, *mein* means "noodles," and the two most popular types are lo mein and chow mein. Lo mein are tossed noodles, which are added to a stir-fry at the end of the cooking process so they stay soft and absorb the sauce. Chow mein are fried first so they are crunchy and crisp.

Ham, Barley and Sweet Potato Jambalaya

Makes 6 servings

It's time for a little history lesson. Listen well. Some say the word "jambalaya" came from the French jambon, meaning "ham," the French phrase à la, meaning "in the style of," and the African ya, meaning "rice." However the word originated, jambalaya is a traditional Louisiana one-pot meal — but you can serve it with a nice green salad and French bread.

Tips

Cajun seasoning is available at most supermarkets and specialty food stores. If you can't find it, substitute 1½ tsp (7 mL) ground cumin, 1 tsp (5 mL) each ground thyme and paprika, ¼ tsp (1 mL) cayenne pepper and a pinch of ground allspice.

Rinse the barley in a fine-mesh sieve under cold running water, stirring to make sure it is thoroughly rinsed, then drain well.

- **3½- to 5-quart slow cooker**

1 tbsp	vegetable oil	15 mL
2 cups	cubed Black Forest ham	500 mL
2	cloves garlic, minced	2
2	stalks celery, chopped	2
1	onion, chopped	1
2 tsp	Cajun seasoning	10 mL
1 tsp	dried oregano	5 mL
1 tsp	salt	5 mL
½ tsp	freshly ground black pepper	2 mL
1	can (28 oz/796 mL) diced tomatoes, with juice	1
3 cups	chicken broth	750 mL
1 cup	pearl barley, rinsed	250 mL
2	large sweet potatoes, peeled and cut into ½-inch (1 cm) cubes	2
2	bay leaves	2
1	green bell pepper, finely chopped	1
8 oz	large cooked peeled shrimp (optional)	250 g
2 tbsp	chopped fresh parsley	30 mL
	Hot pepper sauce	

1. In a large skillet, heat oil over medium heat. Sauté ham, garlic, celery, onion, Cajun seasoning, oregano, salt and pepper for about 5 minutes or until ham is browned all over and onion is tender and translucent. Stir in tomatoes with juice, broth and barley; bring to a boil. Transfer to slow cooker stoneware. Stir in sweet potatoes and bay leaves.

2. Cover and cook on Low for 6 to 8 hours or on High for 3 to 4 hours, until most of the liquid is absorbed.

3. Using a fork, stir in green pepper and shrimp (if using). Cover and cook on High for 20 minutes or until green pepper is tender and shrimp are heated through. Discard bay leaves. Sprinkle with parsley. Serve with hot pepper sauce (you can add a few dashes directly to the jambalaya if you know all your diners like heat).

Variation

Try this dish with smoked turkey in place of the ham.

Make Ahead

This dish can be assembled up to 2 days in advance. Complete step 1, omitting the barley, cover and refrigerate. When ready to cook, place stoneware in slow cooker, add barley and proceed with step 2.

Pearl barley is a popular grain and a great alternative to rice. It has been hulled, steamed and polished, meaning the bran has been removed. It has an oval shape with a dull white color. When cooked, it has a creamy, chewy texture. Barley can be found near the dried peas and beans in the supermarket.

Stuffed Zucchini with Ham and Rice

Makes 4 servings

This dish is best made in a large oval slow cooker, which will hold both of the zucchini. Look for smaller zucchini, but if you can't find them, trim and cut the zucchini into smaller chunks and spoon the rice mixture over the chunks.

Variation

In place of the ham, you can use smoked turkey or chicken.

• **Minimum 5-quart slow cooker (preferably oval)**

2	zucchini (about 7 inches/18 cm long)	2
	Salt	
2	thick slices Black Forest ham, finely chopped	2
1	small onion, finely chopped	1
1	can (14 oz/398 mL) diced tomatoes, with juice	1
1 cup	cooked long-grain white rice	250 mL
½ tsp	paprika	2 mL
½ tsp	dried oregano	2 mL
½ cup	crumbled feta cheese	125 mL

1. Remove ends of zucchini, then cut each in half lengthwise, scoop out seedy pulp and discard. Sprinkle zucchini with salt and set aside.

2. Meanwhile, in a large bowl, combine ham, onion, tomatoes with juice, rice, paprika and oregano. Mound rice mixture in scooped-out zucchini and place in slow cooker stoneware.

3. Cover and cook on Low for 4 to 5 hours or until zucchini are tender. Sprinkle with cheese. Cover and cook for 5 to 10 minutes or until cheese has melted.

Make Ahead

This dish can be assembled up to 12 hours in advance. Prepare through step 2, cover and refrigerate overnight. The next day, place stoneware in slow cooker and proceed with step 3.

Unstuffed Sweet-and-Sour Cabbage

Makes 4 servings

Making Eastern European–style cabbage rolls is a time-consuming endeavor. This unorthodox method, which uses dried cranberries and ground pork, is much easier — and, I like to think, tastes even better.

Tip

I like to use savoy cabbage for this dish. With its flavorful crinkled leaves, this cabbage is one of the best for cooking. Its loose leaves have lace-patterned veins and vary in color from dark to light green. They are tender and have a milder, sweeter flavor than those of green cabbage. You can also use red cabbage.

- **Minimum 5-quart slow cooker (preferably oval)**

1	head green cabbage (about 2 lbs/1 kg), quartered lengthwise and cored	1
1/4 cup	sodium-reduced chicken broth	60 mL
3	cloves garlic, thinly sliced, divided	3
1 tsp	salt, divided	5 mL
1 tbsp	olive oil	15 mL
1	large onion, thinly sliced	1
1 lb	lean ground pork or turkey (or 8 oz/250 g of each)	500 g
1/2 tsp	freshly ground black pepper	2 mL
1	can (28 oz/796 mL) diced tomatoes, with juice	1
1/3 cup	dried cranberries or cherries	75 mL
1 tbsp	packed dark brown sugar	15 mL
3 tbsp	red wine vinegar	45 mL
2 tbsp	chopped fresh flat-leaf (Italian) parsley	30 mL

1. Place cabbage in slow cooker stoneware. Add broth, one-third of the garlic and 1/4 tsp (1 mL) of the salt.

2. Meanwhile, in a large nonstick skillet, heat oil over medium-high heat. Sauté onion for about 3 minutes or until tender and translucent. Add the remaining garlic and sauté for 1 minute. Add pork, the remaining salt and pepper; cook, breaking up pork with the back of a wooden spoon, for about 3 minutes or until pork is no longer pink. Stir in tomatoes with juice, cranberries, brown sugar and vinegar. Pour into stoneware.

3. Cover and cook on Low for 8 to 10 hours or on High for 4 to 5 hours, until bubbling. Transfer to a serving dish and sprinkle with parsley.

Make Ahead

This dish can be assembled up to 12 hours in advance. Prepare through step 2, letting pork mixture cool before adding it to stoneware. Cover and refrigerate overnight. The next day, place stoneware in slow cooker and proceed with step 3.

Uptown Pork and Beans

Makes 4 to 6 servings

Residents of the city of Waterloo, Ontario, call our downtown area "Uptown." We are also famous for our sausages, served frequently during autumn, when we celebrate Canada's largest Bavarian festival, Oktoberfest, which celebrates the German heritage of many of the region's settlers. This recipe is a nod to our world-renowned festival and great city!

Tip

Leftovers from this tasty meal can be served over spaetzle noodles or on soft kaiser rolls. (You could call the latter "Sloppy Johanns"!)

- **4- to 6-quart slow cooker**

1 lb	fresh Oktoberfest-style sausages or other mild fresh sausages	500 g
6	thick slices bacon, chopped	6
2	cans (each 14 oz/398 mL) baked beans in tomato sauce	2
2	cloves garlic, minced	2
2	carrots, cut into ½-inch (1 cm) chunks	2
1	onion, finely chopped	1
1	stalk celery, chopped	1
1 cup	ketchup	250 mL
1 cup	unsweetened apple cider or apple juice	250 mL
2 tbsp	cider vinegar	30 mL
2 tbsp	Oktoberfest-style mustard or honey mustard	30 mL
2 tbsp	pure maple syrup	30 mL

1. In a large skillet, cook sausage over medium-high heat, turning often, for 10 minutes or until browned all over. Remove from heat and cut into 1-inch (2.5 cm) slices. Transfer to slow cooker stoneware.

2. Stir in bacon, beans, garlic, carrots, onion, celery, ketchup, apple cider, vinegar, mustard and maple syrup.

3. Cover and cook on Low for 6 to 8 hours or on High for 3 to 4 hours, until bubbling.

Make Ahead

This dish can be assembled up to 12 hours in advance. Prepare through step 2, letting sausage cool before adding it to stoneware. Cover and refrigerate overnight. The next day, place stoneware in slow cooker and proceed with step 3.

Oktoberfest mustard is a traditional Russian-style sweet mustard. While some mustards have a sharp, pungent flavor, this mustard is tangy, with a touch of sweetness. A sweet brown mustard or honey mustard is a good alternative. Independent butcher shops and gourmet food shops usually have a good selection of specialty mustards.

Sausage Lasagna

Makes 8 servings

This meat sauce starts quickly on the stove, but hours in the slow cooker add a real depth of flavor. Use sheets of fresh lasagna; that way, you can trim them easily with scissors to fit either oval or round slow cookers.

Tips

To fit lasagna noodles into a round slow cooker, break off corners as needed. You don't have to precook the noodles. When the lasagna's done, they'll be ready too.

Cooking times are approximate and can vary among slow cookers. Lasagna can be prone to overcooking, so begin to check for doneness at the minimum cooking time, if possible.

- **Minimum 5-quart slow cooker (preferably oval)**

1 lb	mild or hot fresh Italian sausage, casings removed	500 g
2	carrots, finely chopped	2
2	cloves garlic, minced	2
1	onion, finely chopped	1
2 tsp	dried basil leaves	10 mL
1/2 tsp	salt	2 mL
1/4 tsp	freshly ground black pepper	1 mL
1	can (28 oz/796 mL) tomato pasta sauce	1
2 cups	shredded mozzarella cheese, divided	500 mL
1 cup	ricotta cheese	250 mL
1 cup	freshly grated Parmesan cheese	250 mL
1/4 cup	basil pesto	60 mL
4 to 6	sheets fresh lasagna (or 15 oven-ready lasagna noodles)	4 to 6

1. In a large pot or Dutch oven, cook sausage over medium-high heat, breaking it up with the back of a wooden spoon, for 6 to 8 minutes or until browned. Add carrots, garlic, onion, basil, salt and pepper; sauté for 3 to 5 minutes or until onion is tender and translucent. Stir in pasta sauce. Set aside.

2. In a bowl, combine 1 cup (250 mL) of the mozzarella, ricotta, Parmesan and pesto.

3. Spoon one-quarter of the sausage mixture into slow cooker stoneware. Top with 1 fresh lasagna sheet (or 5 oven-ready noodles, broken into pieces to fit), breaking an extra lasagna sheet into pieces if necessary to cover sausage mixture completely. Spread with half the cheese mixture, then one-quarter of the sausage mixture. Repeat the layers twice more, ending with sausage mixture.

4. Cover and cook on Low for 4 to 6 hours or until lasagna is tender and heated through.

5. Sprinkle the remaining mozzarella over lasagna in stoneware. Turn off heat, cover and let stand for about 10 minutes or until cheese is melted.

Seven-Layer Sausage Rigatoni Casserole

Makes 8 servings

A slow cooker is ideal for pasta casseroles. During the long cooking, the flavors blend and the sauce melts into every corner of the pasta. If you're letting it cook for longer than 6 hours, you'll want to make sure your slow cooker switches to Warm mode when it should, so the pasta doesn't overcook.

Tip

A generous amount of salt in the cooking water seasons the pasta internally as it absorbs the water and swells. The claim that salted water cooks food faster (because the salt increases the boiling temperature) is exaggerated: you're not adding enough salt to raise the boiling temperature by more than about 1°F (1°C).

- **4- to 6-quart slow cooker, stoneware greased**

3 cups	rigatoni pasta	750 mL
1 lb	mild or hot fresh Italian sausage, casings removed	500 g
3	cloves garlic, minced	3
1	can (28 oz/796 mL) crushed tomatoes	1
1	can (10 oz/284 mL) condensed cream of mushroom soup	1
1 tbsp	dried basil	15 mL
1	jar (13 oz/370 mL) roasted red bell peppers, drained and chopped (see tip, page 327)	1
2	zucchini, coarsely chopped	2
2½ cups	shredded mozzarella cheese	625 mL
½ cup	freshly grated Parmesan cheese	125 mL
½ cup	fresh bread crumbs	125 mL
2 tbsp	melted butter	30 mL

1. In a large pot of boiling salted water, cook rigatoni for 7 to 8 minutes or until firm but tender (al dente). Drain.

2. Meanwhile, in a large skillet, cook sausage over medium-high heat, breaking it up with the back of a wooden spoon, for about 6 to 8 minutes or until browned. Remove from heat.

3. In a bowl, combine garlic, tomatoes, soup and basil.

4. Place half the pasta in bottom of prepared slow cooker stoneware. Top with half the sausage, then half the red peppers and zucchini. Spread with half the tomato mixture. Sprinkle with half the mozzarella. Repeat the layers with the remaining ingredients.

5. In a bowl, combine Parmesan and bread crumbs. Sprinkle evenly over pasta mixture. Drizzle with butter.

6. Cover and cook on Low for 4 to 6 hours or on High for 2 to 3 hours, until bubbling.

Abruzzi-Style Spaghetti

Makes 6 to 8 servings

One night while watching a cooking show on television, my kitchen assistant Leslie saw a celebrity chef prepare a rustic pasta sauce with pork ribs and sausage. "Why don't we try making something similar in the slow cooker?" she asked. When I developed this hearty Italian-style dinner, it was a huge hit with everyone, including my household's hungry teenagers. Serve bowls of this pasta with fresh bread and a green salad.

Tips

Tomato paste is now available in tubes in many supermarkets and delis. These tubes are great, because you can just use as much as you need and the rest keeps for months in the refrigerator.

To prevent soft, mushy pasta, do not allow it to be in the water any longer than necessary. Add it only when the water is at a full boil, and keep it at a steady boil while it cooks.

- **Minimum 4-quart slow cooker**

1½ lbs	pork spareribs	750 g
1 lb	mild fresh Italian sausage	500 g
4	cloves garlic, minced	4
¾ cup	freshly grated Parmesan cheese	175 mL
½ cup	Italian-seasoned dry bread crumbs	125 mL
2 tbsp	dried basil	30 mL
1 tbsp	granulated sugar	30 mL
½ tsp	freshly ground black pepper	2 mL
1	can (48 oz/1.42 L) tomato juice	1
1	can (5½ oz/156 mL) tomato paste	1
1½ lbs	spaghetti	750 g
	Chopped fresh flat-leaf (Italian) parsley	
	Grated Parmesan cheese (optional)	

1. Cut spareribs into two- or three-rib portions. Cut sausage into 3-inch (7.5 cm) lengths. Set aside.

2. In slow cooker stoneware, combine garlic, cheese, bread crumbs, basil, sugar and pepper. Whisk in tomato juice and tomato paste until blended. Add spareribs and sausage, spooning sauce evenly over meat.

3. Cover and cook on Low for 4 to 6 hours or on High for 8 to 10 hours, until pork is falling off the bones.

4. Meanwhile, in a large pot of boiling salted water, cook spaghetti for 8 to 10 minutes or until tender but firm (al dente). Drain.

5. Using a slotted spoon, transfer spareribs and sausage to a platter, arranging them around the edge. Skim off fat from sauce. Toss spaghetti with 2 cups (500 mL) of the sauce, then transfer to center of platter. Sprinkle spaghetti with parsley and additional cheese, if desired. Serve the remaining sauce on the side.

Make Ahead

This dish can be assembled up to 12 hours in advance. Cut the spareribs and sausage as described in step 1 and refrigerate each separately. Prepare the cheese mixture and refrigerate it separately. The next day, assemble ingredients in slow cooker stoneware and proceed with step 3.

Rubbed 'n' Dipped Caribbean Spiced Ribs

Makes 4 servings

This recipe uses a traditional dry rub spice blend to flavor the ribs, followed by a slow simmer in a sweet yet tangy barbecue sauce.

Tips

Look for well-trimmed ribs at the market or grocery store. Ask the butcher to remove the silverskin (the membrane at the back of the ribs) to save you time. But if you purchase untrimmed cuts, which can be quite a cost savings, it is easy enough to do this yourself. The membrane is located on the underside (the concave side) of the rack of ribs. Holding a piece of paper towel to help you grip, wiggle your fingers underneath the membrane and gently pull it away from the meat.

You can also use 2 lbs (1 kg) country-style ribs, cut into individual rib portions, for this recipe. Country-style ribs are the meatiest cut of pork ribs.

- **Minimum 5-quart slow cooker, stoneware greased**

3 lbs	pork back ribs	1.5 kg
2 tbsp	dried minced onion	30 mL
1 tsp	dry mustard	5 mL
1 tsp	hot pepper flakes	5 mL
1/2 tsp	ground allspice	2 mL
1/2 tsp	ground cinnamon	2 mL
1/2 tsp	garlic powder	2 mL
1	onion, sliced	1
1 1/2 cups	barbecue sauce	375 mL

1. Cut ribs into three- or four-rib portions. Remove silverskin from underside of ribs, if necessary (see tip, at left).

2. In a small bowl, combine onion, mustard, hot pepper flakes, allspice, cinnamon and garlic powder. Rub onion mixture into ribs. Place ribs in prepared slow cooker stoneware, then tuck onion slices between ribs. Pour 1/2 cup (125 mL) water around ribs.

3. Cover and cook on Low for 8 to 9 hours, until ribs are tender. Using a slotted spoon, gently remove ribs from stoneware, draining well. Discard cooking liquid.

4. Pour barbecue sauce into a shallow bowl. Dip ribs in sauce, then return to stoneware. Pour any remaining sauce over ribs. Cover and cook on Low for 1 hour or until ribs are glazed.

Make Ahead

This dish can be assembled up to 12 hours in advance. Prepare through step 2, cover and refrigerate overnight. The next day, place stoneware in slow cooker and proceed with step 3.

Mexican Pork Ribs

Makes 4 to 6 servings

Tomatillos are small green fruits surrounded by papery husks, and they are a staple in Mexican cuisine. Green tomatoes or firm plum (Roma) tomatoes seasoned with lemon juice can be used as a substitute. Serve with Mexican Rice (page 257).

Tips

Store fresh ripe tomatillos with their husks on in a paper bag in the refrigerator for up to 1 month. Just make sure they don't get wet, or the inside of the husk may become a little slimy. When you are ready to use them, peel off the husks and wash the tomatillos to remove any stickiness.

Tomatillos may also be frozen whole or sliced. Thawed tomatillo will be soft, but fine for use in this sauce.

- **3- to 5-quart slow cooker**
- *Preheat broiler, with rack set 6 inches (15 cm) below heat source*
- *Blender*
- *Broiler pan or rimmed baking sheet, lined with foil*

1 lb	tomatillos, husks removed, washed (or one 11-oz/325 mL can, drained)	500 g
4 lbs	country-style pork ribs, cut into individual ribs, if possible	2 kg
2 tbsp	olive oil	30 mL
	Salt and freshly ground black pepper	
3	cloves garlic, minced	3
2	jalapeño peppers, seeded and finely chopped	2
1	onion, finely chopped	1
2	cans (each 4½ oz/127 mL) diced mild green chiles	2
1 tbsp	dried oregano	15 mL
⅓ cup	chopped fresh cilantro (approx.)	75 mL
	Shredded Cheddar cheese	
	Lime wedges	
	Fresh cilantro leaves (optional)	

1. In blender, purée tomatillos until smooth. Set aside.

2. Rub ribs with oil and place in prepared broiler pan. Season with salt and pepper. Broil, turning once, for 10 to 15 minutes or until browned. Drain and transfer to slow cooker stoneware.

3. Stir in tomatillos, garlic, jalapeños, onion, chiles, oregano, ½ tsp (2 mL) salt, ¼ tsp (1 mL) pepper and ½ cup (125 mL) water.

4. Cover and cook on Low for 5 hours or on High for 2½ hours, stirring twice to coat ribs, until ribs are tender.

5. Stir in cilantro. Serve sprinkled with cheese, and with lime wedges to squeeze over top. Garnish with additional cilantro leaves, if desired.

> The term "country-style ribs" is a bit confusing, as they are not really ribs at all. This cut comes from the rib end of the loin. The butcher cuts across and through the loin, then opens up the loin like a book. The "ribs" are sold as a slab with bones on the end, but sometimes they come in small chunks. Either way, they will cook up perfectly in the slow cooker.

Boneless Pork Ribs Braised with Fennel and Olives

Makes 6 to 8 servings

Because country-style pork ribs are meaty and thick, they don't really lend themselves to being eaten with your hands, like back ribs do. They are, however, beautifully suited to braising in the slow cooker. Fragrant with fennel and olives, this dish works well for an evening with guests. Serve it with risotto or roasted garlic potatoes, and have a warm loaf of crusty French bread nearby, for soaking up the extra sauce.

Tip

Flat-leaf (Italian) parsley is more fragrant and less bitter than the curly variety.

- **Minimum 5-quart slow cooker**

¼ cup	all-purpose flour	60 mL
2 tsp	ground fennel seeds	10 mL
1 tsp	coarse salt	5 mL
¼ tsp	freshly ground black pepper	1 mL
3 lbs	country-style pork ribs, cut into individual ribs, if possible	1.5 kg
⅓ cup	olive oil (approx.), divided	75 mL
1	large fennel bulb, stems and fronds removed, cut lengthwise into ½-inch (1 cm) slices	1
1	onion, sliced	1
6	cloves garlic, minced	6
1 tsp	dried rosemary	5 mL
1 cup	chicken broth	250 mL
1 cup	diced tomatoes	250 mL
1 tsp	grated orange zest	5 mL
½ cup	freshly squeezed orange juice	125 mL
½ cup	pitted kalamata olives	125 mL
2 tbsp	chopped fresh flat-leaf (Italian) parsley	60 mL

1. On a plate, combine flour, fennel seeds, salt and pepper. Dredge ribs in flour mixture to coat, brushing off excess. Reserve the remaining flour mixture.

2. In a large nonstick skillet, heat 2 tbsp (30 mL) of the oil over medium-high heat. Cook ribs in batches, adding more oil as necessary, for about 3 minutes per side or until browned all over. Transfer to a plate.

3. Dredge fennel slices in the reserved flour mixture. Reserve any remaining flour mixture. Add the remaining oil to skillet. Cook fennel slices for about 2 minutes per side or until lightly browned. Arrange in slow cooker stoneware. Place ribs over fennel.

4. Reduce heat to medium. Add onion to skillet and cook for about 3 minutes or until tender and translucent. Stir in garlic, rosemary and the reserved flour mixture until onions are coated. Stir in broth and bring to a boil. Add tomatoes and orange juice; cook, stirring, for about 5 minutes or until slightly thickened. Pour over ribs.

Tip

To zest an orange, use a Microplane-style rasp grater or citrus zester, ensuring that you don't grate the white pith underneath. Microplanes have tiny razor-like edges, which make quick and easy tasks of grating and cleaning. If you use a zester, finely chop the zest before adding it to the recipe. Microplanes and zesters are widely available at specialty kitchenware shops.

5. Cover and cook on Low for 5 hours or on High for $2\frac{1}{2}$ hours, until ribs are tender.

6. Sprinkle with olives, parsley and orange zest. Cover and cook for 6 to 8 minutes or until olives are heated though.

Fennel bulb, a vegetable commonly found in Mediterranean-style dishes, has a licorice flavor that is mellowed by cooking. It has a grapefruit-size bulb with stalks and fronds poking out from the top. To prepare fennel bulb, simply trim the hard, hollow stalks from the top (saving the feathery fronds for garnish, if you like). Cut the bulb in half lengthwise, then slice it vertically.

Jerk Pork Ribs and Sweet Potatoes

Makes 6 servings

Jerk seasoning, a fiery spice blend, comes to us from the island of Jamaica. While some purist "jerks" may crave the heat, it is actually the flavor notes of thyme and allspice you want to capture in this dish. Serve it with Mango Salad (see recipe, opposite) — the colors are beautiful.

Tips

I used a dry jerk rub for this recipe, but a liquid seasoning would work well too.

Country-style ribs are the meatiest cut of pork ribs, but side ribs or spareribs will also work in this recipe. To help reduce the fat in the finished dish, cut the slab into five- or six-rib portions, place in a large pot of water and bring to a boil, then reduce heat and simmer for 30 to 45 minutes. Continue with step 1 as directed.

- **Minimum 4-quart slow cooker**
- *Preheat broiler, with rack set 6 inches (15 cm) below heat source*
- *Broiler pan or rimmed baking sheet, lined with foil*

3 lbs	country-style pork ribs, cut into individual ribs, if possible	1.5 kg
1 tsp	salt	5 mL
1/2 tsp	freshly ground black pepper	2 mL
2 tbsp	Jamaican jerk seasoning	30 mL
1/4 cup	dark rum	60 mL
2 tbsp	vegetable oil	30 mL
2 tbsp	butter, softened	30 mL
2 lbs	sweet potatoes, peeled and cut into 1/2-inch (1 cm) slices	1 kg
1	onion, sliced	1
2 tbsp	packed brown sugar	30 mL
3	green onions, sliced	3
1	tomato, finely chopped	1

1. Place ribs on prepared broiler pan and season with salt and pepper. Broil, turning once, for 10 to 15 minutes or until browned. Transfer to a plate lined with paper towels and let drain.

2. In a bowl, combine jerk seasoning, rum and oil. Set aside.

3. Spread butter over bottom of slow cooker stoneware. Arrange potatoes and onion on top. Sprinkle with brown sugar. Place ribs on top. Spoon jerk mixture over ribs.

4. Cover and cook on Low for 6 to 8 hours or on High for 3 to 4 hours, until ribs are tender. Using a slotted spoon, transfer potatoes and ribs to a warmed platter and tent with foil to keep warm.

5. Skim fat from cooking liquid, then stir in green onions and tomato. Spoon over ribs.

> Originating in Jamaica, jerk seasoning is used to season meat for grilling. The ingredients vary from cook to cook, but it is generally a combination of hot chile peppers and allspice, with additional seasonings such as cinnamon, cloves, thyme, garlic and onions.

This crisp, colorful salad provides a refreshing contrast to the jerk flavors from the pork ribs. Together, they make a great entertaining menu, as you can start the ribs earlier in the day and toss the salad together at the end. For an extra-peppery flavor, use baby arugula or watercress in place of the Boston lettuce in the salad.

Tip

When it comes to mangos, color is not an indication of freshness. Instead of looking at color, choose fruit that is slightly soft to the touch. Store unripe mangos at room temperature. Once they are ripe, store them in the refrigerator for up to 5 days.

Mango Salad

3	green onions, thinly sliced	3
2	ripe mangos, peeled and cubed	2
1	head Boston lettuce, leaves separated and torn	1
1	red bell pepper, thinly sliced	1
1 cup	shredded red cabbage	250 mL
1/4 cup	chopped fresh cilantro	60 mL
1/2 cup	extra virgin olive oil	125 mL
1 tbsp	liquid honey	15 mL
	Grated zest and freshly squeezed juice of 1 lime	
	Salt and freshly ground black pepper	

1. In a large bowl, toss together green onions, mangos, lettuce, red pepper and cabbage.

2. In a jar with a tight-fitting lid, combine cilantro, oil, honey, lime zest and lime juice. Add to mango mixture and toss gently to coat. Let stand for 10 minutes to allow the flavors to develop.

Slicing a mango can be a challenge. First, slice the unpeeled mango from stem end to bottom end, parallel to the flat seed. Flip the mango around and repeat on the other side. These slices are known as cheeks. (What's left in the middle is mostly the seed.) Placing the cheeks flesh side up, cut parallel slices into the flesh, being careful not to cut through to the skin. Turn the mango 90 degrees and cut another set of parallel slices, making a checkerboard pattern. Turn the scored cheek inside out by pushing the skin up from underneath. Using a sharp paring knife, scrape the chunks off the skin.

Mediterranean "Pulled" Lamb with Mint Vinegar

Makes 6 to 8 servings

I love the flavor combination of lemon, garlic and herbs with lamb, and this recipe fulfills my taste buds' expectations! This is not meant to be a roast, but it is meant to be fall-apart soft — almost like "pulled" lamb. I serve it over Greek-Style Couscous (see recipe, opposite), but if you're pressed for time, a plain couscous served with a tomato and cucumber salad will work well too.

Tips

Fresh lamb shoulder roasts are sometimes hard to find if you don't have a farmer's market nearby. Ask your butcher to order it in for you, if possible, or look for a frozen roast and thaw it in the refrigerator (it'll take 1 to 2 days).

Fresh mint in the vinegar is what really elevates this lamb dish and finishes it beautifully. I would not recommend substituting dried mint. Take the extra time to chop the fresh herb. Look for small containers of fresh herbs in the produce aisle of the supermarket.

• **Minimum 4-quart slow cooker**

1	boneless lamb shoulder roast (3 to 4 lbs/1.5 to 2 kg), tied	1
1/2 tsp	salt	2 mL
1/4 tsp	freshly ground black pepper	1 mL
4 to 6	cloves garlic, crushed	4 to 6
1/2 cup	freshly squeezed lemon juice	125 mL
1/4 cup	olive oil	60 mL
1 tsp	dried oregano	5 mL
1 tsp	ground nutmeg	5 mL

Mint Vinegar

1/4 cup	white balsamic vinegar	60 mL
1 tbsp	finely chopped fresh mint leaves	15 mL
1 tsp	granulated sugar	5 mL

1. Place lamb in slow cooker stoneware and sprinkle with salt and pepper.

2. In a bowl, combine garlic, lemon juice, oil, oregano and nutmeg. Pour over lamb.

3. Cover and cook on Low for 10 to 12 hours or on High for 5 to 6 hours, until lamb is fork-tender. Transfer lamb to a bowl and cut off strings. Using two forks, pull lamb apart into chunky shreds, discarding excess fat. Arrange on a deep serving platter.

4. *Vinegar:* In a small saucepan, combine vinegar, mint and sugar; bring to a boil. Reduce heat and simmer, stirring, for 1 minute or until sugar is dissolved. Drizzle over lamb.

Using all the flavors and ingredients of a Greek salad, this hearty side dish is a perfect accompaniment for the pulled lamb.

Tip

To get the most juice from a lemon, let it warm to room temperature, then roll it on the counter, pressing down with the palm of your hand, before squeezing it.

Greek-Style Couscous

1 cup	couscous	250 mL
1/4 cup	extra virgin olive oil	60 mL
2 tbsp	freshly squeezed lemon juice	30 mL
1 tsp	dried oregano	5 mL
1	tomato, chopped	1
2 cups	coarsely chopped cucumber	500 mL
1/2 cup	crumbled feta cheese	125 mL
1/2 cup	coarsely chopped pitted black olives	125 mL
	Salt and freshly ground black pepper	

1. In a saucepan, bring 1½ cups (375 mL) water to a boil over high heat. Stir in couscous. Remove from heat, cover and let stand for about 5 minutes or until liquid is absorbed.

2. Meanwhile, in a bowl, whisk together oil, lemon juice and oregano. Add tomato, cucumber, cheese and olives. Add couscous and gently toss to coat. Season to taste with salt and pepper.

African Lamb Tagine

**Makes 4 to
6 servings**

*The stews of North Africa
are traditionally made in
a conical vessel called
a tagine. The lid of the
tagine is tall, and it causes
the steam to build up and
precipitate back down to
the stew so that none of
the aroma or flavor is lost
during cooking. The slow
cooker uses basically the
same principal. Crunchy
peanut butter thickens
the broth at the end of
the cooking time, and the
couscous soaks up the
wonderful flavors.*

Tips

For the best flavor, start
with whole cumin seeds
and allspice berries. Toast
them in a dry skillet over
medium-high heat, stirring
constantly, for about
3 minutes or until fragrant.
Then grind them as finely as
you can in a spice grinder or
using a mortar and pestle.

When browning meat in hot
oil, avoid overfilling the skillet.
If the pan is too full, the meat
will steam rather than brown.
Turn the meat frequently and
cook it as quickly as possible,
then use a slotted spoon to
remove it.

- **Minimum 4-quart slow cooker**

2 tbsp	vegetable oil (approx.)	30 mL
2 lbs	boneless stewing lamb, cut into 1-inch (2.5 cm) cubes	1 kg
4	parsnips, diced	4
2	sweet potatoes, peeled and diced	2
1	onion, finely chopped	1
4	cloves garlic, finely chopped	4
1 tbsp	curry powder	15 mL
1/2 tsp	ground cumin	2 mL
1/4 tsp	ground allspice	1 mL
1 cup	beef broth	250 mL
1	can (14 oz/398 mL) diced tomatoes, with juice	1
1	3-inch (7.5 cm) cinnamon stick	1
1/2 tsp	hot pepper flakes	2 mL
2 tbsp	crunchy peanut butter	30 mL
	Salt	
	Hot cooked couscous	
	Chopped fresh parsley or cilantro	

1. In a large skillet, heat half the oil over medium-high heat. Cook lamb in batches, adding more oil as needed, for 4 minutes or until browned all over. Using a slotted spoon, transfer to slow cooker stoneware, leaving fat in pan.

2. Reduce heat to medium-low. Add parsnips, sweet potatoes and onion to skillet and sauté for about 4 minutes or until starting to soften. Add garlic, curry powder, cumin and allspice; sauté for about 1 minute or until vegetables are coated and spices are fragrant. Using a slotted spoon, transfer to stoneware.

3. Add broth to skillet and bring to a boil, scraping up any brown bits from pan. Pour over lamb mixture. Stir in tomatoes with juice, cinnamon stick and hot pepper flakes.

4. Cover and cook on Low for 6 to 8 hours or on High for 3 to 4 hours, until lamb is tender and stew is bubbling.

The flavors really mingle by the second day, so don't be afraid to cook this stew one day, pop it in the refrigerator, then reheat and eat it the next day.

5. Discard cinnamon stick. Stir in peanut butter until thoroughly combined. Season to taste with salt.

6. Place couscous on a serving platter. Top with stew and sprinkle with parsley.

Couscous, a North African granular pasta, is available in a precooked instant form in most grocery stores. Unless the box instructions tell you otherwise, for 4 servings, bring 1½ cups (375 mL) water to a boil, then stir in 1 cup (250 mL) couscous. Cover, remove from heat and let stand for 5 minutes. Fluff with a fork, then stir in chopped fresh cilantro or parsley. Couscous, enlivened with any fresh herb, is a good complement for most stews.

Lamb Shanks with Oranges and Olives

Makes 4 to 6 servings

The trick to all braised dishes is the very first step: carefully browning the meat to a deep golden brown. This not only ensures delicious, full-flavored meat, but also contributes to a rich and complex sauce. In this recipe, lamb shanks are slowly simmered with rosemary, white wine, onions and orange juice until the meat falls from the bone. Serve over hot mashed potatoes to sop up the sauce.

Tip

You can find the popular Greek black kalamata olives in most large grocery stores or gourmet food shops. Look for the fresh ones in the deli, rather than the canned variety. They're salty and very flavorful.

- **Minimum 4-quart slow cooker**

¹⁄₄ cup	all-purpose flour	60 mL
1 tsp	salt	5 mL
¹⁄₂ tsp	freshly ground black pepper	2 mL
4 lbs	large meaty sliced or whole lamb shanks	2 kg
2 tbsp	olive oil (approx.)	30 mL
4	cloves garlic, minced	4
1	large red onion, finely chopped	1
1 tbsp	dried rosemary	15 mL
1 cup	tomato pasta sauce	250 mL
¹⁄₂ cup	dry white wine	125 mL
¹⁄₂ cup	chicken broth	125 mL
	Grated zest and juice of 1 navel orange	
¹⁄₂ cup	kalamata olives	125 mL

1. On a plate, combine flour, salt and pepper. Dredge lamb shanks in flour mixture to lightly coat, shaking off any excess. Reserve the remaining flour mixture.

2. In a skillet, heat half the oil over medium-high heat. Cook lamb in batches, adding more oil as needed, for 10 to 15 minutes or until lightly browned all over. Using tongs, transfer to slow cooker stoneware, leaving fat in the pan.

3. Reduce heat to medium. Add garlic, red onion, rosemary and the reserved flour mixture to skillet and sauté for about 2 minutes or until garlic is softened. Add pasta sauce, wine, broth and orange juice; cook, stirring, until thickened. Pour over lamb shanks.

4. Cover and cook on Low for 10 to 12 hours or on High for 5 to 6 hours, until lamb is falling off the bone. Turn off heat and let stand for 10 minutes. Transfer to a warmed platter and sprinkle with orange zest and olives.

The shank is the lower portion of the leg. It is almost always sold bone-in. It's not a very tender cut of meat, so it is ideally suited to slow cooking, which allows the ample collagen in the shank to melt, producing a velvety sauce.

Sides and Grains

Braised Roman Artichokes

Makes 4 servings

I love to eat artichokes but hate to wait for them to cook. The long, slow cooking they require makes them especially suitable for the slow cooker. When they are available fresh at my farmer's market, I make a meal out of them with a dipping sauce, good bread and a glass of wine.

Tip

Artichokes are an excellent source of fiber, magnesium and folate and serve up a good dose of vitamin C. For optimal freshness, choose firm artichokes with tightly closed leaves.

- **Minimum 5-quart slow cooker**

4	large globe artichokes (about 2 lbs/1 kg total)	4
1	lemon, cut in half	1
	Ice water	
2	cloves garlic, finely chopped	2
3 tbsp	chopped fresh flat-leaf (Italian) parsley	45 mL
1 tbsp	chopped fresh mint	15 mL
1½ tsp	salt	7 mL
2 cups	hot water (approx.)	500 mL

Lemon Aïoli Dipping Sauce

2	cloves garlic, minced	2
¼ tsp	salt	1 mL
⅔ cup	light mayonnaise	150 mL
1 tsp	freshly squeezed lemon juice	5 mL

1. Work with one artichoke at a time and prevent discoloration by rubbing each cut surface with one of the lemon halves immediately after cutting. Using a sharp knife, trim stem off evenly so artichoke will stand upright. Cut 1 inch (2.5 cm) off the top. Using scissors, snip off all the prickly points. Spread the leaves to gain easier access to the center and, using a melon baller or paring knife, scoop out and discard the fuzzy choke and purplish inner leaves. Squeeze juice from the remaining lemon half into a bowl of ice water, then add lemon half and trimmed artichoke.

2. In a bowl, combine garlic, parsley and mint. Rub into scooped-out centers of artichokes.

3. Set artichokes upright in slow cooker stoneware and sprinkle with salt. Squeeze juice from lemon half used to rub artichokes and drizzle over top. Add enough hot water to come one-third up sides of artichokes.

4. Cover and cook on Low for 4 to 6 hours or until artichoke leaves pull off easily and hearts are tender when pierced.

5. *Dipping Sauce:* Meanwhile, sprinkle garlic and salt on a cutting board. Using the side of a chef's knife or a fork, rub together into a paste. In a small bowl, combine mayonnaise, lemon juice and garlic paste. Cover and refrigerate for up to 4 hours.

6. Using a slotted spoon, transfer artichokes, stem side up, to a serving platter. Let cool until warm or room temperature. Serve with dipping sauce.

Roasted Beets with Mint and Pine Nuts

Makes 4 to 6 servings

I took a class on Mediterranean cooking a few years ago and made a similar salad to this one. No other vegetable can match the ruby intensity of beets. Since they take time to cook in the oven, I love to slow-roast beets in the slow cooker. Combined with mint and pine nuts, this salad tastes great warm or cold.

Tips

If you purchase beets with the tops attached, trim them off but do not discard them. Cook them as you would any other bitter greens. They're a wonderfully potent wake-up call for the palate.

You can also make this dish with golden beets, or a combination of golden and red. If you use both, you can cook them together but, once they're skinned, keep them separate until you serve them, to prevent the red beets from discoloring the gold.

- **4- to 6-quart slow cooker**

2 lbs	beets (about 6)	1 kg
1 tbsp	olive oil	15 mL
	Salt and freshly ground black pepper	
2 tbsp	water	30 mL
1 cup	pine nuts, lightly toasted	250 mL
1/3 cup	crumbled feta cheese	75 mL
1/4 cup	fresh mint leaves	60 mL

Vinaigrette

1	shallot, minced	1
1/4 cup	red wine vinegar	60 mL
1 tsp	Dijon mustard	5 mL
1/3 cup	olive oil	75 mL
1 tbsp	liquid honey (optional)	15 mL

1. Scrub beets well under running water and trim off ends. Place beets in slow cooker stoneware. Add oil, salt and pepper to taste and 2 tbsp (30 mL) water; toss to coat.

2. Cover and cook on Low for 5 to 6 hours or until beets are fork-tender. Using a slotted spoon, transfer to a bowl and let cool. Using your hands or a vegetable peeler, slip off skins. Slice beets into rounds or wedges and transfer to a bowl. Set aside.

3. *Vinaigrette:* Meanwhile, in a bowl, whisk together shallot, vinegar and mustard. Slowly whisk in oil until emulsified. Whisk in honey (if using) until blended.

4. Drizzle about half the vinaigrette over beets and let marinate for about 20 minutes.

5. Place beets on individual serving plates. Top with pine nuts, cheese and mint. Drizzle with the remaining vinaigrette. Season to taste with salt and pepper.

Apricot-Glazed Carrots

Makes 8 to 10 servings

Fresh garden carrots are cooked with a hint of orange, then "kissed" with a little honey and apricot jam in this easy, yet divinely delicious side dish.

Tip

You can substitute a 2-lb (1 kg) bag of ready-cut baby carrots for the large ones. Make sure all the carrots are about the same size, so they will cook evenly. If you have a few larger ones in the bag, cut them in half lengthwise.

- **4- to 6-quart slow cooker**

12	large carrots, thinly sliced	12
1	onion, thinly sliced	1
2 tbsp	freshly squeezed orange juice	30 mL
1 tbsp	olive oil	15 mL
½ tsp	salt	2 mL
⅓ cup	liquid honey	75 mL
⅓ cup	apricot jam or marmalade	75 mL
2 tbsp	chopped fresh parsley	30 mL

1. In slow cooker stoneware, toss together carrots, onion, orange juice, oil and salt.

2. Cover and cook on Low for 6 hours or on High for 3 hours, until carrots are tender. Drain off cooking liquid.

3. In a small bowl, combine honey and jam. Pour over carrot mixture in stoneware. Cover and cook on High for 10 to 15 minutes or until hot. Sprinkle with parsley. (Carrots will hold on Low for up to 2 hours; stir occasionally.)

Roasted Orange Cauliflower

Makes 4 servings

Ordinary cauliflower will be anything but when it's served with a hint of orange zest. Slow roasting adds a depth of flavor you just don't get by boiling this vegetable.

Tip

Save time by buying precut cauliflower florets, found in the produce section of the supermarket. You may need to cut them a little smaller, but most of the work will already be done.

- **4- to 6-quart slow cooker**

4 cups	cauliflower florets (about $\frac{1}{2}$ head), cut into 1-inch (2.5 cm) pieces	1 L
2 tbsp	olive oil	30 mL
$\frac{1}{2}$ tsp	salt	2 mL
$\frac{1}{4}$ tsp	freshly ground black pepper	1 mL
$\frac{1}{2}$ tsp	grated orange zest	2 mL
1 cup	shredded Asiago cheese	250 mL
1 tbsp	snipped fresh chives	15 mL

1. Place cauliflower in slow cooker stoneware. Drizzle with oil and sprinkle with salt, pepper and orange zest; toss to coat.

2. Cover and cook on Low for 5 to 6 hours or on High for $2\frac{1}{2}$ to 3 hours, until tender. Sprinkle with cheese and chives.

Corn on the Cob with Chili Lime Butter

Makes 6 to 8 servings

Everyone loves corn on the cob. By steaming it in its own juices, you cook the kernels to perfection, and there is no big pot left on the stove to clean up. Have the kids husk the corn for you — they will, of course, leave a mess behind, but the hard part will be done.

Tip

A large slow cooker works best to cook the corn. If you have a smaller one, break cobs in half to fit.

Refrigerate any leftover butter mixture in an airtight container for up to 2 weeks.

- **Minimum 6-quart slow cooker**

6 to 8	ears corn, husked	6 to 8

Chili Lime Butter

1/4 cup	butter, softened	60 mL
2 tbsp	coarsely chopped fresh cilantro	30 mL
1/2 tsp	grated lime zest	2 mL
1 1/2 tbsp	freshly squeezed lime juice	7 mL
1/4 tsp	chili powder	1 mL

1. Wrap each cob of corn with foil and place in slow cooker stoneware.

2. Cover and cook on High for 2 to 2 1/2 hours, until corn is just tender. (Do not overcook.)

3. *Chili Lime Butter:* In a small bowl, combine butter, cilantro, lime zest, lime juice and chili powder.

4. Unwrap corn cobs, draining off any liquid. Spread hot cobs with chili lime butter.

Triple-Pepper Corn Gratin

Makes 6 to 8 servings

This is a seriously decadent recipe, especially if you are looking for something special. It's a wonderful match for Mexican dishes such as chicken mole or enchiladas.

Tip

Some ingredients, such as milk and lower-fat creams (5% and 10%), do not hold up well to slow cooking. Higher-fat cream (18% and 35%) and evaporated milk, however, hold up extremely well and do not curdle when hot. (Don't confuse evaporated milk with the sweetened condensed milk used in desserts and candies.)

- **4- to 5-quart slow cooker, stoneware greased**

1/2 cup	butter	125 mL
1	onion, finely chopped	1
1/2 cup	all-purpose flour	125 mL
1 tsp	chili powder	5 mL
1/2 tsp	salt	2 mL
1/2 tsp	freshly ground black pepper	2 mL
2 cups	table (18%) cream or evaporated milk	500 mL
2	eggs, lightly beaten	2
2 cups	shredded Monterey Jack cheese	500 mL
1 cup	shredded Cheddar cheese	250 mL
1	bag (2 lbs/1 kg) frozen corn kernels, thawed	1
1	can (4 1/2 oz/127 mL) diced mild green chiles	1
1	jalapeño pepper, seeded and minced	1
1	red bell pepper, finely chopped	1
1/4 cup	chopped fresh cilantro	60 mL

Crunchy Bran Topping

1 cup	bran cereal, such as bran flakes	250 mL
2 tsp	butter	10 mL
1 tsp	minced garlic	5 mL

1. In a large saucepan, melt butter over medium heat. Sauté onion for 3 to 4 minutes or until tender and translucent. Stir in flour, chili powder, salt and pepper until blended into thick paste. Gradually whisk in cream and cook, whisking constantly, for 2 to 3 minutes or until slightly thickened. Remove from heat. Whisk in eggs until blended. Stir in Monterey Jack, Cheddar, corn, green chiles, jalapeños and red pepper. Transfer to prepared slow cooker stoneware.

2. Cover and cook on Low for 3 1/2 to 4 hours or until set and a knife inserted in the center comes out clean. Turn off heat and let stand for 5 to 10 minutes.

3. *Crunchy Bran Topping:* Meanwhile, preheat broiler, with the rack set about 4 inches (10 cm) below the heat source. In food processor, combine cereal, butter and garlic; pulse until cereal is crushed.

4. Remove stoneware from slow cooker. Sprinkle with cilantro, then cereal mixture. Broil for about 2 minutes or until browned.

Edamame Succotash

Makes 6 to 8 servings

I can only think of Sylvester the Cat when I say "succotash," but it actually refers to a mixture of corn and lima beans usually served around Thanksgiving — though it is delicious anytime. In this updated version, I have replaced the lima beans with edamame (shelled soybeans), which are an excellent source of protein. If you can't find them, substitute frozen lima beans.

Tip

To ripen tomatoes, place them in a brown paper bag and store at room temperature. Never store tomatoes in the refrigerator, as it destroys their delicate flavor.

• **4- to 5-quart slow cooker**

4	large plum (Roma) tomatoes, chopped	4
1	onion, chopped	1
1	zucchini, diced	1
2 cups	frozen shelled edamame, thawed	500 mL
2 cups	frozen corn kernels, thawed	500 mL
2 tbsp	olive oil	30 mL
1 tsp	dried Italian seasoning	5 mL
1/2 tsp	salt	2 mL
1/2 tsp	freshly ground black pepper	2 mL
3 tbsp	chopped fresh basil or chives	45 mL

1. In slow cooker stoneware, toss together tomatoes, onion, zucchini, edamame, corn, oil, Italian seasoning, salt and pepper.

2. Cover and cook on Low for 4 to 4 1/2 hours or on High for 2 to 2 1/2 hours, until onion and zucchini are tender. Stir in basil and season to taste with salt and pepper.

> Edamame, also known as green or sweet soybeans, have been a major source of protein in East Asia for more than 2,000 years and are becoming a popular ingredient in North America. They are picked while they're still green and sweet. Shelled edamame are delicious simmered in soups and stews. Look for them in the freezer section of your grocery store. Lima beans are a good alternative if you can't find edamame.

Stewed Green Beans with Bacon

Makes 6 to 8 servings

Slowly simmered green beans with bacon is a dish famous in the American South and, as odd as it sounds, it is wonderful as part of a Thanksgiving meal. Using the slow cooker frees up much-needed stovetop or oven space.

Tip

Ready-to-use broth in convenient Tetra-Paks is a handy ingredient and doesn't need to be diluted. Avoid using cubes and powders, which tend to be very salty.

- 3- to 5-quart slow cooker

6	slices bacon, thinly sliced crosswise	6
2½ lbs	green beans, trimmed and cut into 1-inch (2.5 cm) lengths	1.25 kg
1 cup	chicken or vegetable broth	250 mL
	Coarse salt and freshly ground black pepper	

1. In a large skillet, cook bacon over medium-high heat, stirring, for 6 to 8 minutes or until crisp. Using a slotted spoon, transfer to slow cooker stoneware. Stir in beans and broth.

2. Cover and cook on Low for 3 to 4 hours or until beans are very tender. Season to taste with salt and pepper.

Perfect Southern Greens

Makes 6 to 8 servings

This recipe yields the best-tasting greens I have ever eaten. It has the potential to convert those who think they don't like greens, and may even inspire them to talk with a cute Southern accent.

Tips

Blanching the kale before adding it to the slow cooker can help remove some of its natural bitterness. Add torn greens to a pot of boiling salted water and cook for 4 to 5 minutes. Drain well. This will reduce the cooking time to 4 hours on Low or 2 hours on High.

You can also substitute beet, collard or mustard greens for the kale.

- **4- to 6-quart slow cooker**

1 lb	mild Italian sausage, casings removed	500 mL
8 cups	kale, tough ribs and stems removed, torn into 2-inch (5 cm) pieces	2 L
1 tsp	salt	5 mL
½ tsp	freshly ground black pepper	2 mL
2 to 3 tsp	red wine vinegar (optional)	10 to 15 mL

1. In a large skillet, cook sausage over medium-high heat, breaking it up with the back of a wooden spoon, for about 6 to 8 minutes or until browned. Using a slotted spoon, transfer to slow cooker stoneware. Stir in kale, salt, pepper and 2 cups (500 mL) water.

2. Cover and cook on Low for 6 hours or on High for 3 hours, until kale is tender. Stir in vinegar (if using). Serve hot.

A member of the cabbage family, kale has beautiful dark green, curly leaves. It has been dubbed a "superfood" for its cancer-fighting phytonutrients. Although it can be found year-round in the supermarket, it is in season from the middle of winter through the beginning of spring, a time when quality green foods can otherwise be difficult to find.

Layered Cheese Ravioli Lasagna (page 307)

Barbecue Burger Sliders (page 316)

Petite Pot Roast (page 342)

Pineapple Ginger Pork (page 348)

Green Tea–Poached Winter Fruits (page 388)

Warm Chocolate Lava Cake (page 394)

Ginger Crème Brûlée (page 402)

Pumpkin Croissant Pudding with Tipsy Caramel Sauce (page 404)

Rutabaga and Pear Crisp

Makes 8 to 10 servings

The pears in this purée sweeten the rutabaga and temper its bite. This is an earthy, savory-sweet side that is perfect at any holiday meal and makes a surprising alternative to mashed potatoes. The celery root adds to the earthy flavor. This dish is a wonderful accompaniment to prime rib or roast chicken.

Tip

To extract the most juice from a lemon, let it warm to room temperature, then roll it on the counter, pressing down with the palm of your hand, before squeezing it. Or microwave a whole lemon on High for 30 seconds, then roll it. The juice can be frozen in ice cube trays, then the frozen cubes stored in sealable plastic bags for later use. Lemon zest can also be wrapped and frozen for later use.

- 4- to 5-quart slow cooker
- *Food processor*

2 cups	diced peeled rutabaga	500 mL
2 cups	diced peeled celery root	500 mL
2	ripe pears, peeled and diced	2
2 tbsp	melted butter	30 mL
2 tbsp	liquid honey	30 mL
1/4 cup	freshly squeezed lemon juice	60 mL
1/2 tsp	salt	2 mL
1/4 tsp	freshly ground white pepper	1 mL
1/4 cup	chopped fresh parsley	60 mL
1/2 cup	toasted sliced almonds	125 mL

1. In slow cooker stoneware, combine rutabaga and celery root. Add enough water to cover.

2. Cover and cook on Low for 5 to 7 hours or on High for $2\frac{1}{2}$ to $3\frac{1}{2}$ hours, until rutabaga and celery root are tender.

3. Stir in pears. Cover and cook on High for 1 hour. Drain.

4. In food processor, in batches if necessary, purée rutabaga mixture, butter, honey and lemon juice until silky smooth. Season with salt and white pepper. Fold in parsley.

5. Transfer to a warmed serving bowl and top with toasted almonds.

Make Ahead

This dish can be prepared through step 3 up to 24 hours in advance. Place cooked purée in a lightly greased casserole dish, cover and refrigerate overnight. Reheat, covered, in a 350°F (180°C) oven for 30 to 45 minutes or until hot. Top with toasted almonds before serving.

Celery root is a vegetable from the celery family. It resembles a brown and lumpy, misshapen turnip. The brown outer skin should be washed and peeled before the celery root is cooked. Choose firm tubers without fleshy spots or discolorations. Smaller roots will taste better, while larger roots are woodier and more suitable for roasting or long stewing.

Caramelized Orange Shallots

Makes 4 servings

Slow cooking makes these sweet-and-sour shallots exceptionally tender. They are marvelous beside any simple grilled meat or fish.

Tips

To easily peel shallots, place them in a bowl of warm water and soak until the skins loosen (they will look a little wrinkled and cracked). Use a paring knife to slip the skins off, leaving the stem end intact.

If your shallots are large, cut them in half lengthwise for this recipe.

* **3- to 4-quart slow cooker**

1 lb	small shallots (about 12), peeled, leaving stem ends intact (see tips, at left)	500 g
3 tbsp	packed brown sugar	45 mL
3 tbsp	balsamic vinegar, divided	45 mL
1 tsp	grated orange zest	5 mL
2 tbsp	freshly squeezed orange juice	30 mL
1/2 tsp	salt	2 mL
1/4 tsp	freshly ground black pepper	1 mL

1. In slow cooker stoneware, toss together shallots, brown sugar, 2 tbsp (30 mL) of the vinegar, orange juice, salt and pepper.

2. Cover and cook on High for 3 to 3½ hours, stirring once, until tender.

3. Stir in orange zest and the remaining vinegar. Season to taste with salt and pepper. Using a slotted spoon, transfer shallots to a warmed serving dish. Drizzle with cooking liquid.

> Shallots have a sweeter, more delicate flavor than onions, which makes them a nice substitute in a variety of dishes.

Slow-Cooked Yellow Summer Squash

Makes 4 servings

Summer squash are picked when they are quite young, and slow cooking concentrates their sweet, nutty flavor. If you can't find the yellow variety, you can substitute zucchini, the most prevalent and prolific summer squash.

Tip

Resist the urge to lift the lid and taste or smell whatever is inside the slow cooker as it's cooking. Every peek will increase the cooking time by 20 minutes.

- **4- to 5-quart slow cooker**

4	yellow summer squash, sliced	4
1	onion, halved and thinly sliced	1
2 tbsp	olive oil	30 mL
½ tsp	dried thyme	2 mL
¼ tsp	lemon pepper	1 mL
	Coarse salt and freshly ground black pepper	

1. In slow cooker stoneware, toss together squash, onion, oil, thyme and lemon pepper.
2. Cover and cook on Low for 2 to 3 hours or until tender. Season to taste with salt and pepper.

Make-Your-Own Lemon Pepper

Lemon pepper fuses black peppercorns and grated lemon zest into a seasoning blend. It can be purchased commercially in the spice aisle of the supermarket, but you can easily make it yourself. Using a citrus zester, remove the zest (avoiding the white pith) from 1 lemon and place it in a small bowl. Add 2 tsp (10 mL) freshly cracked black peppercorns. Using a wooden spoon, mash them together to release the citrus oils and infuse them into the pepper. Spread mixture on a rimmed baking sheet and bake in a 200°F (100°C) oven for 4 to 6 hours. Transfer to a coffee grinder or a small food processor and grind until pulverized. Store in an airtight container for up to 1 month.

Spiced Sweet Potatoes

Makes 4 to 6 servings

If I have one guilty food pleasure, it is sweet potato fries. Whenever I see them on a restaurant menu, I order a side. This version is a great combination of savory and sweet, it's a lot healthier than deep-fried potatoes, and it's perfect for a summer menu with grilled chicken or fish — and you won't heat up the kitchen.

Tip

To get the most juice from a lime, let it warm to room temperature, then roll it on the counter, pressing down with the palm of your hand, before squeezing it. Or microwave a whole lime on High for 30 seconds, then roll, cut and squeeze it. Juice can be frozen in ice cube trays, then kept in the freezer in sealable plastic bags for later use. Zest can also be wrapped and frozen for later use.

- **4- to 6-quart slow cooker**

2¼ lbs	sweet potatoes (about 5)	1.125 kg
2 tbsp	olive oil	30 mL
1 tbsp	freshly squeezed lime juice	15 mL
1 tsp	chili powder	5 mL
½ tsp	ground cumin	2 mL
½ tsp	salt	2 mL
¼ tsp	ground cinnamon	1 mL

1. Peel sweet potatoes and cut into 2-inch (5 cm) long, ½-inch (1 cm) thick sticks.

2. In slow cooker stoneware, toss together sweet potatoes, oil, lime juice, chili powder, cumin, salt and cinnamon.

3. Cover and cook on Low for about 3 hours or until sweet potatoes are tender but still hold their shape. Drain off any remaining liquid before serving.

Granola Streusel–Topped Sweet Potatoes

Makes 8 to 10 servings

Everyone in my household loves sweet potatoes, especially as a side dish at Thanksgiving. Using the slow cooker frees up the oven or stovetop when you have many other dishes to cook. Crunchy granola breakfast cereal and sweet maple syrup are the secrets to this delicious dish.

Tip

Cooking times can vary a great deal between slow cooker manufacturers. Always let your food cook for the minimum amount of time before testing for doneness.

- **4- to 6-quart slow cooker, stoneware greased**

6	sweet potatoes, peeled and cut into 1-inch (2.5 cm) pieces	6
½ cup	heavy or whipping (35%) cream	125 mL
¼ cup	pure maple syrup	60 mL
2 tbsp	butter, melted	30 mL
½ tsp	salt	2 mL
1 cup	granola cereal	250 mL
¼ cup	chopped pecans (optional)	60 mL
2 tbsp	butter or margarine	30 mL

1. Place sweet potatoes in prepared slow cooker stoneware. In a bowl, whisk together cream, maple syrup, butter and salt. Pour over sweet potatoes.

2. Cover and cook on High for 2½ to 3 hours, stirring once or twice, until fork-tender and fragrant. Mash slightly, if desired.

3. In a bowl, combine granola, pecans and butter. Spoon evenly over sweet potatoes in stoneware. Cover and cook on Low for 20 to 30 minutes or until heated through. Serve hot.

Make Ahead

This dish can be assembled up to 24 hours in advance. Prepare through step 1, cover and refrigerate. The next day, place stoneware in slow cooker and proceed with step 2.

Warm Caesar Potato Salad

Makes 6 to 8 servings

At restaurants, Caesar salad is requested more than any other. Here's a twist on that old favorite: toss the creamy salad dressing on hot, braised potatoes for an irresistibly delicious side dish.

Tip

If mini potatoes are not available, use larger ones cut into quarters.

• **4- to 5-quart slow cooker**

2 lbs	red or white mini potatoes	1 kg
1	onion, chopped	1
2 tbsp	olive oil	30 mL
1/2 tsp	salt	2 mL
1/4 tsp	freshly ground black pepper	1 mL
6	slices bacon, cooked crisp and crumbled	6
3	green onions, sliced	3
2	cloves garlic, minced	2
1/2 cup	freshly grated Parmesan cheese	125 mL
1/2 cup	creamy Caesar salad dressing	125 mL
1/4 cup	chopped fresh basil	60 mL

1. In slow cooker stoneware, combine potatoes, onion, oil, salt, pepper and 2 tbsp (30 mL) water.

2. Cover and cook on Low for 3 to 3 1/2 hours or until potatoes are tender.

3. Discard cooking liquid and transfer potato mixture to a large bowl. Add bacon, green onions, garlic, cheese and dressing; toss to coat. Sprinkle with basil and serve warm.

Make Ahead

This dish can be fully prepared up to 2 days in advance. Cover and refrigerate. Serve cold or let warm to room temperature.

Authentic Parmesan cheese (Parmigiano-Reggiano) is expensive, but its flavor is certainly worth the price. Well-wrapped in the refrigerator, a block keeps for months, and it goes a long way when you freshly grate it as you need it. Grated versions found on supermarket shelves have a soapy, salty taste that can't compare with freshly grated Parmesan.

Curried Potatoes and Peas

Makes 4 to 6 servings

This Indian classic, known as alu matter or aloo matar, is an excellent way to cook new potatoes slowly in their own juices. It is a wonderful side dish, but you can also serve it as a main course, along with a bowl of dal (lentils) and a green vegetable.

Tips

Leave the skins on the potatoes, scrub them thoroughly and dry with paper towels. Halve those larger than 1 inch (2.5 cm) in diameter.

Madras curry powder has a higher heat level than basic supermarket curry powder. If you are unaccustomed to hot food, be sparing with Madras curry.

- 4- to 5-quart slow cooker

2 tbsp	vegetable oil	30 mL
2 lbs	fingerling potatoes	1 kg
2	onions, finely chopped	2
1	clove garlic, minced	1
1 tsp	curry powder, preferably Madras	5 mL
1/2 tsp	salt	2 mL
1/2 tsp	freshly ground black pepper	2 mL
1/2 cup	water or vegetable broth	125 mL
1 cup	frozen peas, thawed	250 mL
2 tbsp	freshly squeezed lemon juice	30 mL
1/4 cup	finely chopped fresh cilantro	60 mL

1. In a skillet, heat oil over medium-high heat. In batches, sauté potatoes until just beginning to brown. Using a slotted spoon, transfer to slow cooker stoneware.

2. Reduce heat to medium. Add onions to skillet and sauté for about 3 minutes or until tender and translucent. Add garlic, curry powder, salt and pepper; sauté for 1 minute. Increase heat to high, add water and bring to a boil. Pour over potatoes.

3. Cover and cook on Low for 8 hours or on High for 4 hours, until potatoes are tender.

4. Stir in peas and lemon juice. Cover and cook on High for 10 to 15 minutes or until heated through. Serve sprinkled with cilantro.

Make Ahead

This dish can be assembled up to 12 hours in advance. Prepare through step 2, cover and refrigerate overnight. The next day, place stoneware in slow cooker and proceed with step 3.

Creamy Blue Cheese Grits

Makes 6 to 8 servings

When we travel south to the Sunshine State, I get my fill of grits wherever I can. When I asked my friend Kristine in Knoxville, Tennessee, to send me a recipe, she turned to her friend Suzanne. According to Suzanne, grits is an acronym for Girls Raised in the South. No wonder I love them so much! Blue cheese grits are great served alongside a grilled steak.

Variation

If you prefer something more mainstream, use 1 cup (250 mL) shredded Cheddar, smoked Gouda or Monterey Jack cheese instead of the blue cheese.

- **3- to 4-quart slow cooker**

1 cup	grits or coarse cornmeal	250 mL
¼ cup	butter	60 mL
1 tsp	coarse salt	5 mL
¼ cup	crumbled blue cheese	60 mL
¼ cup	sour cream	60 mL

1. In slow cooker stoneware, combine grits, butter, salt and 5 cups (1.25 L) water.

2. Cover and cook on Low for 4 to 5 hours or on High for 2 to 2½ hours, until thickened.

3. Stir in cheese and sour cream. Serve immediately.

Grits are dried corn kernels ground fine, medium or coarse. They are often simmered with water or milk until fairly thick. Quick grits (a very fine grind that has been presteamed) are available in supermarkets, but don't use them in this recipe. If you have difficulty finding grits, look for coarse or stone-ground cornmeal in a specialty, bulk food or health food store.

Pecorino and Parsley Polenta

Makes 6 servings

Polenta is the name given to both the popular Italian dish of cornmeal mush and the cornmeal used to make the dish. Like risotto, polenta requires constant stirring when it's cooked on the stovetop; this way, the slow cooker does all the work.

Tip

Good-quality Pecorino Romano cheese is imported from Italy and is made from sheep's milk. It is straw white in color and has an aromatic but pleasantly sharp taste. It is an excellent grating cheese and melts into sauces well without becoming too stringy.

- **4- to 5-quart slow cooker**

3 tbsp	butter, softened	45 mL
2 cups	yellow cornmeal or polenta	500 mL
2 tsp	salt	10 mL
½ cup	freshly grated Pecorino Romano cheese	125 mL
3 tbsp	chopped fresh parsley	45 mL
	Freshly ground black pepper	

1. Brush 1 tbsp (15 mL) of the butter evenly over bottom and sides of slow cooker stoneware. Add the remaining butter, cornmeal and salt. Stir in 8 cups (2 L) water.

2. Cover and cook on Low for 4 hours or on High for 2 hours, stirring occasionally, until thickened and creamy.

3. Just before serving, stir in cheese and parsley. Season to taste with pepper.

Make Ahead

This dish can be fully prepared up to 24 hours in advance. Pour into a buttered 13- by 9-inch (33 by 23 cm) baking dish. Let cool, cover and refrigerate overnight. To reheat, slice into squares and place on a greased baking sheet. Drizzle with olive oil and bake in a 400°F (200°C) oven for 15 to 20 minutes, turning once, until golden.

Chorizo and Pecan Cornbread Stuffing

Makes 10 servings

Sausage is a wonderful addition to stuffing because the meat is so highly seasoned. This recipe has a nice Southwestern twist, and using the slow cooker makes it fuss-free.

Tips

To grease stoneware, use a nonstick vegetable spray or use the cake pan grease available in specialty cake decorating shops or bulk food stores.

To toast pecans, spread a single layer of nuts in a shallow baking pan. Bake in a 350°F (180°C) oven for 5 to 10 minutes or until golden brown and fragrant.

- **Minimum 6-quart slow cooker, stoneware greased**

1 lb	fresh chorizo sausage, casings removed	500 g
3	stalks celery, finely chopped	3
1	large onion, finely chopped	1
½ cup	dry white wine	125 mL
2	eggs, beaten	2
12 cups	cubed cornbread (see recipe, opposite)	3 L
3 tbsp	finely chopped fresh sage	45 mL
½ tsp	salt	2 mL
¼ tsp	freshly ground black pepper	1 mL
1½ cups	hot chicken broth	375 mL
2 tbsp	melted butter	30 mL
1½ cups	coarsely chopped pecans, toasted	375 mL

1. In a large nonstick skillet, cook sausage over medium-high heat, breaking it up with the back of a wooden spoon, for 5 to 7 minutes or until starting to brown. Add celery and onion; sauté for about 5 minutes or until softened. Add wine and boil, stirring, for 3 to 5 minutes or until evaporated. Transfer to a large bowl.

2. Gently toss in eggs, cornbread, sage, salt and pepper (cornbread will break down into smaller pieces). The sausage mixture should be moist but not soggy; if necessary, add up to ½ cup (125 mL) of the hot broth. Transfer to prepared slow cooker stoneware.

3. Combine the remaining broth and butter. Drizzle over sausage mixture.

4. Cover and cook on Low for 3 hours or until heated through. Gently stir in pecans. (The stuffing will hold on Low or Warm for up to 1 hour before serving.)

If you have difficulty finding store-bought cornbread, here's an easy-to-make recipe that is perfect for the stuffing on page 298.

Tip

Use this simple substitute if you don't have any buttermilk: Pour 2½ tbsp (37 mL) white vinegar or freshly squeezed lemon juice into a measuring cup. Add enough milk to make 2½ cups (625 mL). Let stand for 5 minutes, then stir before adding it to the eggs.

Quick and Easy Cornbread

- *Preheat oven to 425°F (220°C)*
- *9-inch (23 cm) square glass baking dish*

½ cup	butter, divided	125 mL
1½ cups	cornmeal	375 mL
1½ cups	all-purpose flour	375 mL
¼ cup	granulated sugar	60 mL
2 tsp	baking soda	10 mL
2 tsp	salt	10 mL
3	eggs	3
2½ cups	buttermilk	625 mL

1. Spread 2 tbsp (30 mL) of the butter over bottom and sides of baking dish. Melt the remaining butter. Set aside.

2. In a bowl, whisk together cornmeal, flour, sugar, baking soda and salt. In another bowl, whisk together eggs, buttermilk and melted butter. Add cornmeal mixture to buttermilk mixture and stir just until moistened (do not overmix). Spread in prepared baking dish.

3. Bake in preheated oven for 15 to 20 minutes or until golden and a tester inserted in the center comes out clean. Let cool in dish on a wire rack for 10 minutes before slicing.

Fruited Wild Rice and Sourdough Dressing

Makes 14 servings

Gatherings in my husband's family are always potluck events. My brother-in-law Bob looks after the roast turkey, my mother-in-law, Mary, brings the mashed potatoes, and my sister-in-law Dianne looks after the salad and side vegetable. I started to bring the slow cooker dressing when Bob no longer wanted to stuff the bird. This one takes a little extra effort, but the flavor is well worth it.

Tip

I like to purchase predried bread cubes to make this recipe a little faster to prepare. However, if you're using fresh sourdough bread, cut it into 1-inch (2.5 cm) cubes. Spread a single layer of cubes over a rimmed baking sheet and bake in a 300°F (150°C) oven for 10 to 15 minutes or until lightly toasted. Set aside until ready to use. Bread cubes will keep for 24 hours before use. A quick tip is to bake them in the oven as directed and then turn the oven off and leave the bread overnight to finish drying out. The next day, the cubes will be thoroughly dried, perfect for the dressing.

- **Minimum 6-quart slow cooker**

½ cup	wild rice	125 mL
3½ cups	chicken broth, divided	875 mL
1 tsp	grated orange zest	5 mL
1 cup	freshly squeezed orange juice	250 mL
2 tbsp	butter or margarine	30 mL
1	onion, finely chopped	1
1 cup	coarsely shredded carrot	250 mL
2 tbsp	chopped fresh parsley	30 mL
2 tsp	crumbled dried marjoram	10 mL
1 tsp	dried thyme	5 mL
½ tsp	salt	2 mL
¼ tsp	ground black pepper	1 mL
8 cups	cubed dried sourdough bread (1-inch/2.5 cm cubes)	2 L
⅔ cup	dried sour (tart) cherries	150 mL
⅔ cup	chopped green onions	150 mL
½ cup	coarsely chopped pecans, toasted (see tip, page 298)	125 mL
	Sliced green onions (optional)	

1. In slow cooker stoneware, combine wild rice and 3 cups (750 mL) of the broth. Cover and cook on High for about 3 hours or until wild rice is tender.

2. Meanwhile, in a glass measuring cup, combine the remaining broth and orange juice. Set aside.

3. In a large nonstick skillet, melt butter over medium-high heat. Sauté onion and carrot for about 5 minutes or until softened. Add orange zest, parsley, marjoram, thyme, salt and pepper; sauté for about 1 minute or until fragrant. Stir into rice, along with bread cubes, cherries, chopped green onions and pecans. Slowly add the reserved orange juice mixture, tossing gently to combine.

4. Cover and cook on Low for 3 to 4 hours or until heated through. (Dressing will hold on Low or Warm for up to 2 hours.) Garnish with sliced green onions, if desired.

Make Ahead

Step 1 can be completed up to 1 day in advance. Cover and refrigerate until ready to use.

Wild rice is not actually rice at all but a long grain harvested from marsh grass native to the Great Lakes region of North America. It takes longer to cook than rice. Cooked perfectly, wild rice has a nutty flavor and tender, plump, chewy grains that are butterflied.

Fennel and Rice Pilaf

Makes 6 servings

A little fennel and orange jazz up a simple rice pilaf. Save the fennel fronds to use as a garnish.

Tips

Use long-grain parboiled rice (also known as converted rice) for best results in the slow cooker. The process of parboiling, or converting, the rice helps keep the kernels from sticking together, resulting in an evenly cooked product.

To remove the zest from the orange, use a citrus zester. Zesters are inexpensive and widely available at specialty kitchenware shops.

- **3- to 4-quart slow cooker**

2 tbsp	butter	30 mL
1	small fennel bulb, chopped	1
1	onion, chopped	1
1½ cups	long-grain parboiled (converted) white rice	375 mL
2	strips orange zest (each about 6 inches/15 cm long by ½ inch/1 cm wide)	2
1	bay leaf	1
¾ tsp	coarse salt	3 mL
2¾ cups	chicken broth	675 mL

1. In a skillet, melt butter over medium heat. Sauté fennel and onion for about 6 minutes or until softened. Transfer to slow cooker stoneware. Stir in rice, orange zest, bay leaf, salt and broth.

2. Cover and cook on Low for 2¾ to 3 hours or until broth is absorbed and rice fluffs easily with a fork. Discard orange zest and bay leaf.

Multigrain Asian Pilaf

Makes 10 to 12 servings

Pilaf dates back to ancient times and is common in Asia, the Middle East and South America. Packed with grains and wild rice, this filling side dish has a rich, nutty taste and texture. The slow cooker not only makes a fluffy pilaf, but keeps it warm until you're ready to serve it.

Tip

Frozen edamame are found in the frozen-foods aisle of the supermarket or health food store. If you prefer, you can substitute frozen lima beans.

- 4- to 6-quart slow cooker

²/₃ cup	wheat berries	150 mL
½ cup	pearl barley, rinsed	125 mL
½ cup	wild rice	125 mL
4	cloves garlic, minced	4
1	red bell pepper, chopped	1
1	onion, finely chopped	1
¾ cup	frozen shelled edamame or lima beans, thawed	175 mL
1 tbsp	chopped fresh sage	15 mL
½ tsp	dried thyme	2 mL
½ tsp	salt	2 mL
¼ tsp	freshly ground black pepper	1 mL
2½ cups	vegetable broth	625 mL
1 tbsp	butter, melted	15 mL

1. In a colander, thoroughly rinse wheat berries, barley and rice under cold running water. Drain and transfer to slow cooker stoneware.

2. Stir in garlic, red pepper, onion, edamame, sage, thyme, salt, pepper, broth and butter.

3. Cover and cook on Low for 6 to 8 hours or on High for 3 to 4 hours, until grains are tender and broth is absorbed. Stir once before serving.

Wheat berries are entire wheat kernels, each comprising the bran, germ and endosperm. They are tan to reddish brown in color and are sometimes labeled "hard" or "soft." The hard variety tends to be available in natural health and gourmet food stores, while supermarkets carry the soft type (although they may not say that on the label). Both types are interchangeable, but soft wheat berries cook a little faster, so you may want to check for doneness at the minimum cooking time. Wheat berries are not only a healthy "whole grain," but are also an excellent source of fiber.

Saffron Risotto

Makes 4 to 6 servings

Risotto in a slow cooker? Absolutely. It's an effortless way to make this Italian specialty. There's no constant stirring and no guesswork, but you must cook the rice in oil or butter first and be home to take it out of the slow cooker as soon as it's done, so don't skip any steps.

Tips

Arborio rice is the most common variety of rice used to make risotto, but you can also use carnaroli or vialone nano.

Serve the risotto as soon as it is cooked. Otherwise, you will end up with an unappealing lump.

- 3- to 4-quart slow cooker

2 tbsp	olive oil	30 mL
1	small onion, chopped	1
1½ cups	Arborio rice	375 mL
¾ cup	white wine	175 mL
½ tsp	saffron threads	2 mL
3½ cups	chicken broth	875 mL
½ cup	freshly grated Parmesan cheese	125 mL
2 tbsp	butter	30 mL
	Salt and freshly ground black pepper	

1. In a large skillet, heat oil over medium-high heat. Reduce heat to medium and sauté onion for 3 to 4 minutes or until tender and translucent. Stir in rice and cook, stirring frequently, for 3 to 4 minutes or until opaque. Stir in wine and bring to a boil. Transfer to slow cooker stoneware. Stir in saffron and broth.

2. Cover and cook on High for 2¼ to 2½ hours or until liquid is absorbed but rice is still moist. Stir in cheese and butter. Season to taste with salt and pepper. Serve immediately.

Saffron is the most expensive spice in the world, by weight. Saffron threads are the stigmas of a particular kind of crocus, and must be picked by hand during a short fall harvest. There are only three stigmas per blossom, and it takes about 75,000 stigmas to yield 1 lb (500 g) of saffron. Fortunately, a pinch (about 20 threads) is usually all it takes to impart saffron's distinctive yellow color and vaguely metallic, bittersweet flavor.

Big-Batch Dinners for a Crowd

Go Big and Come Home!

Everyone's coming to your house after the game. But not to worry — you have the slow cooker on your side. The recipes in this chapter make anywhere from 8 to 16 servings of party-food favorites, savory casseroles and entrées, hearty sandwiches and chilis.

Today's slow cookers come in handy 6- to 7-quart sizes, and making big batches not only saves time, but is economical too. Whether you're looking to feed a crowd or stash servings in the freezer for convenient reheating, hot meals are a snap to prepare. Best of all, slow-cooked meals are evenly cooked and ready when you are.

Another great way to make use of the slow cooker's ability to cook big batches is to join a communal kitchen or share your slow cooker dishes with friends. Meet to plan, shop for and prepare several meals together. Everyone can take meals home to freeze for times when they don't feel like shopping or cooking.

If you're planning to freeze some of your big batch and reheat it later, here are some tips to remember:

- Have storage containers on hand that accommodate the meal or portion size you'll want later. For example, if you want reheatable single servings for lunches or dinners, choose small plastic containers with lids or sealable freezer bags.
- Use containers or bags that are easy to label, and date each before putting it in the freezer. You'll want to use most foods within 3 or 4 months at most.
- Always let food cool completely before freezing it. This helps the food retain flavor and wards off bacterial growth. But never leave prepared food at room temperature for longer than 2 hours before freezing it.
- Rotate the containers of frozen food so you eat the oldest ones first: first in, first out.
- Don't defrost food at room temperature. This encourages bacterial growth and uneven thawing. Instead, place containers on a tray in the refrigerator and let thaw (it may take a day or two for larger portions), or microwave on a low or Defrost power setting until thawed.

Layered Cheese Ravioli Lasagna

Makes 10 to 12 servings

To give you great lasagna without as much layering, this recipe uses fresh cheese ravioli, topped with loads of cheese and red peppers. It is the perfect pasta for cheese lovers, a perfect potluck take-along and an easy-to-make entrée that friends and family will find hard to resist.

Tip

The size of the ravioli will vary depending on the brand, but don't worry, it doesn't really matter: with smaller ravioli, the layers will be more pasta than cheese; with larger ones, the dish will be cheesier.

Variation

To lower the carbohydrate content (glycemic load) of this dish, you can substitute whole wheat spinach and cheese ravioli, which also delivers more nutrition and fewer calories.

- Minimum 6-quart slow cooker, stoneware greased

Pasta Sauce

1 tbsp	olive oil	15 mL
1	onion, chopped	1
2	cloves garlic, minced	2
1	carrot, shredded	1
1 tsp	dried Italian seasoning	5 mL
1	jar (28 oz/796 mL) tomato pasta sauce	1
1	can (28 oz/796 mL) diced tomatoes, with juice	1

Ravioli Lasagna

2 cups	shredded provolone cheese	500 mL
1 cup	shredded mozzarella cheese	250 mL
2 tbsp	freshly grated Parmesan cheese	30 mL
1	jar (14 oz/398 mL) sliced roasted red peppers, drained	1
1	package (2 lbs/1 kg) fresh cheese ravioli	1

1. *Sauce:* In a large nonstick skillet, heat oil over medium-high heat. Sauté onion for 4 to 6 minutes or until tender and translucent. Add garlic, carrot and Italian seasoning; sauté for 1 to 2 minutes or until fragrant. Stir in pasta sauce and tomatoes with juice; bring to a boil. Reduce heat and simmer, stirring occasionally, for about 10 minutes or until slightly thickened. Remove from heat.

2. *Lasagna:* In a large bowl, combine provolone, mozzarella and Parmesan. Set aside.

3. Spread 1 cup (250 mL) of the pasta sauce evenly over bottom of prepared slow cooker stoneware. Spread one-third of the ravioli evenly over sauce. Spread one-third of the red peppers evenly over ravioli. Top with one-third of the remaining sauce and sprinkle with one-third of the cheese mixture. Repeat layers two more times with the ravioli, red peppers, sauce, then cheese.

4. Cover and cook on Low for 4 to 5 hours or until bubbling. Remove stoneware from slow cooker and let stand for 10 minutes before serving.

Polish Pierogies with Caramelized Onions

Makes 8 to 10 servings

This is the next best thing to making your own pierogies and so much better than buying frozen ones. It's a meatless affair that uses lasagna noodles instead of pierogi dough, layering them with mashed potatoes and cottage cheese. In Poland, pierogies were a traditional peasant food, but in time, their popularity spread to all social classes. This is a perfect potluck dish.

Tip

If you use sweet onions, such as Spanish or Vidalia, there's no need to add sugar when caramelizing the onions. If your onions are strong and not sweet, stir in some granulated or raw sugar about 10 minutes after cooking starts. Use about 1 tbsp (15 mL) sugar per onion. Watch closely throughout cooking and stir occasionally, reducing the heat if necessary to ensure that the sugar does not burn.

Make Ahead

Prepare the caramelized onions in advance. See box, page 209.

- Minimum 6-quart slow cooker, stoneware greased

2 tbsp	olive oil	30 mL
4	large onions, thinly sliced	4
	Salt and freshly ground black pepper	
3	large baking potatoes, peeled and diced	3
1 cup	shredded Cheddar cheese	250 mL
2 cups	4% cottage cheese	500 mL
1	egg, lightly beaten	1
1/4 tsp	onion salt	1 mL
1	package (12 oz/340 g) fresh lasagna sheets (or 12 oven-ready lasagna noodles)	1
	Chopped fresh dill	
	Sour cream	

1. In a large skillet, heat oil over medium-high heat. Reduce heat to medium-low and cook onions, stirring occasionally, for 30 to 45 minutes or until golden and just beginning to caramelize. Season to taste with salt and pepper. Set aside.

2. Meanwhile, in a large pot, cover potatoes with cold water and season with salt. Bring to a boil over high heat. Reduce heat to medium and boil gently for 12 to 15 minutes or until tender. Drain and mash. Stir in Cheddar, 1 tsp (5 mL) salt and 1/2 tsp (2 mL) pepper. Set aside.

3. In a bowl, combine cottage cheese, egg and onion salt.

4. Spread half the onions over bottom of prepared slow cooker stoneware. Cover with 1 lasagna sheet, breaking another sheet if necessary to cover onions completely (or use 3 oven-ready noodles). Spread potato mixture evenly on top. Cover with another lasagna sheet. Spread cottage cheese mixture evenly on top. Cover with another lasagna sheet. Spread the remaining onions evenly on top.

5. Cover and cook on Low for 4 to 6 hours or until bubbling. Remove stoneware from slow cooker and let stand for 10 minutes before serving. Serve with chopped fresh dill and a dollop of sour cream.

Smoky Chicken Chipotle Soft Tacos

Makes 14 to 16 servings

These perfect party tacos make a great excuse to gather friends and family for a Friday night appetizer. I love the rich, smoky flavor the peppers add to the chicken. Serving the tacos with guacamole and sour cream helps combat the heat of the peppers. Leftovers can be served over nachos or as a topping for baked potatoes or cooked pasta.

Tips

After opening canned chipotle chiles, transfer the peppers and their sauce to a glass jar with an airtight lid, close tightly and store in the refrigerator for up to 1 month. For longer storage, transfer peppers and sauce to a freezer bag and gently press out the air, then seal the bag. Manipulate the bag to separate the peppers so that it will be easy to break off a frozen section of pepper and sauce without thawing the whole package. Freeze for up to 6 months.

To warm tortillas, stack them, wrap the stack in foil and heat in a 350°F (180°C) oven for 15 to 20 minutes.

- 5- to 6-quart slow cooker

5 lbs	boneless skinless chicken thighs	2.5 kg
2	onions, chopped	2
2	chipotle peppers in adobo sauce, minced, with 1 tbsp (15 mL) sauce	2
1	Cubanelle pepper, seeded and finely chopped	1
1	can (5½ oz/156 mL) tomato paste	1
¾ cup	chili sauce	175 mL
2 tbsp	unsweetened cocoa powder	30 mL
1 tsp	ground cumin	5 mL
¾ tsp	salt	3 mL
½ tsp	ground cinnamon	2 mL
Pinch	ground nutmeg	Pinch
Pinch	ground coriander	Pinch
14 to 16	6- or 7-inch (15 or 18 cm) flour tortillas, warmed (see tip, at left)	14 to 16

Toppings

Shredded Cheddar cheese or Tex-Mex cheese blend

Diced tomatoes

Diced onions

Sour cream

Guacamole

Shredded lettuce

Salsa

Lime wedges

1. Place chicken in slow cooker stoneware. Stir in onions, chipotle peppers with sauce, Cubanelle pepper, tomato paste, chili sauce, cocoa powder, cumin, salt, cinnamon, nutmeg and coriander.

2. Cover and cook on Low for 6 to 7 hours or until juices run clear when chicken is pierced with a fork.

3. Using two forks, shred chicken in stoneware. Stir with sauce to combine. (Chicken mixture will hold on Low or Warm heat for up to 2 hours; stir occasionally.)

4. Spoon ⅓ cup (75 mL) of the chicken mixture along the center of each tortilla. Sprinkle with desired toppings, squeeze lime juice over top, if desired, and roll up.

Tex-Mex Chicken and Beans

Makes 10 to 12 servings

This memorable fix-and-forget casserole feeds a crowd after a full day of activities. Use good-quality salsa to save time without skimping on flavor. Serve with nacho chips or cornbread for scooping or sopping up every last bit from the bottom of the bowl.

Tips

If you like food with a little kick, adjust the heat level by using a hotter salsa.

Yes, you really do add all the ingredients to the slow cooker at once. The water and juice from the chicken help cook the beans so they won't have a pasty mouth feel.

- **Minimum 6-quart slow cooker**

2 cups	dried pinto beans, rinsed	500 mL
3 cups	mild or medium salsa	750 mL
2 to 3	chipotle peppers in adobo sauce, minced, with 1 tbsp (15 mL) sauce	2 to 3
¼ cup	all-purpose flour	60 mL
3 lbs	boneless skinless chicken thighs	1.5 kg
	Salt and freshly ground black pepper	
1	red onion, chopped	1
1	red bell pepper, chopped	1
	Sour cream	
	Chopped fresh cilantro	

1. In slow cooker stoneware, stir together beans, 2 cups (500 mL) water, salsa, chipotle peppers and flour. Sprinkle chicken with salt and pepper and arrange on salsa mixture. Sprinkle with red onion and red pepper.

2. Cover and cook on Low for 8 hours or until beans are tender and juices run clear when chicken is pierced with a fork. (Do not lift lid or stir.)

3. Using a slotted spoon, transfer chicken to a plate. Using two forks, shred into large pieces. Stir back into stew. Divide evenly among individual serving bowls. Top each with a dollop of sour cream and sprinkle with cilantro.

Sandy's Big White Curry

Makes 8 to 10 servings

This recipe comes to me from my sister in Kelowna, British Columbia, who has two growing boys. While it makes a generous pot of curry, in her house this dish is eaten in one sitting, thanks to her boys. Sandy gets the slow cooker started before they head to the ski hill. When they return, the aroma entices everyone to dive in.

Variation

To make a vegetarian version, omit the chicken and stir in 2 cups (500 mL) cooked or canned chickpeas (see page 120), drained and rinsed. (Or, for extra protein, use both chickpeas and chicken.)

- **Minimum 6-quart slow cooker**

2 tbsp	vegetable oil (approx.)	30 mL
12	boneless skinless chicken thighs, cut into chunks	12
1	onion, chopped	1
2	cloves garlic, minced	2
2 tbsp	minced gingerroot	30 mL
1	large sweet potato, peeled and diced	1
1	large potato, peeled and diced	1
1	small head cauliflower, chopped	1
1	can (28 oz/796 mL) diced tomatoes, with juice	1
¼ cup	packed brown sugar	60 mL
¼ cup	mild curry paste	60 mL
1 cup	frozen peas, thawed	250 mL
½ cup	chopped fresh cilantro (optional)	125 mL
½ cup	cream (any type)	125 mL

1. In a large nonstick skillet, heat half the oil over medium-high heat. Cook chicken in batches, adding more oil as needed, for 2 to 4 minutes or until browned all over. Using a slotted spoon, transfer to slow cooker stoneware.

2. Add onion to skillet and sauté for 3 to 5 minutes or until tender and translucent. Add garlic and ginger; sauté for 1 minute. Pour over chicken. Stir in sweet potato, potato, cauliflower, tomatoes, brown sugar, curry paste and ½ cup (125 mL) water.

3. Cover and cook on Low for 5 to 6 hours or on High for 3 to 4 hours, until juices run clear when chicken is pierced with a fork. About 20 minutes before the end of cooking, stir in peas, cilantro (if using) and cream.

Curry pastes are complex blends of freshly ground spices and herbs preserved in vegetable oil to seal in freshness. Some are hot, but many, such as tandoori or tikka masala, are mild blends that can be mixed with broth, yogurt or canned tomatoes to create a delicious sauce for meat, poultry, seafood or vegetables. After they're opened, curry pastes can be stored, tightly covered, in the refrigerator for up to 6 months.

10-Alarm Turkey Chili

Makes 8 to 10 servings

Heads up! This chili is crazy spicy — in a good way! If you like a little less heat, use only 2 chipotle peppers.

Tips

If you've purchased good-quality chocolate, don't worry if you add a little too much — it will only add to the richness of the sauce.

This dish tastes especially good if you toast and grind cumin seeds yourself rather than using ground cumin. Toast the seeds in a dry skillet over medium-high heat, stirring, for about 3 minutes or until fragrant. Use a mortar and pestle or a spice grinder to grind the seeds as finely as you can.

Because ground turkey has such a mild flavor, I often find I need to add extra seasoning to it.

- **Minimum 5-quart slow cooker**

2 tbsp	vegetable oil	30 mL
4 lbs	lean ground turkey or chicken	2 kg
4	cloves garlic, minced	4
1	large onion, chopped	1
4	chipotle peppers in adobo sauce, minced, with 1 tbsp (15 mL) sauce	4
2	red and/or yellow bell peppers, chopped	2
2	carrots, chopped	2
1	can (28 oz/796 mL) crushed tomatoes	1
1	can (28 oz/796 mL) diced tomatoes, drained	1
2 cups	cooked or canned pinto beans (see page 120), drained and rinsed	500 mL
2 cups	cooked or canned red kidney beans (see page 120), drained and rinsed	500 mL
1 cup	corn kernels, thawed if frozen	250 mL
2 tbsp	chili powder	30 mL
2 tsp	ground cumin	10 mL
1 tbsp	Worcestershire sauce	15 mL
1 oz	dark chocolate (at least 70% cacao), broken into small pieces	30 g
	Salt	
	Sour cream (optional)	

1. In a large nonstick skillet, heat oil over medium-high heat. Cook turkey, garlic and onion, breaking up meat with the back of a wooden spoon, for 3 to 5 minutes or until turkey is no longer pink. Using a slotted spoon, transfer to slow cooker stoneware.

2. Stir in chipotle peppers with sauce, red and/or yellow peppers, carrots, crushed tomatoes, diced tomatoes, pinto beans, kidney beans, corn, chili powder, cumin and Worcestershire sauce.

3. Cover and cook on Low for 6 to 8 hours or on High for 3 to 4 hours, until bubbling. Stir in chocolate until melted. Season to taste with salt.

4. Spoon into individual serving bowls and top each with a dollop of sour cream (if using).

Chili Mac and Jack

Makes 16 servings

This is traditional mac and cheese with a little sass! Chili improves with age, so some say this dish tastes even better the next day. Semisweet chocolate enriches and enhances the chili. Use the leftovers the next day for your children's lunches. In the morning, warm the chili in the microwave or on the stove, then pop each portion into a Thermos. They will be so pleased!

Tips

When handling hot peppers, keep your hands away from your eyes and skin. Better yet, wear rubber gloves and wash your hands and utensils afterwards.

Always use a large, deep pot to boil pasta. You need at least 1 quart (1 L) water per 3½ oz (100 g) dry pasta. And always salt the water, because this seasons the pasta internally as it absorbs the liquid and swells. You'll need about 1 tbsp (15 mL) salt for a large pot of boiling water. Chefs prefer to use sea salt or kosher salt because it is easier to control the amount you add and it dissolves faster than table salt.

- **Minimum 6-quart slow cooker**

2 lbs	lean ground beef or turkey	1 kg
2	large onions, chopped	2
1	jalapeño pepper, seeded and chopped	1
1	jar (28 oz/796 mL) tomato pasta sauce	1
2 cups	cooked or canned red kidney beans (see page 120), drained and rinsed	500 mL
2 tbsp	chili powder	30 mL
2 tbsp	semisweet chocolate chips	30 mL
1 tbsp	cider vinegar	15 mL
1 tsp	ground cinnamon	5 mL
¼ tsp	ground allspice	1 mL
2 cups	diced Monterey Jack cheese	500 mL
1 lb	short pasta, such as ziti, wagon wheels or gemelli	500 g
	Shredded Monterey Jack cheese (optional)	
	Chopped onion (optional)	

1. In a large nonstick skillet, cook beef and onions over medium-high heat, breaking up beef with the back of a wooden spoon, for 3 to 5 minutes or until beef is no longer pink. Using a slotted spoon, transfer to slow cooker stoneware.

2. Stir in jalapeño, pasta sauce, beans, chili powder, chocolate chips, vinegar, cinnamon, allspice and ½ cup (125 mL) water.

3. Cover and cook on Low for 6 to 8 hours or on High for 3 to 4 hours, until bubbling.

4. In a pot of boiling salted water, cook ziti according to package directions until tender but firm (al dente). Drain.

5. Toss ziti and diced cheese into beef mixture in stoneware. Cover and cook on Low for 10 to 15 minutes or until cheese is melted.

6. Ladle into individual serving bowls. Sprinkle with shredded cheese and onion (if using).

Nationals Chili Dogs

Makes 10 servings

My husband is on a quest to visit every major-league ballpark across the country. When I get to tag along, I look for the ballpark food specialty. At Nationals Park, we were served a Cincinnati-style chili over steamed hot dogs, which was my inspiration for this recipe. Kids love them, and they make a great choice for tailgate parties. Enjoy some laughs, beer and good dogs. What could be better than that?

Tip

Any type of hot dog wiener will work, but slightly firmer all-beef or turkey hot dogs are best.

- **5- to 6-quart slow cooker**

Chili Sauce

2 lbs	lean ground beef	1 kg
1	large onion, chopped	1
3	cloves garlic, minced	3
1	can (14 oz/398 mL) diced tomatoes, with juice	1
1	can (4½ oz/127 mL) diced mild green chiles	l
1 tbsp	chili powder	15 mL
1 tsp	granulated sugar	5 mL
1 tsp	paprika	5 mL
½ tsp	ground cumin	2 mL
½ tsp	celery seeds	2 mL
¼ tsp	salt	2 mL
¼ tsp	freshly ground black pepper	1 mL
1 tbsp	prepared mustard	15 mL
1 tsp	Worcestershire sauce	5 mL
20	hot dog wieners (or 10 jumbo-size), warmed	20
20	hot dog buns (or 10 jumbo-size), split and toasted	20
	Shredded Cheddar cheese (optional)	
	Chopped onion (optional)	
	Prepared mustard (optional)	

1. *Chili Sauce:* In a large skillet, cook beef, onion and garlic over medium-high heat, breaking up beef with the back of a wooden spoon, for 6 to 8 minutes or until vegetables are tender and beef is no longer pink. Drain off excess fat. Stir in tomatoes with juice, chiles, chili powder, sugar, paprika, cumin, celery seeds, salt, pepper, mustard and Worcestershire sauce.

2. Arrange wieners in slow cooker stoneware. Spoon beef mixture over top.

3. Cover and cook on Low for 4 to 5 hours or on High for 2 to 2½ hours, until bubbling.

4. Using tongs, transfer wieners to buns. Top each with about ⅓ cup (75 mL) sauce and garnish with cheese, onion and mustard (if using).

Crock o' Reubens

Makes
24 sandwiches

The next time you are hosting a casual party, wow everyone with a pot of corned beef and sauerkraut. After it is cooked, it will stay warm for hours, leaving you free to mingle with your guests and have a good time!

Tips

Corned beef brisket is a cut from the shank end. It is cured in a seasoned brine and found in the deli department of the supermarket. While some packages may tell you to cook right in the bag, I remove the brisket with the seasoning and place it in the slow cooker.

If you have difficulty finding a large enough corned beef brisket, buy two smaller ones.

Choose hearty, rustic rolls such as German pumpernickel, Jewish rye, light rye or American rye.

Small holes in Swiss cheese indicate that it hasn't been aged for very long. Large-holed Swiss Emmentaler cheese is a good choice for this recipe.

- **Minimum 6-quart slow cooker**

2 to 3 lbs	corned beef brisket with brine and spices (see tip, at left), trimmed	1 to 1.5 kg
1	jar (28 oz/796 mL) sauerkraut, drained	1
1	small onion, finely chopped	1
½ cup	regular or light mayonnaise	125 mL
2 tbsp	chili sauce	30 mL
½ tsp	paprika	2 mL
24	small rye or whole wheat rolls, split	24
3 cups	shredded Swiss cheese	750 mL

1. Place brisket in slow cooker stoneware (cutting into pieces to fit, if necessary). Sprinkle with spices from packet. Spread sauerkraut over brisket.

2. In a bowl, combine onion, mayonnaise, chili sauce and paprika. Spread over sauerkraut.

3. Cover and cook on Low for 4 to 6 hours or on High for 2 to 3 hours, until brisket is tender. Using tongs, transfer brisket to a cutting board. Let cool for 15 minutes.

4. Thinly slice brisket across the grain. Stir into cooking liquid in stoneware.

5. Using a slotted spoon, spoon corned beef mixture onto bottom half of each roll. Top with cheese, then cover with top half of roll.

Barbecue Burger Sliders

Makes 24 mini burgers

"If you can do meatballs in the slow cooker, why not burgers?" I asked myself. Now you can have a great barbecue-flavored burger without the hassle of making your way out to the grill, especially, if like me, you live somewhere with long, snowy winters. It's a good idea to toast the buns first, so the sauce doesn't soak through, but it's not necessary. Add any of your favorite burger toppings.

Tips

If you don't want to go to the effort of making barbecue sauce, simply use 2 cups (500 mL) bottled barbecue sauce.

Look for small rolls in the bakery section of your supermarket to fit the mini patties perfectly.

You can make regular-size burgers instead of the sliders. Prepare as directed above, dividing the meat mixture into 12 portions and using 12 regular hamburger buns.

- **Minimum 6-quart slow cooker**

4 lbs	lean ground beef or turkey	2 kg
4	eggs, lightly beaten	4
2	onions, finely chopped	2
2 cups	fine dry bread crumbs	500 mL
2 tbsp	Dijon mustard	30 mL
2 tbsp	Worcestershire sauce	30 mL
2 tsp	dried oregano	10 mL
2 cups	Barbecue Sauce (see recipe, opposite)	500 mL
24	mini hamburger buns, split	24

1. In a large bowl, combine beef, eggs, onions, bread crumbs, mustard, Worcestershire sauce and oregano. Using your hands, gently form about ¼ cup (60 mL) of the beef mixture into a 1-inch (2.5 cm) thick patty. Make 24 of these mini patties and layer them in slow cooker stoneware. Pour barbecue sauce over top.

2. Cover and cook on Low for 4 to 6 hours or until burgers are firm and an instant-read thermometer inserted in the center registers at least 160°F (71°C).

3. Transfer each burger to a bun. Skim fat off sauce. Spoon a little sauce on each burger and serve the remaining sauce on the side.

**Makes 2 cups
(500 mL)**

There are plenty of store-bought barbecue sauces, but nothing compares to this lip-smacking sauce. The chipotle pepper gives it a little kick.

Tip

Once opened, transfer canned chipotle peppers and their sauce to a glass jar with a tight-fitting lid and store in the refrigerator for up to 10 days. For longer storage, transfer the peppers and sauce to a freezer bag and gently press out the air, then seal the bag. Manipulate the bag to separate the peppers, so it will be easy to break off a frozen section of pepper and sauce without thawing the whole package.

Barbecue Sauce

2 tbsp	olive oil	30 mL
1	onion, finely chopped	1
2	cloves garlic, minced	2
1½ cups	ketchup	375 mL
1 cup	beef broth or beer	250 mL
¼ cup	light (fancy) molasses	60 mL
½	chipotle pepper in adobo sauce, seeded and minced	½
1 tbsp	mustard	15 mL

1. In a small skillet, heat oil over medium-high heat. Sauté onion for about 5 minutes or until tender and translucent. Add garlic and sauté for 1 to 2 minutes or until fragrant. Stir in ketchup, broth, molasses, chipotle pepper and mustard; bring to a boil. Reduce heat and simmer, stirring occasionally, for about 40 minutes or until thickened to consistency of bottled barbecue sauce.

2. Remove from heat and let cool. Refrigerate in a tightly sealed jar for up to 2 weeks.

Baba's Russian Mennonite Borscht

Makes 8 to 10 servings

My friend Sheila received this recipe from her old college roommate. It was a favorite from his grandmother, a Russian immigrant who would make it for her family when they were homesick. In Mennonite cuisine, borscht is a soup with cabbage, beef, potato and tomato, but no beets, and, unlike in many cultures, it is served hot. Baba's borscht is an economical, tasty and filling soup. Serve it with thick, dark bread, such as pumpernickel.

Tip

When browning meat in hot oil, avoid overfilling the skillet. If the pan is too full, the meat will steam rather than brown. Turn the meat frequently and cook it as quickly as possible, then use a slotted spoon to remove it.

- **Minimum 6-quart slow cooker**

1/4 cup	all-purpose flour	60 mL
1 tsp	dried basil	5 mL
1 tsp	dried dillweed	5 mL
1/2 tsp	dried savory	2 mL
2 lbs	stewing beef, cut into 1-inch (2.5 cm) cubes	1 kg
2 tbsp	vegetable oil (approx.)	30 mL
2 cups	chicken or vegetable broth	500 mL
6	carrots, sliced	6
4	potatoes, peeled and diced	4
4	tomatoes, chopped	4
3	onions, chopped	3
1/2	small head cabbage, chopped (about 5 cups/1.25 L)	1/2
1	envelope (1 1/2 oz/45 g) onion soup mix	1
1	can (14 oz/398 mL) tomato sauce	1
1 tbsp	Worcestershire sauce	15 mL
	Sour cream	
	Finely chopped fresh dill (optional)	

1. In a heavy plastic bag, combine flour, basil, dill and savory. In batches, add beef to bag and toss to coat with flour mixture. Discard any excess flour mixture.

2. In a large nonstick skillet, heat half the oil over medium-high heat. Cook beef in batches, adding more oil as needed, for 5 minutes or until browned all over. Using a slotted spoon, transfer to slow cooker stoneware.

3. Add broth to skillet and bring to a boil, scraping up any brown bits from pan. Transfer to stoneware. Stir in carrots, potatoes, tomatoes, onions, cabbage, onion soup mix, tomato sauce and Worcestershire sauce.

4. Cover and cook on Low for 10 to 12 hours or on High for 5 to 6 hours, stirring once if possible, until beef and vegetables are tender.

5. Ladle into individual serving mugs. Top each with a dollop of sour cream and sprinkle with fresh dill (if using).

Pork Carnitas

Makes 10 to 12 servings

Enter any taqueria in California and you'll find carnitas on the menu, usually pork shoulder (butt) roast, slow-braised, pulled apart, then roasted over high heat to caramelize it. This is a great way to use the slow cooker and the oven to create an authentic Mexican dish to feed a crowd. Add some sangría or margaritas, and you'll have a Mexican party-in-a-pot!

Tip

Carnitas means "little meats," a type of Mexican braised or roasted pork. Carnitas are sometimes served with refried beans and thinly sliced radishes. You can add the radishes to this recipe, if you choose.

- **Minimum 6-quart slow cooker**
- *Rimmed baking sheet*

4 lbs	boneless pork shoulder blade (butt) roast, trimmed and cut into large cubes	2 kg
8	cloves garlic, minced	8
1 tsp	salt	5 mL
½ tsp	freshly ground black pepper	2 mL
1 cup	freshly squeezed orange juice	250 mL
2 tbsp	olive oil	30 mL
1	can (14 oz/398 mL) refried beans, warmed (optional)	1
20 to 24	6- or 7-inch (15 or 18 cm) corn or flour tortillas, warmed	20 to 24
	Fresh cilantro leaves	
1	large white onion, thinly sliced	1
4	avocados, peeled and diced	4
20 to 24	lime wedges	20 to 24

1. In slow cooker stoneware, combine pork, garlic, salt, pepper and 8 cups (2 L) water.

2. Cover and cook on Low for 10 to 12 hours or on High for 5 to 6 hours, until pork is fork-tender. Discard cooking liquid.

3. Preheat oven to 400°F (200°C). Break pork into smaller chunks and spread on baking sheet. Drizzle with orange juice and oil. Roast, stirring occasionally, for 15 to 20 minutes or until browned and crisp.

4. Spread a layer of refried beans (if using) on each tortilla. Top with pork, cilantro, onion and avocado. Serve with a lime wedge to squeeze over top.

Make Ahead

This dish can be assembled up to 12 hours in advance. Prepare through step 1, cover and refrigerate overnight. The next day, place stoneware in slow cooker and proceed with step 2.

Pulled Pork Sammies with Radish Slaw

Makes 8 to 10 servings

Forget any worries about feeding a large crowd when you make this slow cooker all-time favorite. It starts with a dry rub to season the meat, then slow-cooks it in tangy apple juice to tenderize it. A Habitat for Humanity group conducting a local build were the lucky recipients of my recipe test, and everyone gave it a "hammers up" rating!

Tips

A boneless pork shoulder is an inexpensive cut of pork that turns into a tender, juicy and succulent piece of meat after low and slow cooking.

Tomato paste is now available in tubes in many supermarkets and delis. It keeps for months in the refrigerator.

To get the most juice from a lime, let it warm to room temperature, then roll it on the counter, pressing down with the palm of your hand, before squeezing it. Or microwave a whole lime on High for 30 seconds, then roll, cut and squeeze it. Juice can be frozen in ice cube trays, then kept in the freezer in sealable plastic bags for later use. Zest can also be wrapped and frozen for later use.

- **Minimum 6-quart slow cooker**

1/4 cup	garlic powder	60 mL
1/4 cup	paprika	60 mL
2 tbsp	chili powder	30 mL
2 tbsp	dried oregano	30 mL
2 tbsp	coarse salt	30 mL
1 tbsp	freshly ground black pepper	15 mL
1 tbsp	celery seeds	15 mL
3 lbs	boneless pork shoulder blade (butt) roast, trimmed	1.5 kg
1	large onion, sliced	1
5	cloves garlic, minced	5
4	sprigs fresh thyme	4
1	bay leaf	1
2 cups	unsweetened apple juice	500 mL

Barbecue Sauce

1/2 cup	smoky-flavored barbecue sauce	125 mL
1 tbsp	tomato paste	15 mL
1	clove garlic, minced	1
1	chipotle pepper in adobo sauce, minced (optional)	1

Radish Slaw

1/3 cup	light mayonnaise	75 mL
1 tbsp	granulated sugar	15 mL
3 tbsp	white wine vinegar	45 mL
3 tbsp	freshly squeezed lime juice	45 mL
	Salt and freshly ground black pepper	
1	small green cabbage (about 2 lbs/1 kg), halved, cored and thinly sliced	1
1	bunch radishes, halved and thinly sliced (about 1 1/2 cups/375 mL)	1
24	small hamburger buns, toasted	24

1. In a small bowl, combine garlic powder, paprika, chili powder, oregano, salt, pepper and celery seeds. Place pork in a bowl and rub all over with spice mixture. Let marinate at room temperature for 15 to 30 minutes.

Tip

Cooking times can vary a great deal between slow cooker manufacturers. Always let your food cook for the minimum amount of time before testing for doneness.

2. Arrange onion over bottom of slow cooker stoneware. Place pork on top. Add garlic, thyme, bay leaf and apple juice.

3. Cover and cook on Low for 8 to 10 hours or on High for 4 to 6 hours, until pork is fork-tender and falling apart. Transfer pork to a cutting board and let cool slightly.

4. Remove any butcher's string holding the roast together. Using two forks, shred pork.

5. Skim fat from cooking liquid. Reserve 1 cup (250 mL) cooking liquid and set aside. Discard bay leaf and the remaining cooking liquid. Return pork to stoneware.

6. *Sauce:* In a bowl, combine the reserved cooking liquid, barbecue sauce, tomato paste, garlic and chipotle pepper (if using). Stir into pork. Keep warm on Low heat.

7. *Slaw:* Meanwhile, in a large bowl, whisk together mayonnaise, sugar, vinegar and lime juice. Season to taste with salt and pepper. Add cabbage and radishes; toss to coat. Cover and refrigerate for at least 1 hour.

8. Spoon pork mixture on the bottom half of each bun and top with a big scoop of slaw. Cover with top half of bun.

Make Ahead

The radish slaw can be prepared up to 1 day ahead.

Pass-the-Hot-Potato Bar

Makes 12 servings

The potato-bar choices in this recipe elevate the standard baked potato to a whole new level. This is a great way to bring people together to talk, eat and have fun. This bar creates a lot of excitement, as everyone gets to choose their own topping combos.

Tip

If these toppings seem too adult-friendly, choose toppings you know everyone will enjoy. Try leftover chili, salsa, ranch dressing, sour cream, shredded Cheddar cheese, crumbled goat cheese, shredded cooked chicken, sliced black olives or chopped fresh parsley or cilantro.

Keep in mind that the more potatoes you have in the cooker, the longer the cooking time.

- Minimum 6-quart slow cooker

12	baking potatoes	12
¼ cup	olive oil	60 mL
	Salt	

Red Onion Jam

2 tbsp	butter	30 mL
2	large red onions, thinly sliced	2
½ cup	red wine	125 mL
3 tbsp	granulated sugar	45 mL
3 tbsp	balsamic or red wine vinegar	45 mL
2 tbsp	grenadine (optional)	30 mL

Chopped chives
Crumbled crisply cooked bacon
Chopped pistachios

1. Using a fork or the tip of a sharp knife, prick potatoes all over and rub with oil. Sprinkle each with salt, wrap in foil and place in slow cooker stoneware. (Do not add water.)

2. Cover and cook on Low for 6 to 7 hours or on High for 3 to 4 hours, until tender. Reduce heat to Low, if necessary, or Warm, if possible. (Potatoes will hold for up to 2 hours before serving.)

3. *Jam:* Meanwhile, in a large skillet, melt butter over medium-low heat. Sauté onions for 12 to 15 minutes or until tender but not browned. Add wine, sugar, vinegar and grenadine (if using). Reduce heat to low and cook, stirring occasionally, for 10 to 12 minutes or until thickened and jammy.

4. Open corners of foil to expose the tops of potatoes. Slice an X in each, then squeeze the bottom of the potato to open the cuts. Top each potato with jam, chives, bacon and pistachios.

Meals for Two

Slow Cooking for Two or Just You

If you are your own dinner partner or one of a party of two, you may find preparing nutritious, tasty meals a challenge, especially if you're used to cooking for a family, or you may find it hard to get motivated to cook for just yourself. Slow cooker to the rescue!

Making dinners for one or two has never been easier. Manufacturers now make 3- to 4-quart slow cookers, which are perfect for the smaller household. They take up less storage space, use less energy, are easier to clean and hold just the right amount of food for one or two.

This chapter is dedicated to recipes designed for the smaller slow cooker. No longer will you have to cut a recipe in half or freeze large quantities of leftovers. With a little extra planning, you can enjoy tasty, healthful meals with a minimum of effort.

Dining alone doesn't have to be lonely or burdensome. Make the most of your meals and budget by planning ahead, making your cooking count and making every meal an experience. Here are some tips that will help make it easy:

- Save money and preparation time by buying foods that can be easily divided into portions for one or two.
- Immediately place perishable foods — fresh vegetables and fruit, milk products and fresh meat, fish and poultry — in the refrigerator or freezer.
- Store fresh vegetables and fruit separately. Fruit can give off gases that speed up ripening in vegetables and hasten spoilage.
- Buy bulk packs of meat, fish and poultry. When you get home, divide them into single portions, then wrap and freeze them for later use. Remember to thaw meat in the refrigerator before putting it in the slow cooker.
- You can extend the shelf life of dry goods, such as crackers and cereal, by storing them in well-sealed containers that keep out moisture and air.
- When possible, purchase foods such as pasta, rice and oatmeal in bulk. These versatile dry goods can be combined with other simple ingredients to create a multitude of meals in the slow cooker.
- Dried beans, peas and lentils are a great source of fiber and an inexpensive source of protein. They are easy to prepare in the slow cooker (see page 120), then freeze in 1-cup (250 mL) portions for use in salads, chilis, stews and soups. You can purchase dried beans and lentils in bulk; they have a long shelf life in your pantry.
- Don't freeze more than you can eat within 2 to 3 months. Consider exchanging frozen portions of soups, casseroles, stews and meatloaf with friends.

Mediterranean Minestrone

Makes 2 servings

Ground lamb gives this soup extra flavor. The topping of fresh mint and feta cheese adds to its Mediterranean essence.

Tips

If you can only purchase 1 lb (500 g) of ground lamb or more, divide it into 8-oz (250 g) portions. Use one for this recipe. Wrap the other portions and freeze in heavy-duty freezer bags.

To prevent soft, mushy pasta, do not allow it to be in the water any longer than necessary. Add it only when the water is at a full boil, and keep it at a steady boil while it cooks.

- **3- to 4-quart slow cooker**

8 oz	lean ground lamb	250 g
3	cloves garlic, minced	3
1/2	stalk celery, finely chopped	1/2
1/4 cup	chopped onion	60 mL
1/4 cup	finely chopped carrot	60 mL
1	tomato, chopped	1
2 cups	cooked or canned white kidney beans (see page 120), drained and rinsed	500 mL
2 cups	beef broth	500 mL
3/4 cup	coarsely chopped zucchini	175 mL
2 tsp	freshly squeezed lemon juice	10 mL
1/2 tsp	dried oregano	2 mL
1/2 tsp	hot pepper flakes	2 mL
1/8 tsp	freshly ground black pepper	0.5 mL
1	bay leaf	1
1/4 cup	elbow macaroni or other small pasta	60 mL
1 tbsp	snipped fresh mint	15 mL
2 tbsp	crumbled feta cheese	30 mL

1. In a nonstick skillet, cook lamb, garlic, celery, onion and carrot over medium-high heat, breaking up lamb with the back of a wooden spoon, for 4 minutes or until onion is translucent and tender and lamb is no longer pink. Using a slotted spoon, transfer to slow cooker stoneware.

2. Stir in tomato, beans, broth, zucchini, lemon juice, oregano, hot pepper flakes, black pepper and bay leaf.

3. Cover and cook on Low for 4 to 6 hours or on High for 2 to 3 hours, until bubbling and vegetables are tender. Discard bay leaf.

4. Meanwhile, cook pasta according to package directions until tender but firm (al dente). Drain. About 10 minutes before the end of cooking, stir pasta into lamb mixture.

5. Just before serving, stir in mint. Ladle into individual serving bowls and sprinkle with cheese.

Make Ahead

This dish can be assembled up to 12 hours in advance. Prepare through step 2, cover and refrigerate overnight. The next day, place stoneware in slow cooker and proceed with step 3.

Pantry Corn Chowder

Makes 2 servings

There is nothing more satisfying on a cool evening than a steaming bowl of this hearty classic. It's so simple to prepare, using basic pantry essentials: frozen corn, potatoes, bacon and cream. In this recipe, evaporated milk replaces the cream, with the same creamy results.

Tips

If you have not thawed the corn, quickly defrost it in the microwave.

Evaporated milk holds up extremely well in the slow cooker and will not curdle when it is cooked over a long period of time. Don't confuse evaporated milk with the sweetened condensed milk used in desserts and candies.

Most leftover canned and jarred ingredients can be transferred to an airtight container, covered and stored in the refrigerator. Transfer the remaining evaporated milk to a glass jar with a tight-fitting lid and refrigerate for up to 7 days. Freezing is not recommended, as the solids tend to separate from the water, and no amount of stirring, shaking or blending will help blend it back together. Be sure to mark the date and amount on the jar for easy use next time.

- **3- to 4-quart slow cooker**

2 cups	frozen corn kernels, thawed	500 mL
¾ cup	evaporated milk	175 mL
3	slices bacon, minced	3
1	small onion, minced	1
3	small red potatoes, diced	3
2	cloves garlic, minced	2
2 cups	chicken broth	500 mL
1	bay leaf	1
⅛ tsp	dried thyme	0.5 mL
	Salt and freshly ground black pepper	

1. In a food processor or blender, process 1 cup (250 mL) of the corn and the evaporated milk until fairly smooth. Set aside.

2. In a nonstick skillet, sauté bacon and onion over medium heat for 5 to 7 minutes or until onion is tender and translucent. Using a slotted spoon, transfer to slow cooker stoneware.

3. Stir in puréed corn mixture, the remaining corn, potatoes, garlic, broth, bay leaf and thyme.

4. Cover and cook on Low for 8 to 10 hours or on High for 4 to 6 hours, until bubbling and potatoes are tender. Discard bay leaf. Season to taste with salt and pepper.

Roasted Red Pepper Soup

Makes 2 servings

Using roasted red peppers from a jar makes putting this soup together quick and easy. It has a slightly smoky, sweet flavor from the peppers and is a knock-'em-dead start to any meal. For a complete meal, serve with a simple grilled cheese sandwich or panini.

Tip

For convenience, roasted red bell peppers are available in jars or can be found fresh in the deli section of some supermarkets. To make your own, preheat broiler. Cut peppers in half and remove stem and seeds. Place cut side down on rimmed baking sheet. Broil until skins have blackened. Transfer to a paper bag, close it, and let peppers sweat for about 30 minutes. Peel off skins and chop flesh. Roasted peppers can be stored in plastic freezer bags in the freezer for up to 3 months. You will need 4 or 5 whole roasted peppers for this recipe.

- **3- to 4-quart slow cooker**

1 tsp	butter	5 mL
1	onion, finely chopped	1
1	clove garlic, minced	1
1	jar (13 oz/370 mL) roasted red peppers, drained and chopped	1
1 cup	vegetable broth	250 mL
1/2 cup	freshly squeezed orange juice	125 mL
1/8 tsp	salt	0.5 mL
1/2 cup	half-and-half (10%) cream	125 mL
1 tbsp	chopped fresh basil	15 mL
1/4 cup	crumbled blue cheese	60 mL

1. In a small skillet, melt butter over medium heat. Sauté onion and garlic for about 5 minutes or until onion is tender and translucent. Transfer to slow cooker stoneware. Stir in roasted peppers, broth, orange juice and salt.

2. Cover and cook on Low for 4 to 6 hours or on High for 2 to 2 1/2 hours, until bubbling.

3. Using an immersion blender, or in a food processor or blender, in batches as necessary, purée soup until smooth. (If using food processor or blender, return purée to stoneware.)

4. Stir in cream and basil. Cover and cook on High for 10 minutes or until heated through.

5. Ladle into bowls and sprinkle with cheese.

Hearty Drumstick "Stoup" with Parsley Dumplings

Makes 2 servings

I couldn't decide whether this satisfying recipe was a soup or a stew, so I settled on calling it "stoup." You can cheat and substitute prepared refrigerated biscuits for the Parsley Dumplings.

Tips

Turkey drumsticks can vary in size. Oval slow cookers easily fit an elongated cut of meat such as a drumstick. Round slow cookers may be more challenging. If you have difficulty fitting a drumstick into the stoneware, substitute a meaty turkey thigh.

A mini food processor is perfect for smaller portions. It takes up less storage space, uses less energy, is easier to clean and holds just the right amount of ingredients for one or two.

- **3- to 4-quart slow cooker (preferably oval)**
- *Food processor*

1	turkey drumstick (about 12 oz/375 g)	1
2	cloves garlic, minced	2
1	carrot, diced	1
1	stalk celery, diced	1
1	small onion, finely chopped	1
1	bay leaf	1
1/2 tsp	poultry seasoning	2 mL
1/2 tsp	dried thyme	2 mL
2 cups	chicken broth	500 mL
2 tbsp	chopped fresh parsley	30 mL
	Salt and freshly ground black pepper	

Parsley Dumplings

1	slice white bread, quartered	1
1 tbsp	chopped fresh parsley	15 mL
1/4 cup	all-purpose flour	60 mL
1/4 tsp	baking powder	1 mL
1/8 tsp	salt	0.5 mL
2 tbsp	milk	30 mL
1 tbsp	butter, melted	15 mL

1. In slow cooker stoneware, combine turkey, garlic, carrot, celery, onion, bay leaf, poultry seasoning and thyme. Pour in broth and 1 cup (250 mL) water.

2. Cover and cook on High for 5 to 6 hours or until meat is falling off the bones. Discard bay leaf. Using a slotted spoon, transfer turkey to a cutting board and let cool.

3. Remove and discard turkey skin and bones. Using two forks, shred turkey and return to stoneware, along with parsley. Season to taste with salt and pepper.

4. *Parsley Dumplings:* Meanwhile, in food processor, pulse bread and parsley to medium-size crumbs. Add flour, baking powder and salt; process until just combined. Add milk and butter; pulse until just blended.

5. Drop mounded spoonfuls of batter into soup. Cover and cook on High for 12 to 15 minutes or until a tester inserted in the center of a dumpling comes out clean.

Creamy Herbed Chicken Stew

Makes 2 to 3 servings

I have a soft spot for this creamy stew. It reminds me of chicken pot pie without the crust. Creamy sauce and juicy chunks of chicken and vegetables combine to make it the ultimate comfort food.

Tip

You can substitute boneless skinless chicken breasts for the chicken thighs, but you will need to reduce the cooking time to 3 to 4 hours on Low. Cooking times for poultry may be shorter for smaller slow cookers and/or when there is a relatively high proportion of white to dark meat. When cooking mostly white-meat dishes, be sure to avoid overcooking.

- **3- to 4-quart slow cooker**

6	white mushrooms, quartered	6
1 cup	baby carrots	250 mL
1/4 cup	chopped onion	60 mL
1/4 cup	sliced celery	60 mL
1/2 tsp	dried thyme, divided	2 mL
1/4 tsp	dried sage	1 mL
1/8 tsp	salt	0.5 mL
1/8 tsp	freshly ground black pepper	0.5 mL
8 oz	boneless skinless chicken thighs (about 4)	250 g
3/4 cup	chicken broth	175 mL
1/4 cup	frozen peas, thawed	60 mL
1/4 cup	heavy or whipping (35%) cream	60 mL
2 tbsp	all-purpose flour	30 mL
	Chopped fresh parsley	

1. In slow cooker stoneware, combine mushrooms, carrots, onion and celery. Sprinkle with half the thyme, sage, salt and pepper. Place chicken on top. Pour broth over chicken.

2. Cover and cook on Low for 6 to 8 hours or until vegetables are tender and juices run clear when chicken is pierced.

3. Stir in peas. Cover and cook for 10 to 15 minutes or until heated through.

4. Using a slotted spoon, transfer chicken and vegetables to a serving bowl and keep warm.

5. In a bowl, whisk together cream, flour and the remaining thyme. Stir into cooking liquid in stoneware. Cover and cook on High for about 10 minutes or until thickened into sauce. Pour over chicken and vegetables. Sprinkle with parsley.

Beef Stew for Two

Makes 2 servings

Soups and stews don't always have to feed a crowd. This heartwarming dish was designed just for two. Serve it with a crisp green salad and a few crusty rolls for soaking up the extra juice.

Tips

Select lean stewing beef or trim any excess fat from the meat. Trimming takes a little extra time, but it's worth it.

Store any leftovers in an airtight container in the refrigerator for up to 3 days or freeze for up to 3 months. If the consistency of leftover stew seems too thick, reheat it first, as it can thin considerably once it is warmed. If the warmed stew is still too thick, thin it down by gradually adding water or beef broth until the desired consistency is achieved.

- **3- to 4-quart slow cooker**

2 tbsp	all-purpose flour	30 mL
1/2 tsp	paprika	2 mL
1/2 tsp	dried thyme	2 mL
1/8 tsp	salt	0.5 mL
1/8 tsp	freshly ground black pepper	0.5 mL
1 lb	boneless stewing beef, cut into 1-inch (2.5 cm) cubes	500 g
1 tbsp	vegetable oil (approx.)	15 mL
1 cup	beef broth	250 mL
1	can (7 1/2 oz/213 mL) tomato sauce	1
1	carrot, chopped	1
1	stalk celery, chopped	1
1	clove garlic, minced	1
1/2 cup	diced peeled potatoes	125 mL
1/2 cup	frozen peas, thawed	125 mL

1. In a heavy plastic bag, combine flour, paprika, thyme, salt and pepper. In batches, add beef to bag and toss to coat with flour mixture. Discard excess flour mixture.

2. In a nonstick skillet, heat oil over medium-high heat. Cook beef in batches, adding more oil as needed, for 5 minutes or until browned all over. Using a slotted spoon, transfer to slow cooker stoneware.

3. Add broth to skillet and bring to a boil, scraping up any brown bits from pan. Transfer to stoneware. Stir in tomato sauce, carrot, celery, garlic and potatoes.

4. Cover and cook on Low for 8 to 10 hours or on High for 4 to 5 hours, until bubbling and vegetables are tender.

5. Stir in peas. Cook for 15 to 20 minutes or until heated through.

Multi-Bean Vegetarian Chili for Two

Makes 2 to 3 servings

It's hard to find a recipe for chili that doesn't make a huge pot. My mom and dad like this recipe because it uses a can of mixed beans, so you get a nice variety without a huge quantity. Can you spot the secret ingredient? No, the chocolate syrup is not a mistake. It really does add an interesting element to the sauce for this chili.

Tip

Cajun seasoning is a combination of chiles, pepper, garlic, onions and herbs, and is found in the spice section of the supermarket. It has a little heat, so use as much or as little as your palate can handle. If you can't find it, substitute ¾ tsp (3 mL) ground cumin, ½ tsp (2 mL) each ground thyme and paprika and a pinch of cayenne pepper and ground allspice.

- 3- to 4-quart slow cooker

1	can (19 oz/540 mL) mixed beans, drained and rinsed	1
1	can (14 oz/398 mL) diced tomatoes, with juice	1
1	can (4½ oz/127 mL) diced mild green chiles	1
1	small zucchini, diced	1
½ cup	frozen corn kernels, thawed	125 mL
½ cup	beer or chicken broth	125 mL
1 tbsp	chocolate syrup	15 mL
1 tbsp	chili powder	15 mL
1 tsp	Cajun seasoning	5 mL
	Sour cream (optional)	
	Shredded Cheddar cheese (optional)	

1. In slow cooker stoneware, stir together beans, tomatoes with juice, green chiles, zucchini, corn, beer, chocolate syrup, chili powder and Cajun seasoning.

2. Cover and cook on Low for 6 to 8 hours or on High for 3 to 4 hours, until bubbling.

3. Ladle into bowls, top each with a dollop of sour cream (if using) and sprinkle with cheese (if using).

Make Ahead

This dish can be assembled up to 12 hours in advance. Prepare through step 1, cover and refrigerate overnight. The next day, place stoneware in slow cooker and proceed with step 2.

White-Hot Chicken Chili

Makes 2 to 3 servings

Chili doesn't have to be the traditional red dish most people think of. The added chili powder gives this one a slightly speckled shade, but it is considered a white chili, nevertheless. Spoon it over a slab of Southwest Cornbread (page 73) or inside crunchy taco shells, and serve a green salad on the side.

Tip

To prepare jalapeño peppers, wash them well and remove the stems and seeds. When cutting hot peppers, wear rubber gloves and don't touch your eyes or skin. Continue to wear the gloves while cleaning the cutting board, knife and gloves.

- **3- to 4-quart slow cooker**

4 tsp	vegetable oil (approx.), divided	20 mL
1	onion, finely chopped	1
1	stalk celery, chopped	1
1¼ lbs	boneless skinless chicken breasts, cut into 1-inch (2.5 cm) pieces	625 g
2	cloves garlic, minced	2
1	jalapeño pepper, seeded and finely chopped	1
1	can (19 oz/540 mL) white kidney beans, drained and rinsed	1
1 cup	chicken broth	250 mL
1 tbsp	chili powder	15 mL
½ tsp	ground cumin	2 mL
½ tsp	dried oregano	2 mL
½ tsp	salt	2 mL
¼ tsp	hot pepper flakes	1 mL
¼ cup	chopped fresh cilantro or flat-leaf (Italian) parsley	60 mL
	Shredded jalapeño Monterey Jack cheese	

1. In a large skillet, heat half the oil over medium heat. Sauté onion and celery for 5 minutes or until tender. Using a slotted spoon, transfer to slow cooker stoneware.

2. Increase heat to high. Add the remaining oil to skillet. Cook chicken in batches, adding more oil as needed, for about 5 minutes or until browned all over. Using a slotted spoon, transfer to stoneware.

3. Stir in garlic, jalapeño, beans, broth, chili powder, cumin, oregano, salt and hot pepper flakes.

4. Cover and cook on Low for 5 to 6 hours or on High for 2½ to 3 hours, until bubbling. Taste and adjust seasoning, if necessary.

5. Ladle into bowls and sprinkle with cilantro and cheese.

Make Ahead

This dish can be assembled up to 12 hours in advance, as long as the chicken is left out. Complete step 1, skip over step 2, then complete step 3. Cover and refrigerate overnight. The next day, brown the chicken as directed in step 2. Place stoneware in slow cooker, add chicken and proceed with step 4.

Chunky Fireside Chili for Two

Makes 2 to 3 servings

After a busy day, unwind with a quiet meal built around a dynamite bowl of red chili. Set out the toppings on a tray and enjoy a cozy fireside dinner.

Tip

I like to think of chipotle peppers in adobo sauce as "canned heat." For less heat, scrape the ribs and seeds out of the peppers before adding them to a dish.

You can substitute chipotle hot sauce for the peppers

- **3- to 4-quart slow cooker**

1 tbsp	vegetable oil (approx.)	15 mL
1 lb	boneless beef round steak or pork shoulder blade (butt) roast, trimmed and cut into ½-inch (1 cm) cubes	500 g
1	small red bell pepper, diced (about ½ cup/125 mL)	1
1	small onion, chopped	1
1	can (14 oz/398 mL) baked beans in tomato sauce	1
1	can (14 oz/398 mL) diced tomatoes, with juice	1
¼ cup	beef broth	60 mL
2 tsp	minced garlic	10 mL
1 to 2 tsp	finely chopped chipotle pepper in adobo sauce	5 to 10 mL
½ tsp	salt	2 mL
¼ tsp	ground cumin	1 mL
¼ tsp	dried oregano	1 mL
	Shredded Tex-Mex cheese blend	
	Chopped avocado	
	Crushed tortilla chips (optional)	
	Sour cream (optional)	

1. In a large nonstick skillet, heat half the oil over medium-high heat. Cook beef in batches, adding more oil as needed, for about 5 minutes or until browned all over. Using a slotted spoon, transfer to slow cooker stoneware.

2. Stir in red pepper, onion, beans, tomatoes with juice, broth, garlic, chipotle pepper, salt, cumin and oregano.

3. Cover and cook on Low for 6 to 8 hours or on High for 3 to 4 hours, until beef is tender.

4. Ladle into bowls and top with cheese, avocado, tortilla chips (if using) and sour cream (if using).

Make Ahead

The ingredients in step 2 can be assembled in the stoneware up to 12 hours in advance. Cover and refrigerate overnight. The next day, brown the beef as directed in step 1. Place stoneware in slow cooker, add beef and proceed with step 3.

Zucchini Ratatouille

Makes 2 to 3 servings

I make this on a regular basis in the summer when I'm harvesting zucchini from my vegetable garden. If I have any leftovers, I like to heat up a bowl for lunch and serve it over rotini. It also makes a great side for grilled chicken or sausage.

Tips

Because eggplant skin can be tough, you may want to peel the eggplant before cubing and cooking it. Alternatively, you can peel it in stripes, leaving some of the skin intact.

Italian seasoning can be purchased premixed in the spice aisle of the grocery store. You can also mix your own from crumbled dried herbs. Combine 2 tsp (10 mL) each basil, marjoram and oregano and 1 tsp (5 mL) dried sage. Store in an airtight container away from heat, moisture and sunlight for up to 1 year.

- **3- to 4-quart slow cooker**

1	can (7 $\frac{1}{2}$ oz/213 mL) pizza sauce or tomato sauce	1
1 $\frac{1}{2}$ cups	cubed peeled baby eggplant (see tip, at left)	375 mL
$\frac{1}{2}$ cup	coarsely chopped zucchini or yellow summer squash	125 mL
$\frac{1}{2}$ cup	coarsely chopped tomato	125 mL
$\frac{1}{3}$ cup	coarsely chopped red bell pepper	75 mL
$\frac{1}{4}$ cup	finely chopped onion	60 mL
1	clove garlic, minced	1
2 tsp	granulated sugar	10 mL
$\frac{1}{2}$ tsp	dried Italian seasoning	2 mL
$\frac{1}{4}$ tsp	salt	1 mL
$\frac{1}{8}$ tsp	freshly ground black pepper	0.5 mL
1 tbsp	snipped fresh basil	15 mL
3 tbsp	freshly grated Parmesan cheese	45 mL

1. In slow cooker stoneware, combine pizza sauce, eggplant, zucchini, tomato, red pepper, onion, garlic, sugar, Italian seasoning, salt and pepper.

2. Cover and cook on Low for 4 $\frac{1}{2}$ to 5 hours or on High for 2 to 2 $\frac{1}{2}$ hours, until bubbling and vegetables are tender.

3. Just before serving, stir in basil. Ladle into bowls and sprinkle with cheese.

Smokin' Mac and Cheese

Makes 2 to 3 servings

This updated version of a comfort-food classic gets its exquisite flavor from a touch of smoked cheese. If you have finicky eaters, replace the smoked Gouda with an equal amount of Cheddar. It will still be delicious, just not as poetic. Round it out with a tossed green salad and whole wheat dinner rolls.

Tip

When preparing pasta for the slow cooker, undercook it in boiling salted water first, to remove some of the starch. It will continue to cook in the slow cooker, and the consistency will be perfect rather than overdone.

- **3- to 4-quart slow cooker, stoneware greased**

2 cups	elbow macaroni	500 mL
1	egg, lightly beaten	1
1	can (12 oz/370 mL) evaporated milk	1
¼ cup	milk	60 mL
¼ tsp	salt	1 mL
¼ tsp	freshly ground black pepper	1 mL
¼ tsp	dry mustard	1 mL
⅛ tsp	smoked paprika (optional)	0.5 mL
1 cup	shredded smoked Gouda cheese	250 mL
1	small tomato, chopped	1

1. In a pot of boiling salted water, cook macaroni for 5 minutes. Drain and transfer to prepared slow cooker stoneware.

2. In a bowl, combine egg, evaporated milk, milk, salt, pepper, mustard and paprika (if using). Pour over macaroni. Stir in cheese and tomato.

3. Cover and cook on Low for 5 to 6 hours or until set.

Gouda, Holland's most famous exported cheese, has a yellow interior dotted with a few holes. The smoked variety is made by placing the rounds over smoldering hickory chips, which gives the rind a brown color without affecting the color of the creamy yellow interior.

Braised Salmon with Springtime Vegetables

Makes 2 servings

In this simple one-dish meal, delicate salmon fillets are poached in a fragrant herb sauce alongside new potatoes, carrots and peas.

Tips

Although it's slightly more expensive, I like to use boneless salmon fillets rather than bone-in salmon steaks, because I don't like having to watch out for tiny bones when I am eating (although even with the fillets you may occasionally discover a tiny pin bone). Fresh salmon fillets are found at the seafood counter in the supermarket and usually weigh in at about 5 oz (150 g) each.

Because of its higher fat content, salmon is quite forgiving in the slow cooker. Don't worry if you let it cook 20 to 30 minutes longer than directed.

- **3- to 4-quart slow cooker**

6	baby new potatoes, cut in half lengthwise	6
1	carrot, peeled and cut into thin strips	1
½	small onion, sliced	½
¼ cup	frozen peas, thawed	60 mL
1 cup	vegetable broth	250 mL
1 tbsp	soy sauce	15 mL
2	boneless skinless salmon fillets (each about 5 oz/150 g)	2
1 tbsp	chopped fresh tarragon (or 1 tsp/5 mL dried)	15 mL
¼ cup	heavy or whipping (35%) cream	60 mL
1 tbsp	snipped fresh chives	15 mL
	Salt and freshly ground black pepper	

1. In slow cooker stoneware, combine potatoes, carrot, onion and peas.

2. In a small saucepan, bring broth and soy sauce to a simmer over medium-high heat. Pour over potato mixture.

3. Cover and cook on Low for 4 to 6 hours or on High for 2 to 3 hours, until vegetables are tender.

4. Place salmon on potato mixture and sprinkle with tarragon. Cover and cook on High for 30 to 40 minutes or until salmon flakes easily when tested with a fork. Using a slotted spoon, transfer salmon and vegetables to a platter.

5. Stir cream into cooking liquid in stoneware. Season to taste with salt and pepper. Drizzle sauce over salmon and vegetables and garnish with chives.

Creamy Pesto Chicken and Asparagus

Makes 2 servings

This simple chicken and pesto pasta dish can be quickly assembled and put in the slow cooker before you hit the golf course or curling rink. It will be ready for the quick finishing touches when you return.

Tip

Look for fettuccini or linguine pasta packaged like nests — they make it easy to cook only what you need for 2 servings.

- **3- to 4-quart slow cooker**

4	boneless skinless chicken thighs, cut into 1-inch (2.5 cm) cubes	4
	Freshly ground black pepper	
½ cup	chicken broth	125 mL
2 tbsp	basil pesto or sun-dried tomato pesto	30 mL
4 oz	asparagus, chopped	125 g
¼ cup	heavy or whipping (35%) cream	60 mL
2 tbsp	freshly grated Parmesan cheese	30 mL
	Salt	
	Hot cooked fettuccini or rotini pasta	
	Additional freshly grated Parmesan cheese (optional)	

1. Arrange chicken in slow cooker stoneware and sprinkle with ¼ tsp (1 mL) pepper.

2. In a glass measuring cup, combine broth and pesto. Pour over chicken.

3. Cover and cook on Low for 5 to 6 hours or until juices run clear when chicken is pierced.

4. Stir in asparagus, cream and cheese. Cover and cook on High for 15 minutes or until liquid is slightly thickened and asparagus is tender. Season to taste with salt and pepper.

5. Serve over fettuccine, sprinkled with additional cheese, if desired.

Italian Chicken Braciola

Makes 2 to 3 servings

These stuffed chicken thighs are so easy to prepare and so tasty served over pasta or Pecorino and Parsley Polenta (page 297). Complete the meal with crusty bread for soaking up the sauce and mixed greens tossed with a light vinaigrette.

Tip

Authentic Italian Parmesan cheese (Parmigiano-Reggiano) is expensive, but its flavor is certainly worth the price. Well-wrapped in the refrigerator, a block keeps for months, and it goes a long way when you freshly grate it as you need it.

- **3- to 4-quart slow cooker**

4	slices bacon, diced	4
1	clove garlic, minced	1
1/2 cup	finely chopped onion	125 mL
1	egg, lightly beaten	1
1/4 cup	fine dry bread crumbs	60 mL
1/4 cup	freshly grated Parmesan cheese	60 mL
1 tbsp	chopped fresh rosemary (or 1 tsp/5 mL dried)	15 mL
6	boneless skinless chicken thighs	6
1 tbsp	olive oil	15 mL
1 tbsp	butter	15 mL
1	can (19 oz/ 540 mL) diced tomatoes with Italian seasonings, with juice	1
3 tbsp	tomato paste	45 mL

1. In a skillet, cook bacon over medium-high heat, stirring frequently, until crisp. Add garlic and onion; sauté for 2 to 3 minutes or until softened. Remove from heat and stir in egg, bread crumbs, cheese and rosemary.

2. Unfold chicken thighs and place smooth side down on a work surface. Spoon about 2 tbsp (30 mL) of the bacon mixture over each thigh, fold over to enclose filling and secure with a toothpick.

3. In the same skillet, heat oil and butter over medium-high heat. Cook thighs for 2 to 3 minutes per side or until browned all over. Transfer to slow cooker stoneware.

4. In a bowl, combine tomatoes with juice and tomato paste. Pour over chicken.

5. Cover and cook on Low for 5 to 6 hours or on High for 2 1/2 to 3 hours, until juices run clear when chicken is pierced with a fork.

No-Hurry Mango Chicken Curry

Makes 2 servings

Not all slow cooker meals look pretty as they cook, but this one is an exception. Simple chicken curry mixed with sweet mangos and red peppers is assembled quickly but simmered slowly. It will satisfy all your curry cravings. Serve over hot basmati or jasmine rice.

Tip

To store gingerroot, peel it and place it in a jar with a tight-fitting lid. Add enough sherry to cover. The sherry will saturate and preserve the ginger. Refrigerate for up to 1 month. Use the infused wine to flavor other chicken dishes, or check out the recipe for Mary's Australian Ginger Beer (page 33).

- **3- to 4-quart slow cooker**

1 tsp	vegetable oil	5 mL
4	boneless skinless chicken thighs	4
½	red bell pepper, chopped	½
1 cup	frozen mango chunks, thawed and drained	250 mL
½ cup	chopped onion	125 mL
1 tbsp	raisins	15 mL
1	clove garlic, minced	1
½ cup	unsweetened applesauce	125 mL
2 tsp	hot or mild curry paste	10 mL
½ tsp	finely grated gingerroot (or ¼ tsp/1 mL ground ginger)	2 mL
¼ tsp	salt	1 mL
⅛ tsp	freshly grated black pepper	0.5 mL
⅓ cup	plain yogurt	75 mL
1 tsp	chopped fresh cilantro or parsley	5 mL

1. In a nonstick skillet, heat oil over medium-high heat. Cook chicken for 2 to 3 minutes per side or until browned all over. Transfer to slow cooker stoneware.

2. Stir in red pepper, mango, onion and raisins.

3. In a bowl, combine garlic, applesauce, curry paste, ginger, salt and pepper. Pour into stoneware.

4. Cover and cook on Low for 6 to 8 hours or on High for 3 to 4 hours, until juices run clear when chicken is pierced with a fork. Just before serving, stir in yogurt and sprinkle with cilantro.

Make Ahead

The ingredients in steps 2 and 3 can be assembled in the stoneware up to 2 days in advance. Cover and refrigerate. When ready to cook, brown the chicken as directed in step 1. Place stoneware in slow cooker, add chicken and proceed with step 4.

Spicy Lemon Coconut Chicken

Makes 2 to 3 servings

This Thai-influenced chicken treat has lots of exotic flavors, but is so simple to create. The crunch of the green beans and red peppers contrasts nicely with the moist meat.

Tips

One of the perks of cooking bone-in chicken is that the meat retains its tenderness.

Squeezing fresh lemon juice over the chicken enhances the Thai flavors — it really does make a difference to the finished dish.

- **3- to 4-quart slow cooker**

1 tbsp	all-purpose flour	15 mL
½ tsp	ground coriander	2 mL
¼ tsp	ground cumin	1 mL
¼ tsp	salt	1 mL
⅛ tsp	ground allspice	0.5 mL
Pinch	freshly ground black pepper	Pinch
2	chicken leg quarters (about 1½ lbs/750 g)	2
1 tbsp	olive oil	15 mL
¼ cup	chicken broth	60 mL
2 tsp	Thai red curry paste	10 mL
1	small red bell pepper, cut into strips	1
4 oz	green beans, stem ends removed, cut into 1-inch (2.5 cm) lengths	125 g
¼ cup	unsweetened coconut milk	60 mL
	Hot cooked jasmine rice, basmati rice or stir-fried noodles	
½	lemon, cut into wedges	½

1. In a bowl, combine flour, coriander, cumin, salt, allspice and pepper. Coat chicken with flour mixture and set aside.

2. In a nonstick skillet, heat oil over medium-high heat. Cook chicken for 6 to 8 minutes per side or until browned all over. Transfer to slow cooker stoneware.

3. In a bowl, combine broth and curry paste. Pour around chicken in stoneware. Sprinkle with red pepper.

4. Cover and cook on Low for 6 to 8 hours or on High for 3 to 3½ hours, until juices run clear when chicken is pierced with a fork.

5. Stir in green beans and coconut milk. Cover and cook on High for 25 to 30 minutes or until beans are tender.

6. Mound rice on a platter. Spoon chicken, vegetables and sauce on top and squeeze juice from lemon wedges over chicken.

Mu Shu for Two

Makes 2 servings

This is one of my son's favorite dinners. Since it only serves two, I originally made it on an evening when just he and I were home, and Jack loved it — any meal wrapped in a tortilla is fine by him. I served it with some lightly blanched asparagus spears, drizzled with an Asian dressing.

Tip

There is no need to peel gingerroot before grating it. Simply scrub it and use a standard box grater with fine holes. You can wrap any unused gingerroot in plastic wrap and freeze it for up to 6 months, then grate the frozen gingerroot as you need it.

- **3- to 4-quart slow cooker**

4	boneless skinless chicken thighs	4
1/4 tsp	salt	1 mL
1/8 tsp	freshly ground black pepper	0.5 mL
1	clove garlic, minced	1
1 tsp	minced gingerroot (or 1/4 tsp/1 mL ground ginger)	5 mL
1/4 cup	soy sauce	60 mL
2 tsp	sesame oil	10 mL
4	10-inch (25 cm) whole wheat flour tortillas	4
1/4 cup	hoisin sauce	60 mL
1 cup	broccoli slaw mix	250 mL
1/4	red bell pepper, thinly sliced	1/4

1. Arrange chicken in slow cooker stoneware. Sprinkle with salt and pepper.

2. In a small bowl, combine garlic, ginger, soy sauce, sesame oil and 1/4 cup (50 mL) water. Pour over chicken.

3. Cover and cook on Low for 6 to 7 hours or on High for 3 to 3 1/2 hours, until juices run clear when chicken is pierced with a fork. Using a slotted spoon, transfer chicken to a cutting board. Using two forks, shred meat. Return meat to sauce in stoneware.

4. Preheat oven to 350°F (180°C). Stack tortillas and wrap them in foil. Warm in oven for 10 minutes.

5. Spread 1 tbsp (15 mL) hoisin sauce over each tortilla, then top with one-quarter of the chicken mixture, 1/4 cup (60 mL) of the broccoli slaw and red pepper. Fold or roll up tortillas.

Hoisin sauce is a thick, soy-based sauce that is regularly used in Chinese dishes and stir-fries. The typical ingredients are soybean paste, garlic, vinegar and various seasonings, such as chile peppers. The flavor is sweet, salty and spicy.

Petite Pot Roast

Makes 2 servings

Even two people can enjoy a pot roast without days of leftovers. A cross rib or chuck pot roast has a nice compact size that lends itself to a two-person meal. Surrounded by hearty, home-style vegetables, this roast is delicious and satisfying.

Tip

Slow cooking tenderizes less expensive cuts of meat. Pot roasts benefit from long cooking on Low. If you need to cook this faster, a minimum of 4 hours of simmering on High will produce fork-tender meat.

- **3- to 4-quart slow cooker**

1 tbsp	all-purpose flour	15 mL
1/4 tsp	salt	1 mL
1/8 tsp	freshly ground black pepper	0.5 mL
1	boneless beef cross rib or chuck roast (1 to 1 1/2 lbs/500 to 750 g)	1
1 tbsp	vegetable oil	15 mL
4	baby new potatoes, cut in half	4
2	carrots, cut into 1-inch (2.5 cm) pieces	2
1	small parsnip, cut into 1-inch (2.5 cm) pieces	1
1	small onion, cut into wedges	1
1	clove garlic, minced	1
1	bay leaf	1
1 tbsp	tomato paste	15 mL
1 tsp	soy sauce	5 mL
1/2 tsp	fresh thyme	2 mL
1/2 cup	fresh or frozen peas, thawed if frozen	125 mL

1. In a bowl, combine flour, salt and pepper. Pat beef dry with paper towels and coat all over with flour mixture.

2. In a large skillet, heat oil over medium-high heat. Cook beef, turning with two wooden spoons, for 7 to 10 minutes or until browned all over. Transfer to slow cooker stoneware.

3. Add potatoes, carrots, parsnip, onion, garlic, bay leaf, tomato paste, soy sauce and thyme to stoneware.

4. Cover and cook on Low for 8 to 10 hours or on High for 4 to 5 hours, until beef is fork-tender. Transfer beef to a warmed platter, cover with foil and let stand for 15 minutes.

5. Meanwhile, stir peas into vegetable mixture in stoneware. Cover and cook on High for 10 to 15 minutes or until heated through. Discard bay leaf.

6. Cut beef across the grain into 6 slices. Using a slotted spoon, arrange vegetables around beef. Spoon cooking liquid over top.

Make Ahead

The ingredients in step 3 can be assembled in the stoneware up to 2 days in advance. Cover and refrigerate. When ready to cook, coat and brown the beef as directed in steps 1 and 2. Place stoneware in slow cooker, add beef and proceed with step 4.

Cranberry Chipotle Pot Roast

Makes 2 to 3 servings

When you're making a pot roast for a small household, either buy a large roast and cut it in half (freeze what you don't need) or look for smaller cuts of beef. The butcher will often cut one for you, if you ask. This recipe was a real hit with my parents' condo neighbors — it got a four-fork rating! Mashed potatoes are a must on the side.

Tip

If the sauce is not thick enough for your liking, here is a quick way to thicken it. Transfer the cooking liquid to a small saucepan and bring it to a boil over medium-high heat. In a small bowl, combine 1 tbsp (15 mL) all-purpose flour and 1 tbsp (15 mL) softened butter; whisk into sauce and cook, stirring, until thickened. Spoon over meat when serving.

- **3- to 4-quart slow cooker**

1	boneless beef cross rib, chuck or rump roast (1½ to 2 lbs/750 g to 1 kg)	1
1	clove garlic, minced	1
½ tsp	dried thyme	2 mL
	Salt and freshly ground black pepper	
2 tsp	vegetable oil	10 mL
1	small onion, cut into thin wedges	1
¾ cup	whole berry cranberry sauce	175 mL
½ to 1 tsp	finely chopped chipotle pepper in adobo sauce	2 to 5 mL

1. Sprinkle beef with garlic, thyme and ⅛ tsp (0.5 mL) each salt and pepper.

2. In a large skillet, heat oil over medium-high heat. Cook beef, turning with two wooden spoons, for 7 to 10 minutes or until browned all over. Transfer to slow cooker stoneware. Arrange onion around beef.

3. In a bowl, combine cranberry sauce and chipotle pepper. Pour over beef.

4. Cover and cook on Low for 8 to 10 hours or on High for 4 to 5 hours, until beef is fork-tender. Using a slotted spoon, transfer beef and onion to a warmed platter, cover with foil and let stand for 10 minutes.

5. Skim off any fat from cooking liquid. Season to taste with salt and pepper. Pour into a gravy boat. Slice roast across the grain and serve with gravy on the side.

Italian Beef Sandwiches

Makes 2 to 3 servings

Flank steak is an underused cut of meat that works really well in the slow cooker. If you have a hard time finding a small steak, just cut one in half and freeze the rest for another recipe. Once the meat is cooked, it shreds easily with two forks. My friend's mom, Sheila, taste-tested this one for me one night. She cooked some noodles the next night and spooned warmed leftover meat and sauce on top for a second great meal.

Tips

Look for reduced-sodium tomato sauce.

To shred meat, hold a fork in each hand and insert the tines, back to back and straight down, into the meat. Gently pull the forks apart, shredding the meat into long, thin strands.

- **3- to 4-quart slow cooker**

1 lb	flank steak	500 g
1	clove garlic, minced	1
1 tbsp	chopped sun-dried tomatoes	15 mL
1/2 tsp	dried oregano	2 mL
1/4 tsp	dried rosemary	1 mL
Pinch	hot pepper flakes	Pinch
1	can (7 1/2 oz/213 mL) tomato sauce	1
1/4 cup	roasted red bell pepper, cut into strips	60 mL
2	4-inch (10 cm) pieces of baguette (or 2 crusty panini rolls), split and toasted	2
1/4 cup	shredded provolone cheese	60 mL
1/2	small green bell pepper, cut into thin strips	1/2

1. Place steak in slow cooker stoneware. Sprinkle with garlic, sun-dried tomatoes, oregano, rosemary and hot pepper flakes. Pour tomato sauce over top.

2. Cover and cook on Low for 7 to 8 hours or on High for 3 1/2 to 4 hours, until steak is fork-tender. Using a slotted spoon, transfer steak to a cutting board. Using two forks, shred meat. Stir roasted red pepper into shredded steak.

3. Spread steak mixture over bottom halves of bread. Drizzle with cooking liquid and sprinkle with cheese and green pepper. Cover with top halves of bread. Serve the remaining cooking liquid on the side, for dipping.

Steak and Mushroom Pub Pie

Makes 2 servings

On a family trip to Wales, my son ordered a pie similar to this in a quaint pub. Jack loved it so much, he polished off the whole thing. I've recreated it for the slow cooker, with great results. Adding a little butter to the sauce gives an extra richness to the filling.

Tips

Serve with boiled new potatoes, just as they would in Wales.

If you prefer a browner crust, you can bake the topping in the oven. Top the cooked stew as directed, then transfer stoneware to a 400°F (200°C) oven and bake for 30 to 35 minutes or until topping is golden brown.

Beer has wonderful tenderizing properties, so it's a great addition to a dish that includes less tender cuts of meat, such as stewing beef. Although dark beers, such as stout and porter, have a strong flavor, they will not overpower the cooked dish. You can substitute lighter or non-alcoholic beer, but the flavor might not be quite as good.

- **3- to 4-quart slow cooker**

Filling

2 tbsp	all-purpose flour	30 mL
1/2 tsp	dried thyme	2 mL
1/4 tsp	salt	1 mL
1/8 tsp	freshly ground black pepper	0.5 mL
1 lb	stewing beef, cut into 1/2-inch (1 cm) cubes	500 g
2 tsp	vegetable oil	10 mL
1	bottle (12 oz/341 mL) dark beer, such as Guinness	1
1 cup	quartered button mushrooms	250 mL
3/4 cup	chopped onion	175 mL
1 tsp	Worcestershire sauce	5 mL
1 tbsp	butter	15 mL

Topping

1 cup	prepared biscuit mix	250 mL
1/3 cup	milk	75 mL
2 tbsp	shredded Cheddar cheese	30 mL
1/4 tsp	dried thyme	1 mL

1. *Filling:* In a bowl, combine flour, thyme, salt and pepper. Add beef and toss to coat with flour mixture.

2. In a large nonstick skillet, heat oil over medium-high heat. Cook beef until browned all over. Using a slotted spoon, transfer to slow cooker stoneware.

3. Add beer to skillet and cook, scraping up any brown bits from pan. Transfer to stoneware. Stir in mushrooms, onion, Worcestershire sauce and butter.

4. Cover and cook on Low for 8 to 10 hours or on High for 4 to 5 hours, until beef is fork-tender.

5. *Topping:* In a bowl, stir together biscuit mix, milk, cheese and thyme until a lumpy dough forms. (Do not overmix.) Drop spoonfuls of dough over stew.

6. Cover and cook on High for 20 to 25 minutes or until a tester inserted in center of topping comes out clean.

Stuffed Mexican Sweet Peppers

Makes 2 servings

Stuffed red bell peppers and Mexican seasonings liven up an easy dinner that starts with ground beef or turkey.

Tip

The hole in the bottom of each pepper allows moisture and steam to penetrate the stuffing, promoting even cooking.

- **3- to 4-quart slow cooker**

2	small to medium red bell peppers	2
8 oz	lean ground beef or turkey	250 g
1	clove garlic, minced	1
½	small onion, diced	½
½ cup	black bean or chunky salsa	125 mL
½ cup	shredded jalapeño Monterey Jack cheese, divided	125 mL
2 tbsp	long-grain parboiled (converted) white rice	30 mL
½ tsp	dried oregano	2 mL
	Chopped fresh cilantro (optional)	

1. Trim out stem, core and seeds from the top of peppers. Cut a small hole in the bottom of each pepper.

2. In a large skillet, cook beef, garlic and onion over medium heat, breaking up beef with the back of a wooden spoon, for 7 minutes or until no longer pink. Drain off fat. Stir in salsa, half the cheese, rice and oregano. Spoon evenly into peppers, mounding if necessary (do not pack tightly).

3. Set peppers upright in slow cooker stoneware. Pour ½ cup (125 mL) water around peppers.

4. Cover and cook on Low for 6 to 7 hours or on High for 3 to 3½ hours, until peppers are tender.

5. Using a slotted spoon, transfer peppers to a serving platter. Top with the remaining cheese and sprinkle with cilantro (if using).

Peachy Pork Chops

Makes 2 servings

A pleasing combination of peach jam, soy sauce, rice vinegar and fresh ginger gives these chops an exotic Asian flavor. Serve with brown rice and a green vegetable, such as broccoli, for a dinner that welcomes you home at the end of the day.

Tip

You can use pork shoulder (blade) butt chops in this recipe, but you will need to increase the cooking time to 6 to 8 hours on Low or 3 to 4 hours on High. Since these chops tend to release more juices when cooked longer, the sauce will be a little thinner. To thicken it at the end of cooking, combine 2 tsp (10 mL) cornstarch and 1 tbsp (15 mL) cold water; stir into cooking liquid in stoneware (after you've removed the chops). Cover and cook on High for 15 to 20 minutes or until thickened into sauce.

- **3- to 4-quart slow cooker**

2	bone-in pork loin rib chops (about 3/4 inch/2 cm thick), trimmed	2
2 tsp	vegetable oil	10 mL
1/2	small onion, sliced	1/2
1/2 tsp	grated gingerroot	2 mL
1/2 tsp	dry mustard	2 mL
1/4 tsp	salt	1 mL
1/8 tsp	freshly ground black pepper	0.5 mL
1/4 cup	peach jam	60 mL
1 tbsp	soy sauce	15 mL
1 tbsp	rice vinegar	15 mL
1/2 cup	long-grain brown rice	125 mL

1. In a nonstick skillet, heat oil over medium-high heat. Cook pork chops for about 5 minutes per side or until browned all over. Transfer to slow cooker stoneware. Arrange onion on top. Sprinkle with ginger, mustard, salt and pepper.

2. In a small bowl, combine jam, soy sauce and vinegar. Pour over pork chops.

3. Cover and cook on Low for 4 to 5 hours or on High for 2 to 2½ hours, until fork-tender.

4. Meanwhile, cook rice according to package directions. Mound rice on a serving platter. Arrange pork chops on top and drizzle with cooking liquid.

Pineapple Ginger Pork

Makes 2 servings

My family has always loved this easy weeknight meal, served over lots of steamed rice. The smell is heavenly, especially when you've been out of the house all day.

Tips

You could also use a pork shoulder chop, cut into pieces, for this dish.

I used a lunch-pack size can of pineapple, which is perfect for this two-person dish. If you have difficulty finding that size, measure out ⅔ cup (150 mL) pineapple and ¼ cup (50 mL) pineapple juice from a regular can, then save the remainder to make a small fruit salad for dessert.

- **3- to 4-quart slow cooker**

12 oz	pork tenderloin, cut into 1-inch (2.5 cm) cubes	375 g
2 tsp	cornstarch, divided	10 mL
2 tbsp	soy sauce, divided	30 mL
1 tsp	sesame oil	5 mL
1	small onion, thinly sliced	1
1	clove garlic, minced	1
1 tbsp	packed brown sugar	15 mL
1 tsp	minced gingerroot (or ¼ tsp/1 mL ground ginger)	5 mL
1	can (5 oz/142 mL) pineapple tidbits, drained, reserving juice	1
¼ cup	chicken broth or water	60 mL
2 tbsp	ketchup	15 mL
1 tbsp	rice vinegar	15 mL
1 tbsp	hoisin sauce	15 mL
½	red bell pepper, thinly sliced	½
½	green bell pepper, thinly sliced	½

1. In a bowl, toss together pork, half the cornstarch, half the soy sauce and sesame oil. Let stand for 30 minutes. Transfer to slow cooker stoneware.

2. In a bowl, combine onion, garlic, brown sugar, ginger, the remaining cornstarch, the remaining soy sauce, pineapple juice, broth, ketchup, vinegar and hoisin sauce. Pour over pork.

3. Cover and cook on Low for 6 to 8 hours or until pork is tender.

4. Add pineapple, red pepper and green pepper to stoneware. Cover and cook on High for 15 minutes or until peppers are tender-crisp and pineapple is warmed through.

Barbecue Pork Chili Ribs

Makes 2 servings

There's no need to fire up the grill for these ribs — they simmer away on their own in a spunky barbecue sauce. Serve with a side of potato salad for an authentic taste of summer. Shred any leftover meat to fill grilled panini the next day.

Tip

Here's a foolproof way to chop an onion: Peel the onion and halve it from top to base. Place each half cut side down on a cutting board. Slice horizontally across each half. Holding the slices together, slice vertically.

- **3- to 4-quart slow cooker**

1½ lbs	pork back ribs, trimmed	750 g
1	small onion, finely chopped	1
1	clove garlic, minced	1
2 tbsp	packed brown sugar	30 mL
½ tsp	chili powder	2 mL
¼ tsp	smoked paprika	1 mL
¼ tsp	celery seeds	1 mL
½ cup	ketchup	125 mL
½ tsp	Worcestershire sauce	2 mL
¼ tsp	hot pepper sauce	1 mL

1. Place ribs in slow cooker stoneware. In a small bowl, combine onion, garlic, brown sugar, chili powder, paprika, celery seeds, ketchup, Worcestershire sauce, hot pepper sauce and ½ cup (125 mL) water. Pour over ribs.

2. Cover and cook on Low for 10 to 12 hours or on High for 5 to 6 hours, until ribs are tender. Using a slotted spoon, transfer ribs to a serving platter and keep warm.

3. Skim off any fat from cooking liquid in stoneware. Transfer cooking liquid to a saucepan and bring to a boil. Reduce heat slightly and boil gently for 5 to 7 minutes or until thickened. Serve sauce on the side.

> Smoked paprika is made by grinding peppers that have undergone a smoking process. You can find it in various heat levels (from mild to hot). Be careful how much you use, because smoky seasonings can easily overpower the flavor of a dish.

One-Pot Sausage Supper

Makes 2 servings

All this German-style meal needs is some crusty rolls and your favorite mustard. You can use smoked Polish sausage for this recipe, but I like the fresh variety a little better.

Tip

If there is not much liquid in the ingredients, it is a good idea to grease your stoneware with nonstick cooking spray. Otherwise, when the stoneware heats up, the food can stick, making cleanup difficult. If food does stick, soak the stoneware in hot, soapy water to help remove it.

- **3- to 4-quart slow cooker, stoneware greased**

1 tbsp	vegetable oil	15 mL
2	fresh Oktoberfest or bratwurst sausages	2
1 1/2 cups	frozen hash brown potatoes	375 mL
1	small red bell pepper, chopped (about 1/2 cup/125 mL)	1
1/2	red-skinned apple, sliced	1/2
1/4 tsp	caraway seeds	1 mL
1/4 tsp	salt	1 mL
1/8 tsp	freshly ground black pepper	0.5 mL
1/3 cup	unsweetened apple juice or apple cider	75 mL
2 tsp	cider vinegar	10 mL
1 cup	drained sauerkraut	250 mL
1 tbsp	chopped fresh parsley	15 mL

1. In a nonstick skillet, heat oil over medium-high heat. Cook sausages, turning, for 6 to 8 minutes or until browned all over. (To make them easier to slice, sausages should not be cooked through.) Transfer to a cutting board. Using a sharp knife, slice into 1-inch (2.5 cm) chunks.

2. In prepared slow cooker stoneware, combine hash browns and red pepper. Arrange sausage, then apple, on top. Sprinkle with caraway seeds, salt and pepper.

3. In a measuring cup, combine apple juice and vinegar. Pour over sausage mixture.

4. Cover and cook on Low for 5 to 6 hours or on High for 2 1/2 to 3 hours, until heated through.

5. Spread sauerkraut over sausage mixture. Cover and cook on High for 25 to 30 minutes or until sauerkraut is heated through. Transfer to a serving dish and sprinkle with parsley.

Double-Duty Dinners

Cook Once, Eat Twice

If the daily dinner dilemma is stressing you out, and you're frequently defaulting to the nearest drive-through to feed your famished family, maybe it's time to chill. You can turn tonight's delicious dinner into tomorrow's feast. This chapter is filled with recipes designed to yield extras that come together quickly in a simple second meal on Day Two.

Whether you are slow-cooking a ham or braising chicken thighs, it doesn't take any

longer to make a little more. Then you can turn the leftovers into something new and different the whole family will love: a French dip sandwich from pot roast; nachos from leftover turkey breast or ground meat.

With a bit of advance planning and the inspiring recipes from this chapter, you can banish the remark "Not *that* again!" You'll have two delicious meals for the work of one.

Martha's Maple Chipotle Chicken

Day One

Makes 4 servings, plus leftovers

Meaty chicken thighs star in this hearty dish. Chicken thighs cook so well in the slow cooker, imparting lots of flavor to the dish while staying moist and juicy. The sweet maple syrup balances nicely with the smokiness of the chipotle peppers.

Tip

Tomato paste is now available in tubes in many supermarkets and delis. It keeps for months in the refrigerator.

● **Minimum 5-quart slow cooker**

2	red bell peppers, cut into 1-inch (2.5 cm) pieces	2
2	carrots, coarsely chopped	2
1	onion, cut into thin wedges	1
3 lbs	boneless skinless chicken thighs	1.5 kg
1	can (19 oz/540 mL) chili-style stewed tomatoes, with juice	1
3 tbsp	tomato paste	45 mL
2 to 3 tbsp	finely chopped chipotle peppers in adobo sauce	30 to 45 mL
2 tbsp	pure maple syrup or packed brown sugar	30 mL
1 tsp	salt	5 mL
	Hot buttered egg noodles	

1. Arrange red peppers, carrots and onion in slow cooker stoneware. Place chicken on top.

2. In a bowl, combine tomatoes with juice, tomato paste, chipotle peppers, maple syrup and salt. Pour over chicken and vegetables.

3. Cover and cook on Low for 8 to 9 hours or on High for 4 to 4½ hours, until juices run clear when chicken is pierced.

Tip

Resist the urge to lift the lid and taste or smell whatever is inside the slow cooker as it's cooking. Every peek will increase the cooking time by 20 minutes.

4. For Day Two, transfer 8 chicken thighs and 1 cup (250 mL) sauce to separate airtight containers. Let cool, then refrigerate for up to 3 days.

5. Serve the remaining chicken and sauce over hot buttered noodles.

Make Ahead

This dish can be assembled up to 12 hours in advance. Prepare through step 2, cover and refrigerate overnight. The next day, place stoneware in slow cooker and proceed with step 3.

Friday Night Chicken Quesadillas

`Day Two`

Makes 4 servings

When convenience counts, this recipe is the perfect solution. Leftover chicken and sauce make it a snap to put together. Serve with a spinach salad and enjoy a lime-flavored beer on the side.

Tip

Quesadillas can also be pan-fried. Set a large skillet (preferably nonstick or well-seasoned cast iron) over medium-low heat. Add enough vegetable oil to barely coat the bottom. Place the quesadilla in the skillet. When the cheese begins to melt (after about 2 minutes), flip the quesadilla over. Cook for 1 to 2 minutes or until the bottom is warm and lightly toasted.

- *Preheat oven to 400°F (200°C)*
- *Rimmed baking sheet*

8	reserved chicken thighs from Day One	8
1 cup	reserved sauce from Day One	250 mL
8	10-inch (25 cm) flour tortillas	8
2	green onions, sliced	2
1	jalapeño pepper, seeded and diced (optional)	1
2 cups	shredded Monterey Jack or mild Cheddar cheese	500 mL
1 cup	frozen corn kernels, thawed	250 mL
	Hot or mild salsa	
	Sour cream	

1. Place chicken on a cutting board. Using two forks, shred meat; transfer to a bowl. Add sauce and toss to coat.

2. Place 4 tortillas on baking sheet. Top each with chicken mixture, green onions, jalapeño (if using), cheese and corn. Cover each with another tortilla.

3. Bake in preheated oven, turning once, for 15 to 20 minutes or until tortillas are golden and cheese is melted. Transfer to a cutting board and cut into wedges. Serve with salsa and sour cream.

Indian Orange-Spiced Chicken Thighs

Day One

Makes 6 servings, plus leftovers

I just can't get enough of chicken in a flavorful curry sauce, and if I can eat it two ways, I'm even happier. Bone-in thighs are best for this dish, as they stay moist and tender.

Tips

To zest an orange, use the fine side of a box cheese grater, making sure not to grate the white pith underneath. Or use a zester, then finely chop the zest. Zesters are inexpensive and are widely available at specialty kitchenware shops.

For this recipe, use a mild curry paste, such as tandoori or tikka masala. Look for it where Indian foods are shelved in the supermarket.

• **Minimum 5-quart slow cooker**

2 tbsp	vegetable oil (approx.)	30 mL
4 lbs	bone-in skinless chicken thighs	2 kg
4	onions, thinly sliced	4
½ cup	chicken broth	125 mL
	Finely grated orange zest	
½ cup	freshly squeezed orange juice	125 mL
8	cloves garlic, minced	8
3 tbsp	mild curry paste	45 mL
1 tbsp	minced gingerroot	15 mL
¼ tsp	ground cinnamon	1 mL
¼ tsp	ground allspice	1 mL
2 tbsp	all-purpose flour	30 mL
1 cup	plain yogurt	250 mL
3 cups	hot cooked jasmine rice or basmati rice	750 mL
	Snipped fresh mint	
	Toasted slivered almonds	

1. In a large skillet, heat half the oil over medium-high heat. Cook chicken in batches, adding more oil as needed, for 4 to 6 minutes or until browned all over. Using a slotted spoon, transfer to slow cooker stoneware.

2. Reduce heat to medium. Add onions to skillet and sauté for 8 to 10 minutes or until tender and translucent. Spoon over chicken.

3. In a glass measuring cup, whisk together broth, orange juice, garlic, curry paste, ginger, cinnamon and allspice. Pour over chicken mixture.

4. Cover and cook on Low for 7 to 8 hours or on High for 3½ to 4 hours, until juices run clear when chicken is pierced.

5. For Day Two, use a slotted spoon to transfer 12 chicken thighs and 1 cup (250 mL) of the onions (about half) to separate airtight containers. Let cool, then refrigerate for up to 3 days.

6. Using a slotted spoon, transfer the remaining chicken to a platter and cover to keep warm.

Tip

Cooking times can vary a great deal between slow cooker manufacturers. Always let your food cook for the minimum amount of time before testing for doneness.

7. In a bowl, whisk together flour and yogurt. Stir into cooking liquid in stoneware. Cover and cook on High for 15 to 20 minutes or until thickened.

8. Serve chicken and sauce over rice, sprinkled with mint, orange zest and almonds.

Quick Coconut Chicken Curry

Day Two

Makes 6 servings

A can of coconut milk and some curry powder is all it takes to sauce this dish of chicken and vegetables.

Tips

To ensure the best flavor and ripeness, select a plump, firm mango with taut skin and a pleasant aroma from the stem end.

You can substitute 1½ cups (375 mL) thawed frozen mango chunks for the fresh mango.

12	reserved chicken thighs from Day One	12
1 cup	reserved onions from Day One	250 mL
1 tbsp	cornstarch	15 mL
½ tsp	curry powder	2 mL
1	can (14 oz/398 mL) unsweetened coconut milk	1
¼ cup	raisins	60 mL
2	mangos, diced (see box, page 273)	2
3 cups	hot cooked couscous	750 mL
	Toasted shredded coconut (optional)	

1. In a large skillet, warm chicken and onions over medium heat, stirring, until heated through.

2. In a glass measuring cup, combine cornstarch and curry powder. Whisk in coconut milk. Stir into chicken mixture. Stir in raisins and bring to a boil, stirring. Reduce heat and simmer, stirring often, for 5 to 7 minutes or until thickened and bubbling. Stir in mango and simmer until heated through.

3. Spoon over couscous and sprinkle with coconut (if using).

Couscous is a staple in North African cooking, and while many people think of it as a grain, it is actually a granular semolina. It is easy to prepare, has a nutty taste and absorbs the flavors it is cooked with. The "instant" variety found in supermarkets in North America can be prepared in about 5 minutes.

Creamy Chicken with Lemon and Leeks

Day One

Makes 4 servings, plus leftovers

The subtle, earthy flavor of leeks naturally complements chicken. Serve this easy entertaining dish with mashed potatoes or rice.

Tips

Leeks contain a lot of sand and must be cleaned carefully. Remove most of the green part and halve the white part lengthwise. Rinse thoroughly under cold running water, spreading leaves apart, and drain in a colander, then slice.

The peel of a citrus fruit contains two parts: the zest and the pith. The zest is the shiny, bright-colored outer layer. The volatile oils found in zest make it extremely flavorful. The pith is the white, fibrous membrane directly below the zest that protects the fruit inside. It can impart a bitter taste if it is not removed.

- **Minimum 5-quart slow cooker**

1	lemon	1
1/3 cup	all-purpose flour	75 mL
3/4 tsp	salt, divided	3 mL
1/2 tsp	freshly ground black pepper	2 mL
6	bone-in skinless chicken breasts (about 2 1/2 lbs/1.25 kg)	6
3 tbsp	butter	45 mL
8	cloves garlic, thinly sliced	8
6	leeks, thinly sliced	6
1 1/2 cups	chicken broth	375 mL
2 tbsp	all-purpose flour	30 mL
1 cup	heavy or whipping (35%) cream	250 mL
	Finely chopped fresh parsley	

1. Finely grate 1/2 tsp (2 mL) zest from lemon, transfer to an airtight container and refrigerate for Day Two. Using a sharp knife, remove the remaining peel (including the white pith) and discard. Seed and thinly slice lemon. Set aside.

2. In a shallow dish, combine the 1/3 cup (75 mL) flour, 1/2 tsp (2 mL) of the salt and pepper. Dredge chicken in flour mixture to coat. Discard any excess flour mixture

3. In a large skillet, melt butter over medium heat. Cook chicken in batches, turning, for 3 to 4 minutes or until browned all over. Drain off fat.

4. Arrange garlic and leeks in slow cooker stoneware. Sprinkle with the remaining salt. Place chicken on top. Arrange the reserved lemon slices over chicken. Pour broth over chicken and vegetables.

5. Cover and cook on Low for 6 to 8 hours or on High for 3 to 4 hours, until chicken is no longer pink inside.

6. For Day Two, remove 2 chicken breasts and let cool. Chop, transfer to an airtight container and refrigerate for up to 3 days.

7. Using a slotted spoon, transfer the remaining chicken to individual serving plates. Spoon leeks over chicken. Cover to keep warm.

Tips

Resist the urge to lift the lid of the slow cooker — every peek will increase the cooking time by 20 minutes.

8. Transfer $\frac{1}{2}$ cup (125 mL) of the cooking liquid to a saucepan. (Discard the remaining cooking liquid.) In a bowl, whisk together the 2 tbsp (30 mL) flour and cream until blended. Pour into saucepan and bring to a boil, whisking. Reduce heat and simmer, whisking, for 3 to 4 minutes or until thickened.

9. Spoon sauce over chicken and leeks. Sprinkle with parsley.

Chicken and Portobello Risotto

Day Two

Makes 4 servings

This is pure comfort food. Although it requires a lot of stirring, the delicious result is worth the effort!

Tips

To prepare the chicken broth, pour it into a large saucepan and bring to a boil over high heat. Cover and reduce heat to low to keep it hot.

If desired, you can sprinkle the finished risotto with additional grated Parmesan cheese.

1 tbsp	olive oil	15 mL
1 tbsp	butter	15 mL
2	large portobello mushrooms, chopped	2
1	onion, chopped	1
1½ cups	Arborio rice	375 mL
½ cup	dry white wine	125 mL
5½ cups	hot chicken broth (see tip, at left)	1.375 mL
	Reserved chopped chicken from Day One	
	Reserved grated lemon zest from Day One	
½ cup	freshly grated Parmesan cheese	125 mL
	Freshly ground black pepper	
	Chopped fresh parsley	

1. In a large skillet, heat oil and butter over medium-high heat. Cook mushrooms and onion, stirring occasionally, for about 8 minutes or until onion is tender and translucent. Add rice and cook, stirring, for 2 minutes.

2. Stir wine into mushroom mixture, loosening rice from bottom of pan. Cook, stirring frequently, for about 2 minutes or until wine is absorbed. Add 1 cup (250 mL) of the broth, reduce heat to medium and simmer, stirring frequently, until broth is absorbed. Continue to add broth, $\frac{1}{2}$ cup (125 mL) at a time, and cook, stirring frequently, until each addition is absorbed before adding the next, until rice is tender. This will take 25 to 30 minutes. While cooking, the mixture should be gently bubbling, so adjust heat as necessary to maintain a simmer.

3. Stir in chicken, lemon zest, Parmesan and $\frac{1}{4}$ tsp (1 mL) pepper; cook, stirring frequently, until heated through but still creamy.

4. Ladle into individual serving bowls and sprinkle with pepper and parsley.

Honey Mustard Chicken

Makes 6 servings, plus leftovers

This tangy-sweet favorite is quick to put together. Cooking the whole meal at once makes things less hectic at dinnertime. Serve with white or brown rice.

Tips

Cooking times for poultry may be longer for larger slow cookers and/or where there is a relatively high proportion of dark to white meat. For predominantly white-meat dishes, be sure to avoid overcooking.

Before measuring honey, rub the inside of the measuring cup with a little vegetable oil. After measuring, the honey will pour out easily, without leaving a sticky mess.

- **Minimum 5-quart slow cooker**

2	large sweet potatoes	2
1	large onion, halved lengthwise and sliced	1
1	large red bell pepper, chopped	1
8	bone-in skinless chicken breasts (about 4$\frac{1}{2}$ lbs/2.25 kg)	8
$\frac{1}{2}$ tsp	salt	2 mL
$\frac{1}{4}$ tsp	freshly ground black pepper	1 mL
$\frac{1}{4}$ cup	liquid honey	60 mL
$\frac{1}{4}$ cup	Dijon mustard	60 mL
2 tbsp	curry powder	30 mL
2 tbsp	butter, softened	30 mL
2 tbsp	cornstarch	30 mL
2 tbsp	cold water	30 mL

1. Cut each sweet potato in half lengthwise, then in half crosswise. Cut each quarter into three wedges. In slow cooker stoneware, combine sweet potatoes, onion and red pepper. Arrange chicken on top. Sprinkle with salt and pepper.

2. In a bowl, combine honey, mustard, curry powder and butter. Pour over chicken and vegetables.

3. Cover and cook on Low for 5 to 6 hours or on High for 2$\frac{1}{2}$ to 3 hours, until chicken is no longer pink inside.

4. For Day Two, transfer 2 chicken breasts, 1 cup (250 mL) of the vegetables and $\frac{1}{2}$ cup (125 mL) of the cooking liquid to separate airtight containers. Let cool, then refrigerate for up to 3 days.

5. Using a slotted spoon, transfer the remaining chicken and vegetables to a serving platter and cover to keep warm.

6. Strain cooking liquid into a saucepan, discarding solids. In a small bowl, combine cornstarch and water. Bring cooking liquid to a boil over medium-high heat. Whisk in cornstarch mixture. Reduce heat and simmer, stirring, for 2 to 3 minutes or until thickened. Spoon over chicken and vegetables.

Asian Chicken Salad

Makes 4 servings

This crunchy, wonderfully satisfying salad uses reserved chicken from the Honey Mustard Chicken. Even the dressing is made from the previous day's cooking liquid.

Tip

Chow mein noodles are usually found in the Asian food section of supermarkets, but some clever grocers stock them in the produce section, since they are often added to salads for extra crunch.

Dressing

¹/₂ cup	reserved cooking liquid from Day One	125 mL
¹/₂ cup	mayonnaise	125 mL

Salad

2	reserved chicken breasts from Day One	2
1 cup	reserved vegetables from Day One	250 mL
3 cups	shredded napa cabbage or iceberg lettuce	750 mL
1¹/₂ cups	broccoli slaw mix	375 mL
¹/₂ cup	snow peas, trimmed and thinly sliced lengthwise	125 mL
¹/₂ cup	crunchy chow mein noodles	125 mL

1. *Dressing:* In a small bowl, whisk together cooking liquid and mayonnaise until smooth. Set aside.

2. *Salad:* Remove chicken from bones, discarding bones. Chop chicken and reserved vegetables.

3. In a large bowl, combine chicken, vegetables, cabbage, broccoli slaw, snow peas and noodles. Add dressing and toss to coat.

> Broccoli slaw is a type of coleslaw made with shredded broccoli, carrots and red cabbage. Look for it in the produce department of the supermarket. It is delicious tossed with your favorite coleslaw dressing or with added fruit such as apples and dried cranberries.

Thai Chicken Noodle Bowls

Day One

Makes 4 servings, plus leftovers

Thai food is known for its symphony of flavors — sweet, salty, spicy and sour. With this slow-simmered dish, you can enjoy two Thai-inspired meals in one week.

Tips

Sriracha chili sauce is found in the Asian food section of the supermarket or in Asian or gourmet food stores. It is a smooth paste of ground sun-ripened chiles and garlic. It adds a delicious spiciness to Thai food, but it's not overpowering.

Canned coconut milk is made from grated soaked coconut pulp — it's not the liquid found inside the coconut. It can be found in the Asian food section of the supermarket or in Asian food stores. Be sure you don't buy coconut cream, often used to make tropical drinks such as piña coladas.

- **Minimum 5-quart slow cooker**

3	large red bell peppers, cut into strips	3
2	onions, sliced	2
1 to 2	serrano chile peppers, seeded and finely chopped	1 to 2
8 oz	cremini mushrooms, sliced	250 g
6	cloves garlic, minced	6
2 tsp	minced gingerroot	10 mL
6	boneless skinless chicken breasts	6
1 cup	tomato sauce	250 mL
1/4 cup	fish sauce	60 mL
2 tbsp	granulated sugar	30 mL
2 tbsp	freshly squeezed lime juice	30 mL
2 tbsp	Sriracha chili sauce	30 mL
1 cup	coconut milk	250 mL
1½ cups	bean sprouts	375 mL
2 tbsp	cornstarch	30 mL
2 tbsp	cold water	30 mL
1	package (6 oz/175 g) rice stick noodles	1
½ cup	chopped peanuts	125 mL
	Chopped fresh cilantro	

1. Arrange red peppers, onions, serrano chiles to taste and mushrooms in slow cooker stoneware. Sprinkle with garlic and ginger. Place chicken on top.

2. In a glass measuring cup, combine tomato sauce, fish sauce, sugar, lime juice and chili sauce. Pour over chicken and vegetables.

3. Cover and cook on Low for 6 to 7 hours or on High for 3 to 3½ hours, until chicken is no longer pink inside.

4. Stir in coconut milk and bean sprouts. Cover and cook on High for about 30 minutes or until heated through.

5. For Day Two, transfer 2 chicken breasts, 1 cup (250 mL) of the vegetables and ¼ cup (60 mL) of the cooking liquid to separate airtight containers. Let cool, then refrigerate for up to 2 days.

6. Using a slotted spoon, transfer the remaining chicken breasts to a cutting board. Slice, cover to keep warm and set aside. Transfer vegetables to a bowl and cover to keep warm.

7. In a small bowl, whisk together cornstarch and water. Transfer the remaining cooking liquid to a saucepan and bring to a boil over medium-high heat. Reduce heat to medium. Whisk in cornstarch mixture and cook, stirring, for 3 to 5 minutes or until thickened.

8. Meanwhile, in a large pot of boiling salted water, cook noodles according to package directions until tender but firm (al dente). Drain and return to pot.

9. Add 1/2 cup (125 mL) of the sauce and the reserved vegetables to the noodles and toss to coat. Transfer to a serving platter. Top with sliced chicken and spoon the remaining sauce over top. Sprinkle with peanuts and cilantro.

Thai Chicken Pizza Day Two

Makes 4 servings

If you are looking for a pizza that has lots of flavor and is a little different from the rest, this will become one of your favorites. The cilantro on top is a must!

- Preheat oven to 475°F (240°C), with rack positioned at bottom

1/4 cup	reserved cooking liquid from Day One	60 mL
1 tbsp	peanut butter	15 mL
1 tsp	sesame oil	15 mL
Pinch	hot pepper flakes (optional)	Pinch
1	12-inch (30 cm) baked pizza base or flatbread	1
2	reserved chicken breasts from Day One, chopped	2
1 cup	reserved vegetables from Day One	250 mL
1/2	red onion, thinly sliced	1/2
3 cups	shredded mozzarella cheese	750 mL
1/4 cup	chopped fresh cilantro	60 mL

1. In a saucepan, combine cooking liquid, peanut butter, sesame oil and hot pepper flakes. Cook over medium heat, stirring often, until heated through. Set aside.

2. Spread sauce over pizza base. Top evenly with chicken, reserved vegetables, red onion, then cheese.

3. Place directly on lowest rack in preheated oven and bake for 10 to 12 minutes or until cheese is bubbling and brown. Sprinkle with cilantro.

Turkey Breast with Sweet Cranberry Soy Gravy

Day One

Makes 6 servings, plus leftovers

Don't wait for the holidays to make a turkey roast. This delicious recipe can be made as a weeknight meal without any special-occasion fuss. Serve it with rice or mashed potatoes and a sauté of colorful peppers on the side.

Tip

If you're using a smaller slow cooker, substitute 2 bone-in turkey breasts (each 3 lbs/1.5 kg).

- **Minimum 6-quart oval slow cooker (see tip, at left)**

1	bone-in double turkey breast (6 to 7 lbs/3 to 3.5 kg)	1
1	can (14 oz/398 mL) whole berry cranberry sauce	1
1	envelope (1½ oz/45 g) onion soup mix	1
	Grated zest and juice of 1 orange	
3 tbsp	cornstarch	45 mL
3 tbsp	soy sauce	45 mL
1 tbsp	granulated sugar	15 mL
1½ tsp	cider vinegar	7 mL
	Salt and freshly ground black pepper	

1. Place turkey, meat side up, in slow cooker stoneware.

2. Transfer 2 tbsp (30 mL) of the cranberry sauce to an airtight container and refrigerate for Day Two. In a bowl, combine the remaining cranberry sauce, soup mix, orange zest and orange juice. Pour over turkey.

3. Cover and cook on High for 3½ to 5 hours or until a meat thermometer inserted into the thickest part of the breast registers 165°F (74°C) and juices run clear when turkey is pierced. Transfer turkey to a cutting board and let stand for 15 minutes.

4. Cut turkey off the bone and thinly slice. Chop 1½ cups (375 mL) for Day Two and transfer to an airtight container. Let cool, then refrigerate for up to 3 days. Cover the remaining sliced turkey to keep warm.

5. Transfer cooking liquid to a saucepan. In a small bowl, whisk together cornstarch and soy sauce until smooth. Stir into cooking liquid, along with sugar and vinegar. Season to taste with salt and pepper. Bring to a boil, then reduce heat and simmer, stirring, for 2 to 3 minutes or until slightly thickened. Spoon over sliced turkey.

Crunchy Turkey and Cranberry Pie

Makes 6 servings

This quiche-like recipe is a great way to use up leftover turkey and cranberry sauce, and is a family favorite in my home. If you have enough turkey left from the previous night, make two pies and freeze the second one for a third meal. Serve with a spinach salad.

Tips

Quiche is a great way to use up leftovers. In most cases, egg and cream or milk are the main components of the custard layer, which sits in a flaky bottom crust. But instead of using a pie crust, you could also line the sides and bottom of a pie plate with large croissants that have been split in half.

This dish can be served hot or at room temperature.

* *Preheat oven to 400°F (200°C)*

1	9-inch (23 cm) deep-dish pie shell (unbaked)	1
1 tbsp	Dijon mustard	15 mL
2 tbsp	reserved cranberry sauce from Day One	30 mL
1 cup	shredded Swiss cheese	250 mL
1 cup	shredded Cheddar cheese	250 mL
1 tbsp	butter or margarine	15 mL
1	onion, chopped	1
1	stalk celery, chopped	1
1/4 cup	slivered almonds	60 mL
1 1/2 cups	chopped reserved turkey from Day One	375 mL
3	eggs	3
3/4 cup	evaporated milk	175 mL
1/4 tsp	dried sage	1 mL

1. Bake pie shell in preheated oven for 5 to 7 minutes or until crust is light golden. Remove from oven, leaving oven on, and let cool slightly. Using a pastry brush, brush mustard over inside of pie shell. Spread cranberry sauce over mustard.

2. In a bowl, combine Swiss cheese and Cheddar. Sprinkle half the cheese mixture over cranberry sauce. Set aside.

3. In a nonstick skillet, melt butter over medium heat. Sauté onion, celery and almonds for 3 to 5 minutes or until vegetables are softened.

4. In prepared pie shell, evenly layer onion mixture, turkey and the remaining cheese.

5. In a bowl, whisk eggs until blended; whisk in evaporated milk and sage. Slowly pour into pie shell.

6. Bake for 15 minutes. Reduce heat to 375°F (190°C) and bake for 25 to 30 minutes or until set. (Cover edges of crust with foil, if necessary, to prevent excess browning during the last 10 to 15 minutes.) Let stand for 10 minutes before slicing.

Adobo Barbecue Turkey Thighs

Makes 6 servings, plus leftovers

Turkey thighs become so tender in this low, slow, Southwest simmer with big, bold flavors. Continue the theme by making the enchiladas for your Day Two dinner.

Tips

For an authentic Southwestern flair, serve this over hominy instead of rice. You can find hominy, either dried or in cans, in the Latin food section of many supermarkets. If you purchase it in cans, just drain, rinse and heat it.

You can freeze the cooked turkey thighs for use at a later time. Transfer to an airtight container and freeze for up to 1 month. When ready to use, let thaw in the refrigerator overnight.

Enchilada sauce is a cooked tomato and chile sauce. Look for it in the Mexican food section of the supermarket.

- Minimum 5-quart slow cooker

5	skinless turkey thighs (about 5 lbs/2.5 kg)	5
1	large red or green bell pepper, chopped	1
6	cloves garlic, minced	6
1	can (28 oz/796 mL) crushed tomatoes	1
1	can (10 oz/284 mL) enchilada sauce	1
¼ cup	red wine vinegar	60 mL
2 tbsp	finely chopped chipotle peppers in adobo sauce	30 mL
1 tbsp	chili powder	15 mL
2 tsp	crumbled dried oregano	10 mL
1 tsp	ground cumin	5 mL
1 tsp	salt	5 mL
½ tsp	ground cinnamon	2 mL
3 cups	hot cooked rice	750 mL
	Sour cream (optional)	

1. Arrange turkey thighs in slow cooker stoneware and sprinkle with red pepper.

2. In a bowl, combine garlic, tomatoes, enchilada sauce, vinegar, chipotle peppers, chili powder, oregano, cumin, salt and cinnamon. Pour over turkey.

3. Cover and cook on Low for 8 to 10 hours or on High for 4 to 6 hours, until juices run clear when turkey is pierced and meat is very tender and falling off the bones. Using a slotted spoon, transfer turkey to a cutting board. Skim fat from sauce.

4. For Day Two, transfer 2 turkey thighs and 1 cup (250 mL) of the sauce to separate airtight containers. Let cool, then refrigerate for up to 3 days.

5. Cut the remaining turkey thighs from bones, discarding bones, and cut in half. Serve turkey over rice, topped with sour cream (if using). Serve the remaining sauce on the side.

Make Ahead

This dish can be assembled up to 12 hours in advance. Prepare through step 2, cover and refrigerate overnight. The next day, place stoneware in slow cooker and proceed with step 3.

Amazing Turkey Enchiladas

Makes 6 servings

This rolled tortilla casserole comes together easily. It's a fast fix with loads of family appeal!

Tip

Serve these enchiladas with a selection of garnishes, such as sliced radishes or avocado, chopped tomatoes, shredded lettuce and sour cream. Or try them with Mexican Rice (page 257) alongside.

- *Preheat oven to 350°F (180°C)*
- *13- by 9-inch (33 by 23 cm) glass baking dish, greased*

2	reserved turkey thighs from Day One	2
4 oz	light cream cheese	125 g
3	green onions, finely chopped	3
1 cup	reserved sauce from Day One	250 mL
½ cup	plain low-fat yogurt	125 mL
6	10-inch (25 cm) flour tortillas	6
1½ cups	salsa verde	375 mL
1½ cups	shredded Cheddar or Monterey Jack cheese	375 mL
2 tbsp	chopped fresh cilantro or parsley	30 mL

1. Place turkey on a cutting board. Using two forks, shred meat. Discard bones.

2. In large microwave-safe bowl, soften cream cheese on Medium (50%) power for 1 minute. Stir well. Stir in green onions, sauce, yogurt and turkey.

3. Spread about ½ cup (125 mL) of the cream cheese mixture along the center of each tortilla and roll up. Arrange tortillas in a single layer, seam side down, in prepared baking dish.

4. Spread salsa over tortillas and sprinkle with cheese. Bake in preheated oven for 30 to 35 minutes or until heated through. Sprinkle with cilantro.

Make Ahead

You can assemble this dish up to 24 hours in advance. Prepare through step 3, cover and refrigerate overnight. When ready to cook, proceed with step 4.

Salsa verde is Spanish for "green salsa." Green salsas are almost always milder than red salsas. In salsa verde, tomatillos replace the tomatoes used in red salsa. The tomatillos give a tangy, zesty flavor to green salsa, which also has underlying flavors of hearty roasted green chiles and onions.

Caramelized Onion and Mushroom Pot Roast

Day One

Makes 4 servings, plus leftovers

This slow cooker dish, with its braised caramelized onions, is perfect after work on a cold or rainy evening.

Tips

Slow cooking tenderizes less expensive cuts of meat. Pot roast benefits from long, slow cooking on Low, but if you're short of time, count on 5 to 6 hours on High to produce fork-tender meat.

Store mushrooms in a paper bag, with the top loosely folded over once or twice, or place them in a glass container and cover it with a tea towel or moist paper towel. Be sure to allow air circulation. Store in the refrigerator (but not in the crisper) and use within a few days — or a week, if they are packaged and unopened.

To prepare mushrooms, first trim off the bottoms of the stems, then wipe off the mushrooms. Don't rinse or soak the mushrooms, or they'll absorb water and turn mushy when you cook them.

- Minimum 5-quart slow cooker

2 tbsp	vegetable oil	30 mL
1	boneless beef cross rib, rump or chuck roast (3 to 4 lbs/1.5 to 2 kg)	1
5	large onions, halved lengthwise and sliced $1/4$ inch (0.5 cm) thick	5
2 tbsp	packed brown sugar	30 mL
$1/2$ tsp	ground cinnamon	2 mL
1 tsp	dried thyme	5 mL
1	bay leaf	1
4	cloves garlic, minced	4
8 oz	mushrooms, halved	250 g
2 tbsp	balsamic vinegar	30 mL
1 cup	beef broth	250 mL
2 tbsp	cornstarch	30 mL
2 tbsp	cold water	30 mL
	Salt and freshly ground black pepper	

1. In a large skillet, heat oil over medium-high heat. Cook roast, turning with two wooden spoons, for 7 to 10 minutes or until browned all over. Transfer to slow cooker stoneware.

2. Add onions, brown sugar, cinnamon, thyme and bay leaf to skillet and sauté for 12 to 15 minutes or until onions are tender and translucent. Add garlic and mushrooms; sauté for 1 minute. Add vinegar and cook for 2 to 3 minutes or until evaporated. Transfer to stoneware. Pour in broth.

3. Cover and cook on Low for 10 to 12 hours or on High for 5 to 6 hours, until beef is fork-tender. Transfer beef to a cutting board. Slice off two-thirds of the beef, cover to keep warm and set aside.

4. For Day Two, using two forks, shred the remaining beef and transfer to an airtight container. Using a slotted spoon, transfer 1 cup (250 mL) of the vegetables to another airtight container. Transfer $1\frac{1}{2}$ cups (375 mL) of the cooking liquid to a third airtight container. Let beef, vegetables and cooking liquid cool, then refrigerate for up to 3 days.

5. Transfer the remaining vegetables to a bowl and cover to keep warm. Strain the remaining cooking liquid into a saucepan. In a small bowl, whisk together cornstarch and water. Pour into cooking liquid and bring to a boil. Reduce heat to medium and cook, whisking, for 6 to 8 minutes or until thickened into gravy. Season to taste with salt and pepper. Pour into a gravy boat to serve on the side.

6. Slice the reserved beef, arrange on a serving platter and surround with vegetables.

Make Ahead

Complete Step 2, cover and refrigerate for up to 2 days. When ready to cook, complete step 1 and proceed with step 3.

Philippe's French Dip Sandwiches

Day Two

Makes 4 servings

This sandwich was invented by accident. As the story goes, a policeman ordered a sandwich at his favorite Los Angeles deli, owned by a Frenchman named Philippe Mathieu. While he was preparing the sandwich, Philippe accidentally dropped it into some pan juices, but the policeman said he'd eat it anyway. It was a hit! I love serving these sandwiches with french fries, and they are good dipped into the sauce, too. Bon appétit!

- *Preheat broiler, with rack set 3 to 4 inches (7.5 to 10 cm) below heat source*

	Reserved shredded beef from Day One	
1 cup	reserved vegetables from Day One	250 mL
4	crusty French-style rolls, split	4
4	slices provolone cheese, cut in half	4
2 tbsp	Dijon mustard	30 mL
1½ cups	reserved cooking liquid from Day One	375 mL

1. Evenly divide beef and vegetables over bottom halves of rolls. Top each with 2 half-slices of cheese. Spread mustard on top halves. Place, open face, on a baking sheet.

2. Broil for 2 to 3 minutes or until cheese is melted and sandwiches are heated through. Close sandwiches.

3. Meanwhile, in a saucepan, heat reserved cooking liquid over medium-high heat for 3 to 4 minutes or until heated through. Ladle into small bowls for dipping and serve with sandwiches.

Chili-Glazed Meatloaf

Day One

Makes 6 servings, plus leftovers

I wouldn't like to tinker with your favorite meatloaf recipe, and I have always included a few in my collection, but this recipe works well for two meals. The trick to making a good meatloaf is to use a blend of meats and work with a light touch when you shape the loaf by hand. Serve this with mashed potatoes and a steamed green vegetable, such as broccoli.

Tips

You can also line the stoneware with a layer of cheesecloth that's large enough to extend up the sides and over the rim.

Meatloaf can be frozen for later use. Let cool to room temperature, wrap in foil and place in a sealable plastic bag. Mark the bag with the date and recipe name and freeze for up to 3 months. Let thaw in the refrigerator overnight.

- **Minimum 5-quart slow cooker**

1½ lbs	lean ground beef	750 g
1½ lbs	lean ground pork	750 g
3	eggs, lightly beaten	3
1	large onion, finely chopped	1
2 cups	fresh bread crumbs	500 mL
2 tsp	salt	10 mL
½ tsp	freshly ground black pepper	2 mL

Chili Sauce Glaze

½ cup	ketchup	125 mL
¼ cup	chili sauce	60 mL
2 tbsp	packed brown sugar	30 mL
½ tsp	dry mustard	2 mL

1. Cut three 2-foot (60 cm) lengths of heavy foil and fold each one in half lengthwise. Place one strip lengthwise along bottom of slow cooker stoneware, bringing the ends up the sides and over the rim. Place two strips widthwise across bottom of stoneware, bringing the ends up the sides and over the rim.

2. In a large bowl, using your hands, combine beef, pork, eggs, onion, bread crumbs, salt and pepper. Shape into two 5-inch (12.5 cm) loaves. Place loaves on foil strips in stoneware.

3. *Glaze:* In a bowl, combine ketchup, chili sauce, brown sugar and mustard. Spread over loaves.

4. Tucking strip ends under lid, cover and cook on Low for 7 to 8 hours or on High for 3½ to 4 hours, until a meat thermometer inserted in center of loaf registers 170°F (77°C). Remove lid and grasp strip ends to carefully lift out loaves. Transfer one loaf to a serving platter.

5. For Day Two, transfer the other loaf to an airtight container. Let cool, then refrigerate for up to 3 days.

Italian Meatloaf Parmesan

Day Two

Makes 4 to 6 servings

This is a fantastic way to use up leftover meatloaf. It is so easy to prepare, and even the fussiest eaters will enjoy it. Serve over cooked pasta, such as linguine, and add a tossed green salad on the side.

Tip

Authentic Italian Parmesan cheese (Parmigiano-Reggiano) is expensive, but its flavor is certainly worth the price. Well-wrapped in the refrigerator, a block keeps for months, and it goes a long way when you freshly grate it as you need it.

- *Preheat oven to 350°F (180°C)*
- *Rimmed baking sheet, lined with parchment paper*

	Reserved meatloaf from Day One	
2	eggs, lightly beaten	2
1/4 cup	milk	60 mL
1/2 cup	Italian-seasoned fine dry bread crumbs	125 mL
1/4 cup	freshly grated Parmesan cheese	60 mL
2 cups	tomato pasta sauce	500 mL
1 cup	shredded mozzarella cheese	250 mL

1. Cut meatloaf into 6 slices. Set aside.

2. In a shallow bowl, combine eggs and milk. In another shallow bowl, combine bread crumbs and Parmesan.

3. Dip each meatloaf slice in egg mixture, then in bread crumb mixture, coating evenly. Transfer to prepared baking sheet.

4. Bake in preheated oven for 20 minutes. Spoon pasta sauce evenly over meatloaf slices and sprinkle with mozzarella. Bake for about 15 minutes or until cheese is melted and sauce is heated through.

Picadillo

Makes 4 to 6 servings, plus leftovers

A traditional dish in many Latin American countries, picadillo is made with ground meat, tomatoes and other regional ingredients. It's a great alternative to chili, and it freezes well. The Puerto Rican and Cuban versions include olives and, on occasion, capers. Cubans omit the chili powder. Picadillo is usually served with black beans and rice.

Tip

Picadillo is sometimes served with cubed cooked potatoes, which you can substitute for the rice, if you wish.

Variation

Stir in 1 cup (250 mL) thawed frozen green peas with the olives.

- **4- to 6-quart slow cooker**

1 tbsp	olive oil	15 mL
3 lbs	lean ground beef	1.5 kg
4	cloves garlic, minced	4
2	onions, chopped	2
1	green bell pepper, chopped	1
2 tsp	dried oregano	10 mL
1 tsp	ground cinnamon	5 mL
1/2 tsp	ground cloves	2 mL
1/2 tsp	hot pepper flakes	2 mL
1	can (19 oz/540 mL) diced tomatoes, with juice	1
2 tbsp	tomato paste	30 mL
2 tbsp	cider vinegar	30 mL
1/2 cup	raisins (optional)	125 mL
1/2 cup	slivered almonds (optional)	125 mL
1/4 cup	pimento-stuffed green olives, sliced	60 mL
1 tsp	salt	5 mL
1/2 tsp	freshly ground black pepper	2 mL
	Hot cooked rice	

1. In a large, heavy saucepan, heat oil over medium-high heat. Cook beef, breaking it up with the back of a wooden spoon, for about 7 minutes or until no longer pink. Add garlic, onions, green pepper, oregano, cinnamon, cloves and hot pepper flakes; sauté for 4 to 5 minutes or until vegetables are tender. Using a slotted spoon, transfer to slow cooker stoneware. Stir in tomatoes with juice, tomato paste and vinegar.

2. Cover and cook on Low for 6 to 8 hours or on High for 4 to 6 hours, until bubbling.

3. Stir in raisins (if using), almonds (if using) and olives. Cover and cook for 5 to 10 minutes or until heated through. Stir in salt and black pepper.

4. For Day Two, transfer 2 cups (500 mL) of the picadillo to an airtight container. Let cool, then refrigerate for up to 3 days.

5. Serve the remaining picadillo over rice.

Picadillo Nachos

Makes 4 to 6 servings

This recipe has all the fun and flavor of a restaurant favorite.

Tip

If your diners prefer different toppings, divide the chips into serving-size piles on the baking sheet and let them add their own toppings.

- *Preheat oven to 425°F (220°C)*
- *Rimmed baking sheet, lined with parchment paper*

1	bag (8 oz/250 g) tortilla chips or scoops	1
1½ cups	shredded Monterey Jack or Cheddar cheese, divided	375 mL
2 cups	reserved picadillo from Day One	500 mL
1 cup	corn kernels	250 mL
1 cup	cooked or canned black beans (see page 120), drained and rinsed	250 mL
1	avocado, cut into cubes	1
1 cup	grape tomatoes, quartered	250 mL
¼ cup	chopped fresh cilantro	60 mL
	Sour cream	

1. Arrange chips, slightly overlapping, on prepared baking sheet. Sprinkle with half the cheese, picadillo, corn, beans, avocado, tomatoes, then the remaining cheese.

2. Bake in preheated oven for about 10 minutes or until cheese is melted and picadillo is heated through. Sprinkle with cilantro and serve with sour cream.

Other Ways to Use Leftover Picadillo
- Stuff it into tortillas for quick burritos. Just roll up with some shredded lettuce, chopped tomatoes and shredded Cheddar or Monterey Jack cheese.
- Serve it over pasta or baked potatoes.
- Use it as a filling for quesadillas or baked stuffed bell peppers.

Chinese Five-Spice Beef Short Ribs

Day One

Makes 4 servings, plus leftovers

Unlike back ribs, which have more bone than meat, short ribs are covered with generous layers of meat and fat, and require long, moist-heat cooking to release their succulent flavor. When preparing this recipe, first broil the short ribs to render the excess fat. This allows the intriguing Asian flavors to develop as the ribs simmer in the slow cooker.

Tips

Ready-to-use broth in convenient Tetra-Paks is a handy ingredient and doesn't need to be diluted. Avoid using cubes and powders, which tend to be very salty.

Five-spice powder is commonly used in Chinese-style cooking. Its main components are ground fennel seeds, cloves, cinnamon, star anise (which has a wonderful licorice flavor) and Szechuan peppercorns. While you may find it at some supermarkets, I recommend purchasing it from an Asian market — you will pay a little less, and the flavor will be more authentic.

- **Minimum 5-quart slow cooker**
- *Preheat broiler, with rack set 6 inches (15 cm) below heat source*
- *Broiler pan or rimmed baking sheet, lined with foil*

6 lbs	beef short ribs or braising ribs, cut into 3-inch (7.5 cm) sections	3 kg
2	large red onions, sliced	2
⅔ cup	beef broth	150 mL
¼ cup	soy sauce	60 mL
¼ cup	rice vinegar	60 mL
2 tbsp	liquid honey	30 mL
1 tbsp	Chinese five-spice powder	15 mL
1 tsp	ground ginger	5 mL
4	cloves garlic, minced	4
2 cups	hot cooked rice	500 mL

1. Place ribs on prepared pan. Broil, turning often, for 10 to 15 minutes or until browned all over. Transfer to a plate lined with paper towels and let drain.

2. Arrange red onions in slow cooker stoneware. Place ribs on top.

3. In a bowl, combine broth, soy sauce, vinegar, honey, five-spice powder, ginger and garlic. Pour over ribs.

4. Cover and cook on Low for 11 to 12 hours or on High for 5½ to 6 hours, until ribs are tender. Using a slotted spoon, remove ribs and onions and set aside. Pour cooking liquid into a glass measuring cup and skim off fat.

5. For Day Two, transfer half the ribs, half the onions and half the cooking liquid to separate airtight containers. Let cool, then refrigerate for up to 3 days.

6. Serve the remaining ribs, onions and cooking liquid over rice.

Shanghai Beef Stuffed Spuds

Day Two

Makes 4 servings

Stuffed baked potatoes are a popular meal in my house, especially with my two teenagers. You can make the potatoes ahead of time, then just reheat and fill them with the hot beef topping. They are perfect for those nights when everyone is on a different schedule. Serve these spuds with a tossed green salad and some corn on the cob for a great family-friendly meal!

Tips

To bake potatoes: Bake in a 400°F (200°C) oven for 1 hour or until potatoes give slightly when squeezed.

To microwave potatoes: Arrange potatoes 1 inch (2.5 cm) apart in a circle on a roasting rack or paper towel in the microwave. Microwave on High, turning halfway through, until potatoes are tender when pierced with a skewer. For 1 large baking potato, cook for 4 to 5 minutes; for two, 6 to 8 minutes; for four, 10 to 12 minutes.

- *Preheat oven to 350°F (180°C)*
- *Shallow baking dish*

4	large baking potatoes (each about 10 oz/300 g), scrubbed	4
	Reserved ribs from Day One	
	Reserved onions from Day One	
	Reserved cooking liquid from Day One	
½ cup	buttermilk	125 mL
1 cup	shredded Cheddar cheese	250 mL
2 tbsp	chopped fresh parsley	30 mL
	Salt and freshly ground black pepper	

1. Using a fork, pierce skin of each potato several times. Bake or microwave potatoes (see tips, at left).

2. Meanwhile, remove meat from ribs, discarding bones, and, using two forks, shred to make about 1½ cups (375 mL). In a saucepan, combine beef, onions and cooking liquid. Cook over medium-high heat, stirring often, until heated through.

3. Cut potatoes in half lengthwise. Carefully scoop out flesh and transfer to a bowl, leaving a ¼-inch (0.5 cm) shell around each half. Set shells aside.

4. Beat buttermilk into potato flesh until smooth. Stir in beef mixture, half the cheese and parsley. Season to taste with salt and pepper. Spoon into shells. Top with the remaining cheese.

5. Arrange in baking dish and bake in preheated oven for 15 minutes or until cheese is melted.

Cubano Pork Roast

Day One

Makes 6 servings, plus leftovers

This roast features a winning combination of the warm flavors and spices of Cuba: orange, lime, honey, garlic and cumin. Use the leftovers to make South Beach Pork Panini on Day Two.

Tip
After opening canned chipotle chiles, transfer the peppers and their sauce to a glass jar with an airtight lid, close tightly and store in the refrigerator for up to 1 month. For longer storage, transfer peppers and sauce to a freezer bag and gently press out the air, then seal the bag. Manipulate the bag to separate the peppers so that it will be easy to break off a frozen section of pepper and sauce without thawing the whole package. Freeze for up to 6 months.

- **5- to 6-quart slow cooker**

1	boneless pork loin roast (3½ to 4 lbs/1.75 to 2 kg), trimmed	1
2	cloves garlic, minced	2
1	onion, chopped	1
1	chipotle pepper in adobo sauce, finely chopped	1
1 cup	orange marmalade	250 mL
1 tbsp	liquid honey	15 mL
½ tsp	grated lime zest	2 mL
1 tbsp	freshly squeezed lime juice	15 mL
1 tsp	ground cumin	5 mL
½ tsp	crumbled dried oregano	2 mL
½ tsp	salt	2 mL
¼ tsp	freshly ground black pepper	1 mL
½ cup	chicken broth	125 mL

1. Place pork roast in slow cooker stoneware.

2. In a bowl, stir together garlic, onion, chipotle pepper, marmalade, honey, lime zest, lime juice, cumin, oregano, salt and pepper. Spread over pork. Pour broth around pork.

3. Cover and cook on Low for 5 to 5½ hours or on High for 2½ to 3 hours, until pork is fork-tender. Transfer pork to a cutting board.

4. For Day Two, slice off about one-third of the pork and transfer to an airtight container. Let cool, then refrigerate for up to 3 days.

5. Slice the remaining pork and transfer to a serving platter. If desired, strain cooking liquid and drizzle some on top. (Discard the remaining cooking liquid.)

Make Ahead
This dish can be assembled up to 12 hours in advance. Prepare through step 2, cover and refrigerate overnight. The next day, place stoneware in slow cooker and proceed with step 3.

South Beach Pork Panini

Makes 6 servings

Tasty toasted pork sandwiches are Miami's favorite snack and are quickly becoming an icon of American pop food culture.

Tip

If using a skillet, you may wish to press the sandwiches as they cook. Place sandwiches, butter side down, in skillet. Cover with foil and top with a dinner plate. (If necessary, weigh down the plate with 2 to 3 full cans of food.)

* *Preheat panini grill (optional)*

1/3 cup	mayonnaise or roasted garlic mayonnaise	75 mL
1/2	chipotle pepper in adobo sauce, finely chopped	1/2
12	slices sourdough bread	12
1/3 cup	prepared mustard	75 mL
	Reserved pork from Day One, cut into 6 slices	
6	slices Swiss cheese	6
8 oz	shaved Black Forest ham	250 g
6	lengthwise dill pickle slices	6
3 tbsp	butter or margarine, softened	45 mL

1. In a small bowl, combine mayonnaise and chipotle pepper. Spread evenly on 6 of the bread slices and spread mustard on the other 6 slices. On each slice spread with mustard, place 1 slice pork, 1 slice cheese, one-sixth of the ham and 1 slice pickle. Cover with the remaining bread slices. Dividing half the butter evenly, lightly spread over one side of each sandwich.

2. In batches, arrange sandwiches, butter side down, on panini grill (or in a large skillet over medium heat). Lightly spread tops of sandwiches with the remaining butter. Cook for about 8 minutes (or for about 4 minutes per side in skillet) or until cheese has slightly melted and bread is toasted. Cut sandwiches in half.

Family Fun Italian Sausage Sliders

Day One

Makes 6 servings, plus leftovers

With sliders, you get all the fun of a full-size sausage on a bun in an easy-to-hold package. These are perfect for tailgating, picnics or any other occasion when you want to serve food without the fuss of cutlery or plates. A large Caesar salad will round out the meal.

Tips

In the slow cooker, whole-leaf dried herbs, such as basil and oregano, release their flavor slowly throughout the long cooking process, so they are a better choice than ground herbs.

Adding a little balsamic vinegar to tomato pasta sauce adds richness and brings all the flavors together.

- **Minimum 5-quart slow cooker**
- *Rimmed baking sheet*

10	fresh hot or mild Italian sausages (about 2 lbs/1 kg)	10
6	cloves garlic, minced	6
1	can (28 oz/796 mL) fire-roasted diced tomatoes or San Marzano tomatoes, with juice	1
2 cups	tomato pasta sauce	500 mL
1 tbsp	balsamic vinegar	15 mL
2 tsp	crumbled dried basil	10 mL
1 tsp	dried oregano	5 mL
½ tsp	salt	2 mL
¼ tsp	freshly ground black pepper	1 mL
¼ tsp	hot pepper flakes	1 mL
12	small French-style dinner rolls or hoagie buns, split	12
12	slices provolone cheese, cut in half	12
¾ cup	bottled roasted red peppers, drained and cut into thin strips	175 mL

1. In a large nonstick skillet, cook sausages over medium-high heat, turning, for 6 to 8 minutes or until browned all over. Transfer to slow cooker stoneware.

2. Stir in garlic, tomatoes with juice, pasta sauce, vinegar, basil, oregano, salt, black pepper and hot pepper flakes.

3. Cover and cook on Low for 6 to 8 hours or on High for 3 to 4 hours, until bubbling.

4. For Day Two, transfer 4 sausages and 4 cups (1 L) of the sauce to separate airtight containers. Let cool, then refrigerate for up to 3 days.

5. Preheat broiler, with rack set 4 to 5 inches (10 to 12 cm) below heat source. Place roll halves, cut side up, on baking sheet. Cut the remaining sausages in half crosswise. Place 1 sausage half on each bottom roll half. Spoon about 1 tbsp (15 mL) sauce over each and top with 1 half-slice of cheese. Place the remaining half-slices of cheese on top roll halves.

Tips

Resist the urge to lift the lid and taste or smell whatever is inside the slow cooker as it's cooking. Every peek will increase the cooking time by 20 minutes.

6. Broil for 2 to 3 minutes or until cheese is bubbling. Top each sausage with roasted red peppers. Cover with top roll halves. Serve the remaining sauce on the side for dipping.

San Marzano plum tomatoes are grown in the volcanic soil near Salerno, Italy, long known for producing the most flavorful tomatoes. Deep red and sweet, they are packed in tomato juice and have been the traditional choice of generations of Italian cooks. The production and labeling of this product is restricted by law under the European Union Protected Designation of Origin (DOP). Each can carries a seal of authenticity and is individually numbered.

Saucy Sausage Pasta

Day Two

Makes 6 servings

This rich tomato sauce is highly seasoned by the simmering Italian sausage. Add a few vegetables, and you've got a flavorful pasta sauce that's great over any shape of noodle. A nice Chianti wine and some warm Italian bread complete this quick and easy dinner.

Tip

Authentic Italian Parmesan cheese (Parmigiano-Reggiano) is expensive, but its flavor is certainly worth the price. Well-wrapped in the refrigerator, a block keeps for months, and it goes a long way when you freshly grate it as you need it.

1 tbsp	olive oil	15 mL
1	onion, finely chopped	1
1	large carrot, diced	1
1	red bell pepper, finely chopped	1
4	reserved sausages from Day One, cut into 1-inch (2.5 cm) chunks	4
1	can (14 oz/398 mL) tomato sauce	1
4 cups	reserved sauce from Day One	1 L
1 lb	rotini or penne pasta	500 g
	Freshly grated Parmesan cheese	

1. In a large skillet, heat oil over medium-high heat. Sauté onion, carrot and red pepper for 5 to 7 minutes or until tender. Add sausages, tomato sauce and reserved sauce; bring to a boil. Reduce heat and simmer, stirring occasionally, for 10 to 15 minutes or until sauce is heated through.

2. Meanwhile, in a large pot of boiling salted water, cook pasta according to package directions until tender but firm (al dente). Drain. Toss in sauce to coat pasta.

3. Divide evenly among individual serving bowls and sprinkle with Parmesan.

Ham with Fruited Bourbon Sauce

Day One

Makes 6 to 8 servings, plus leftovers

A beautiful glazed ham is a joy to behold on any special occasion. Enjoy this elegant roast one night for dinner, then make the leftovers into a simple frittata for a second meal. Serve with scalloped potatoes and a steamed green vegetable.

Tips

If you prefer not to use the bourbon, you can substitute additional apple juice or orange juice.

Cooking times can vary a great deal between slow cooker manufacturers. Always let your food cook for the minimum amount of time before testing for doneness.

- Minimum 4-quart slow cooker, stoneware greased

1	boneless ham (about 4 lbs/2 kg)	1
1/4 cup	packed dark brown sugar	60 mL
1/2 cup	unsweetened apple juice	125 mL
1 tsp	ground cinnamon	5 mL
1/2 tsp	ground ginger	2 mL
1/4 tsp	hot pepper flakes	1 mL
1/3 cup	dried cranberries	75 mL
1/4 cup	cornstarch	60 mL
2 tbsp	cold water	30 mL
2 tbsp	bourbon or amber rum	30 mL

1. Place ham, cut side up, in slow cooker stoneware.

2. In a bowl, combine brown sugar, apple juice, cinnamon, ginger and hot pepper flakes. Pour over ham.

3. Cover and cook on Low for 9 to 10 hours or on High for 4½ to 5 hours, until meat is tender and sauce is bubbling. About 30 minutes before the end of cooking, add cranberries. At the end of cooking, transfer ham to a cutting board. Let stand for 15 minutes. Carve into slices.

4. For Day Two, cube enough of the ham to make 1½ cups (375 mL). Transfer to an airtight container, let cool and refrigerate for up to 3 days.

5. Place the remaining ham on a serving platter and cover to keep warm.

6. Pour cooking liquid into large glass measuring cup and let stand for 5 minutes. Skim off fat and pour liquid into a saucepan. In a small bowl, whisk together cornstarch and water. Bring cooking liquid to a boil over medium-high heat. Whisk in cornstarch mixture. Reduce heat and simmer, stirring, for about 3 minutes or until thickened. Remove from heat and whisk in bourbon. Spoon over sliced ham.

Make Ahead

This dish can be assembled up to 24 hours in advance. Prepare through step 2, cover and refrigerate. When ready to cook, place stoneware in slow cooker and proceed with step 3.

Ham, Potato and Herb Frittata

Day Two

Makes 6 servings

Nothing beats a delicious frittata for a special-occasion breakfast, brunch or supper. A frittata is an Italian version of an omelet. Unlike its finicky cousin, which needs careful flipping and turning, a frittata doesn't require any skill other than stirring, so it's almost impossible to ruin it.

Tips

I like to cook the potatoes whole for this recipe, because they maintain a cubed shape better if cut after cooking. Place scrubbed potatoes in a large saucepan, add salt and enough water to cover, and bring to a boil. Reduce heat and simmer for 20 to 30 minutes or until tender. If you don't have the patience for this, you can microwave the potatoes: prick scrubbed potatoes all over with a fork and place on a microwave-safe plate. Microwave on High for 5 minutes. Turn potatoes over and cook for 5 minutes or until tender.

If your skillet's handle is not ovenproof, wrap it in a double layer of foil to protect it.

- *Preheat oven to 375°F (190°C)*
- *Large ovenproof skillet*

2 tbsp	butter	30 mL
2	green onions, finely chopped	2
1	small red bell pepper, finely chopped	1
1 cup	cubed peeled cooked potatoes (1/2-inch/1 cm cubes)	250 mL
1 1/2 cups	reserved cubed ham from Day One	375 mL
8	eggs, lightly beaten	8
2 tbsp	milk	30 mL
2 tbsp	chopped fresh parsley	30 mL
1 tbsp	chopped fresh chives	15 mL
2 tsp	chopped fresh thyme, oregano or basil	10 mL
1/2 tsp	salt	2 mL
1/4 tsp	freshly ground black pepper	2 mL
1 cup	shredded Cheddar, Edam or Havarti cheese	250 mL
	Salt and freshly ground black pepper	

1. In a skillet, melt butter over medium high-heat. Sauté green onions, red pepper and potatoes for about 5 minutes or until red pepper is tender. Reduce heat to medium-low and stir in ham.

2. In a large bowl, beat eggs, milk, parsley, chives, thyme, salt and pepper. Pour over green onion mixture and cook, stirring gently, for about 1 minute or until beginning to set (eggs will appear semi-scrambled). Stir in cheese.

3. Bake in preheated oven for 15 to 20 minutes or until center is just set. Let cool for 5 minutes. Turn out onto a large serving plate and cut into wedges.

Greek Lamb Roast Dinner

Day One

Makes 4 servings, plus leftovers

Greek cooks usually roast lamb in liquid until it is well-done and mouth-wateringly tender and juicy. If you have difficulty finding fresh lamb roasts, look for frozen roasts in the supermarket and thaw overnight in the refrigerator. An oval slow cooker works best for this recipe, as you need to fit two small lamb roasts in.

Tips

If the lamb roasts are tied, remove string before sprinkling and rubbing with the shallot mixture, then retie each with butcher's twine.

To zest a lemon, use the fine side of a box grater, making sure not to grate the white pith underneath. Or use a zester, then finely chop the zest. Zesters are inexpensive and widely available at specialty kitchenware shops.

- **Minimum 5-quart oval slow cooker**

1	shallot, minced	1
1 tsp	grated lemon zest	5 mL
1 tsp	garlic powder	5 mL
1 tsp	dried oregano	5 mL
½ tsp	dried mint	2 mL
½ tsp	dried rosemary	2 mL
½ tsp	salt	2 mL
¼ tsp	freshly ground black pepper	1 mL
2	boneless lamb shoulder roasts (each 2 to 2½ lbs/1 to 1.25 kg), trimmed	2
4	carrots, halved lengthwise and cut into 3-inch (7.5 cm) sticks	4
2	white or red potatoes, quartered	2
1	large onion, cut into wedges	1
½ cup	chicken broth	125 mL

1. In a small bowl, combine shallot, lemon zest, garlic powder, oregano, mint, rosemary, salt and pepper. Sprinkle evenly over lamb roasts, rubbing into the meat.

2. In slow cooker stoneware, combine carrots, potatoes, onion and broth. Place roasts on top.

3. Cover and cook on Low for 8 to 9 hours or on High for 4 to 5 hours, until lamb is tender and cooked to desired doneness.

4. For Day Two, transfer one roast to a bowl and let cool. Using two forks, shred lamb and transfer to an airtight container. Refrigerate for up to 3 days.

5. Transfer the other roast to a serving platter and carve into slices. Using a slotted spoon, remove vegetables from stoneware and arrange around meat.

6. Strain cooking liquid into a glass measuring cup and skim off fat. Spoon some of the cooking liquid over meat and vegetables. (Discard the remaining cooking liquid.)

Make Ahead

This dish can be assembled up to 12 hours in advance. Prepare through step 2, cover and refrigerate overnight. The next day, place stoneware in slow cooker and proceed with step 3.

Warm Lamb Gyros with Tzatziki

Makes 4 servings

My favorite part of a gyro (a Greek sandwich made with lamb, tomatoes and onions) is the tzatziki. Serve with a chickpea side salad.

Tip

Use pitas without pockets, since you will be wrapping the pitas around the filling.

- *Preheat oven to 275°F (140°C)*
- *Microwave-safe baking dish*

4	pitas	4
1	reserved shredded lamb roast from Day One	1
2 cups	shredded lettuce	500 mL
2	tomatoes, sliced	2
1/2	red onion, sliced	1/2
1 cup	tzatziki (store-bought or see recipe, below)	250 mL
1/2 cup	crumbled feta cheese	125 mL

1. Stack pitas and wrap in foil. Bake in preheated oven for 10 to 15 minutes or until heated through.

2. Place lamb in baking dish. Cover and microwave on High for 2 1/2 to 3 1/2 minutes, stirring halfway through, until heated through.

3. Place 1 pita on each individual serving plate. Top with lettuce, tomatoes, red onion, lamb, tzatziki and cheese. Wrap up on either side.

Makes about 2 cups (500 mL)

Cucumber, lemon and yogurt combine in this refreshing sauce, which goes perfectly with lamb.

Tzatziki

3 cups	low-fat plain yogurt	750 mL
1	cucumber (unpeeled)	1
1 tsp	salt	5 mL
2 tsp	minced garlic	10 mL
2 tsp	freshly squeezed lemon juice or red wine vinegar	10 mL

1. Line a colander with a large coffee filter or a double layer of paper towels and set over a bowl. Place yogurt in colander and let drain in the refrigerator for 4 hours or until reduced to 1 1/2 cups (375 mL).

2. Meanwhile, grate cucumber, sprinkle with salt and let stand for 20 minutes. Transfer to a sieve and drain, pressing with your palm to squeeze out excess moisture.

3. In a bowl, combine yogurt, cucumber, garlic and lemon juice. Use immediately or cover and refrigerate for up to 5 days.

Storage Tips for Prepared Foods

- Give your leftovers time to cool before packing them up and refrigerating them, but be sure to refrigerate them within 2 hours. If you have a large amount of hot food left over, divide it into smaller portions in shallow containers so it will cool more quickly.
- Store food in leak-proof containers — preferably clear, so you can see the contents. And don't pack the refrigerator; cool air must be able to circulate to keep food safe.
- If you can't use the leftovers the next day, you may wish to freeze them for later use. Most prepared foods freeze well, provided they are wrapped or packaged airtight and your freezer temperature is below 32°F (0°C).
- Use an appliance thermometer in your refrigerator and freezer to ensure food stays at 40°F (4°C) in the refrigerator and 0°F (−18°C) in the freezer. You can pick up thermometers at kitchen, houseware or hardware stores.
- Use containers or bags that are easy to label, and date each before putting it in the freezer. You'll want to use most foods within 3 or 4 months at most.
- Rotate the containers of frozen food so you eat the oldest ones first: first in, first out.
- Don't defrost food at room temperature. This encourages bacterial growth and uneven thawing. Instead, place containers on a tray in the refrigerator and let thaw (it may take a day or two for larger portions), or microwave on a low or Defrost power setting until thawed.
- Do not reheat cooked food in the slow cooker. Reheat in a conventional oven or in a microwave oven, using approved microwave-safe lids or plastic wrap for thorough heating.
- Bring leftover sauces, soups and gravies to a boil in a saucepan on the stove. Heat all other leftovers thoroughly to 165°F (74°C).

Desserts

Braised Apricots with Vanilla Mascarpone

Makes 4 servings

A ripe apricot is a thing of beauty, sweetly fragrant and delicious. While apricots are delicious as is, they also braise beautifully. To add a little luxury, this dessert is served with a dollop of vanilla-infused mascarpone, but you can substitute sweetened whipped cream.

Tips

You can substitute 1 tsp (5 mL) vanilla extract for the vanilla bean.

When apricots are not in season, you can use one 14-oz (398 mL) can of apricots, drained. You can also substitute 4 fresh or canned peaches for the apricots.

• **3- to 4-quart slow cooker**

1	vanilla bean, split lengthwise	1
1/4 cup	packed brown sugar	60 mL
2 tbsp	butter, melted	30 mL
1 tbsp	freshly squeezed lemon juice or brandy	15 mL
8	firm ripe apricots, halved and pitted	8
1/2 cup	mascarpone cheese	125 mL
1 tbsp	confectioner's (icing) sugar	15 mL
	Raspberries	

1. In slow cooker stoneware, combine vanilla bean, brown sugar, butter and lemon juice. Add apricots, turn to coat with butter mixture and arrange cut side down in a single layer.

2. Cover and cook on Low for 3 to 4 hours or on High for 1 1/2 to 2 hours, until apricots are tender.

3. Using tongs, remove vanilla bean. Using a sharp paring knife, scrape seeds into a small bowl. Discard pod. Stir mascarpone and confectioner's sugar into vanilla seeds.

4. Using a slotted spoon, transfer apricots to individual serving dishes. Serve warm or at room temperature, topped with mascarpone mixture and raspberries and drizzled with cooking liquid.

> Vanilla beans are found in glass tubes in the baking aisle of the supermarket. They can be tough pods to open, so a sharp paring knife is a must. Steaming the pod first softens it and makes it a little easier to slice open. Lay the pod flat on a cutting board. Insert the tip of the blade at the center and slice toward one end, then repeat to slice to other end. Once the pod is split open, scrape out the tiny seeds with the blade. They are a little sticky and jammy, so you'll need to scrape them from your blade.

Almost Cherries Jubilee

Makes 4 to 6 servings

This is a great dessert to serve after a hearty meal. Unlike the traditional version, which must be prepared and served immediately, in this recipe the cherries simmer away in the slow cooker, then are ignited and served.

Tips

I like to make this in the early summer, when cherries are in season, but you can substitute canned cherries if you like. Use two 14-oz (398 mL) cans sweet cherries. Drain and reserve the juice, then substitute it for the water in the recipe. Reduce the sugar to 2 tbsp (30 mL).

If you don't have a cherry pitter, a paper clip will do the job. Simply unfold it at its center, then, depending on the size of the cherry, insert either the large or the small end of the clip through the top of the stemmed cherry, loosen the pit and pull it out.

- **3- to 4-quart slow cooker**

3 cups	sweet black cherries, pitted	750 mL
½ cup	granulated sugar	125 mL
2 tbsp	cornstarch	30 mL
2	½-inch (1 cm) wide strips orange zest	2
1½ cups	water or freshly squeezed orange juice	375 mL
1 tsp	vanilla extract	5 mL
¼ cup	brandy or kirsch (optional)	60 mL
	Vanilla ice cream	

1. Place cherries in slow cooker stoneware.

2. In a saucepan, combine sugar and cornstarch. Whisk in orange zest, water and vanilla; cook over medium heat, stirring, for about 4 minutes or until sugar is dissolved and sauce is slightly thickened. Pour over cherries.

3. Cover and cook on High for 2 to 3 hours or until cherries are tender. Transfer to a heatproof serving dish.

4. If using brandy, pour into a small saucepan and heat over medium heat until just warm. Remove from heat. With a long match, ignite brandy and pour, still flaming, over cherries. When flames die, serve immediately over vanilla ice cream.

How to Make Citrus Strips

Hold the fruit firmly in one hand and press the blade of a zester into the peel. (If your zester also has a channel knife, use that to get long strips.) Slowly twist the fruit, holding the zester steady. If you apply the right amount of pressure, you'll get a nice deep cut without puncturing the fruit. Keep twisting until you have removed all of the peel or the amount you need. (If you don't have a zester, you can use a sharp paring knife to peel the fruit.) Scrape any white pith from the zest, as the pith is bitter.

Susan's Spiced Peaches

Makes 6 servings

When my children say, "Mom, you have to get so-and-so's recipe!" I don't hesitate. If they will eat it, I will make it. So when my daughter told me to ask for her best friend's mother's spiced peaches recipe, I called right away. It was not a slow cooker recipe, but I adapted it, with great results. These spiced peaches are delicious on their own, or you can serve them over slices of angel food or pound cake, or with vanilla ice cream.

Tip

Transfer extra peaches and syrup to an airtight container and refrigerate for up to 1 week. Serve warm or cold.

- **4- to 5-quart slow cooker**

1/2 cup	freshly squeezed lemon juice, divided	125 mL
12	peaches (about 3 1/2 lbs/1.75 kg)	12
	Cold water	
1 cup	granulated sugar	250 mL
1 tsp	hot pepper flakes	5 mL
4	1/2-inch (1 cm) wide strips orange zest	4
4	1/2-inch (1 cm) thick slices gingerroot	4
2	whole cloves	2
2	star anise pods	2
1	3-inch (7.5 cm) cinnamon stick, broken	1

1. In a large bowl, combine 2 cups (500 mL) water and 2 tbsp (30 mL) of the lemon juice to make acidulated water. Set aside.

2. Using the tip of a sharp knife, score an X into the base of each peach. In a saucepan of boiling water, working with 2 or 3 peaches at a time, submerge peaches for 30 seconds. Using a slotted spoon, transfer to a bowl of cold water and let stand until chilled. Peel off skins and transfer peaches to acidulated water. Cut large peaches into quarters and small ones in half, discarding pits.

3. In slow cooker stoneware, combine sugar, hot pepper flakes, orange zest, ginger, cloves, star anise, cinnamon, the remaining lemon juice and 2 cups (500 mL) water. Add peaches.

4. Cover and cook on Low for 4 to 6 hours or on High for 2 to 3 hours, until peaches are tender. Discard orange zest, cinnamon and star anise.

> Star anise is a star-shaped pod that has eight points, with a seed in each point. It lends a licorice flavor to dishes such as stir-fries and desserts. You can add it whole and simmer it in dishes as they cook, as in this recipe, or grind it in a clean coffee or spice grinder. Look for it in specialty food stores or Asian supermarkets.

Root Beer–Poached Pears

Makes 4 servings

Root beer's aromatic, spicy sweetness makes it a great poaching liquid for the pears, which are best served cool or at room temperature, with the whipped cream on the side. This is the perfect dessert to make ahead, and makes an elegant finish to a grand meal.

Tips

To check for ripeness, gently press your thumb against the pear near the stem; if the flesh gives, the pear is ready to eat. Ripe pears often emit a delicious, sweet aroma. Let pears ripen at room temperature, then refrigerate.

For the best results, use a gourmet or artisanal microbrewed root beer. It will add both a subtle sweetness and a spicy touch, contributing to the complexity of flavors in the finished dish. Look for packs of 6 or 12 bottles in the soda aisle of the supermarket.

- **4-quart slow cooker**

4	firm ripe Bosc pears, peeled leaving stems intact	4
2	bottles (each 12 oz/355 mL) root beer (preferably an artisanal brand)	2
1	vanilla bean, split lengthwise	1
	Grated zest of 1 lemon	

Ginger Whipped Cream

1/2 cup	whipping (35%) cream	125 mL
1 tbsp	confectioner's (icing) sugar	15 mL
1/2 tsp	ground ginger (or 1 tbsp/15 mL chopped candied ginger)	2 mL

1. Using a melon baller, remove core from bottom end of each pear, then set pears upright in slow cooker stoneware. Add root beer, vanilla bean and lemon zest.

2. Cover and cook on Low for 4 to 6 hours or until pears are tender. Using a slotted spoon, transfer pears to a plate. Cover to keep warm.

3. Pour cooking liquid into a saucepan and bring to a boil over medium-high heat. Boil for about 15 minutes or until reduced to about 3/4 cup (175 mL) syrup. (Watch syrup carefully toward the end of cooking; it can burn quickly.)

4. *Whipped Cream:* Meanwhile, in a bowl, combine cream and confectioner's sugar. Whip until soft peaks form. Fold in ginger. Cover and refrigerate until ready to use.

5. Place pears on individual serving plates. Drizzle with syrup and garnish with whipped cream.

Make Ahead

The pears and syrup may be prepared up to 4 hours ahead and kept at room temperature. If the cooled syrup gets too thick, reheat it before serving. You can also cook pears, then transfer to a bowl with the cooking liquid. Cover and refrigerate for up to 24 hours. Just before serving, reduce cooking liquid as directed.

Green Tea–Poached Winter Fruits

Makes 6 to 8 servings

When the selection of fresh fruit is lacking in the winter, poaching dried fruit in a lemon-infused green tea creates luscious fruit compote. Serve with lemon or vanilla yogurt and chopped pistachios, for breakfast or dessert.

Tips

You can substitute fruit-flavored green teas, such as lemon and mango, to add flavor to the fruit.

Packages of dried mixed fruit are available in the supermarket, or you can make your own mix of apples, apricots, peaches, pears, figs and prunes.

- **3- to 4-quart slow cooker**

3 cups	boiling water	750 mL
3	green tea bags	3
2 tbsp	granulated sugar	30 mL
2 tsp	grated lemon zest	10 mL
4 cups	mixed dried fruit	1 L

1. Pour boiling water into slow cooker stoneware. Add tea bags and steep for 3 to 5 minutes. Discard tea bags.

2. Stir sugar and lemon zest into tea. Cut any large pieces of dried fruit in half or into quarters. Add fruit to tea mixture.

3. Cover and cook on Low for $3\frac{1}{2}$ to 4 hours or on High for $1\frac{1}{2}$ to 2 hours, until fruit is plump and tender and tea is thickened into syrup. Transfer to a bowl and let cool. Cover and refrigerate until chilled.

Green tea is the favored tea in many Asian countries. It is produced from leaves that are steamed and dried but not fermented. This process produces a greenish yellow tea with a flavor that's slightly bitter and close to the taste of the fresh leaf. Green tea is packed with many antioxidant powers.

Cran-Raspberry Ambrosia with Warm Dumpling Topping

Makes 4 to 6 servings

Raspberries are truly the "fruit of the gods," and while true ambrosia is a cold dessert, I couldn't resist using that name for this warm version. The airy dumplings form a cake-like topping. If you omit the dumplings, you'll have a wonderful fruit sauce to serve over ice cream or frozen yogurt.

Tip

There is no need to defrost frozen berries. As the slow cooker heats up, it will thaw and cook the fruit evenly.

- **3- to 4-quart slow cooker**

3 cups	fresh or frozen raspberries	750 mL
1 cup	fresh or frozen cranberries	250 mL
1/2 cup	granulated sugar	125 mL
1/2 cup	cranberry-raspberry cocktail or unsweetened apple juice	125 mL
2 tbsp	cornstarch	30 mL

Dumplings

1 cup	all-purpose flour	250 mL
2 tbsp	granulated sugar	30 mL
1 1/4 tsp	baking powder	6 mL
1/4 tsp	salt	1 mL
3 tbsp	butter, cubed	45 mL
1	egg, lightly beaten	1
1/2 cup	milk	125 mL
2 tbsp	packed brown sugar	30 mL
	Whipped cream or frozen yogurt	

1. In slow cooker stoneware, combine raspberries, cranberries, sugar, cranberry-raspberry cocktail and cornstarch.

2. Cover and cook on Low for 5 to 6 hours or on High for 2 1/2 to 3 hours, until bubbling.

3. *Dumplings:* In a bowl, combine flour, granulated sugar, baking powder and salt. Using a pastry blender or two knives, cut in butter until mixture resembles coarse crumbs.

4. In a small glass measuring cup, whisk together egg and milk. Pour into flour mixture and stir until a soft dough forms.

5. Drop spoonfuls of dough on raspberry mixture in stoneware. Sprinkle evenly with brown sugar. Cover and cook on High for 30 to 60 minutes or until a tester inserted in the center of a dumpling comes out clean. Serve warm, with dollops of whipped cream.

Bumbleberry Cobbler

Makes 6 servings

Bags of frozen mixed berries (or "bumbleberries") are readily available in the supermarket, which makes this dessert a year-round favorite. It is delicious on its own, but if you want to treat yourself, you can add a scoop of ice cream, frozen yogurt or whipped cream.

Tip

To zest a lemon, use the fine side of a box grater, making sure not to grate the white pith underneath. Or use a zester, then finely chop the zest. Zesters are inexpensive and widely available at specialty kitchenware shops.

- **3- to 4-quart slow cooker, stoneware greased**

1	package (21 oz/600 g) frozen mixed berries	1
½ cup	granulated sugar	125 mL
2 tbsp	cornstarch	30 mL
2 tsp	grated lemon zest	10 mL

Topping

1½ cups	all-purpose flour	375 mL
½ cup	packed brown sugar	125 mL
2¼ tsp	baking powder	11 mL
¼ tsp	ground nutmeg	1 mL
¾ cup	milk	175 mL
⅓ cup	butter, melted	75 mL

1. In prepared slow cooker stoneware, gently combine berries, sugar, cornstarch and lemon zest.

2. *Topping:* In a bowl, combine flour, brown sugar, baking powder and nutmeg. Stir in milk and butter just until blended into batter. Drop spoonfuls of batter on berry mixture.

3. Cover and cook on Low for 4 to 5 hours or until a tester inserted in the center of a dumpling comes out clean. Uncover and let stand for about 30 minutes before serving.

Peach and Blueberry Cobbler with Spiced Pecan Topping

Makes 4 to 6 servings

Bags of frozen fruit are so convenient to have on hand. Quick desserts like this one are so easy to put together, you can make a family pleaser even on weeknights. I like this served with a dollop of vanilla-bean ice cream.

Tip

There is no need to defrost frozen berries. As the slow cooker heats up, it will thaw and cook the fruit evenly.

- **3- to 4-quart slow cooker, stoneware greased**

²⁄₃ cup	all-purpose flour	150 mL
½ cup	packed brown sugar	125 mL
1½ tsp	ground cinnamon, divided	7 mL
⅛ tsp	salt	0.5 mL
¼ cup	butter, cut into cubes	60 mL
²⁄₃ cup	coarsely chopped pecans	150 mL
3 cups	fresh or frozen blueberries	750 mL
2 cups	frozen peaches (or about 3 fresh, halved, pitted and sliced)	500 mL
½ cup	granulated sugar	125 mL
¼ tsp	ground nutmeg	1 mL

1. In a small bowl, combine flour, brown sugar, ½ tsp (2 mL) of the cinnamon and salt. Using your fingers, work in butter until mixture readily clumps when pressed. Add pecans and mix until crumbly.

2. In a large bowl, combine blueberries, peaches, granulated sugar, nutmeg and the remaining cinnamon. Transfer to prepared slow cooker stoneware and sprinkle with flour mixture.

3. Cover and cook on Low for 6 to 8 hours or on High for 3 to 4 hours, until fruit is tender and juice is bubbling.

Pineapple Rhubarb Crumble

Makes 6 to 8 servings

Go ahead and dish out double portions of this warm, sweetly tart crumble; otherwise, everyone will want seconds! Don't be alarmed by the pinch of cayenne — it helps bring out the flavor of the fruit. Serve warm, with a scoop of vanilla ice cream.

Tips

If you use frozen rhubarb for this recipe, increase the cornstarch to 2 tbsp (30 mL), as the rhubarb will get quite watery when it is cooked.

To toast pecans, place in a single layer on a rimmed baking sheet and bake in a 350°F (180°C) oven for 5 to 10 minutes or until golden brown and fragrant.

- **3- to 4-quart slow cooker**

4 cups	chopped rhubarb	1 L
3 cups	chopped fresh pineapple	750 mL
3 tbsp	granulated sugar	45 mL
1 tbsp	cornstarch	15 mL
1 cup	all-purpose flour	250 mL
2/3 cup	packed brown sugar	150 mL
1 tsp	finely grated orange zest	5 mL
1 tsp	ground ginger	5 mL
1/4 tsp	ground cinnamon	1 mL
1/4 tsp	ground nutmeg	1 mL
Pinch	cayenne pepper	Pinch
1/3 cup	butter, cut into cubes	75 mL
1/2 cup	chopped pecans, toasted	125 mL

1. In slow cooker stoneware, gently toss together rhubarb, pineapple, granulated sugar and cornstarch.

2. In a bowl, whisk together flour, brown sugar, orange zest, ginger, cinnamon, nutmeg and cayenne. Using a pastry blender or two knives, cut in butter until mixture resembles small peas. Sprinkle over rhubarb mixture. Sprinkle evenly with pecans.

3. Cover and cook on Low for 6 to 8 hours or on High for 3 to 4 hours, until fruit is tender and juice is bubbling. Serve warm.

> Rhubarb may be used as a fruit, but it is botanically a vegetable. Its thick pink, celery-like stalks are the only edible portion of the plant. The leaves contain oxalic acid and can be toxic. In the spring and early summer, you can find field-grown rhubarb (perhaps from your own garden), but throughout the rest of the year rhubarb is hothouse-grown. You can also find bags of flash-frozen rhubarb in the supermarket.

Double Chocolate Carrot Cake

Makes 8 to 10 servings

Made with cocoa powder and chocolate chips, this cake has an intense chocolate flavor with bright orange highlights. It's as easy to make as a store-bought mix and every bit as moist.

Tips

To line the bottom of the stoneware, set it on parchment paper and trace around the edge. Remove stoneware and cut out paper, then place in the bottom.

Do not be tempted to use the Low setting to bake this cake. It requires high heat to bake properly.

This cake freezes well. Wrap the cooled cake in plastic wrap, then in foil, and freeze for up to 1 month.

- 3- to 4-quart slow cooker, stoneware greased, bottom lined with parchment paper

2 cups	all-purpose flour	500 mL
¾ cup	unsweetened cocoa powder	175 mL
1 tsp	baking soda	5 mL
½ tsp	baking powder	2 mL
¼ tsp	salt	1 mL
1½ cups	granulated sugar	375 mL
½ cup	butter, softened	125 mL
3	eggs	3
2 tsp	vanilla extract	10 mL
2 cups	shredded carrots	500 mL
½ cup	semisweet chocolate chips	125 mL
	Confectioner's (icing) sugar	

1. In a bowl, combine flour, cocoa powder, baking soda, baking powder and salt.

2. In another bowl, using an electric mixer, cream sugar and butter until light and fluffy. Beat in eggs and vanilla until smooth. Using a rubber spatula, gently fold in flour mixture just until blended. Fold in carrots and chocolate chips. Spoon batter into prepared slow cooker stoneware.

3. Cover and cook on High for 2 to 2½ hours or until a tester inserted in center of cake comes out clean.

4. Transfer stoneware to a wire rack and let cool for 10 minutes. Run a knife around sides to loosen cake. Turn out onto wire rack and let cool. Dust top with confectioner's sugar before slicing.

Warm Chocolate Lava Cake

Makes 8 servings

This decadent dessert is supremely rich and incredibly delicious. It originally developed from a kitchen error: the chef simply had no more time to bake the cake, so he called it a "lava" cake. Sometimes less time is a delicious thing!

Tips

Most recipes use large eggs. If a recipe doesn't specify a size, assume you need large.

Do not be tempted to use the Low setting to bake this cake. It requires high heat to bake properly.

- **4-quart slow cooker, stoneware greased**

2 cups	semisweet chocolate chips	500 mL
¾ cup	butter, cut into cubes	175 mL
6	eggs	6
⅔ cup	granulated sugar	150 mL
2 tsp	vanilla extract	10 mL
2 tbsp	all-purpose flour	30 mL
	Coffee or vanilla ice cream	

1. In a large microwave-safe glass bowl or an 8-cup (2 L) glass measuring cup, combine chocolate chips and butter. Microwave on Medium (50%) for 2½ to 3 minutes, stirring every minute, until melted and smooth.

2. Whisk in eggs, sugar and vanilla until smooth. Whisk in flour until blended and smooth. Spread evenly in prepared slow cooker stoneware.

3. Cover and cook on High for 2 to 2½ hours or until edges are set but center is slightly runny. Serve immediately with ice cream.

Snickerdoodle Cheesecake

Makes 6 to 8 servings

This popular dessert is often served in restaurants, but this is my own version. This method makes a perfect cheesecake every time, without any cracks. Make sure to use a large, oval slow cooker that accommodates the springform pan. Serve with a dollop of whipped cream and some fresh strawberries on the side.

Tips

If you can't find a small springform pan, you can use a straight-sided baking dish or soufflé dish that fits in the stoneware. The cheesecake won't come out of the dish as cleanly, but it will still taste good.

This cake is best made 1 day ahead. You can also freeze it for up to 2 weeks.

- **Minimum 6-quart oval slow cooker**
- *7- or 8-inch (18 or 20 cm) springform pan*
- *Vegetable steamer or low rack to fit in stoneware*

Crust

¾ cup	chocolate wafer cookie crumbs	175 mL
1 tbsp	granulated sugar	15 mL
2 tbsp	melted butter	30 mL

Cheesecake

1 lb	cream cheese, softened	500 g
2 tbsp	granulated sugar	30 mL
2	eggs	2
½ cup	heavy or whipping (35%) cream	125 mL
½ tsp	vanilla extract	2 mL
2	Snickers candy bars (each 2 oz/59 g), cut into ½-inch (1 cm) pieces, divided	2

Topping

¼ cup	heavy or whipping (35%) cream	60 mL
2 oz	semisweet chocolate, chopped	60 g

1. *Crust:* In a bowl, combine cookie crumbs, sugar and butter. Press evenly over bottom of springform pan. Chill until ready to use.

2. *Cheesecake:* In a large bowl, using an electric mixer or food processor, combine cream cheese and sugar; beat or process until smooth. One at a time, beat in eggs, mixing well after each addition. Beat in cream and vanilla.

3. Spread three-quarters of the candy pieces evenly over crust. Pour cream cheese mixture evenly over top. Wrap entire pan tightly with foil, securing with an elastic band. Place pan on steamer in slow cooker stoneware. (Do not add any water.)

4. Cover and cook on High for 3 to 3½ hours or until edges are set and center is slightly jiggly. Turn off heat, uncover and let cool for at least 1 hour. Remove from stoneware.

5. *Topping:* In a small saucepan, heat cream and chocolate over medium-low heat, stirring, until smooth. Using a spatula, spread over top of cheesecake. Cover and refrigerate for 4 hours, until chilled, or overnight.

6. Gently run a knife around inside edge of pan to loosen cake. Remove side. Garnish cake with the remaining candy pieces.

Blueberry Orange Coffee Cake

Makes 6 to 8 servings

You will find it hard to believe that this addictive coffee cake was made in the slow cooker. Share it with good friends, along with steaming lattes.

Tips

To grease stoneware, use a nonstick vegetable spray or use the cake pan grease available in specialty cake decorating shops or bulk food stores.

There is no need to defrost frozen berries. As the slow cooker heats up, it will thaw and cook the fruit evenly.

To zest an orange, use a Microplane-style rasp grater or citrus zester, ensuring that you don't grate the white pith underneath. Microplanes have tiny razor-like edges, which make quick and easy tasks of grating and cleaning. If you use a zester, finely chop the zest before adding it to the recipe. Microplanes and zesters are widely available at specialty kitchenware shops.

- 3- to 4-quart round slow cooker, stoneware greased

Topping

¼ cup	packed brown sugar	60 mL
¼ cup	chopped walnuts	60 mL
½ tsp	ground cinnamon	2 mL
2 tbsp	butter, softened	30 mL

Cake

1½ cups	all-purpose flour	375 mL
1 tsp	baking powder	5 mL
1 tsp	ground cinnamon	5 mL
½ tsp	ground nutmeg	2 mL
¼ tsp	baking soda	1 mL
¼ tsp	salt	1 mL
1 cup	fresh or frozen blueberries	250 mL
½ cup	granulated sugar	125 mL
½ cup	butter, softened	125 mL
2	eggs	2
½ cup	sour cream or plain yogurt	125 mL
1 tsp	vanilla extract	5 mL
½ tsp	grated orange zest	2 mL
½ cup	chopped walnuts	125 mL

1. *Topping:* In a bowl, using your fingers, combine brown sugar, walnuts, cinnamon and butter until crumbly. Set aside.

2. *Cake:* In a bowl, combine flour, baking powder, cinnamon, nutmeg, baking soda and salt.

3. Place blueberries in another bowl and add 1 tbsp (15 mL) of the flour mixture; gently toss to coat. Set aside.

4. In a large bowl, using an electric mixer, cream sugar and butter until light and fluffy. Add eggs, one at a time, beating well after each addition. Beat in sour cream, vanilla and orange zest until blended. Using a wooden spoon, stir in flour mixture until just until blended. Gently fold in blueberries and walnuts (the batter will be thick).

5. Spoon batter into prepared slow cooker stoneware. Sprinkle with topping.

6. Cover and cook on High for about 2 hours or until a tester inserted in the center comes out clean. (Do not overcook.) Transfer stoneware to a wire rack and let cool for 15 minutes. Run a knife around sides to loosen cake. Using a spatula, gently ease cake out of stoneware and transfer to a serving plate. Let cool completely before cutting into wedges.

Manufacturers designed a kitchen rasp after they discovered that chefs were using the woodworking version to grate citrus fruits. I prefer the citrus zester, which is one of my favorite kitchen tools.

Mugga Bittersweet Brownie Decadence

I couldn't resist trying this recipe when I saw something similar in a magazine. I often pick up a package of gourmet brownie mix for a quick treat. Using it as a base for this slow cooker dessert makes these decadent brownies so moist and chocolatey they disappear in no time.

Tip

Store cocoa powder in an airtight container in a cool, dark place for up to 2 years.

- **Minimum 5-quart slow cooker**
- *6 mugs (each about 6 oz/175 mL), lightly greased*

3	eggs, beaten	3
1	package (18 oz/520 g) brownie mix (about 2½ cups/625 mL)	1
1	package (4-serving size) instant chocolate pudding mix	1
½ cup	semisweet chocolate chips	125 mL
¼ cup	butter, melted	60 mL
2 tbsp	packed brown sugar	30 mL
2 tbsp	unsweetened cocoa powder	30 mL
	Vanilla ice cream or whipped cream	

1. Set prepared mugs in slow cooker stoneware.

2. In a large bowl, combine eggs, brownie mix, pudding mix, chocolate chips and butter (the batter will be very thick). Divide batter evenly among mugs.

3. In a small saucepan, whisk together brown sugar, cocoa powder and ¾ cup (175 mL) water; bring to a boil over medium-high heat. Reduce heat and simmer, stirring, for about 1 minute or until sugar is dissolved. Divide evenly over batter in each mug.

4. Cover and cook on High for 2½ to 3 hours or until a tester inserted in the center of a brownie comes out clean. Turn off heat and let mugs stand in covered stoneware for 30 minutes. Top each mug with ice cream, place on a plate and serve warm.

Cocoa powder delivers such a rich, deep chocolate flavor, it's hard to beat. Cacao beans are processed into a paste, which is then dried and ground into powder. Dutch-process cocoa powder is a little richer and darker than natural unsweetened cocoa powder, because it has been treated with an alkali, which helps neutralize cocoa's natural acidity.

Creamy Caramel Blondies

Makes 4 to 6 servings

My son, Jack, and I are caramel and butterscotch fanatics! Blondies are often described as brownies without chocolate, which I find silly: blondies have their own unique, delicious personality. While brownies depend on chocolate for their flavor, with blondies it's all about the brown sugar. This tasty dessert combines a cake top over a creamy caramel sauce. Be sure to serve with a big scoop of vanilla ice cream.

Tip

It is best to use individually wrapped soft caramels, but you can substitute ½ cup (125 mL) butterscotch chips.

- **4- to 5-quart slow cooker**

1 cup	all-purpose flour	250 mL
1 tsp	baking powder	5 mL
½ tsp	salt	2 mL
1 cup	packed brown sugar, divided	250 mL
¼ cup	butter, softened	60 mL
1 tsp	vanilla extract	5 mL
½ cup	milk	125 mL
½ cup	soft caramels, wrappers removed	125 mL
1 cup	boiling water	250 mL

1. In a bowl, combine flour, baking powder and salt.

2. In another bowl, using an electric mixer, beat half the brown sugar and butter until creamy. Stir in vanilla. Add flour mixture alternately with milk, making three additions of each and beating well after each addition. Stir in caramels. Spread batter evenly in slow cooker stoneware.

3. In a glass measuring cup, combine the remaining brown sugar and boiling water, stirring until sugar is dissolved. Pour evenly over batter.

4. Cover and cook on High for 2½ to 3 hours or until a toothpick inserted in the center comes out clean.

Elephant Ears with Hot Caramel Sauce

Makes about 6 to 8 servings

My friend Chris described this sauce as "heaven in a pot." I like to use it as a dessert fondue for dipping the simple French cookies known as palmiers. While the sauce is cooking, you can easily bake a batch of these quick cookies.

Tips

Puff pastry package sizes vary between brands, ranging from 14 to 18 oz (397 to 511 g). If your package is slightly larger or smaller, it will still work fine for this recipe.

Refrigerate any leftover sauce in an airtight container for up to 2 weeks. It can be reheated in a mini slow cooker or microwave.

- 1½- to 3-quart slow cooker
- *Baking sheets, lined with parchment paper*

Caramel Sauce

1½ cups	packed brown sugar	375 mL
1¼ cups	heavy or whipping (35%) cream	300 mL
¼ tsp	ground cinnamon	1 mL
2 tsp	butter	10 mL
1 tsp	vanilla extract	5 mL

Elephant Ears

	Granulated sugar	
1	package (14 oz/397 g) puff pastry, thawed	1

1. *Sauce:* In slow cooker stoneware, combine brown sugar, cream and cinnamon. Cover and cook on Low for 2½ hours, stirring once or twice. Uncover and cook for 30 to 60 minutes or until thickened slightly. Stir in butter and vanilla.

2. *Elephant Ears:* Meanwhile, sprinkle about ¼ cup (60 mL) sugar over work surface. Roll out pastry into a 12- by 10-inch (30 by 25 cm) rectangle. Sprinkle another ¼ cup (60 mL) sugar over pastry. Roll the left short side inward, stopping in the middle of the dough. Roll up the right side so the two rolls meet in the middle. Press the two rolls together gently. Wrap and refrigerate for 30 minutes.

3. Preheat oven to 400°F (200°C). Cut dough crosswise into slices about ½ inch (1 cm) thick. Lightly sprinkle sugar on each side. Pinch and press the sides of the two rolls together to ensure that they don't unroll during baking. Transfer to prepared baking sheets, placing cookies about 2 inches (5 cm) apart. (They swell dramatically during baking, so only bake 12 at a time.)

4. Bake one sheet at a time for 10 to 15 minutes or until sugar is caramelized and pastry is flaky. Transfer to a wire rack and let cool for 10 minutes.

5. Pour warm sauce into a small serving dish and surround with cookies for dipping.

To-Die-For Butterscotch Custard

Makes 6 servings

Butterscotch pudding is traditionally made with butter and a little Scotch whisky. In this über-creamy version (which is a bit of a cheat), I use butterscotch chips to simplify the recipe. The result is so flavorful, even purists won't complain.

Tips

The cooked custard can also be refrigerated for up to 4 hours or overnight and served cold.

For individual servings, spoon the cream mixture into 6 lightly greased heatproof mugs. Omit foil strips and place mugs in stoneware. Add water and cook as directed.

- **Minimum 5-quart slow cooker**
- *6-cup (1.5 L) soufflé dish or heatproof bowl, lightly greased*

3½ cups	heavy or whipping (35%) cream, divided	875 mL
½	vanilla bean, split lengthwise (see box, page 384)	½
1 cup	butterscotch chips	250 mL
5	egg yolks	5
1½ tsp	packed dark brown sugar	7 mL
½ tsp	salt	2 mL
2 tsp	amaretto (optional)	10 mL
	Whipped cream	
	Caramel sauce	

1. In a heavy saucepan, bring cream and vanilla bean to a simmer over medium heat. Simmer for 3 minutes. Remove from heat and, using tongs, remove vanilla bean. Using a sharp knife, scrape seeds into cream mixture, discarding pod. Add butterscotch chips and let stand for 3 minutes. Whisk until smooth.

2. In a large bowl, whisk together egg yolks, brown sugar, salt and 1 tsp (5 mL) water. Gradually add cream mixture, whisking constantly. Whisk in amaretto (if using). Pour into prepared soufflé dish. Cover tightly with foil and secure with an elastic band.

3. Cut a 2-foot (60 cm) length of foil in half lengthwise to make two strips. Fold each strip in half lengthwise. Crisscross strips on bottom of slow cooker stoneware, bringing the ends up the sides and over the rim. Place soufflé dish in stoneware and pour in enough water to come 1 inch (2.5 cm) up sides of dish. (If dish fits snugly in stoneware, add water before inserting it; see page 14.)

4. Tucking strip ends under lid, cover and cook on High for 2 to 3 hours or until custard is set. Remove lid and grasp strip ends to lift out dish.

5. Spoon into individual serving dishes. Top each with a dollop of whipped cream and drizzle with caramel sauce.

Ginger Crème Brûlée

Makes 4 servings

One of the most popular choices in any fine restaurant, crème brûlée is a rich dessert of soft custard with a crisp caramel top. It takes a little work, but is a superb finale to any special meal.

Tips

Straining the cream mixture through a fine-mesh wire sieve filters out any solid eggy bits to ensure a smooth consistency. Rinse the sieve under cold running water before washing it — hot water will cook the egg particles into the mesh, making cleanup difficult.

If you don't have individual soufflé dishes or ramekins, you can cook the custard in a 4-cup (1 L) heatproof dish that fits inside the stoneware. The servings won't look as pretty, but they will still taste great.

- **Minimum 6-quart slow cooker**
- *Four 6-oz (175 mL) soufflé dishes or ramekins*

2 cups	heavy or whipping (35%) cream	500 mL
4 oz	peeled gingerroot, cut into chunks	125 g
1	vanilla bean, split lengthwise	1
5	egg yolks	5
1/2 cup	granulated sugar	125 mL
3 to 4 tbsp	packed brown sugar	45 to 60 mL

1. Set soufflé dishes in slow cooker stoneware.

2. In a saucepan, bring cream, ginger and vanilla bean to a simmer over medium heat. Remove from heat and let stand for at least 15 minutes or for up to 1 hour. Discard ginger chunks. Remove vanilla bean and, using a sharp knife, scrape seeds into cream mixture, discarding pod.

3. In a bowl, whisk together egg yolks and granulated sugar. Whisk in cream mixture. Strain through a fine-mesh sieve. Pour into dishes in stoneware. Add enough hot water to come 1 inch (2.5 cm) up sides of dishes. (Don't pour any water into dishes.)

4. Cover and cook on High for 2 to 2½ hours or until custards are set but centers are slightly jiggly. Turn off heat, uncover and let cool. Remove from stoneware, cover with plastic wrap and refrigerate for at least 2 hours, until chilled, or overnight.

5. Preheat broiler with rack set 3 inches (7.5 cm) below heat source. Sprinkle brown sugar evenly over custards. Broil for 2 to 3 minutes or until sugar is melted and caramelized.

Thai Coconut Tapioca Pudding

Makes 6 servings

For many people, tapioca pudding was a favorite childhood dessert. Infused with Thai-inspired flavors, this version is updated but still resembles that familiar comfort food. Traditionally, it was served chilled, but we all loved it warm, too.

Tips

Make sure you use pearl tapioca, not instant. Pearl tapioca and Thai basil are readily available at Asian supermarkets. Pearl tapioca is also available at health food markets.

When choosing a mango, color is less important than texture — the softer it is, the riper it is. Some varieties of mango wrinkle a little at the stem when perfectly ripe. An unripe mango will ripen if left at room temperature for a day or two. Once it is ripe, store it in the refrigerator until ready to use.

- **3- to 4-quart slow cooker**

4 cups	whole milk	1 L
1/2 cup	pearl tapioca	125 mL
1/2 cup	granulated sugar	125 mL
1 tsp	grated gingerroot	5 mL
1/4 tsp	grated lime zest	1 mL
Pinch	cayenne pepper	Pinch
1	4-inch (10 cm) cinnamon stick	1
2	eggs, lightly beaten	2
1	can (14 oz/398 mL) unsweetened coconut milk	1
1	large mango	1
1 tbsp	freshly squeezed lime juice	15 mL
	Thai basil sprigs (optional)	

1. In slow cooker stoneware, combine milk, tapioca, sugar, ginger, lime zest, cayenne and cinnamon stick.

2. Cover and cook on Low for 3 to 4 hours or until thickened, milk is absorbed and most of the tapioca is translucent.

3. In a bowl, whisk together eggs and coconut milk. Stir in 2 to 3 tbsp (30 to 45 mL) of the hot milk mixture and beat well. Pour into stoneware.

4. Cover and cook for 30 minutes. Turn off heat and let cool in covered stoneware for 30 minutes. Discard cinnamon stick.

5. Spoon into individual serving dishes, cover with plastic wrap and refrigerate for at least 2 hours, until chilled, or for up to 3 days. (Or, if desired, serve warm.)

6. Peel mango and cut into cubes. In a bowl, combine mango and lime juice. Spoon over each serving and garnish with a basil sprig.

Pumpkin Croissant Pudding with Tipsy Caramel Sauce

Makes 6 servings

This bread pudding recipe came to me from my colleague Dana Shortt, who has a fantastic ready-made food shop and catering business. She serves this up to her customers over the holidays, and it is always a hit. I adapted it to the slow cooker, with delicious results.

Tips

For an extra-boozy hit, soak the raisins in a little rum overnight before using.

You can use dried cranberries in place of the raisins.

Make Ahead

This dish can be assembled up to 24 hours in advance. Complete step 1, cover and refrigerate. Complete step 3, transfer sauce to an airtight container and refrigerate. When ready to cook, place stoneware in slow cooker and proceed with step 2. Just before serving, return sauce to a saucepan and warm over medium-low heat, stirring, until bubbling.

- **4- to 5-quart slow cooker, stoneware greased**

2	eggs	2
1	can (14 oz/398 mL) pumpkin purée (not pie filling)	1
1 cup	packed brown sugar	250 mL
1½ tsp	pumpkin pie spice	7 mL
1½ tsp	ground cinnamon	7 mL
2 cups	table (18%) cream	500 mL
1½ tsp	vanilla extract	7 mL
1	bag (12 oz/375 g) mini croissants (about 24), torn into pieces	1
½ cup	golden raisins	125 mL
½ cup	coarsely chopped pecans	125 mL
	Whipped cream (optional)	

Tipsy Caramel Sauce

1¼ cups	packed brown sugar	300 mL
½ cup	unsalted butter	125 mL
½ cup	heavy or whipping (35%) cream	125 mL
¼ cup	amber or light rum	60 mL

1. In a large bowl, whisk together eggs, pumpkin purée, brown sugar, pumpkin pie spice, cinnamon, cream and vanilla. Fold in croissant pieces and raisins. Spoon into prepared slow cooker stoneware. Sprinkle with pecans.

2. Cover and cook on Low for 3 to 3½ hours or on High for 1½ to 2 hours, until custard is set and a tester inserted in the center comes out clean.

3. *Sauce:* Meanwhile, in a heavy saucepan, whisk brown sugar and butter over medium heat until butter is melted. Whisk in cream and cook, stirring, for about 3 minutes or until sugar is dissolved and sauce is smooth. Remove from heat and stir in rum.

4. Spoon pudding into a serving dish and drizzle with sauce. Garnish with whipped cream (if using).

Mexican Chocolate Bread Pudding

**Makes 6 to
8 servings**

*This Mexican dessert,
called* capirotadas, *is
traditionally served during
Lent. It is full of texture
and flavor, and with a few
savory garnishes, such as
sour cream or thin slices of
aged Cheddar or Monterey
Jack cheese, it also makes
a wonderful breakfast or
brunch dish.*

Tips

Regardless of which bread
you use, it's important that it
is stale. The staler the bread,
the more readily it absorbs
the custard mixture and the
more tender and flavorful the
pudding will be. I often cube
leftover bread, then leave it
out, uncovered, to dry.

Challah (pronounced
HAH-lah) is a traditional
Jewish bread made with
eggs, yeast, flour and water.
It has a distinct yellow interior
because of the yolks used
to make it. Challah is one of
the best breads to use for
bread pudding, because you
can easily cut it into thick
slices and it absorbs the egg
mixture quickly.

- **4- to 5-quart slow cooker, stoneware greased**

2 cups	light (5%) cream	500 mL
4 oz	unsweetened chocolate, coarsely chopped	125 g
2	eggs, beaten	2
1/2 cup	packed brown sugar	125 mL
3/4 tsp	ground cinnamon	3 mL
1/2 tsp	ground allspice	2 mL
1/8 tsp	salt	0.5 mL
1 tsp	vanilla extract	5 mL
1/2 cup	dried currants	125 mL
4	thick slices stale egg bread or challah, crusts removed, cut into 1-inch (2.5 cm) cubes (about 4 cups/2 L)	4
1/3 cup	slivered almonds	75 mL
	Sour cream (optional)	

1. In a heavy saucepan, bring cream to a simmer over medium heat. Remove from heat. Add chocolate and let stand for 2 to 3 minutes. Stir until chocolate is melted. Let cool slightly.

2. In a large bowl, whisk together eggs, brown sugar, cinnamon, allspice, salt and vanilla. Stir in currants. Stir in cream mixture. Gently fold in bread cubes. Pour into prepared slow cooker stoneware. Sprinkle evenly with almonds.

3. Cover and cook on High for 3 to 4 hours or until a tester inserted in the center comes out clean.

4. Serve warm or chilled. Top each serving with generous dollop of sour cream, if desired.

Make Ahead

This dish can be assembled up to 24 hours in advance. Prepare through step 2, cover and refrigerate. When ready to cook, place stoneware in slow cooker and proceed with step 3.

Chocolate Pâté with Raspberry Sauce

Makes 10 to 12 servings

I have to admit that I'm not a big chocolate lover. What can I say? I prefer caramel. But this flourless chocolate pâté is so good, even I'm a huge fan. The recipe is a good choice when you're entertaining, because it tastes best when it's made a day ahead. You need to serve it at room temperature, so take it out of the fridge at least an hour before serving.

Tips

Use a good-quality bittersweet chocolate in this recipe. The cocoa content can range anywhere from 35% to 99%, so check out the ingredients list to see what else is included. A high percentage of solids doesn't guarantee quality, but it does mean there are a lot less fillers. Your best test is your mouth. A good-quality bittersweet chocolate will have an almost chalky mouth feel, but it will coat your mouth evenly, without waxiness or grittiness. It should also have an array of undertones, such as coffee, fruit or acidic notes.

When whipping cream, be sure it is well chilled — and for best results, chill the bowl and beaters, too.

- **Minimum 6-quart slow cooker**
- *7- or 8-inch (18 or 20 cm) springform pan*
- *Vegetable steamer or low rack to fit in stoneware*

Raspberry Sauce

1	bag (21 oz/600 g) frozen raspberries, partially thawed	1
1/3 cup	confectioner's (icing) sugar	75 mL

Chocolate Pâté

2 oz	bittersweet chocolate, coarsely chopped	60 g
2 cups	semisweet chocolate chips	500 mL
1 cup	unsalted butter	250 mL
6	eggs	6
1 1/2 tbsp	granulated sugar	22 mL

Fresh raspberries (optional)
Whipped cream

1. *Sauce:* In a blender or food processor, purée raspberries and confectioner's sugar until smooth. If desired, strain through a fine-mesh sieve to remove seeds. Cover and refrigerate for up to 2 days.

2. *Pâté:* In a large microwave-safe glass bowl, combine unsweetened chocolate, chocolate chips and butter. Microwave on Medium (50%) for 1 1/2 to 2 minutes, stirring after 1 minute, until melted and smooth when stirred. (Or melt in a double boiler over hot water.) Whisk in eggs, one at a time, then sugar.

3. Wrap outside of springform pan with foil to prevent leaks. Spread chocolate mixture evenly in pan. Cover top of pan with foil and secure with an elastic band. Place pan on steamer in slow cooker stoneware. (Do not add any water.)

4. Cover and cook on High for 3 hours or until edges are slightly firm but center is still soft and moist. Turn off heat, uncover and let stand for about 30 minutes or until pan is cool enough to handle.

5. Remove pan from stoneware and remove foil. Transfer pan to a wire rack and let cool for 1 hour. Cover and refrigerate for 3 to 4 hours, until chilled and set, or for up to 24 hours. (Pâté is best when made 24 hours ahead.)

6. Let sauce and pâté come to room temperature before serving. Gently run a knife around inside edge of springform pan. Unlatch side and remove ring. Slice pâté with a warm knife. Drizzle each slice with sauce and garnish with raspberries, if desired, and whipped cream.

Caramelized Banana Splits

Makes 4 servings, plus extra sauce

With its warm, gooey goodness, this dessert will bring to mind those lazy days of summer. You'll have some sauce left over, which is handy because — I assure you — you'll be in the mood to have this again the next night, if not sooner!

Tip

To store the extra sauce, transfer it to an airtight container and refrigerate for up to 2 weeks. To serve warm, reheat in the microwave on Medium (50%) power or in a saucepan over low heat.

- 1$\frac{1}{2}$- to 3-quart slow cooker

Warm Raspberry Chocolate Sauce

1 lb	bittersweet or semisweet chocolate, chopped	500 g
1 cup	heavy or whipping (35%) cream	250 mL
$\frac{1}{3}$ cup	seedless raspberry jam	75 mL
1 tsp	vanilla extract	5 mL

Banana Splits

3 tbsp	butter	45 mL
3	firm ripe bananas, cut diagonally into $\frac{1}{2}$-inch (1 cm) slices	3
$\frac{1}{4}$ cup	lightly packed brown sugar	60 mL
	Cinnamon or vanilla ice cream	
$\frac{1}{2}$ cup	chopped walnuts, toasted	125 mL

1. *Sauce:* In slow cooker stoneware, combine chocolate, cream and jam. Cover and cook on Low for 1$\frac{1}{2}$ to 2 hours, stirring two or three times, until chocolate is melted and sauce is smooth and hot. Whisk in vanilla.

2. *Banana Splits:* In a large, heavy skillet, melt butter over medium heat. Add bananas in a single layer and sprinkle with brown sugar. Increase heat to medium-high and cook, shaking skillet occasionally and gently turning bananas once, for 3 to 4 minutes or until sugar is caramelized.

3. Divide bananas among individual serving bowls. Top with scoops of ice cream, drizzle with sauce and sprinkle with walnuts.

Index